America Firsthand

Volume One
Readings from Settlement to Reconstruction

America Firsthand

Eighth Edition

Volume One
Readings from Settlement to Reconstruction

Robert D. Marcus
*Late of the State University
of New York College at Brockport*

David Burner
State University of New York at Stony Brook

Anthony Marcus
*University of Melbourne
John Jay College of Criminal Justice
of the City University of New York*

BEDFORD/ST. MARTIN'S
Boston ◆ New York

FOR BEDFORD/ST. MARTIN'S

Publisher Editor for History: Mary V. Dougherty
Executive Editor: William J. Lombardo
Senior Editor: Louise Townsend
Editorial Assistants: Katherine Flynn, Jennifer Jovin
Production Associate: Ashley Chalmers
Executive Marketing Manager: Jenna Bookin Barry
Project Management: Books By Design, Inc.
Cover Design: Billy Boardman
Cover Photo: *Early New Mexico Newspaper*. © Bettmann/Corbis.
Composition: Achorn International
Printing and Binding: R.R. Donnelley & Sons Company

President: Joan E. Feinberg
Editorial Director: Denise B. Wydra
Director of Marketing: Karen R. Soeltz
Director of Editing, Design, and Production: Marcia Cohen
Assistant Director of Editing, Design, and Production: Elise S. Kaiser
Manager, Publishing Services: Emily Berleth

Library of Congress Control Number: 2008933819

Manufactured in the United States of America.

4 3 2 1 0 9
f e d c b a

For information, write: Bedford/St. Martin's, 75 Arlington Street, Boston, MA 02116   (617-399-4000)

ISBN-10: 0-312-48906-4
ISBN-13: 978-0-312-48906-9

Acknowledgments

Acknowledgments and copyrights appear at the back of the book on pages 323–24, which constitute an extension of the copyright page.

It is a violation of the law to reproduce these selections by any means whatsoever without the written permission of the copyright holder.

This book is dedicated to Robert Marcus, who died in October 2000; he was one of the two creators and coeditors of America Firsthand. At the time of Bob's death, his doctoral sponsor Robert Wiebe—soon to pass away himself—eulogized that Bob had "a first-rate mind, was ingenious, versatile, and brimming over with fresh ideas." We remember Bob as an original thinker, a thoughtful scholar, and a true friend.

Preface

When *America Firsthand* was launched in the late 1980s, Ronald Reagan was president; the personal computer was not yet tied to the limitless global information web we now call the Internet; educators were becoming concerned about fostering students' critical thinking skills; and U.S. history instructors were just beginning to introduce social history methods into undergraduate classes. In these last two efforts, *America Firsthand* led the way, successfully bringing the resources and tools for learning, interpreting, and writing about U.S. history to students in classrooms across the United States and Canada, while providing a uniquely personal view of how ordinary Americans lived, witnessed, and made history.

Now, more than twenty years later, we live in what is commonly called the Information Age. Students and instructors are confronted by a staggering array of historical sources, resources, and images, available on millions of Web sites put up by community groups, political organizations, governments, universities, and just about anybody willing to manage a blog. The sources one can draw on are increasingly diverse, fragmented, particular, and de-contextualized. It is for this reason that *America Firsthand* remains more than ever a crucial classroom resource. Whether used as a companion to a survey text or as a stand-alone, this collection, covering the broad sweep of U.S. history from new world encounters to the twenty-first century, provides a common ground where students can ponder and debate key historical moments and topics and test their ideas against other ideas in the classroom and in the world beyond. The editors of *America Firsthand* are proud to provide the intellectual space in which students can discover the pleasures and challenges of primary documents while developing the critical skills necessary to read, interpret, and understand America's past.

The eighth edition continues *America Firsthand*'s emphasis on individuals making and living history, adding newly uncovered and rediscovered documents with more of the voices and topics that reviewers have asked for: more from Asian Americans and Native Americans, and more on religion, popular and political culture, technology, and the environment. In Volume One, students read the words of Pueblo Indians in revolt against the Spanish empire and those of a Scots-Iroquois leader fighting for the British; they learn about the experiences of Jews in colonial America and of deists and revivalists in the nineteenth century; and they experience the back and forth mudslinging of political propaganda through revolutionary era cartoons; in Volume Two, they encounter naturalist

John Muir fighting to preserve his beloved American wilderness; they learn what it was like to move to a single-family home for the first time in a place called "the suburbs" in the 1940s; and they read an account by a fledgling dot.com-er who risks it all in the 1990s high-tech boom. This is but a small sampling from the rich array of new documents and old favorites contained in this edition.

The eighth edition retains our popular Points of View, part-opening features that juxtapose readings on a specific event or topic, providing students with opportunities for critical thinking and analysis of different perspectives from the past. For instance, in Volume One, students encounter contrasting views of the conquest of Mexico by conquistador Hernando Cortés and Nahua natives, and in Volume Two multiple perspectives on the creation and dropping of the atomic bomb on Hiroshima and Nagasaki during World War II. Critical thinking questions at the close of the documents help students sift through the evidence, make connections, and analyze the readings in relation to one another.

Volume One offers two new Points of View, one contrasting the experiences of colonial women, the other juxtaposing the views of Frederick Douglass and a Southern slaveholder at the close of the Civil War, as both men contemplate the future. Volume Two also contains two new Points of View, one featuring accounts of the Battle of Little Bighorn by Native Americans and by an Italian American soldier of fortune who was present at "Custer's last stand," the other featuring witnesses to the Guantánamo Bay Detention Center and their public battle over the legacy of George W. Bush's war on terror.

This edition also includes one new visual portfolio in each volume, with commentary, background information, and critical-thinking questions to help students engage in meaningful analysis of the images. The first volume features a set of patriot and loyalist propaganda cartoons, exposing students to the kind of visual propaganda and powerful imagery that was and remains an important means of influencing the public. The second volume includes a new portfolio on "The Peopling of the West" with broadsides, photographs, and cartoons that convey the incredible ethnic diversity that characterized the West during the second half of the nineteenth century.

In addition to the visual portfolios that appear in each volume, we include stand-alone visual documents throughout, sources that are treated the same as the textual documents, with headnotes and questions to help students make sense of these images as evidence. Volume One, for example, gives students the opportunity to analyze an early French map that suggests the relationship between mapmaking and colonialism, while Volume Two features photographs, both provocative and challenging, of the 1992 Los Angeles riots in the wake of the Rodney King verdict.

Throughout, we retain sources that users have said they wanted and dropped less successful ones. New selections in the first volume include Mary Rowlandson's captivity narrative (the first example of a colonial woman's autobiographical writing); the views of Elihu Palmer, often described as America's first atheist; and a description of the events that led Henry "Box" Brown, once a relatively well-off urban slave, to abandon everything and mail himself to freedom in a box. Fresh selections in the second volume include tales of life on the road during the Great Depression, inside views of the feminist and Puerto Rican ethnic rights movements of the 1960s, and Al Gore's speech on global warming when he accepted the Nobel Prize in 2007.

As in previous editions, carefully written headnotes preceding the selections prepare students for each reading and help locate personalities in their times and places. Questions to Consider immediately following the headnotes offer points to reflect on when reading and encourage in-depth analysis. This time around we have added even more gloss notes at the base of the page within the accounts to identify unfamiliar names and terms.

To better equip students with the tools for working with all the sources in this collection—visual as well as textual—we have revised and expanded the student introduction on Studying and Writing History. And to ensure that instructors get the support *they* need, the *Instructor's Resource Manual* has been thoroughly revised and updated by Margaret Rung of Roosevelt University. Available online at bedfordstmartins.com/marcusburner, this manual includes discussion of the main themes and topics in each part, references to and summaries of relevant books and articles, strategies for teaching with the documents including in-class learning activities and Suggestions for Collaborative Learning Exercises for each Points of View feature, as well as ample discussion and essay questions.

America Firsthand, Eighth Edition, presents the American experience through the perspectives of diverse people who have in common a vivid record of the world they inhabited and of the events they experienced. We hope that this collection will continue to provide a rich and rewarding intellectual space for students, one in which they can develop their own interest in firsthand sources to further their own historical knowledge, bringing that knowledge to bear in the classroom, in their lives, and in the world beyond.

ABOUT THE AUTHORS

The eighth edition of *America Firsthand* has been brought to press by Anthony Marcus, who replaced his father, Robert Marcus, after his untimely death in October 2000, joining co-author David Burner. Burner, a Guggenheim Fellow and emeritus scholar at the State University of New York at Stony Brook, together with his longtime friend and collaborator Robert Marcus brought *America Firsthand* into the world and nurtured it over several successful editions. Anthony Marcus is an historian and anthropologist who has taught college students for over fifteen years and published on race, ethnicity, and public policy in the United States, Latin America, Australia, and Indonesia. With the eighth edition, he seeks to continue *America Firsthand*'s tradition of pedagogical excellence and to uphold his father's oft-stated commitment to "include people from many groups whose experience has been, until recently, largely lost in mainstream history."

ACKNOWLEDGMENTS

We would like to thank all the instructors who graciously provided helpful comments for improving *America Firsthand*: Lesley Gordon, University of Akron; John Wigger, University of Missouri; Richard Meixsel, James Madison University; Sharon Anderson, Tennessee Tech University; Jennifer Helgren, University of the Pacific; Martha K. Robinson, Clarion University; Steven Kite, Fort Hays State University; Tim Lehman, Rocky Mountain College; Kathleen Clark, University of Georgia; Deborah Blackwell, Texas A&M International University; Sharon Rubin, Ramapo College of New Jersey; Craig Smith, Missouri State University; Margaret Rung, Roosevelt University; Nikki Taylor, University of Cincinnati; Mary Ann Bodayla, Southwest Tennessee Community College; Wendy Castro, University of Central Arkansas; Melinda Barr, Oklahoma City Community College; Joyce Goldberg, University of Texas–Arlington; Scott Newman, Loyola University–Chicago; and Laurie Chin, California State University–Long Beach. And finally, thanks to Gerald Sider, whose 2003 book *Between History and Tomorrow: Making and Breaking Everyday Life in Rural Newfoundland* provided the inspiration for the title of Chapter 7 in Volume Two.

We are also grateful to all the members of the Bedford/St. Martin's staff who have been involved with the development of the reader from start to finish and have made this edition of *America Firsthand* the best that it can be. Thanks to Katherine Flynn and Jennifer Jovin for helping with numerous tasks on this project; to photo researcher Lisa Jelly Smith for help with the expanded visual component; to Donna Dennison and Billy Boardman for creating the new book covers; to Emily Berleth and Nancy Benjamin for turning the manuscript into a book; to Joan Feinberg and Denise Wydra for agreeing to bring out another edition and making sure that it happened; to Mary Dougherty and William Lombardo, who oversaw the business and logistical side; to Jane Knetzger, who oversaw the editorial development of the project; and to Louise Townsend, whose tireless efforts and ability to be maddeningly picky about details, while still getting the big picture, made her exactly the navigator that this project needed at this time.

Introduction: Using Sources to Study the Past

The study of history offers us a way of knowing who we are, where we have come from, and where we are headed. Perhaps because we live in the present it is sometimes easy to assume that people in the past were basically like us, just with different clothing, as is the case in most Hollywood history movies, where protagonists are made sympathetic to contemporary audiences by giving them modern goals and desires. In such "historical dramas" people fight for their nation, even if neither it nor the very idea of a nation exists yet; they make great sacrifices for romantic love, even if this concept has not yet been invented; struggle to protect the innocence of children, even if there is not yet a concept of childhood; and demand personal freedom, in societies where the greatest goal is to have a defined place in the social order. These uses of dramatic license to place modern motivations and values into the past is called historical anachronism, and it usually leads to good movies, but rather poor understanding of how our ancestors made decisions and took actions. History is a systematic attempt to study the differences and similarities between the past and the present, in order to understand how we got from there to here and how we may craft our future.

How, then, do we as students of history or historians approach the study of our past? The first step is to pose a research question about the past. For example:

- What was social life like between African Americans and white Americans in colonial Virginia?

Asking this question is important because so much of our vision of race relations before the civil rights movement of the 1940s–1960s is built on visions of the hardened institutionalized slavery of the mid-nineteenth century and the Jim Crow segregation that followed. Some historians, like Edmund Morgan, have argued that relations between whites and blacks were more fluid and equal in the first century of the British colonization of North America, when slavery was not hereditary or restricted to African Americans, who could still testify in court, cohabit with white women, buy their own freedom, and even own slaves, all providing that they converted to Christianity.

Knowing something about how the nineteenth-century horrors of industrial scale slavery, laws against literacy among slaves, and finally segregation emerged from an earlier, and perhaps less harsh, time can help us understand the nature of race relations in America and tell us something about the potential for changes in the future. Whatever our motivation is for posing questions such as the one above, the first step in trying to address them is to find relevant sources that may provide answers. These come in two broad categories: *primary sources* and *secondary sources*.

PRIMARY SOURCES

Primary sources are documents and artifacts directly produced by the individuals and groups that participated in or witnessed the situation, event, or topic being researched. They are a lot like the evidence and testimony that lawyers use in a courtroom to present different versions of what happened and why. Often answering the question "why" is just as important as figuring out what actually happened. For example, if it is known that a defendant shoved his brother off a roof to his death, it matters to the judge, jury, and district attorney whether the action was self-defense, an accident, or occurred in the heat of anger. If the court can establish that the killer invited his brother to the roof two days after learning that his brother had named him as sole beneficiary in a life insurance policy, the results are likely to be very different than if we discover that it was the dead brother who set up the meeting on the roof and neither stood to benefit from the death.

All the sources included in *America Firsthand* are primary ones, but this is only a small sample of what is possible in primary source research. The types of primary sources are as limitless as the imagination of the historian. Human records of all kinds leave useful information for scholars and students. From a drawing done by an eighteenth-century child showing what was taught to young elites to DNA suggesting that Thomas Jefferson had children with his African American slave, Sally Hemings, or a colonial New York candlestick holder made by a Portuguese Jew with designs borrowed from Native Americans to oral history interviews, every primary source leaves behind clues for the historian. The problem is often sorting out which clues are useful and which are not. This may change depending on what questions are being asked and what techniques are available at the time of research.

Not only can science and technology make old primary sources newly important; social and political changes also open up new possibilities for asking different *kinds* of questions of the evidence. Obviously, Thomas Jefferson's DNA had little value before modern advances in genetics but also, until the study of slavery and sexual relations between whites and blacks had advanced to a certain stage, few historians would have dared ask questions about Jefferson's potential fathering of children by a slave woman. Similarly, historian James Lockhart probably never would have crossed the globe to bring together Nahua descriptions of the conquest of Mexico (Volume One, Document 2) if there had not been an indigenous civil rights movement when he was in school in the 1960s and 1970s that drew attention to the native point of view. There would have been far less interest before September 11, 2001, in why Shams Alwujude

(Volume Two, Document 42) chooses to wear a traditional Middle Eastern head covering. Instead, it probably would have been ignored as an old-fashioned cultural tradition soon to disappear, as did the Italian, Greek, and Jewish female head coverings in the United States during the early twentieth century. Prompted by events of the present, historians are now busy looking for new primary sources to answer research questions pertaining to such questions as whether or not the prevalence and use of Muslim head coverings in the United States has increased over time and if so, why. What type of visual or written primary sources might help historians to answer this question?

Returning to our first question about the social life between African Americans and white Americans in colonial Virginia, the relationship between Sally Hemings and Thomas Jefferson might tell us something important. Although Hemings was born at the very end of the colonial period, the world that she and Jefferson inhabited may have been as much like the seventeenth century as the nineteenth century. Now that it is widely accepted, thanks to DNA testing, that Hemings bore Jefferson a child, much of the controversy revolves around how equal, unequal, voluntary, or coerced the sexual relationship was between an aged former president and the teenage girl who was his legal property. For some the inequality of race and age and the fact that Jefferson owned Hemings is decisive proof that it was a highly coercive relationship. For others, who argue that men and women of every race had legally unequal marriages at that time, the fact that Hemings signed legal documents for Jefferson, traveled with him, and chose to remain with him, even though they lived for a time in France, where she was legally a free woman and may have had many offers of marriage from eligible Frenchmen is proof that this relationship was somewhat mutual.

What kind of evidence do you think would show that this relationship was coercive and unequal? What kind of evidence would show that Hemings was her own woman? Does the fact that she was the half sister of Jefferson's deceased wife say anything about the mixing of races among the elites in colonial America? For some commentators, "the bottom line" is that Jefferson never married Hemings and could not, by law. However, the existence of such key primary sources as laws allow a variety of interpretations. The mere fact that courts started to pass miscegenation (intermarriage between people of different racial background) laws in the eighteenth century is a good sign that a) there were such interracial marriages; b) blacks and whites were increasingly being allocated different positions in society; and c) inequality was becoming increasingly fixed. The historian may find clues in primary sources as complex as philosophic essays and autobiographies and as simple as shopping lists, photographs, and Hemings' signature on Jefferson household payments for animal feed.

SECONDARY SOURCES

Secondary sources are books and articles in scholarly journals that bring together collections of evidence in order to interpret and build arguments around what happened. They offer answers to research questions and provide stories that link together all the evidence into coherent and interesting narratives. Secondary sources provide background about a particular subject, include important references to primary sources through footnotes and bibliographies, and raise questions, topics, and debates that form the foundation for further research. To take the courtroom analogy a step further, it is the lawyer's job, like the historian's, to take the evidence (primary sources) and build a case (secondary source). It is impossible to build a case unless you have some idea of what the other lawyers are saying, what their evidence is, and how they plan to structure their case. This is why courts have a "discovery" process that requires lawyers to share their evidence with opposing counsel before trial. And it is why history teachers send students off to the library to read secondary sources before allowing them to plunge into the difficult task of going through birth records or ship manifests looking for new evidence, trying to rearrange the old evidence, or combining the two to create a new understanding of what happened. The exciting part of history is when you come up with your own questions about the past and find answers that create knowledge and spark new ways of understanding the past, present, and even the future.

APPROACHING SOURCES CRITICALLY

In any courtroom trial, opposing lawyers try many ways to poke holes in each other's argument, but at the end of the day, the jury must decide what evidence is most relevant, whose testimony is the most reliable, and which argument is most convincing. The same standard applies to historical sources. In determining if slavery was economically inefficient, do we trust the tax office's records or the plantation owner's financial records, his complaints to his congressman about how much tax he was paying, or his boastful letters to his sister about cheating on his taxes? Is there a good reason why some or all of these sources may be lying, stretching the truth, or simply misleading? Who is a more reliable witness to slavery, the slave or the slaveholder; the Northern abolitionist or the Southern politician; the poor white farmer who hates the slaveholders or the English gentleman visiting his Georgia cousins? Every person has a unique point of view, set of beliefs, way of seeing things, and reason for giving testimony, and we must critically analyze and evaluate everything and assume nothing. This point of view constitutes the bias of the source. Because all sources are biased, it is important that you develop a set of questions for interrogating primary sources. Some useful questions to ask are these:

- What is the historical context for the document? When was it produced, and how does it relate to important events of the period? (Note: The headnotes for the sources included in this book provide you with background information.)
- Who is the author? What can you tell about that person's background, social status, and so on?
- What can you infer about the purpose of the document? Who was its intended audience?
- What does the style and tone of the document tell you about the author's purpose?

- What main points does the author seek to communicate or express?
- What does the document suggest about the author's point of view and biases? Consider whether the author misunderstood what he or she is relating or had reason to falsify the account on purpose.
- What can you infer about how typical for the period the views expressed in the document are?

Additional thought must be given to visual sources. When working with visual sources, ask the following questions in addition to those above:

- How is the image framed or drawn? What was included? What might have been excluded? What does this tell you about the event, person, or place you are analyzing?
- What medium (drawing, painting, or photograph, etc.) did the creator employ? What constraints did the medium impose on the creator? For example, photographic technology in the nineteenth century was very rudimentary and involved large, bulky cameras with very slow shutter speeds. This tells us something about why people often posed stiffly, without smiles on their faces, for early photographs. Likewise, while there are numerous Civil War photographs, most were posed or created after battles because the camera's shutter speeds did not allow for action photography.
- Do you know if the work was expensive or cheap to produce? What might this suggest about the event, person, or place you are analyzing?

Historians strive not to use the standards of the present to make judgments on the past. When working with both primary and secondary sources, the question of historical context must always be considered. For example, the decision to drop atomic bombs on Hiroshima and Nagasaki is often said to have been made without the same taboos, socio-political fears, and ecological concerns that are today tied to atomic energy and atomic weapons. It was largely assumed, during the entire process of developing atomic weapons, that they would be used. At the time, there was little serious discussion of not using this new war technology to hasten the end of the war with Japan, beyond a few last-minute letters and petitions from the very atomic scientists who had spent years and vast sums of money working to develop this new weapon. This was the historical context in which the decision to drop the atomic bomb was made. To bring in more modern concerns such as nuclear proliferation and environmental impact would be moving beyond this decision's historical context.

However, you should be wary of simply absolving those who made the bomb, gave the orders, and carried out the mission by reducing history to "the way people viewed things back then." It is difficult enough to figure out today's social context or how people view things now; the past is even more uncertain and filled with dissenting views. Many respected and important people during the prewar years had argued passionately against the dropping of bombs on civilian populations. They claimed that it was ethically unforgivable and not a particularly useful or effective practice of war that might strengthen a civilian population's will to fight, rather than soften them up for conquest. These people might have had no knowledge of the devastation of atomic weapons, but they were living at the time that Hiroshima and Nagasaki were bombed, and they certainly would not have viewed it as an acceptable act of warfare. Several international conventions attempted to eliminate bombing of civilians from modern warfare and thousands of journals, letters, autobiographies, movies, novels, and popular songs suggest that throughout the twentieth century many politicians, generals, and bomber pilots were uncomfortable with this peculiarly abstract and violent form of warfare against civilians.

There are, therefore, no easy answers to the question, "How did people view things back then?" Like the present, the past contains a multitude of contested and contradictory norms, values, and perspectives held by a variety of people with different understandings of the context in which people took action and made history. This is the most complicated aspect of historical inquiry and interpretation, taking evidence, finding the right context, and telling a story about the similarities and differences between past and present. Returning to the first question in this introduction, we cannot know whether blacks and whites were once equal in seventeenth-century Virginia, unless we know something about the contemporary values, rules, and social expectations of the time. What did it mean to be equal? If being a member of the Church of England was the key marker of belonging in seventeenth-century Virginia, it may be that African converts to Christianity had more rights than Irish, Jews, and Native Americans. Such a situation would suggest that a fully formed code of caste/color inequality had not yet developed, and we might look for clues a bit later in colonial history.

Because all sources, firsthand primary accounts and secondary works by historians, have unique points of view and reasons for seeing things the way they do, you need to question and critically analyze everything. Read all historical documents with skepticism, taking into account how their authors' points of view fit into the context of the time, the voices of contemporaries, and the way they might have imagined themselves being remembered historically. This last consideration, people's own sense of how they make history, has always been important. But it may have become even more important in the contemporary world that Andy Warhol characterized as providing everybody with "fifteen minutes of fame." Ultimately, the craft of history is as subjective as a trial verdict. We can never know what actually happened. We can establish a fair trial, one with relevant evidence, good witnesses, and brilliant lawyers. This will get us closer to the truth, but never fully beyond a shadow of a doubt. Historians, after all, are asking big and highly charged political questions that go beyond the innocence or guilt of one person to attempt to understand society's most deeply held values, intimate behaviors, and strongly protected interests. Fortunately, we have the ability to reopen any case at any time and work to overturn a verdict that just does not sit right with us. It is just a matter of getting in there, studying the sources, and researching and writing history.

Contents

Preface   vii
Introduction: Using Sources to Study the Past   xi

PART ONE
Indians and Europeans: New World Encounters   1

Points of View: Contact and Conquest (1502–1521)

1. DISPATCHES OF THE CONQUEST FROM THE NEW
   WORLD   3
   Hernando Cortés
   *In a letter to King Charles V of Spain, Hernando Cortés recounts his
   recent conquest of Mexico.*

2. A NAHUA ACCOUNT OF THE CONQUEST OF MEXICO   7
   *An anonymous Nahua account of the conquest of Mexico describes the
   Spanish conquest and suggests possible reasons for their defeat.*

FOR CRITICAL THINKING   12

---

3. DESTRUCTION OF THE INDIES   13
   Bartolomé de Las Casas
   *The Dominican friar Bartolomé de Las Casas's powerful report of the horrors
   of the Spanish conquest is often described as the "Black Legend."*

4. DESCRIPTION OF VIRGINIA   18
   John Smith
   *Captain John Smith describes Virginia and the Powhatan Indians he
   encountered at Jamestown in 1607.*

5. ENCOUNTER WITH THE INDIANS   22
   Father Paul Le Jeune

   The French Jesuit missionary Father Paul Le Jeune reports from Quebec in
   1634, where he lived among North American Indians.

6. CAPTURED BY INDIANS   28
   Mary Rowlandson

   Mary Rowlandson describes her captivity and experiences with the
   Wampanoag Indians during King Philip's War.

VISUAL PORTFOLIO: *New World Images*   **37**

PART TWO
The Colonial Experience: A Rapidly Changing Society   43

Points of View: Women in Colonial America

7. A BUSINESS TRIP ACROSS THE COLONIES   45
   Sarah Kemble Knight

   Kemble Knight records her adventures traveling in New England in
   1704 and 1705.

8. LEAVING AN ABUSIVE HUSBAND   50
   Abigail Abbot Bailey

   Abigail Abbot Bailey finds few legal protections following her marriage
   in 1767.

FOR CRITICAL THINKING   **57**

9. TESTIMONY OF PUEBLO INDIANS   58
   Pedro Naranjo and Josephe

   Pedro Naranjo of the Queres Nation and Josephe, a Spanish-speaking
   Indian, explain why they drove invaders from their villages in the Pueblo
   Revolt of 1680.

10. THE AFRICAN SLAVE TRADE   64
    Olaudah Equiano

    An eyewitness account of the African slave trade by Olaudah Equiano, Ibo
    prince supposedly kidnapped in the early 1760s.

11. ON THE MISFORTUNE OF INDENTURED SERVANTS   69
    Gottlieb Mittelberger

    A young German relates his arrival in Pennsylvania in 1750 and his sale as
    an indentured servant.

12. DEFENDING COLONIAL ACTIVITIES BEFORE PARLIAMENT 73
Benjamin Franklin

Franklin explains colonial opposition to the Stamp Act in 1766.

13. ASSIMILATION AND DISCRIMINATION 80
Jews in the Early Republic

Rebecca Lazarus and Benjamin Nones negotiate their Judaism in the colonies.

14. MAPMAKING AND COLONIALISM IN THE NEW WORLD 86
Amplissima Regionis Mississippi

A 1763 French map of North America reveals much about geography as a cultural and political construct.

PART THREE

Resistance and Revolution: Struggling for Liberty   89

Points of View: The Boston Massacre (1770)

15. A BRITISH OFFICER'S DESCRIPTION 90
Thomas Preston

A British officer stationed in Boston before the American Revolution recalls why his soldiers fired on Americans.

16. COLONIAL ACCOUNTS 94
George Robert Twelves Hewes, John Tudor, and the *Boston Gazette and Country Journal*

A patriot shoemaker, a Boston merchant, and the Boston Gazette and Country Journal *relate this bloody event from the colonists' perspective.*

FOR CRITICAL THINKING 102

VISUAL PORTFOLIO: *Patriot and Loyalist Propaganda*   *103*

17. A SOLDIER'S VIEW OF THE REVOLUTIONARY WAR 110
Joseph Plumb Martin

Martin, who joined the Revolutionary Army before his sixteenth birthday, writes about life as a common soldier.

18. CHOOSING SIDES 117
Boston King

A South Carolina slave escapes to enlist in the British Army and is rewarded with freedom in Canada in 1783.

19. SECRET CORRESPONDENCE OF A LOYALIST WIFE   122
    Catherine Van Cortlandt

    Catherine Van Cortlandt sends letters to her Tory husband behind British
    lines in 1776 and 1777.

20. REPUBLICAN MOTHERHOOD   127
    Abigail Adams

    Abigail Adams dispenses love, wisdom, and advice in letters to her husband
    and son.

21. SHAYS'S REBELLION: PRELUDE TO THE CONSTITUTION   132
    George Richards Minot

    George Richards Minot describes Shays's Rebellion of 1786–1787.

22. CASTING THEIR LOT WITH THE BRITISH   138
    Major John Norton (Teyoninhokarawen)

    A Scots-Iroquois chief supports the British Army in the War of 1812.

Part Four
Defining America: The Expanding Nation   145

Points of View: Religion in the New Nation (1800–1830)

23. THE GREAT REVIVAL OF 1800   147
    James McGready

    A passionate evangelical minister describes camp meeting revivals in
    Kentucky.

24. AN AMERICAN DEIST   132
    Elihu Palmer

    A minister promotes a rationalist revolution in religious thinking and
    deplores the "double despotism of church and state."

25. RELIGION IN AMERICA   157
    Frances Trollope

    A British writer attending a camp revival meeting is amused and
    appalled by what she witnesses.

For Critical Thinking   **162**

26. CROSSING THE CONTINENT   163
    Meriwether Lewis and William Clark

    From 1804 to 1806, braving canoe accidents, native peoples, and the Rockies,
    Lewis and Clark explore the American Northwest.

27. THE TRAIL OF TEARS   171
    John Ross

    John Ross, of mixed Cherokee and white ancestry, protests efforts by
    President Jackson and Congress to remove his tribe from Georgia to
    Oklahoma Territory in the 1830s.

28. PULLING A HANDCART TO THE MORMON ZION   177
    Priscilla Merriman Evans

    An emigrant woman arrives in Salt Lake City, Utah, in 1856, after
    walking one thousand miles from Iowa City, Iowa.

29. HOW THE WEST WAS WON   184
    An Officer of the "Army of the West"

    Dispatches from the U.S. Army describe a mix of power and persuasion
    in taking New Mexico.

30. LIFE IN CALIFORNIA BEFORE THE GOLD DISCOVERY   189
    Guadalupe Vallejo et al.

    Aging Californios *remember their lives in California before the 1846*
    "Bear Flag Revolt" and the 1849 gold rush brought thousands of Anglo
    settlers to the region.

31. MINERS DURING THE CALIFORNIA GOLD RUSH   197
    Daguerreotype by Joseph B. Starkweather

    A photograph from 1852 provides a glimpse of the lives of Chinese and
    Anglo miners in the California gold fields.

PART FIVE

An Age of Reform: Rearranging Social Patterns   **199**

Points of View: Nat Turner's Rebellion (1831)

32. A SLAVE INSURRECTION   200
    Nat Turner

    Nat Turner confesses to leading a slave uprising in Southampton
    County, Virginia, where at least fifty whites were killed.

33. WHO IS TO BLAME?   207
    William Lloyd Garrison et al.

    The abolitionist William Lloyd Garrison, editor of The Liberator; *John*
    Hampden Pleasants, editor of the Richmond Constitutional Whig; *and*
    Virginia governor John Floyd, in a letter to a friend, offer widely
    different reasons for and responses to Nat Turner's slave insurrection.

FOR CRITICAL THINKING   **214**

34. THE LOWELL TEXTILE WORKERS   215
    Mary Paul

    A young factory worker describes coming to Lowell to work in the mills and
    her life afterward on a commune.

35. A FAMILY TORN APART BY SLAVERY   222
    Henry "Box" Brown

    A respected member of Richmond, Virginia's, slave community is deprived
    of his wife and children in 1849 by unscrupulous masters.

36. LIFE OF A FEMALE SLAVE   228
    Harriet Jacobs

    Writing under a pseudonym, Harriet Jacobs tells the story of her sexual
    exploitation under slavery beginning at the age of fifteen.

37. A PIONEER FOR WOMEN'S RIGHTS   236
    Elizabeth Cady Stanton

    Elizabeth Cady Stanton remembers the 1848 Seneca Falls Convention
    and its famous "Declaration of Sentiments."

38. TAKING UP ARMS AGAINST SLAVERY   244
    John Brown

    John Brown, abolitionist and leader of the raid at Harpers Ferry, gives
    his farewell address to the Virginia Court on November 2, 1859, before he
    was hanged. Two portraits give a flavor of his personality, and a popular
    Civil War ballad memorializes him.

VISUAL PORTFOLIO: *Slavery and Freedom*   *251*

PART SIX
Civil War and Reconstruction: The Price of War   261

Points of View: Winding Down the War and an Uncertain Future

39. WHAT THE BLACK MAN WANTS   263
    Frederick Douglass

    In a speech to the Massachusetts Anti-Slavery Society in April 1865,
    former slave and renowned abolitionist Frederick Douglass argues for
    equal rights for African Americans.

40. A SLAVE OWNER'S JOURNAL AT THE END
    OF THE CIVIL WAR   269
    Henry William Ravenel

    A Southern slaveholder describes the effects of emancipation in South
    Carolina after Lee's surrender at Appomattox in 1865.

FOR CRITICAL THINKING   276

41. THREE DAYS OF TERROR   277
    Ellen Leonard

    Visiting family in New York City, Ellen Leonard is caught up in the
    violence of the draft riots of 1863.

42. THE BATTLE OF GETTYSBURG: AT WAR AND AT HOME   286
    Samuel and Rachel Cormany

    A young couple with a new baby record their hopes and fears on Civil War
    battle and home fronts in 1863.

43. FIGHTING FOR THE UNION   295
    Letters from Black Union Soldiers

    African American soldiers express their concerns and hopes in letters
    to the press recounting their experience of fighting for the North.

44. HEALING WOUNDS   302
    Cornelia Hancock

    An intrepid and persistent nurse tends to the wounded during the Civil
    War.

45. AFRICAN AMERICANS DURING RECONSTRUCTION   309
    Felix Haywood et al.

    In interviews conducted in the 1930s, Felix Haywood and other former
    slaves tell about their lives immediately following the Civil War.

46. WHITE SOUTHERNERS' REACTIONS TO RECONSTRUCTION   314
    Caleb G. Forshey and the Reverend James Sinclair

    Testimony by two men before a joint congressional committee in 1866
    shows the reaction of Southern whites to Reconstruction policies.

47. RUINS IN CHARLESTON, SOUTH CAROLINA, 1865 OR 1866   321
    Photograph by George N. Barnard

    A photograph of the ruins of Charleston, South Carolina, by a talented field
    photographer shows some of the devastation wrought by Sherman's march.

PART ONE

Indians and Europeans

New World Encounters

The contact between two worlds, a "new" one and an "old" one, permanently changed the way people on both sides of the Atlantic Ocean lived and thought about themselves. For Europeans who had spent centuries in the impoverished western margins of the Old World, Christopher Columbus's "discovery" of the New World afforded many opportunities to amass fortunes in precious metals, exotic spices, and new intoxicants. More important, the emerging European nations of the North Atlantic would eventually reconfigure the entire world, shifting its center away from the great civilizations in the East and building global empires from the fertile land, cheap labor, and high crop yields of the New World. This age of discovery, exploration, and conquest would touch off a scientific and commercial revolution, making Western Europe the cosmopolitan center of the world by attracting new ideas, technologies, and new forms of wealth and redistributing them across the world.

For the native peoples of what would come to be called the Americas, "discovery" was a catastrophe. European settlers, soldiers, and missionaries, along with Africans, introduced new plants, animals, and technologies that disrupted and radically reoriented life in the New World. Within fifty years of contact, Old World pathogens such as smallpox had killed some thirty million natives of the New World, because of their lack of immunity and the brutal tactics of European conquest.

The Dominican friar Bartolomé de Las Casas's report of the Spanish conquest of the West Indies—islands named by explorers who wrongly believed they had found a Western passage to Asia—captures the horrors of that first colonial encounter between Europeans and Native Americans. This pattern of brutality, violence, and subjugation of indigenous peoples would be repeated many times during the following five centuries. Yet, as the Spanish *conquistador* Hernando Cortés shows in his tale of the conquest of Mexico, the campaign

1

was not merely one of violence and enslavement but was also one of politics and persuasion. For centuries following Columbus's voyage, various indigenous nations played independent and sometimes powerful roles in the diplomacy of the Western Hemisphere. Their adaptations and cultural exchanges with one another and with European settlers continued, even while many tribes maintained distinct political and cultural identities into the present. Since the 1960s native peoples have played increasingly important political and social roles in the Americas, leading both indigenous and nonindigenous scholars to seek new ways of understanding the coming together of these two worlds that go beyond Spanish accounts of triumph and the myth that Europeans were taken as gods by the natives of the New World. Recently discovered as well as long forgotten Nahua accounts of the conquest, like the selection from the Florentine Codex included in this chapter, suggest that these early relationships between indigenous peoples and Europeans, in what is now Mexico, may have been more open and mutual than those occurring later in North America where segregated and unequal societies on both sides brought much bitterness and many prejudices to the encounter. The visual portfolio "New World Images" (pages 37–41) illustrates the way that Europeans viewed Native Americans and suggests some of these transformations.

Captain John Smith's description of Virginia's Indians shows cultural differences, probably both real and imagined, between Europeans and natives. And Father Paul Le Jeune, representing the French empire in the New World, suggests how little understanding often existed even between friendly whites and receptive Native Americans.

Indigenous peoples throughout the colonial era and well into the nineteenth century provoked fear and mystery. Stories about what happened when whites were captured by Indians, beginning perhaps with John Smith's account of his supposed rescue by Pocahontas, remained popular for more than two centuries, making captivity narratives among the first best sellers produced in North America. Mary Rowlandson's account of her captivity among the Wampanoag illustrates how Anglo-Americans domesticated their anxieties about Indians and wrapped them in an aura of romance and danger that often contrasted with surprisingly ordinary, everyday encounters.

1

Dispatches of the Conquest from the New World
Hernando Cortés

The discovery of the Americas by Christopher Columbus set off a speculative economic frenzy in Spain and Portugal. Merchants, military men, and adventurers rushed to equip ships and send soldiers in search of the gold, slaves, and spices promised by this vast new world. Twenty-five years after Columbus's discovery, however, the payoff remained elusive. The Spanish colonies in the New World were little more than a few Caribbean islands with sparse populations of settlers, African slaves, and captive Taino natives, who often died of European diseases for which they had no immunity. It was contact with and conquest of the Aztec empire on the mainland and the creation of New Spain (present-day Mexico and Guatemala) in 1521 that finally brought Europeans and natives some understanding of what they could expect from each other and how the future of this new world might look.

Hernando Cortés, who led the conquest of New Spain, was not unlike many of the adventurers and businessmen who crossed the Atlantic in the first century after Columbus. In 1504, at the age of nineteen, Cortés traveled to Hispaniola (now the Dominican Republic and Haiti), on a convoy of merchant ships. Using his training as a lawyer and family connections, he became the colony notary and received a repartimiento, *a Spanish colonial land grant, which included forced native labor. In 1511, he helped conquer Cuba, becoming clerk of the royal treasury, mayor of Havana, and a wealthy owner of land, Indians, and cattle. In 1517 and 1518, two expeditions to the Yucatán brought back rumors of gold and a great inland empire, and Cortés was asked by colonial authorities to command an exploratory expedition to the mainland.*

When Cortés and his army of 508 soldiers arrived, they found an Aztec empire in deep crisis. Rapid expansion from the center of power at Tenochtitlán, the world's largest city at the time and now present-day Mexico City, had stretched the empire's rigid political structure and low technological development to the breaking point. Unable to fully integrate the vast agricultural hinterlands into the empire, the Aztecs had resorted to increasingly brutal ritualized terror, human sacrifice, and militarization to keep control. The first natives that Cortés and his men encountered at the margins of the empire fought initially, but often quickly changed sides, preferring to take their chances with the Spanish invaders.

Anthony Pagden, ed. and trans., *Hernando Cortés: Letters from Mexico* (New Haven, Conn.: Yale University Press, 1986), 35–36, 84–85, 88, 105, 106, 132.

With the help of Malinche, a native woman who became Cortés's lover, adviser, and interpreter, Cortés and his men swept through town after town, defeating local armies, abolishing human sacrifice and tax collection, and carrying out mass conversions to Christianity. By the time the Spanish finally arrived in Tenochtitlán, Cortés and his mistress were feared and admired as mythical liberators. The conquest required two more years of political maneuvering and bloody battles before culminating in the siege of Tenochtitlán in 1521. Cortés's army, bolstered by as many as 200,000 natives, toppled the Aztec empire and declared the creation of a Christian New Spain.

As word of the conquest filtered back to Cuba, the Spanish royal bureaucracy feared that the upstart Cortés would take all the wealth of the New World for himself, perhaps even establish himself as a king. Colonial officials used every political weapon they could find to sabotage Cortés, including officially relieving him of command, organizing mutinies, and seizing all his possessions in Cuba—all to no avail. Realizing that he could trust no one in Havana, and now having great status as a conquistador, *he wrote directly to King Charles V of Spain about the things he had seen and done in the New World. These passages are from the dispatches that Cortés wrote to his king, in the heat of conquest.*

QUESTIONS TO CONSIDER

1. Consider Hernando Cortés's possible motivations for writing. In what ways did his audience—the king of Spain—affect Cortés's account of the conquest?
2. Why do you think that Cortés and 508 men were able to conquer an empire of millions?
3. Was Cortés a liberator or an oppressor of the natives?

They [the Aztecs] have a most horrid and abominable custom which truly ought to be punished and which until now we have seen in no other part, and this is that, whenever they wish to ask something of the idols, in order that their plea may find more acceptance, they take many girls and boys and even adults, and in the presence of the idols they open their chests while they are still alive and take out their hearts and entrails and burn them before the idols, offering the smoke as sacrifice. Some of us have seen this, and they say it is the most terrible and frightful thing they have ever witnessed.

This these Indians do so frequently that, as we have been informed, and, in part, have seen from our own experience during the short while we have been here, not one year passes in which they do not kill and sacrifice some fifty persons in each temple; and this is done and held as customary from the island of Cozumel to this land where we now have settled. Your Majesties [the King and Queen of Spain and the Roman Empire] may be most certain that, as this land seems to us to be very large, and to have many temples in it, not one year has passed, as far as we have been able to discover, in which three or four thousand souls have not been sacrificed in this manner. . . .

After we had crossed [a] bridge, Moctezuma[1] came to greet us and with him some two hundred lords, all barefoot and dressed in a different costume, but also

---

1. **Moctezuma:** Or, Montezuma; ruler of the Aztecs.

very rich in their way and more so than the others. They came in two columns, pressed very close to the walls of the street, which is very wide and beautiful and so straight that you can see from one end to the other. It is two-thirds of a league long and had on both sides very good and big houses, both dwellings and temples.

Moctezuma came down the middle of this street with two chiefs, one on his right hand and the other on his left. One of these was that great chief who had come on a litter to speak with me, and the other was Moctezuma's brother, chief of the city of Yztapalapa, which I had left that day. And they were all dressed alike except that Moctezuma wore sandals whereas the others went barefoot; and they held his arm on either side. When we met I dismounted and stepped forward to embrace him, but the two lords who were with him stopped me with their hands so that I should not touch him; and they likewise all performed the ceremony of kissing the earth. When this was over Moctezuma requested his brother to remain with me and to take me by the arm while he went a little way ahead with the other; and after he had spoken to me all the others in the two columns came and spoke with me, one after another, and then each returned to his column.

When at last I came to speak to Moctezuma himself I took off a necklace of pearls and cut glass that I was wearing and placed it round his neck; after we had walked a little way up the street a servant of his came with two necklaces, wrapped in a cloth, made from red snails' shells, which they hold in great esteem; and from each necklace hung eight shrimps of refined gold almost a span in length. When they had been brought he turned to me and placed them about my neck, and then continued up the street in the manner already described until we reached a very large and beautiful house which had been very well prepared to accommodate us. . . .

Most Invincible Lord, six days having passed since we first entered this great city of Tenochtitlán, during which time I had seen something of it, though little compared with how much there is to see and record, I decided from what I had seen that it would benefit Your Royal service and our safety if Moctezuma were in my power and not in complete liberty, in order that he should not retreat from the willingness he showed to serve Your Majesty; but chiefly because we Spaniards are rather obstinate and persistent, and should we annoy him he might, as he is so powerful, obliterate all memory of us. Furthermore, by having him with me, all those other lands which were subject to him would come more swiftly to the recognition and service of Your Majesty, as later happened. I resolved, therefore, to take him and keep him in the quarters where I was, which were very strong. . . .

There are, in all districts of this great city, many temples or houses for their idols. They are all very beautiful buildings, and in the important ones there are priests of their sect who live there permanently; and, in addition to the houses for the idols, they also have very good lodgings. . . .

The most important of these idols, and the ones in whom they have most faith, I had taken from their places and thrown down the steps; and I had those chapels where they were cleaned, for they were full of the blood of sacrifices; and I had images of Our Lady and of other saints put there, which caused Moctezuma and the other natives some sorrow. . . .

Moctezuma, who together with one of his sons and many other chiefs who had been captured previously [and] was still a prisoner, asked to be taken out onto the roof of the fortress where he might speak to the captains of his people and tell them to end the fighting. I had him taken out, and when he reached a breastwork which ran out beyond the fortress, and was about to speak to them, he received a blow on his head from a stone; and the injury was so serious that he died three days later. I told two of the Indians who were captive to carry him out on their shoulders to the people. What they did with him I do not know; only the war did not stop because of it, but grew more fierce and pitiless each day. . . .

We already knew that the Indians in the city [Tenochtitlán] were very scared, and we now learnt from two wretched creatures who had escaped from the city and come to our camp by night that they were dying of hunger and used to come out at night to fish in the canals between the houses, and wandered through the places we had won in search of firewood, and herbs and roots to eat. And because we had already filled in many of the canals, and leveled out many of the dangerous stretches, I resolved to enter the next morning shortly before dawn and do all the harm we could. The brigantines departed before daylight, and I with twelve or fifteen horsemen and some foot soldiers and Indians entered suddenly and stationed several spies who, as soon as it was light, called us from where we lay in ambush, and we fell on a huge number of people. As these were some of the most wretched people and had come in search of food, they were nearly all unarmed, and women and children in the main. We did them so much harm through all the streets in the city that we could reach, that the dead and the prisoners numbered more than eight hundred; the brigantines also took many people and canoes which were out fishing, and the destruction was very great. When the captains and lords of the city saw us attack at such an unaccustomed hour, they were as frightened as they had been by the recent ambush, and none of them dared come out and fight; so we returned with much booty and food for our allies. . . .

On leaving my camp, I had commanded Gonzalo de Sandoval to sail the brigantines in between the houses in the other quarter in which the Indians were resisting, so that we should have them surrounded, but not to attack until he saw that we were engaged. In this way they would be surrounded and so hard pressed that they would have no place to move save over the bodies of their dead or along the roof tops. They no longer had nor could find any arrows, javelins or stones with which to attack us; and our allies fighting with us were armed with swords and bucklers, and slaughtered so many of them on land and in the water that more than forty thousand were killed or taken that day. So loud was the wailing of the women and children that there was not one man amongst us whose heart did not bleed at the sound; and indeed we had more trouble in preventing our allies from killing with such cruelty than we had in fighting the enemy. For no race, however savage, has ever practiced such fierce and unnatural cruelty as the natives of these parts. Our allies also took many spoils that day, which we were unable to prevent, as they numbered more than

150,000 and we Spaniards were only some nine hundred. Neither our precautions nor our warnings could stop their looting, though we did all we could. One of the reasons why I had avoided entering the city in force during the past days was the fear that if we attempted to storm them they would throw all they possessed into the water, and, even if they did not, our allies would take all they could find. For this reason I was much afraid that Your Majesty would receive only a small part of the great wealth this city once had, in comparison with all that I once held for Your Highness. Because it was now late, we could no longer endure the stench of the dead bodies that had lain in those streets for many days, which was the most loathsome thing in all the world, we returned to our camps.

2

A Nahua Account of the Conquest of Mexico

"None of the Aztec compositions have survived," asserted historian William H. Prescott in 1843 when he wrote The Conquest of Mexico, *regarded for over a century as one of the greatest history books ever written. Indeed, Prescott was drawing primarily on first-hand accounts by Spaniards such as Bernal Díaz del Castillo's* The Conquest of New Spain *as well as close secondary sources written shortly thereafter. For centuries it had been a well-known part of the "Black Legend" of the horrors of the Spanish conquest (see the Las Casas document on page 13) that the first archbishop of Mexico, Juan de Zumarrga, collected thousands of Nahua manuscripts and burned them. (* Nahua *is the word for the people and the language of the Aztec empire.)*

However, some Nahua documents did survive the archbishop's fires, and others were recreated through oral histories taken shortly after the conquest by sympathetic Spanish priests and Nahua natives trained in anthropological and historical skills. These documents, usually known as codices (a codex is a simple form of book), lay unread and unappreciated for centuries in libraries and private collections across Mexico, Europe, and the United States. In the 1960s, a new generation of social and ethnohistorians traveled far and wide compiling and publishing native voices from the conquest. These accounts, translated into English and Spanish and published in dozens of bilingual and trilingual editions, have added greatly to our understanding of what happened when people from Europe and the New World first made contact.

What have scholars discovered by looking at the conquest from the American side? As far as the "facts" go, Nahua accounts confirm much of what had been written previously by Europeans such as Cortés, Díaz del Castillo, and even Prescott. However, when two

James Lockhart, ed. and trans., *We People Here: Nahuatl Accounts of the Conquest of Mexico* (Berkeley, CA: University of California Press, 1993), 90–104.

civilizations meet in such a dramatic way, with no prior knowledge of each other, the brute facts of who won which battle and how many people were killed are at best a starting point. Scholars studying these codices have focused on everything from the time it took for Spanish verbs to enter the Nahua language in different parts of Mexico to how the experiences of the natives in the imperial center at Tenochtitlán, who believed the conquest was a terrifying cataclysmic change, differed from those in the hinterlands, who tended to see it as just another part of a long local history of conflict, conquest, and adaptation.

The following document is drawn from the Florentine Codex, named for its home in the Laurentian Library in Florence, Italy. Probably the most famous of the Nahua descriptions of the conquest, it was first transcribed from Nahua hieroglyphs by native scholars trained and educated in Latin and Spanish by Fra Bernardino de Sahagún. A Franciscan priest known for his rigorous and respectful study of native custom and history, Sahagún supervised the production of the original bilingual Spanish/Nahua edition in the mid-sixteenth century. His Nahua assistants who translated the hieroglyphs, compiled the oral histories, and searched other sources to write this history remain unknown, and contemporary historians continue to struggle with conflicting accounts, different versions of the same documents, and complex political motivations behind the many views of the conquest.

QUESTIONS TO CONSIDER

1. Some scholars argue that Nahua accounts of the conquest are filled with scapegoats and excuses for the defeat. Which ones can you spot in this document?

2. Does this document contradict or confirm the traditional myth that the Nahua believed the Spanish were gods? Why do you think it matters to historians whether the Nahua believed this?

3. How might accounts of the conquest written by Tlascalans living outside of the capital city of Tenochtitlán differ from those by Mexica living at the center of the empire?

Tenth chapter, where it is said how the Spaniards landed uncontested and came on their way in this direction, and how Moteucçoma[1] left the great palace and went to his personal home.

Then Moteucçoma abandoned his patrimonial home, the great palace, and came back to his personal home.

When at last [the Spaniards] came, when they were coming along and moving this way, a certain person from Cempoallan,[2] whose name was Tlacochcalcatl, whom they had taken when they first came to see the land and the various altepetl,[3] also came interpreting for them, planning their route, conducting them, showing them the way, leading and guiding them.

---

1. **Moteucçoma:** Moctezuma or Montezuma; ruler of the Aztecs.
2. **Cempoallan:** Aztec province.
3. **altepetl:** Nahua word for city or town.

And when they reached Tecoac, which is in the land of the Tlaxcalans,[4] where their Otomis[5] lived, the Otomis met them with hostilities and war. But they annihilated the Otomis of Tecoac, who were destroyed completely. They lanced and stabbed them, they shot them with guns, iron bolts, crossbows. Not just a few but a huge number of them were destroyed.

After the great defeat at Tecoac, when the Tlaxcalans heard it and found out about it and it was reported to them, they became limp with fear, they were made faint; fear took hold of them. Then they assembled, and all of them, including the lords and rulers, took counsel among themselves, considering the reports.

They said, "How is it to be with us? Should we face them? For the Otomis are great and valiant warriors, yet they thought nothing of them, they regarded them as nothing; in a very short time, in the blink of an eyelid, they destroyed the people. Now let us just submit to them, let us make friends with them, let us be friends, for something must be done about the common people."

Thereupon the Tlaxcalan rulers went to meet them, taking along food: turkey hens, eggs, white tortillas, fine tortillas. They said to them, "Welcome, our lords."

[The Spaniards] answered them back, "Where is your homeland? Where have you come from?"

They said, "We are Tlaxcalans. Welcome, you have arrived, you have reached the land of Tlaxcala, which is your home."

(But in olden times it was called Texcallan and the people Texcalans.)

Eleventh chapter, where it is said how the Spaniards reached Tlaxcala, [also] called Texcallan.

[The Tlaxcalans] guided, accompanied, and led them until they brought them to their palace[s] and placed them there. They showed them great honors, they gave them what they needed and attended to them, and then they gave them their daughters.

Then [the Spaniards] asked them, "Where is Mexico?[6] What kind of a place is it? Is it still far?"

They answered them, "It's not far now. Perhaps one can get there in three days. It is a very favored place, and [the Mexica] are very strong, great warriors, conquerors, who go about conquering everywhere."

Now before this there had been friction between the Tlaxcalans and the Cholulans.[7] They viewed each other with anger, fury, hate, and disgust; they could come together on nothing. Because of this they put [the Spaniards] up to killing them treacherously.

They said to them, "The Cholulans are very evil; they are our enemies. They are as strong as the Mexica, and they are the Mexica's friends."

---

4. **Tlaxcalans:** Or, Tlascalans; a large native group that allied with Cortés against the Mexica.
5. **Otomis:** A native group that lived near Tlaxcala.
6. **Mexico:** The Aztec empire.
7. **Cholulans:** A native group that the Spaniards defeated in battle as part of their alliance with the Tlaxcalans.

When the Spaniards heard this, they went to Cholula. The Tlaxcalans and Cempoallans went with them, outfitted for war. When they arrived, there was a general summons and cry that all the noblemen, rulers, subordinate leaders, warriors, and commoners should come, and everyone assembled in the temple courtyard. When they had all come together, [the Spaniards and their friends] blocked the entrances, all of the places where one entered. Thereupon people were stabbed, struck, and killed. No such thing was in the minds of the Cholulans; they did not meet the Spaniards with weapons of war. It just seemed that they were stealthily and treacherously killed, because the Tlaxcalans persuaded [the Spaniards] to do it.

And a report of everything that was happening was given and relayed to Moteucçoma. Some of the messengers would be arriving as others were leaving; they just turned around and ran back. There was no time when they weren't listening, when reports weren't being given. And all the common people went about in a state of excitement; there were frequent disturbances, as if the earth moved and [quaked], as if everything were spinning before one's eyes. People took fright.

And after the dying in Cholula, [the Spaniards] set off on their way to Mexico, coming gathered and bunched, raising dust. Their iron lances and halberds[8] seemed to sparkle, and their iron swords were curved like a stream of water. Their cuirasses[9] and iron helmets seemed to make a clattering sound. Some of them came wearing iron all over, turned into iron beings, gleaming, so that they aroused great fear and were generally seen with fear and dread. Their dogs came in front, coming ahead of them, keeping to the front, panting, with their spittle hanging down.

Twelfth chapter, where it is said how Moteucçoma sent a great nobleman along with many other noblemen to go to meet the Spaniards, and what their gifts of greeting were when they greeted the Captain between Iztactepetl and Popocatepetl.[10]

Thereupon Moteucçoma named and sent the noblemen and a great many other agents of his, with Tzihuacpopocatzin as their leader, to go meet [Cortés] between Popocatepetl and Iztactepetl, at Quauhtechcac. They gave [the Spaniards] golden banners, banners of precious feathers, and golden necklaces.

And when they had given the things to them, they seemed to smile, to rejoice and be very happy. Like monkeys they grabbed the gold. It was as though their hearts were put to rest, brightened, freshened. For gold was what they greatly thirsted for; they were gluttonous for it, starved for it, piggishly wanting it. They came lifting up the golden banners, waving them from side to side, showing them to each other. They seemed to babble; what they said to each other was in a babbling tongue.

---

8. **halberds:** A weapon with an axe and a long spike set on a long pole.
9. **cuirasses:** Type of armor.
10. **Iztactepetl and Popocatepetl:** Third highest mountain in Mexico and an active volcano, respectively, both visible from Mexico City.

And when they saw Tzihuacpopocatzin, they said, "Is this one then Moteucçoma?" They said it to the Tlaxcalans and Cempoallans, their lookouts, who came among them, questioning them secretly. They said, "It is not that one, o our lords. This is Tzihuacpopocatzin, who is representing Moteucçoma."

[The Spaniards] said to him, "Are you then Moteucçoma?" He said, "I am your agent Moteucçoma."

Then they told him, "Go on with you! Why do you lie to us? What do you take us for? You can't lie to us, you can't fool us, [turn our heads], flatter us, [make faces at us], trick us, confuse our vision, distort things for us, blind us, dazzle us, throw mud in our eyes, put muddy hands on our faces. It is not you. Moteucçoma exists; he will not be able to hide from us, he will not be able to find refuge. Where will he go? Is he a bird, will he fly? Or will he take an underground route, will he go somewhere into a mountain that is hollow inside? We will see him, we will not fail to gaze on his face and hear his words from his lips."

Therefore they just scorned and disregarded him, and so another of their meetings and greetings came to naught. Then they went straight back the direct way [to Mexico].

Thirteenth chapter, where it is said how Moteucçoma sent other sorcerers to cast spells on the Spaniards, and what happened to them on the way.

Another group of messengers—rainmakers, witches, and priests—had also gone out for an encounter, but nowhere were they able to do anything or to get sight of [the Spaniards]; they did not hit their target, they did not find the people they were looking for, they were not sufficient.

They just came up against a drunk man in the road; they went to meet him and were dumbfounded at him. The way they saw him, he seemed to be dressed as a Chalcan, feigning to be a Chalcan.[11] He seemed to be drunk, feigning drunkenness. On his chest were tied eight grass ropes. He came quarreling with them, coming ahead of the Spaniards.

He ranted at them, saying to them, "What are you still doing here? What more do you want? What more is Moteucçoma trying to do? Did he come to his senses yesterday? Has he just now become a great coward? He has done wrong, he has [abandoned] the people, he has destroyed people, [he has hit himself on the head and wrapped himself up in relation to people], he has mocked people and deceived them."

When they had seen this and heard what he said, they made an effort to address him humbly; they quickly set up for him a place to attend to him, an earthen platform with a straw bed, but he absolutely would not look at it. In vain they had set out for him the earthen platform they had tried to make for him there.

[It was as though they entered his mouth]; he scolded them, greatly scolded them with angry words, saying to them, "What is the use of your coming here? Mexico will never exist again, it [is gone] forever. Go on with you; it is no

---

11. **Chalcan:** A native group renowned among the Aztecs for their poetry.

longer there. Do turn around and look at what is happening in Mexico, what is going on."

Then they looked back, they quickly looked back, and saw all the temples, the calpulli [buildings], the calmecacs,[12] and all the houses in Mexico burning, and it seemed as though there were fighting.

And when the rainmakers had seen that, their hearts seemed to fail them, they were silent, as though someone had forced something down their throats. They said, "What we have seen was needed to be seen not by us but by Moteucçoma, for that was not just anyone, but the youth Tezcatlipoca."[13]

Then he vanished, and they saw him no more. And after that the messengers did not go to encounter [the Spaniards], did not move in their direction, but the rainmakers and priests turned back there and came to tell Moteucçoma. They came together with those who had first gone with Tzihuacpopocatzin.

And when the messengers got there, they told Moteucçoma what had happened and what they had seen. When Moteucçoma heard it, he just hung his head and sat there, not saying a word. He sat like someone on the verge of death; for a long time it was as though he had lost awareness.

He answered them only by saying to them, "What can be done, o men of unique valor? We have come to the end. We are resigned. Should we climb up in the mountains? But should we run away? We are Mexica. Will the Mexica state flourish [in exile]? Look at the sad condition of the poor old men and women, and the little children who know nothing yet. Where would they be taken? What answer is there? What can be done, whatever can be done? Where are we to go? We are resigned to whatever we will see, of whatever nature."

FOR CRITICAL THINKING

1. The Florentine Codex presents the native population as political agents whereas Cortés tends to depict them as relatively passive victims of conquest. How much do you think these two portrayals derive from the different realities of conquest in the region, and how much are they products of the distinct worldviews and personal agendas of their authors?

2. Many Nahua documents agree with Spanish accounts about Moctezuma acting timidly and losing his empire because he believed that the Spanish were gods. Why might some native chroniclers have an interest in perpetuating this theory?

3. How do these two descriptions of encounters between Europeans and natives compare with contemporary views in popular culture of encounters between Native Americans and British settlers in North America?

---

12. **calmecacs:** Religious schools for boys run by Aztec priests.
13. **Tezcatlipoca:** Aztec god of the night, beauty, war, and material things. He often tempted men to do wicked things as a means of rewarding those who could resist temptations and punishing those who succumbed.

3

Destruction of the Indies
Bartolomé de Las Casas

Bartolomé de Las Casas (1474–1566), a Spanish colonist and later a Dominican friar, saw Christopher Columbus in 1493 when the explorer passed through Seville on his return to Spain after discovering the Americas the previous year. Las Casas's father and two uncles sailed that year on Columbus's second voyage. As news spread throughout Europe about what was believed to be a western route to the East Indies, rumors of an abundance of gold, spices, and other valuables attracted adventurers and others in search of fortune. The Spanish built small colonies on the island of Hispaniola (now the Dominican Republic and Haiti). In 1502, Las Casas himself traveled to the New World to serve as an officer of the king. In exchange for his services, he was given an encomienda, *an estate that included native people to labor for him. Several years later, he was moved by a sermon given by a Dominican priest denouncing the treatment of the Indians by the Spanish. Las Casas returned his serfs to the governor and probably was the first priest ordained in the New World.*

Las Casas spent the rest of his long life attempting to protect the Native Americans against the massacres, tortures, slavery, and forced labor imposed on them by their Spanish conquerors. In 1515, Las Casas returned to Spain and pleaded before King Ferdinand for more humane treatment of the native people. His passionate defense of the indigenous Americans influenced Pope Paul III to declare the natives of America rational beings with souls. Las Casas traveled throughout Spain's new colonies and in the 1540s became bishop of Chiapas (now southern Mexico).

His powerful writings created the image of Spanish conquest often called the "Black Legend," a vision of destruction and cruelty until that time unparalleled. Most modern scholars accept the accuracy of Las Casas's shocking portraits of devastation, many of which he personally witnessed, such as the violent and bloody conquest of Cuba. Today, however, many view these horrors not as the outcome of some peculiar Spanish cruelty but as characteristic of the bloody "Columbian encounter" between Europeans and other cultures in the age of exploration and conquest. Las Casas wrote the following treatise in Seville in 1552.

QUESTIONS TO CONSIDER

1. Was Bartolomé de Las Casas's view of the Native Americans accurate? Why or why not?
2. Do you judge his criticism of the Spanish empire to have been fair and accurate?

Francis Augustus MacNutt, *Bartholomew de Las Casas: His Life, His Apostolate, and His Writings* (New York: G. P. Putnam's Sons, 1909), 314–21.

3. Throughout his life Las Casas remained fiercely loyal to both the Spanish monarch and the Catholic Church. How would you reconcile these feelings with his condemnation of the Spanish empire's actions in the New World?

SHORT REPORT OF THE DESTRUCTION OF THE WEST INDIES

The Indies were discovered in the year fourteen hundred and ninety-two. The year following, Spanish Christians went to inhabit them, so that it is since forty-nine years that numbers of Spaniards have gone there: and the first land, that they invaded to inhabit, was the large and most delightful Isle of Hispaniola, which has a circumference of six hundred leagues.

2. There are numberless other islands, and very large ones, all around on every side, that were all — and we have seen it — as inhabited and full of their native Indian peoples as any country in the world.

3. Of the continent, the nearest part of which is more than two hundred and fifty leagues distant from this Island, more than ten thousand leagues of maritime coast have been discovered, and more is discovered every day; all that has been discovered up to the year forty-nine is full of people, like a hive of bees, so that it seems as though God had placed all, or the greater part of the entire human race in these countries.

4. God has created all these numberless people to be quite the simplest, without malice or duplicity, most obedient, most faithful to their natural Lords, and to the Christians, whom they serve; the most humble, most patient, most peaceful, and calm, without strife nor tumults; not wrangling, nor querulous, as free from uproar, hate and desire of revenge, as any in the world.

5. They are likewise the most delicate people, weak and of feeble constitution, and less than any other can they bear fatigue, and they very easily die of whatsoever infirmity; so much so, that not even the sons of our Princes and of nobles, brought up in royal and gentle life, are more delicate than they; although there are among them such as are of the peasant class. They are also a very poor people, who of worldly goods possess little, nor wish to possess: and they are therefore neither proud, nor ambitious, nor avaricious.

6. Their food is so poor, that it would seem that of the Holy Fathers in the desert was not scantier nor less pleasing. Their way of dressing is usually to go naked, covering the private parts; and at most they cover themselves with a cotton cover, which would be about equal to one and a half or two ells square of cloth. Their beds are of matting, and they mostly sleep in certain things like hanging nets, called in the language of Hispaniola *hamacas*.

7. They are likewise of a clean, unspoiled, and vivacious intellect, very capable, and receptive to every good doctrine; most prompt to accept our Holy Catholic Faith, to be endowed with virtuous customs; and they have as little difficulty with such things as any people created by God in the world.

8. Once they have begun to learn of matters pertaining to faith, they are so importunate to know them, and in frequenting the sacraments and divine

service of the Church, that to tell the truth, the clergy have need to be endowed of God with the gift of pre-eminent patience to bear with them: and finally, I have heard many lay Spaniards frequently say many years ago, (unable to deny the goodness of those they saw) certainly these people were the most blessed of the earth, had they only knowledge of God.

9. Among these gentle sheep, gifted by their Maker with the above qualities, the Spaniards entered as soon as they knew them, like wolves, tigers, and lions which had been starving for many days, and since forty years they have done nothing else; nor do they otherwise at the present day, than outrage, slay, afflict, torment, and destroy them with strange and new, and divers kinds of cruelty, never before seen, nor heard of, nor read of, of which some few will be told below: to such extremes has this gone that, whereas there were more than three million souls, whom we saw in Hispaniola, there are to-day, not two hundred of the native population left.

10. The island of Cuba is almost as long as the distance from Valladolid[1] to Rome; it is now almost entirely deserted. The islands of San Juan [Puerto Rico], and Jamaica, very large and happy and pleasing islands, are both desolate. The Lucaya Isles lie near Hispaniola and Cuba to the north and number more than sixty, including those that are called the Giants, and other large and small Islands; the poorest of these, which is more fertile, and pleasing than the King's garden in Seville, is the healthiest country in the world, and contained more than five hundred thousand souls, but to-day there remains not even a single creature. All were killed in transporting them, to Hispaniola, because it was seen that the native population there was disappearing.

11. A ship went three years later to look for the people that had been left after the gathering in, because a good Christian was moved by compassion to convert and win those that were found to Christ; only eleven persons, whom I saw, were found.

12. More than thirty other islands, about the Isle of San Juan, are destroyed and depopulated, for the same reason. All these islands cover more than two thousand leagues of land, entirely depopulated and deserted.

13. We are assured that our Spaniards, with their cruelty and execrable works, have depopulated and made desolate the great continent, and that more than ten Kingdoms, larger than all Spain, counting Aragon[2] and Portugal, and twice as much territory as from Seville to Jerusalem (which is more than two thousand leagues), although formerly full of people, are now deserted.

14. We give as a real and true reckoning, that in the said forty years, more than twelve million persons, men, and women, and children, have perished unjustly and through tyranny, by the infernal deeds and tyranny of the Christians; and I truly believe, nor think I am deceived, that it is more than fifteen.

15. Two ordinary and principal methods have the self-styled Christians, who have gone there, employed in extirpating these miserable nations and removing them from the face of the earth. The one, by unjust, cruel and tyrannous

---

1. **Valladolid:** A city in northwestern Spain.
2. **Aragon:** An ancient kingdom in what is now northeastern Spain.

wars. The other, by slaying all those, who might aspire to, or sigh for, or think of liberty, or to escape from the torments that they suffer, such as all the native Lords, and adult men; for generally, they leave none alive in the wars, except the young men and the women, whom they oppress with the hardest, most horrible, and roughest servitude, to which either man or beast, can ever be put. To these two ways of infernal tyranny, all the many and divers other ways, which are numberless, of exterminating these people, are reduced, resolved, or sub-ordered according to kind.

16. The reason why the Christians have killed and destroyed such infinite numbers of souls, is solely because they have made gold their ultimate aim, seeking to load themselves with riches in the shortest time and to mount by high steps, disproportioned to their condition: namely by their insatiable avarice and ambition, the greatest, that could be on the earth. These lands, being so happy and so rich, and the people so humble, so patient, and so easily subjugated, they have had no more respect, nor consideration nor have they taken more account of them (I speak with truth of what I have seen during all the aforementioned time) than, — I will not say of animals, for would to God they had considered and treated them as animals, — but as even less than the dung in the streets.

17. In this way have they cared for their lives — and for their souls: and therefore, all the millions above mentioned have died without faith, and without sacraments. And it is a publicly known truth, admitted, and confessed by all, even by the tyrants and homicides themselves, that the Indians throughout the Indies never did any harm to the Christians: they even esteemed them as coming from heaven, until they and their neighbours had suffered the same many evils, thefts, deaths, violence and visitations at their hands.

OF HISPANIOLA

In the island of Hispaniola — which was the first, as we have said, to be invaded by the Christians — the immense massacres and destruction of these people began. It was the first to be destroyed and made into a desert. The Christians began by taking the women and children, to use and to abuse them, and to eat of the substance of their toil and labour, instead of contenting themselves with what the Indians gave them spontaneously, according to the means of each. Such stores are always small; because they keep no more than they ordinarily need, which they acquire with little labour; but what is enough for three households, of ten persons each, for a month, a Christian eats and destroys in one day. From their using force, violence and other kinds of vexations, the Indians began to perceive that these men could not have come from heaven.

2. Some hid their provisions, others, their wives and children: others fled to the mountains to escape from people of such harsh and terrible intercourse. The Christians gave them blows in the face, beatings and cudgellings, even laying hands on the lords of the land. They reached such recklessness and effrontery, that a Christian captain violated the lawful wife of the chief king and lord of all the island.

3. After this deed, the Indians consulted to devise means of driving the Christians from their country. They took up their weapons, which are poor enough and little fitted for attack, being of little force and not even good for defence. For this reason, all their wars are little more than games with sticks, such as children play in our countries.

4. The Christians, with their horses and swords and lances, began to slaughter and practise strange cruelty among them. They penetrated into the country and spared neither children nor the aged, nor pregnant women, nor those in child labour, all of whom they ran through the body and lacerated, as though they were assaulting so many lambs herded in their sheepfold.

5. They made bets as to who would slit a man in two, or cut off his head at one blow: or they opened up his bowels. They tore the babes from their mothers' breast by the feet, and dashed their heads against the rocks. Others they seized by the shoulders and threw into the rivers, laughing and joking, and when they fell into the water they exclaimed: "boil body of so and so!" They spitted the bodies of other babes, together with their mothers and all who were before them, on their swords.

6. They made a gallows just high enough for the feet to nearly touch the ground, and by thirteens, in honour and reverence of our Redeemer and the twelve Apostles, they put wood underneath and, with fire, they burned the Indians alive.

7. They wrapped the bodies of others entirely in dry straw, binding them in it and setting fire to it; and so they burned them. They cut off the hands of all they wished to take alive, made them carry them fastened on to them, and said: "Go and carry letters": that is; take the news to those who have fled to the mountains.

8. They generally killed the lords and nobles in the following way. They made wooden gridirons of stakes, bound them upon them, and made a slow fire beneath: thus the victims gave up the spirit by degrees, emitting cries of despair in their torture.

9. I once saw that they had four or five of the chief lords stretched on the gridirons to burn them, and I think also there were two or three pairs of gridirons, where they were burning others; and because they cried aloud and annoyed the captain or prevented him sleeping, he commanded that they should strangle them: the officer who was burning them was worse than a hangman and did not wish to suffocate them, but with his own hands he gagged them, so that they should not make themselves heard, and he stirred up the fire, until they roasted slowly, according to his pleasure. I know his name, and knew also his relations in Seville. I saw all the above things and numberless others.

4

Description of Virginia

John Smith

Before he became one of the original settlers of Jamestown in 1607, Captain John Smith (1580–1631) was already experienced as a soldier and diplomat, fighting the Spanish in the Netherlands and the Turks in Hungary. At Jamestown he took part in governing the colony—leading it from 1608 to 1609—and in managing relations with the native Americans. His story, told years later, of being saved from death by the friendly interven-tion of Pocahontas, the daughter of Chief Powhatan, has a secure place in American leg-end. Historians and ethnographers disagree about whether the incident happened and, if it did, whether Smith correctly understood its meaning in the context of the native culture. Many suspect that it was part of a ritual inducting Smith into the tribe rather than a rescue.

Smith returned to England in 1609. His later years were given over to promoting both himself and the settlement of the New World he had helped to colonize. His de-scriptions in numerous writings both of British America and of its Native American in-habitants set patterns that continued for centuries.

QUESTIONS TO CONSIDER

1. How would you describe John Smith's account of the New World? What kind of modern writing or communication does it suggest?
2. What adjectives would you apply to Smith's description of the Native Americans? How reliable does his account of the Indians seem to you?

THE COMMODITIES IN VIRGINIA
OR THAT MAY BE HAD BY INDUSTRY

The mildness of the air, the fertility of the soil, and the situation of the rivers are so propitious to the nature and use of man as no place is more convenient for pleasure, profit, and man's sustenance. Under that latitude or climate, here will live any beasts, as horses, goats, sheep, asses, hens, etc. The waters, islands, and shoals are full of safe harbors for ships of war or merchandise, for boats of all sorts, for transportation or fishing, etc.

Captain John Smith of Willoughby by Alford, Lincolnshire; President of Virginia and Admiral of New England. Works: 1608–1631, ed. Edward Arber, The English Scholar's Library, No. 16 (Birming-ham, 1884), 63–67. The text has been modernized by Elizabeth Marcus.

The Bay and rivers have much marketable fish and places fit for salt works, building of ships, making of iron, etc.

Muscovia and Polonia yearly receive many thousands for pitch, tar, soap ashes, rosin, flax, cordage, sturgeon, masts, yards, wainscot, furs, glass, and suchlike; also Swethland[1] for iron and copper. France, in like manner, for wine, canvas, and salt, Spain as much for iron, steel, figs, raisins and sherry. Italy with silks and velvets, consumes our chief commodities. Holland maintains itself by fishing and trading at our own doors. All these temporize with others for necessities, but all as uncertain as to peace or war, and besides the charge, travel and danger in transporting them, by seas, lands, storms and pirates. Then how much has Virginia the prerogative of all those flourishing kingdoms for the benefit of our lands, when as within one hundred miles all those are to be had, either ready provided by nature or else to be prepared, were there but industrious men to labor. Only copper might be lacking, but there is good probability that both copper and better minerals are there to be had if they are worked for. Their countries have it. So then here is a place a nurse for soldiers, a practice for mariners, a trade for merchants, a reward for the good, and that which is most of all, a business (most acceptable to God) to bring such poor infidels to the true knowledge of God and his holy Gospel.

OF THE NATURAL INHABITANTS OF VIRGINIA

The land is not populous, for the men be few, their far greater number is of women and children. Within 60 miles of Jamestown there are about some 5,000 people, but of able men fit for their wars scarce 1,500. To nourish so many together they have yet no means, because they make so small a benefit of their land, be it never so fertile.

Six or seven hundred have been the most that have been seen together, when they gathered themselves to have surprised Captain Smyth at Pamaunke, having but 15 to withstand the worst of their fury. As small as the proportion of ground that has yet been discovered, is in comparison of that yet unknown. The people differ very much in stature, especially in language, as before is expressed.

Since being very great as the Sesquaesahamocks, others very little as the Wighcocomocoes: but generally tall and straight, of a comely proportion, and of a color brown, when they are of any age, but they are born white. Their hair is generally black, but few have any beards. The men wear half their heads shaven, the other half long. For barbers they use their women, who with 2 shells will grate away the hair in any fashion they please. The women are cut in many fashions agreeable to their years, but ever some part remain long.

They are very strong, of an able body and full of agility, able to endure, to lie in the woods under a tree by the fire, in the worst of winter, or in the weeds and grass, in ambush in the summer.

They are inconstant in everything, but what fear constrains them to keep. Crafty, timorous, quick of apprehension and very ingenious. Some are of disposition

1. **Swethland:** Sweden.

fearful, some bold, most cautious, all savage. Generally covetous of copper, beads and such like trash. They are soon moved to anger, and so malicious, that they seldom forget an injury: they seldom steal from one another, lest their conjurors should reveal it, and so they be pursued and punished. That they are thus feared is certain, but that any can reveal their offenses by conjuration I am doubtful. Their women are careful not to be suspected of dishonesty without leave of their husbands.

Each household knows their own lands and gardens, and most live off their own labors.

For their apparel, they are some time covered with the skins of wild beasts, which in winter are dressed with the hair but in summer without. The better sort use large mantles of deerskin not much different in fashion from the Irish mantles. Some embroidered them with beads, some with copper, others painted after their manner. But the common sort have scarce to cover their nakedness but with grass, the leaves of trees or suchlike. We have seen some use mantles that nothing could be discerned but the feathers, that was exceedingly warm and handsome. But the women are always covered about their middles with a skin and are ashamed to be seen bare.

They adorn themselves most with copper beads and paintings. Their women have their legs, hands, breasts and face cunningly embroidered with diverse works, as beasts, serpents, artificially wrought into their flesh with black spots. In each ear commonly they have three great holes, from which they hang chains, bracelets or copper. Some of their men wear in those holes a small green and yellow colored snake, near half a yard in length, which crawling and lapping herself around his neck oftentimes familiarly would kiss his lips. Others wear a dead rat tied by the tail. Some on their heads wear the wing of a bird or some large feather, with a rattle; those rattles are somewhat like the chape of a rapier, but less, which they take from the tails of a snake. Many have the whole skin of a hawk or some strange fowl, stuffed with the wings abroad. Others a broad piece of copper, and some the hand of their enemy dried. Their heads and shoulders are painted red with the root Pocone pounded to a powder mixed with oil; this they hold in summer to preserve them from the heat and in winter from the cold. Many other forms of paintings they use, but he is the most gallant that is the most monstrous to behold.

Their buildings and habitations are for the most part by the rivers or not far distant from some fresh spring. Their houses are built like our arbors of small young springs bowed and tied, and so close covered with mats or the barks of trees very handsomely, that notwithstanding either wind, rain or weather, they are as warm as stoves, but very smokey; yet at the top of the house there is a hole made for the smoke to go into right over the fire.

Against the fire they lie on little mounds of reeds covered with a mat, borne from the ground a foot and more by a mound of wood. On these round about the house, they lie heads and points one by the other against the fire, some covered with mats, some with skins, and some stark naked lie on the ground, from 6 to 20 in a house.

Their houses are in the midst of their fields or gardens; which are small plots of ground, some 20, some 40, some 100, some 200, some more, some less. Sometimes from 2 to 100 of these houses are together, or but a little separated by groves of trees. Near their habitations is a little small wood, or old trees on the ground, by reason of their burning of them for fire. So that a man may gallop a horse among these woods anyway, but where the creeks or rivers shall hinder.

Men, women and children have their several names according to the particular whim of their parents. Their women (they say) are easily delivered of child, yet do they love children dearly. To make them hardy, in the coldest mornings they wash them in the rivers, and by painting and ointments so tan their skins that after a year or two no weather will hurt them.

The men bestow their times in fishing, hunting, wars, and such manlike exercises, scorning to be seen in any woman like exercise, which is the cause that the women be very painful and the men often idle. The women and children do the rest of the work. They make mats, baskets, pots, mortars, pound their corn, make their bread, prepare their victuals, plant their corn, gather their corn, bear all kinds of burdens and suchlike.

5

Encounter with the Indians
Father Paul Le Jeune

In the sixteenth and seventeenth centuries, France's Society of Jesus of the Roman Catholic Church, more commonly known as the Jesuits, energetically proselytized in virtually every Portuguese, Spanish, and French colony. The first Jesuit missionaries arrived in French Canada in 1632 determined to bring Christianity to the Indians by living with them, learning their languages, educating their children, and demonstrating (sometimes at the cost of their lives) that they were as brave as the Native American warriors. The French, though haughty and arrogant at times, were less authoritarian than the Spanish in dealing with natives—and often more successful. The Jesuits played a major role in cementing French alliances with many Native American nations across Canada and into the Ohio Valley. This gave France a strategic position in the New World, hemming the colonies of British North America against the eastern seaboard until French power was destroyed in the mid-eighteenth century. The Jesuits in Canada reported regularly on their ministry. These reports form an important account of American Indian life and greatly influenced the European perception of the New World. (It is regrettable that no Indian accounts of the French Jesuits survived.)

Father Paul Le Jeune, born in France in 1591, became a Jesuit in 1613. He had been a professor of rhetoric as well as Superior of the Jesuit House at Dieppe before he radically changed his activities by going to French North America in 1632. Le Jeune found much to admire in the Native Americans, as well as much that he could neither understand nor accept. The report included here was written from Quebec in August 1634. Le Jeune worked among the Indians until 1649. He died in Paris in 1664.

QUESTIONS TO CONSIDER
1. What were Father Le Jeune's impressions and assessment of Native American religion?
2. What did he consider the Indians' virtues?
3. What did he consider their main vices?

Reuben Gold Thwaites, ed., *The Jesuit Relations and Allied Documents: Travels and Explorations of the Jesuit Missionaries in New France* (Cleveland: Burrows Brothers, 1987).

CHAPTER IV. ON THE BELIEF, SUPERSTITIONS, AND ERRORS OF THE MONTAGNAIS SAVAGES

I have already reported that the Savages believe that a certain one named Atahocam had created the world, and that one named Messou had restored it. I have questioned upon this subject the famous Sorcerer and the old man with whom I passed the Winter; they answered that they did not know who was the first Author of the world, — that it was perhaps Atahocam, but that was not certain; that they only spoke of Atahocam as one speaks of a thing so far distant that nothing sure can be known about it. . . .

As to the Messou, they hold that he restored the world, which was destroyed in the flood; whence it appears that they have some tradition of that great universal deluge which happened in the time of Noë. . . .

They also say that all animals, of every species, have an elder brother, who is, as it were, the source and origin of all individuals, and this elder brother is wonderfully great and powerful. . . . Now these elders of all the animals are the juniors of the Messou. Behold him well related, this worthy restorer of the Universe, he is elder brother to all beasts. If any one, when asleep, sees the elder or progenitor of some animals, he will have a fortunate chase; if he sees the elder of the Beavers, he will take Beavers; if he sees the elder of the Elks, he will take Elks, possessing the juniors through the favor of their senior whom he has seen in the dream. . . .

Their Religion, or rather their superstition, consists of little besides praying; but O, my God, what prayers they make! In the morning, when the little children come out from their Cabins, they shout, *Cacouakhi, Pakhais Amiscouakhi, Pakhais Mousouakhi, Pakhais*, "Come, Porcupines; come, Beavers; come, Elk;" and this is all of their prayers.

When the Savages sneeze, and sometimes even at other times, during the Winter, they cry out in a loud voice, *Etouctaian miraounam an Mirouscamikhi*, "I shall be very glad to see the Spring."

At other times, I have heard them pray for the Spring, or for deliverance from evils and other similar things; and they express all these things in the form of desires, crying out as loudly as they can, "I would be very glad if this day would continue, if the wind would change," etc. I could not say to whom these wishes are addressed, for they themselves do not know, at least those whom I have asked have not been able to enlighten me. . . .

CHAPTER V. ON THE GOOD THINGS WHICH ARE FOUND AMONG THE SAVAGES

If we begin with physical advantages, I will say that they possess these in abundance. They are tall, erect, strong, well proportioned, agile; and there is nothing effeminate in their appearance. Those little Fops that are seen elsewhere are only caricatures of men, compared with our Savages. I almost believed, heretofore, that the Pictures of the Roman Emperors represented the ideal of the painters rather than men who had ever existed, so strong and powerful are their heads; but I see here upon the shoulders of these people the heads of Julius

Caesar, of Pompey, of Augustus, of Otho, and of others, that I have seen in France, drawn upon paper, or in relief on medallions.

As to the mind of the Savage, it is of good quality. I believe that souls are all made from the same stock, and that they do not materially differ; hence, these barbarians having well formed bodies, and organs well regulated and well arranged, their minds ought to work with ease. Education and instruction alone are lacking. Their soul is a soil which is naturally good, but loaded down with all the evils that a land abandoned since the birth of the world can produce. I naturally compare our Savages with certain villagers, because both are usually without education, though our Peasants are superior in this regard; and yet I have not seen any one thus far, of those who have come to this country, who does not confess and frankly admit that the Savages are more intelligent than our ordinary peasants.

Moreover, if it is a great blessing to be free from a great evil, our Savages are happy; for the two tyrants who provide hell and torture for many of our Europeans, do not reign in their great forests,—I mean ambition and avarice. As they have neither political organization, nor offices, nor dignities, nor any authority, for they only obey their Chief through good will toward him, therefore they never kill each other to acquire these honors. Also, as they are contented with a mere living, not one of them gives himself to the Devil to acquire wealth.

They make a pretence of never getting angry, not because of the beauty of this virtue, for which they have not even a name, but for their own contentment and happiness, I mean, to avoid the bitterness caused by anger. The Sorcerer said to me one day, speaking of one of our Frenchmen, "He has no sense, he gets angry; as for me, nothing can disturb me; let hunger oppress me, let my nearest relation pass to the other life, let the Hiroquois, our enemies, massacre our people, I never get angry." What he says is not an article of faith; for, as he is more haughty than any other Savage, so I have seen him oftener out of humor than any of them; it is true also that he often restrains and governs himself by force, especially when I expose his foolishness. I have only heard one Savage pronounce this word, *Ninichcatihin*, "I am angry," and he only said it once. But I noticed that they kept their eyes on him, for when these Barbarians are angry, they are dangerous and unrestrained.

Whoever professes not to get angry, ought also to make a profession of patience; the Savages surpass us to such an extent, in this respect, that we ought to be ashamed. I saw them, in their hardships and in their labors, suffer with cheerfulness. My host, wondering at the great number of people who I told him were in France, asked me if the men were good, if they did not become angry, if they were patient. I have never seen such patience as is shown by a sick Savage. You may yell, storm, jump, dance, and he will scarcely ever complain. I found myself, with them, threatened with great suffering; they said to me, "We shall be sometimes two days, sometimes three, without eating, for lack of food; take courage, *Chihiné*, let thy soul be strong to endure suffering and hardship; keep thyself from being sad, otherwise thou wilt be sick; see how we do not cease to laugh, although we have little to eat." One thing alone casts them down,—

it is when they see death, for they fear this beyond measure; take away this apprehension from the Savages, and they will endure all kinds of degradation and discomfort, and all kinds of trials and suffering very patiently. . . .

They are very much attached to each other, and agree admirably. You do not see any disputes, quarrels, enmities, or reproaches among them. Men leave the arrangement of the household to the women, without interfering with them; they cut, and decide, and give away as they please, without making the husband angry. . . .

CHAPTER VI. ON THEIR VICES
AND THEIR IMPERFECTIONS

The Savages, being filled with errors, are also haughty and proud. Humility is born of truth, vanity of error and falsehood. They are void of the knowledge of truth, and are in consequence, mainly occupied with thought of themselves. They imagine that they ought by right of birth, to enjoy the liberty of Wild ass colts, rendering no homage to any one whomsoever, except when they like. They have reproached me a hundred times because we fear our Captains, while they laugh at and make sport of theirs. All the authority of their chief is in his tongue's end; for he is powerful in so far as he is eloquent; and, even if he kills himself talking and haranguing, he will not be obeyed unless he pleases the Savages. . . .

I have shown in my former letters how vindictive the Savages are toward their enemies, with what fury and cruelty they treat them, eating them after they have made them suffer all that an incarnate fiend could invent. This fury is common to the women as well as to the men, and they even surpass the latter in this respect. I have said that they eat the lice they find upon themselves, not that they like the taste of them, but because they want to bite those that bite them.

These people are very little moved by compassion. When any one is sick in their Cabins, they ordinarily do not cease to cry and storm, and make as much noise as if everybody were in good health. They do not know what it is to take care of a poor invalid, and to give him the food which is good for him; if he asks for something to drink, it is given to him, if he asks for something to eat, it is given to him, but otherwise he is neglected; to coax him with love and gentleness, is a language which they do not understand. As long as a patient can eat, they will carry or drag him with them; if he stops eating, they believe that it is all over with him and kill him, as much to free him from the sufferings that he is enduring, as to relieve themselves of the trouble of taking him with them when they go to some other place. I have both admired and pitied the patience of the invalids whom I have seen among them.

The Savages are slanderous beyond all belief; I say, also among themselves, for they do not even spare their nearest relations, and with it all they are deceitful. For, if one speaks ill of another, they all jeer with loud laughter; if the other appears upon the scene, the first one will show him as much affection and treat him with as much love, as if he had elevated him to the third heaven by his praise. The reason of this is, it seems to me, that their slanders and derision do not come from malicious hearts or from infected mouths, but from a mind

which says what it thinks in order to give itself free scope, and which seeks grati-
fication from everything, even from slander and mockery. Hence they are not
troubled even if they are told that others are making sport of them, or have injured their reputation. All they usually answer to such talk is, *mama irinisiou,* "He
has no sense, he does not know what he is talking about"; and at the first opportunity they will pay their slanderer in the same coin, returning him the like.

Lying is as natural to Savages as talking, not among themselves, but to
strangers. Hence it can be said that fear and hope, in one word, interest, is the
measure of their fidelity. I would not be willing to trust them, except as they
would fear to be punished if they had failed in their duty, or hoped to be rewarded if they were faithful to it. They do not know what it is to keep a secret,
to keep their word, and to love with constancy,—especially those who are not
of their nation, for they are harmonious among themselves, and their slanders
and raillery do not disturb their peace and friendly intercourse. . . .

CHAPTER XII. WHAT ONE MUST SUFFER
IN WINTERING WITH THE SAVAGES

In order to have some conception of the beauty of this edifice, its construction
must be described. I shall speak from knowledge, for I have often helped to
build it. Now, when we arrived at the place where we were to camp, the
women, armed with axes, went here and there in the great forests, cutting the
framework of the hostelry where we were to lodge; meantime the men, having
drawn the plan thereof, cleared away the snow with their snowshoes, or with
shovels which they make and carry expressly for this purpose. Imagine now a
great ring or square in the snow, two, three or four feet deep, according to the
weather or the place where they encamp. This depth of snow makes a white
wall for us, which surrounds us on all sides, except the end where it is broken
through to form the door. The framework having been brought, which consists
of twenty or thirty poles, more or less, according to the size of the cabin, it is
planted, not upon the ground but upon the snow; then they throw upon these
poles, which converge a little at the top, two or three rolls of bark sewed together, beginning at the bottom, and behold, the house is made. The ground
inside, as well as the wall of snow which extends all around the cabin, is covered
with little branches of fir; and, as a finishing touch, a wretched skin is fastened
to two poles to serve as a door, the doorposts being the snow itself. . . .

You cannot stand upright in this house, as much on account of its low roof
as the suffocating smoke; and consequently you must always lie down, or sit flat
upon the ground, the usual posture of the Savages. When you go out, the cold,
the snow, and the danger of getting lost in these great woods drive you in again
more quickly than the wind, and keep you a prisoner in a dungeon which has
neither lock nor key.

This prison, in addition to the uncomfortable position that one must occupy upon a bed of earth, has four other great discomforts,—cold, heat, smoke,
and dogs. As to the cold, you have the snow at your head with only a pine
branch between, often nothing but your hat, and the winds are free to enter in a

thousand places. . . . When I lay down at night I could study through this opening both the Stars and the Moon as easily as if I had been in the open fields.

Nevertheless, the cold did not annoy me as much as the heat from the fire. A little place like their cabins is easily heated by a good fire, which sometimes roasted and broiled me on all sides, for the cabin was so narrow that I could not protect myself against the heat. You cannot move to right or left, for the Savages, your neighbors, are at your elbows; you cannot withdraw to the rear, for you encounter the wall of snow, or the bark of the cabin which shuts you in. I did not know what position to take. Had I stretched myself out, the place was so narrow that my legs would have been halfway in the fire; to roll myself up in a ball, and crouch down in their way, was a position I could not retain as long as they could; my clothes were all scorched and burned. You will ask me perhaps if the snow at our backs did not melt under so much heat. I answer, "no"; that if sometimes the heat softened it in the least, the cold immediately turned it into ice. I will say, however, that both the cold and the heat are endurable, and that some remedy may be found for these two evils.

But, as to the smoke, I confess to you that it is martyrdom. It almost killed me, and made me weep continually, although I had neither grief nor sadness in my heart. It sometimes grounded all of us who were in the cabin; that is, it caused us to place our mouths against the earth in order to breathe. For, although the Savages were accustomed to this torment, yet occasionally it became so dense that they, as well as I, were compelled to prostrate themselves, and as it were to eat the earth, so as not to drink the smoke. I have sometimes remained several hours in this position, especially during the most severe cold and when it snowed; for it was then the smoke assailed us with the greatest fury, seizing us by the throat, nose, and eyes. . . .

As to the dogs, which I have mentioned as one of the discomforts of the Savages' houses, I do not know that I ought to blame them, for they have sometimes rendered me good service. . . . These poor beasts, not being able to live outdoors, came and lay down sometimes upon my shoulders, sometimes upon my feet, and as I only had one blanket to serve both as covering and mattress, I was not sorry for this protection, willingly restoring to them a part of the heat which I drew from them. It is true that, as they were large and numerous, they occasionally crowded and annoyed me so much, that in giving me a little heat they robbed me of my sleep, so that I very often drove them away. . . .

6

Captured by Indians

Mary Rowlandson

The Sovereignty and Goodness of God, *by Mary Rowlandson, first published in 1682, is an English Puritan woman's account of her capture and temporary slavery among Indians during Metacom's (King Philip's) War (1675–1676) in southeastern New England. The first in what would become a best-selling genre of "captivity narratives," Rowlandson's account describes her eighty-day ordeal, which began on February 20, 1676, when King Philip's native army burned her home to the ground, shot her relatives, and took her and her children captive. Only after Puritan English neighbors finally purchased Rowlandson's freedom was she able to return to her husband, minister Joseph Rowlandson. King Philip's War had begun in 1675 after decades of tension between land-hungry settlers and Massachusetts Indians. Wampanoag chief Metacom, known to settlers as King Philip, made a bloody attempt to turn back the incursion of settlers into native lands. This uprising, by the very same Indians who only a half century earlier had participated in the first Thanksgiving dinner, plunged New England into a violent conflict and forced natives from across the region to make difficult choices in allegiance between their fellow Native Americans and longtime European friends, business associates, and relatives by marriage.*

Scholars have speculated about what in Rowlandson's narrative is true and what represents the influence of powerful Puritan elders who had supervised the writing and publication of the manuscript. The text has been variously viewed as an early feminist text about the difficulties of being a woman in colonial America; a titillating tale of hidden social and sexual race-mixing between a minister's wife and the native man who she was given to as a squaw; an attempt to justify settler brutality against Indians during King Philip's War; and even as a story of Europeans becoming American. Whatever else it is, Rowlandson's account reflects the experience of one of the many ordinary people on both sides whose lives were plunged into chaos by the conflict.

QUESTIONS TO CONSIDER
1. Why were captivity narratives such popular reading?
2. Rowlandson calls the Indians "ravenous Beasts" but claims that none of them "ever offered me the least abuse of unchastity." How might you explain this ambiguity?
3. Why were some of the Indians willing to help Rowlandson escape?

Mary Rowlandson, *The Sovereignty and Goodness of God*, ed. Neal Salisbury (Boston: Bedford/St. Martin's, 1997), 68–77, 81–83, 104, 107, 111–12.

4. Who was Rowlandson's intended audience and how did that audience shape what she wrote?

TOGETHER WITH THE FAITHFULNESS OF HIS PROMISES DISPLAYED, BEING A NARRATIVE OF THE CAPTIVITY AND RESTORATION OF MRS. MARY ROWLANDSON

On the tenth of February 1675, Came the *Indians* with great numbers upon *Lancaster* [in Massachusetts, about thirty miles west of Boston]: Their first coming was about Sun-rising; hearing the noise of some Guns, we looked out; several Houses were burning, and the Smoke ascending to Heaven. There were five persons taken in one house, the Father, and the Mother and a sucking Child, they knockt on the head; the other two they took and carried away alive. There were two others, who being out of their Garison upon some occasion were set upon; one was knockt on the head, the other escaped: Another there was who running along was shot and wounded, and fell down; he begged of them his life, promising them Money (as they told me) but they would not hearken to him but knockt him in head, and stript him naked, and split open his Bowels. Another seeing many of the *Indians* about his Barn, ventured and went out, but was quickly shot down. There were three others belonging to the same Garison who were killed; the *Indians* getting up upon the roof of the Barn, had advantage to shoot down upon them over their Fortification. Thus these murtherous wretches went on, burning, and destroying before them.

At length they came and beset our own house, and quickly it was the dolefullest day that ever mine eyes saw. The House stood upon the edge of a hill; some of the *Indians* got behind the hill, others into the Barn, and others behind any thing that could shelter them; from all which places they shot against the House, so that the Bullets seemed to fly like hail; and quickly they wounded one man among us, then another, and then a third. About two hours (according to my observation, in that amazing time) they had been about the house before they prevailed to fire it (which they did with Flax and Hemp, which they brought out of the Barn, and there being no defence about the House, only two Flankers[1] at two opposite corners, and one of them not finished) they fired it once and one ventured out and quenched it, but they quickly fired it again, and that took. Now is that dreadfull hour come, that I have often heard of (in time of War, as it was the case of others) but now mine eyes see it. Some in our house were fighting for their lives, others wallowing in their blood, the House on fire over our heads, and the bloody Heathen ready to knock us on the head, if we stirred out. Now might we hear Mothers & Children crying out for themselves, and one another, *Lord, What shall we do?* Then I took my Children (and one of my sisters, hers)[2] to go forth and leave the house: but as soon as we came to the door and

---

1. **Flankers:** Lateral projecting fortifications or walls.
2. **"my Children (and one of my sisters, hers)":** Rowlandson had three children, Joseph Jr., fourteen, Mary, ten, and Sarah, six. Two of her sisters and their families were among the thirty-seven people living in the Rowlandson garrison.

appeared, the *Indians* shot so thick that the bullets rattled against the House, as if one had taken an handfull of stones and threw them, so that we were fain to give back. We had six stout Dogs belonging to our Garrison, but none of them wou'd stir, though another time, if any *Indian* had come to the door, they were ready to fly upon him and tear him down. The Lord hereby would make us the more to acknowledge his hand, and to see that our help is alwayes in him. But out we must go, the fire increasing, and coming along behind us, roaring, and the Indians gaping before us with their Guns, Spears and Hatchets to devour us. No sooner were we out of the House, but my Brother in Law (being before wounded, in defending the house, in or near the throat) fell down dead, whereat the *Indians* scorn-fully shouted, and hallowed, and were presently upon him, stripping off his cloaths, the bulletts flying thick, one went through my side, and the same (as would seem) through the bowels and hand of my dear Child in my arms.[3] One of my elder Sisters Children, named *William*, had then his Leg broken, which the *Indians* perceiving, they knockt him on head. Thus were we butchered by those merciless Heathen, standing amazed, with the blood running down to our heels. My eldest Sister being yet in the House, and seeing those wo-full sights, the Infidels haling Mothers one way, and Children another, and some wallowing in their blood: and her elder Son telling her that her Son *William* was dead, and my self was wounded, she said, And, *Lord, let me dy with them;* which was no sooner said, but she was struck with a Bullet, and fell down dead over the threshold. I hope she is reaping the fruit of her good labours, being faithfull to the service of God in her place. . . . [T]he *Indians* laid hold of us, pulling me one way, and the Children another, and said, *Come go along with us;* I told them they would kill me: they answered, *If I were willing to go along with them, they would not hurt me.*

Oh the doleful sight that now was to behold at this House! *Come, behold the works of the Lord, what desolations he has made in the Earth.*[4] Of thirty seven persons who were in this one House, none escaped either present death, or a bitter captivity, save only one, who might say as he, *Job* 1. 15. *And I only am escaped alone to tell the News.* There were twelve killed, some shot, some stab'd with their Spears, some knock'd down with their Hatchets. When we are in prosperity, Oh the little that we think of such dreadfull sights, and to see our dear Friends, and Relations ly bleeding out their heart-blood upon the ground. There was one who was chopt into the head with a Hatchet, and stript naked, and yet was crawling up and down. It is a solemn sight to see so many Christians lying in their blood, some here, and some there, like a company of Sheep torn by Wolves. All of them stript naked by a company of hell-hounds, roaring, singing, ranting and insulting, as if they would have torn our very hearts out; yet the Lord by his Almighty power preserved a number of us from death, for there were twenty-four of us taken alive and carried captive.

I had often before this said, that if the *Indians* should come, I should chuse rather to be killed by them than be taken alive but when it came to the tryal my

---

3. **"dear Child in my arms":** Rowlandson's youngest child, Sarah.
4. Psalm 46:8.

mind changed; their glittering weapons so daunted my spirit, that I chose rather to go along with those (as I may say) ravenous Beasts, than that moment to end my dayes; and that I may the better declare what happened to me during that grievous Captivity, I shall particularly speak of the severall Removes we had up and down the Wilderness.

THE FIRST REMOVE

Now away we must go with those Barbarous Creatures, with our bodies wounded and bleeding, and our hearts no less than our bodies. About a mile we went that night, up upon a hill within sight of the Town, where they intended to lodge. There was hard by a vacant house (deserted by the English before, for fear of the *Indians*). I asked them whither I might not lodge in the house that night to which they answered, what will you love *English men* still? This was the dolefullest night that ever my eyes saw. Oh the roaring, and singing and danceing, and yelling of those black creatures in the night, which made the place a lively resemblance of hell. And as miserable was the waste that was there made, of Horses, Cattle, Sheep, Swine, Calves, Lambs, Roasting Pigs, and Fowls (which they had plundered in the Town) some roasting, some lying and burning, and some boyling to feed our merciless Enemies; who were joyfull enough though we were disconsolate. To add to the dolefulness of the former day, and the dismalness of the present night: my thoughts ran upon my losses and sad bereaved condition. All was gone, my Husband gone (at least separated from me, he being in the Bay;[5] and to add to my grief, the *Indians* told me they would kill him as he came homeward) my Children gone, my Relations and Friends gone, our House and home and all our comforts within door, and without, all was gone, (except my life) and I knew not but the next moment that might go too. There remained nothing to me but one poor wounded Babe, and it seemed at present worse than death that it was in such a pitiful condition, bespeaking Compassion, and I had no refreshing for it, nor suitable things to revive it.[6] Little do many think what is the savageness and brutishness of this barbarous Enemy, aye even those that seem to profess[7] more than others among them, when the *English* have fallen into their hands. . . .

THE SECOND REMOVE

But now, the next morning, I must turn my back upon the Town, and travel with them into the vast and desolate Wilderness, I knew not whither. It is not my tongue, or pen can express the sorrows of my heart, and bitterness of my spirit, that I had at this departure: but God was with me, in a wonderfull manner, carrying me along, and bearing up my spirit, that it did not quite fail. One of the *Indians* carried my poor wounded Babe upon a horse; it went moaning all along, I shall dy,

---

5. **the Bay:** In the eastern part of the colony, near the bay known as Massachusetts Bay.
6. English people in the seventeenth century referred to little children by the gender-neutral "it" rather than by "she" or "he."
7. **profess:** To declare one's faith or allegiance.

I shall dy. I went on foot after it, with sorrow that cannot be exprest. At length I took it off the horse, and carried it in my arms till my strength failed, and I fell down with it: Then they set me upon a horse with my wounded Child in my lap, and there being no furniture[8] upon the horse back, as we were going down a steep hill, we both fell over the horses head, at which they like inhumane creatures laught, and rejoyced to see it, though I thought we should there have ended our dayes, as overcome with so many difficulties. But the Lord renewed my strength still, and carried me along, that I might see more of his Power; yea, so much that I could never have thought of, had I not experienced it.

After this it quickly began to snow, and when night came on, they stopt: and now down I must sit in the snow, by a little fire, and a few boughs behind me, with my sick Child in my lap; and calling much for water, being now (through the wound) fallen into a violent Fever. My own wound also growing so stiff, that I could scarce sit down or rise up; yet so it must be, that I must sit all this cold winter night upon the cold snowy ground, with my sick Child in my armes, looking that every hour would be the last of its life; and having no Christian friend near me, either to comfort or help me. Oh, I may see the wonderfull power of God, that my Spirit did not utterly sink under my affliction: still the Lord upheld me with his gracious and mercifull Spirit, and we were both alive to see the light of the next morning.

THE THIRD REMOVE

The morning being come, they prepared to go on their way: One of the Indians *got up upon a horse, and they set me up behind him, with my poor sick Babe in my lap.* A very wearisome and tedious day I had of it; what with my own wound, and my Childs being so exceeding sick, and in a lamentable condition with her wound. It may be easily judged what a poor feeble condition we were in, there being not the least crumb of refreshing that came within either of our mouths, from *Wednesday* night to *Saturday* night, except only a little cold water. . . . I sat much alone with a poor wounded Child in my lap, which moaned night and day, having nothing to revive the body, or cheer the spirits of her, but in stead of that, sometimes one *Indian* would come and tell me in one hour, that your *Master* will knock your Child in the head, and then a second, and then a third, your *Master* will quickly knock your Child in the head.

. . . Thus nine dayes I sat upon my knees, with my Babe in my lap, till my flesh was raw again; my Child being even ready to depart this sorrowful world, they bade me carry it out to another Wigwam (I suppose because they would not be troubled with such spectacles) Whither I went with a very heavy heart, and down I sat with the picture of death in my lap. About two houres in the night, my sweet Babe, like a lamb departed this life, on *Feb. 18. 1675,* It being about six *yeares,* and *five months* old. It was *nine dayes* from the first wounding, in this miserable condition, without any refreshing of one nature or other, except a little cold water. I cannot but take notice, how at another time I could not bear to be

---

8. **furniture:** Saddle or other riding gear.

in the room where any dead person was, but now the case is changed; I must and could ly down by my dead Babe, side by side all the night after. I have thought since of the wonderfull goodness of God to me, in preserving me in the use of my reason and senses, in that distressed time, that I did not use wicked and violent means to end my own miserable life. . . . I went to take up my dead child in my arms to carry it with me, but they bid me let it alone: there was no resisting, but goe I must and leave it. When I had been at my masters *wigwam*, I took the first opportunity I could get, to go look after my dead child: when I came I askt them what they had done with it? then they told me it was upon the hill: then they went and shewed me where it was, where I saw the ground was newly digged, and there they told me they had buried it: *There I left that Child in the Wilderness, and must commit it, and my self also in the Wilderness-condition, to him who is above all.* God having taken away this dear Child, I went to see my daughter *Mary*, who was at this same *Indian Town*, at a *Wigwam* not very far off, though we had little liberty or opportunity to see one another: she was about ten years old, & taken from the door at first by a *Praying Indian* & afterward sold for a gun. When I came in sight, she would fall a weeping; at which they were provoked, and would not let me come near her, but bade me be gone; which was a heart-cutting word to me. I had one Child dead, another in the Wilderness, I knew not where, the third they would not let me come near to. . . .

Now the Indians began to talk of removing from this place, some one way, and some another. There were now besides my self nine *English* Captives in this place (all of them Children, except one Woman). I got an opportunity to go and take my leave of them; they being to go one way, and I another, *I asked them whether they were earnest with God for deliverance;* they told me, they did as they were able, and it was some comfort to me, that the Lord stirred up *Children to look to him.* The Woman *viz.* Goodwife *Joslin*[9] told me, she should never see me again, and that she could find in her heart to run away; I wisht her not to run away by any means, for we were near *thirty miles* from any *English Town*, and she very big with Child, and had but one week to reckon; and another Child in her Arms, two years old, and bad Rivers there were to go over, and we were feeble, with our poor and coarse entertainment. I had my Bible with me, I pulled it out, and asked her whether she would read; we opened the Bible and lighted on *Psal.* 27. in which Psalm we especially took notice of that, *ver. ult.,*[10] *Wait on the Lord, Be of good courage, and he shall strengthen thine heart, wait I say on the Lord.* . . .

THE EIGHTH REMOVE

. . . We travelled on till night; and in the morning, we must go over the River to *Philip's* crew. When I was in the Cannoo, I could not but be amazed at the numerous crew of Pagans that were on the Bank on the other side. When I came ashore, they gathered all about me, I sitting alone in the midst: I observed they asked one another questions, and laughed, and rejoyced over their Gains and

9. Ann Joslin, who was also captured in the Rowlandson garrison.
10. **ver. ult.:** Last verse.

Victories. Then my heart began to fail: and I fell a weeping which was the first time to my remembrance, that I wept before them. Although I had met with so much Affliction, and my heart was many times ready to break, yet could I not shed one tear in their sight: but rather had been all this while in a maze, and like one astonished: but now I may say as, Psal.137. 1. *By the rivers of* Babylon, *there we sat down: yea, we wept when we remembered Zion.* There one of them asked me, why I wept, I could hardly tell what to say: yet I answered, they would kill me: No, said he, none will hurt you. Then came one of them and gave me two spoon-fulls of Meal to comfort me, and another gave me half a pint of Pease; which was more worth than many Bushels at another time. Then I went to see King *Philip*, he bade me come in and sit down, and asked me whether I would smoke (a usual Complement now adayes amongst Saints and Sinners) but this no way suited me. For though I had formerly used Tobacco, yet I had left it ever since I was first taken. *It seems to be a bait, the devil lays to make men loose their precious time*: I remember with shame, how formerly, when I had taken two or three pipes, I was presently ready for another, such a bewitching thing it is: But I thank God, he has now given me power over it; surely there are many who may be better imployed than to ly sucking a stinking Tobacco-pipe.

Now the *Indians* gather their Forces to go against *North-Hampton*: over-night one went about yelling and hooting to give notice of the design. Where-upon they fell to boyling of Ground-nuts, and parching of Corn (as many as had it) for their Provision: and in the morning away they went. *During my abode in this place*, Philip *spake to me to make a shirt for his boy, which* I *did, for which he gave me a shilling:* I *offered the money to my master, but he bade me keep it: and with it* I *bought a piece of Horse flesh.* Afterwards he asked me to make a Cap for his boy, for which he invited me to Dinner. I went, and he gave me a Pancake, about as big as two fingers; it was made of parched wheat, beaten, and fryed in Bears grease, but I thought I never tasted pleasanter meat in my life. There was a *Squaw* who spake to me to make a shirt for her *Sannup*,[11] for which she gave me a piece of Bear. Another asked me to knit a pair of Stockins, for which she gave me a quart of Pease: I boyled my Pease and Bear together, and invited my master and mistress to dinner. . . .

THE TWENTIETH REMOVE

. . . My master after he had had his drink, quickly came ranting into the *Wig-wam* again, and called for Mr. *Hoar*,[12] drinking to him, and saying, *He was a good man:* and then again he would say, *Hang him, Rogue:* Being almost drunk, he would drink to him, and yet presently say he should be hanged. Then he called for me, I trembled to hear him, yet I was fain to go to him, and he drank to me, shewing no incivility. He was the first *Indian* I saw drunk all the while that I was amongst them. At last his *Squaw* ran out, and he after her, round the *Wigwam*,

11. **Sannup:** Married man, in this case her husband.
12. John Hoar was a Concord, Massachusetts, lawyer whom Joseph Rowlandson enlisted to help free his wife.

with his money jingling at his knees: But she escaped him: But having an old *Squaw* he ran to her: and so through the Lords mercy, we were no more troubled that night. *Yet I had not a comfortable nights rest: for I think I can say, I did not sleep for three nights together.* The night before the Letter came from the Council, I could not rest, I was so full of feares and troubles, God many times leaving us most in the dark, when deliverance is nearest: yea, at this time I could not rest, night nor day. The next night I was overjoyed, Mr. *Hoar* being come, and that with such good tidings. The third night I was even swallowed up with all thoughts of things, *viz.* that ever I should go home again; and that I must go, leaving my Children behind me in the *Wilderness*; so that sleep was now almost departed from mine eyes.

On *Tuesday morning* they called their *General Court* (as they call it) to consult and determine, whether I should go home or no: And they all as one man did seemingly consent to it, that I should go home; except *Philip*, who would not come among them. . . .

But to return again to my going home, where we may see a remarkable change of Providence: At first they were all against it, except my Husband would come for me; but afterwards they assented to it, and seemed much to rejoyce in it; some askt me to send them some Bread, others some Tobacco, others shaking me by the hand, offering me a Hood and Scarfe to ride in; not one moving hand or tongue against it. Thus hath the Lord answered my poor desire, and the many earnest requests of others put up unto God for me. . . . O the wonderfull power of God that I have seen, and the experience that I have had: *I have been in the midst of those roaring Lyons, and Salvage Bears, that feared neither God, nor Man, nor the Devil, by night and day, alone and in company: sleeping all sorts together, and yet not one of them ever offered me the least abuse of unchastity to me, in word or action.*[13] . . . So I took my leave of them, and in coming along my heart melted into tears, more than all the while I was with them, and I was almost swallowed up with the thoughts that ever I should go home again. . . .

I have seen the extrem vanity of this World: One hour I have been in health, and wealth, wanting nothing: But the next hour in sickness and wounds, and death, having nothing but sorrow and affliction.

Before I knew what affliction meant, I was ready sometimes to wish for it. When I lived in prosperity, having the comforts of the World about me, my relations by me, my Heart chearfull: and taking little care for any thing; and yet seeing many, whom I preferred before my self, under many tryals and afflictions, in sickness, weakness, poverty, losses, crosses, and cares of the World, I should be sometimes jealous least I should have my portion in this life, and that Scripture would come to my mind, *Heb.* 12. 6. *For whom the **Lord** loveth he chasteneth, and scourgeth every Son whom he receiveth.* But now I see the Lord had his time to scourge and chasten me. The portion of some is to have their afflictions by drops, now one drop and then another; but the dregs of the Cup, the Wine of astonishment: like a sweeping rain that leaveth no food, did the Lord prepare to

---

13. Despite colonial fears of native sexuality, there is no record of sexual violation of captive women by indigenous peoples of eastern North America.

be my portion. Affliction I wanted, and affliction I had, full measure (I thought) pressed down and running over; yet I see, when God calls a Person to any thing, and through never so many difficulties, yet he is fully able to carry them through and make them see, and say they have been gainers thereby. And I hope I can say in some measure, as *David* did, *It is good for me that I have been afflicted.*[14] The Lord hath shewed me the vanity of these outward things. That they are the *Vanity of vanities, and vexation of spirit;*[15] that they are but a shadow, a blast, a bubble, and things of no continuance. That we must rely on God himself, and our whole dependance must be upon him. If trouble from smaller matters begin to arise in me, I have something at hand to check my self with, and say, why am I troubled? It was but the other day that if I had had the world, I would have given it for my freedom, or to have been a Servant to a Christian. I have learned to look beyond present and smaller troubles, and to be quieted under them, as *Moses* said, *Exod.* 14. 13. *Stand still and see the Salvation of the Lord.*

14. Psalm 119:71.
15. Ecclesiastes 1:2, 14.

New World Images

Native Americans did not consider themselves collectively as one group of people or as a single nation before their encounter with Europeans and had no common term for themselves. Upon discovering the need to adopt a common name to differentiate themselves from the new strangers in their midst, Native Americans may have had little choice but to choose one that the whites had applied to them. In the end both sides adopted the term *Indian*, based on Christopher Columbus's geographical error in supposing he had arrived in Asia rather than in a new world.

The next most common term to describe them was much less attractive. Medieval legend had depicted wild club-swinging men of the forest as hairy, naked links between humans and animals. Named in Latin *silvaticus*, "men of the woods," they became *sauvage* in French and *salvage* in English, a word that finally turned into *savage*.

These and other names bestowed on Native Americans by whites, such as *wild-men* and *barbarian*, propagated a belief among Europeans that Indians were essentially their opposites. Defined as "the other," Indians were heathens; they performed human sacrifices and were cannibals; they were dirty, warlike, superstitious, sexually promiscuous, and brutal to their captives and to their women. Evils observed anywhere among Indians, as well as evils not observed but known to be practiced such as Aztec human sacrifice, were generalized to all Indians.

At the same time Europeans, troubled by what they regarded as the decadence of their own society, recognized positive traits in the Indians that Europeans lacked. To many, especially those who never migrated to the New World, Indians seemed direct, innocent, hospitable, courteous, handsome, and courageous. Their independence, proud bearing, and stamina suggested a nobility that Europeans seemed to be losing. From this image came a composite ideal called the "Noble Savage."

The first attempt by a European to depict the domestic lives of Native Americans can be seen in Figure 1, an anonymous German woodcut published around 1505 and based on explorer and geographer Amerigo Vespucci's account of his voyages to the New World. The inscription describes natives as: "naked, handsome, brown, well shaped in body; . . . No one has anything, but all things are in common. And the men have as wives those who please them, be they mothers, sisters or friends. . . . They also fight with each other; and they eat each other. . . . They become a hundred and fifty years old and have no government."

Figure 1. Unknown artist, "First European Attempt to Depict the Domestic Life of Native Americans," Germany, c. 1505.

Not all images of the time presented the Europeans and Native Americans as such opposites. Figure 2 shows a drawing of Cortés and his longtime lover and adviser, Malinche (Doña Marina). Malinche was born and raised an Aztec but was sold to the Maya as a slave and then passed on to another ethnic group in Tabasco, south of the Aztec empire. By the time Cortés arrived on the continent, Malinche spoke many local languages and found that she fit in with the Spanish as well as with any native group. This picture by an indigenous artist from around 1540 suggests a degree of understanding between Europeans and natives that is lacking in many of the more essentializing portraits of "barbarians" and "noble savages" by European artists, both earlier and later.

Figure 2. Unknown artist, drawing of Cortés and Malinche, c. 1540.

Figure 3 shows an engraving made from a drawing by John White, who from 1585 to 1586 lived in Roanoke, Virginia, part of the first English colony

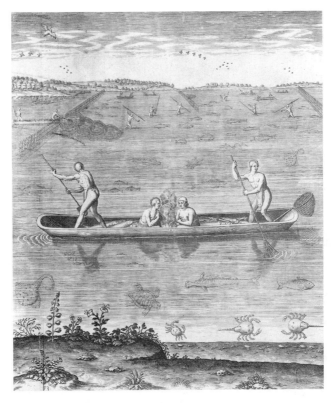

Figure 3. Engraving of John White's drawing, "The Manner of Their Fishing," 1585.

in North America. John White was commissioned to illustrate the first written account of that colony. Thomas Hariot's pamphlet, *A Brief and True Report of the New Found Land of Virginia*, published together with White's images in 1588, was "directed to the investors, farmers, and well-wishers of the project of colonizing and planting there" and emphasized the economic possibilities of the region. The caption to the engraving reads in part:

> It is a pleasing picture to see these people wading and sailing in their shallow rivers. They are untroubled by the desire to pile up riches for their children, and live in perfect contentment with their present state, in friendship with each other, sharing all those things with which God has so bountifully provided them. Yet they do not render Him the thanks which His providence deserves, for they are savage and have no knowledge [of Christianity].

In which readings can you find images of Indians most like that of the German woodcut? In which readings can you find images of Indians similar to White's drawing?

Figure 4 is another domestic scene of Indian life, this time from a French source, François de Creux's *Historia Canadensis*, published in 1664. How does it

Figure 4. Unknown artist, "Huron Woman," 1664.

differ from the way Figure 1 depicts the Indians? Note that both figures in this image are Indian women. Are Indian men described in different terms from Indian women in the various readings?

Figure 5 depicts a conference between Colonel Henry Bouquet and some of the Indians he defeated at the battle of Bushy Run in 1763. Many tribes in the Ohio Valley led by Pontiac, a chief of the Ottawas, rose up against the British in 1763, laying waste to many white settlements in the Ohio Valley. The central focus of the engraving is the return of white captives taken during these raids. The theme of whites, and especially white women, captured by Indians greatly fascinated the colonists and their European counterparts and captivity narratives such as Mary Rowlandson's (Document 6) were best sellers on both sides of the Atlantic.

B. West inv.   Canot sculp.

The Indians delivering up the English Captives to Colonel Bouquet,
near his Camp at the Forks of Muskingum in North America in Nov. 1764.

Figure 5. Unknown artist, "Return of English Captives during a Conference between Colonel Henry Bouquet and Indians on the Muskingum River," 1764.

FOR CRITICAL THINKING

1. What perceptions of the inhabitants of the New World do these images present? How accurate do you think they are? How might Europeans have reacted to these images?
2. Why do you think White's depiction of the Indians on page 39 is so different from that shown in Figure 1?
3. Figure 2 was drawn by an unknown indigenous artist around 1540. How significant is it that this image was made by a Native American?
4. In Figure 4, how might the absence of men in this engraving change the European view of the character of Indians?
5. What attitude toward the Indians and what view of Indian–white relations are suggested by Figure 5?

PART TWO

The Colonial Experience

A Rapidly Changing Society

By the end of the seventeenth century, the closed, firmly fixed religious world of Puritan New England was fading. The Salem witchcraft trials of the 1690s demonstrated that early religious conviction had been reduced to confusion, and as the eighteenth century progressed New England became increasingly integrated into the open, diverse, and commercially oriented societies of the American Atlantic seacoast. Sarah Kemble Knight's journey from Boston to New Haven reveals this changing world and the way in which not just men, but women as well had remarkable opportunities in the dynamic new society. However, Abigail Bailey's account of the terrors of a bad marriage, more than a half century later, shows how much these opportunities for women depended on a combination of class background and the unpredictable temperament of husbands and fathers.

The entire settler population of British America in 1660 would have fit into a baseball stadium, but by 1750 the colonists numbered over one million. Conflict with Indian neighbors initially threatened virtually all of the early colonies, but by midcentury Europeans firmly controlled the eastern seaboard. News of opportunity in the new land brought an increasing number of immigrants from every corner of Europe and even parts of the Middle East. Germans like Gottlieb Mittelberger were among the largest groups to populate the middle colonies. Most signed on as indentured servants to pay their passage, facing extremely harsh circumstances when they arrived. However, some eventually prospered and remade themselves as Americans. Though most saw this as a chance for a new start, some, like Rachel Lazarus, a colonial Jew, worried that increased tolerance and opportunity were leading their coreligionists to discard their Old World customs and identity and assimilate into America. However, Benjamin Nones, a Jewish American Revolutionary War veteran, showed that it was not simply a choice of being either Jewish or American. After being attacked by

43

anti-Semitic federalists in the Philadelphia press, Nones hits back by publicly asserting Jews to be the most American people of all in the new society.

African slaves, involuntary migrants to the New World, contributed enormously to the colonies' prosperity. Slaves imported through the trade in human beings that freedman Olaudah Equiano graphically describes became the critical workforce for the sugar plantations of the West Indies. Supplying these islands with fish, grain, lumber, livestock, and other goods enriched the economies of the middle colonies and New England. After about 1680 African slavery became an important part of Southern plantation agriculture on the mainland. By 1720, African slaves in South Carolina outnumbered whites by about two to one.

However, the colonies that stretched along the Atlantic seaboard side of the Appalachian Mountains were but a tiny portion of a vast continent populated by Spanish, French, and native peoples who had experienced two centuries of living together with all the political conflicts, economic relations, and personal intimacies that characterized settlement. The map reprinted in Document 14 suggests how differently the French viewed eighteenth-century North America, and Pedro Naranjo and Josephe's accounts of the Pueblo rebellion reveal some aspects of the world that would eventually make up an important part of the new nation, once the English colonies of the eastern seaboard finally shook off their king and looked to westward expansion.

Benjamin Franklin may have provided the best assessment of the seeds of this new nation that would eventually reach the Pacific; he testified before the British Parliament and described a people who were still loyal to "their king," but who were becoming too American to remain loyal on any terms except their own.

Women in Colonial America

7

A Business Trip across the Colonies

Sarah Kemble Knight

Born to an affluent merchant family in New England in 1666, Sarah Kemble married Richard Knight at the age of twenty-two and bore the couple's daughter. Knight, a ship-master and successful agent for American business interests in London, was present only sporadically at their Boston home, leaving his wife in charge of family business affairs. Kemble Knight, a woman of tremendous energy and ambition, ran a shop and boarding-house, worked as a court scrivener, and opened her own school. She ended her days as a very wealthy real estate speculator in New London, Connecticut.

The following diary entries recount the difficult and dangerous overland journey Kemble Knight made in 1704 and 1705, from Boston to New Haven (with a side trip south to New York City). Her cousin, Caleb Trowbridge, had died that year and she determined to help settle the estate for his widow. The diary records her thoughts and experiences on this atypical rambling road trip through the wilds of New England, on her own without male relatives or friends.

Perhaps because it was not written for public consumption, Kemble Knight's diary reveals a very different sensibility from that found in most other Puritan New England documents, which are often self-consciously somber and prim in tone. At once judgmental and irreverent, candid and humorous, even playful, this account of her business trip to New Haven provides one of American history's richest sources for understanding the social and economic conditions of early eighteenth-century New England, including the dominant attitudes, customs, and social hierarchies of the time.

QUESTIONS TO CONSIDER

1. What might explain the different attitudes about how a woman should behave held by the eldest daughter at the lodge and Sarah Kemble Knight?
2. How representative is Sarah Kemble Knight of women in colonial America?
3. What does Sarah Kemble Knight believe are the important differences between Boston, New Haven, and New York?

Sarah Kemble Knight, *The Journal of Madam Knight* (Boston: David R. Godine, 1972), 18–22.

MONDAY, OCTB'r Ye SECOND, 1704

About three o'clock afternoon, I begun my Journey from Boston to New-Haven; being about two Hundred Mile. My Kinsman, Capt. Robert Luist, waited on me as farr as Dedham, where I was to meet ye Western post.

I vissitted the Reverd. Mr. Belcher, ye Minister of ye town, and tarried there till evening, in hopes ye post would come along. But he not coming, I resolved to go to Billingses where he used to lodg, being 12 miles further. But being ignorant of the way, Madm Billings, seing no persuasions of her good spouses or hers could prevail with me to Lodg there that night, Very kindly went wyth me to ye Tavern, where I hoped to get my guide, And desired the Hostess to inquire of her guests whether any of them would go with mee. But they being tyed by the Lipps to a pewter engine, scarcely allowed themselves time to say what clownish . . . [the next half page of the manuscript is missing].

. . . to my no small surprise, son John arrose, and gravely demanded what I would give him to go with me? Give you, sais I, are you John? Yes, says he, for want of a Better; And behold! this John look's as old as my Host, and perhaps had bin a man in the last Century. Well, Mr. John, sais I, make your demands. Why, half a pss. of eight and a dram,[1] sais John. I agreed and gave him a Dram (now) in hand to bind the bargain. . . .

. . . My Guide dismounted [in Billinges] and very Compasantly help't me down and shewd the door, signing to me wth his hand to Go in; wch I Gladly did—But had not gone many steps into the Room, ere I was Interogated by a young Lady I understood afterwards was the Eldest daughter of the family, with these, or words to this purpose, (viz.) Law for mee—what in the world brings You here at this time a night?—I never see a woman on the Rode so Dreadfull late, in all the days versall life. Who are You? Where are You going? I'm scar'd out of my witts—with much now of the same Kind. I stood aghast, Prepareing to reply, when in comes my Guide—to him Madam turn'd, Roreing out: Lawfull heart, John, is it You?—how de do! Where in the world are you going with this woman? Who is she? John made no Ansr. but sat down in the corner . . . she then turned agen to mee and fell anew into her silly questions, without asking me to sit down.

I told her shee treated me very Rudely, and I did not think it my duty to answer her unmannerly Questions. But to get ridd of them, I told her I come there to have the post's company with me to-morrow on my Journey &c. Miss star'd awhile, drew a chair, bid me sitt. . . . I paid honest John wth money and dram according to contract, and Dismist him, and pray'd Miss to shew me where I must Lodg. Shee conducted me to a parlour in a little back Lento, wch was almost fill'd wth the bedsted, wch was so high that I was forced to climb on a chair to gitt up to ye wretched bed that lay on it; on wch having Stretcht my tired Limbs, and lay'd my head on a Sadcolourd pillow, I began to think on the transactions of ye past day.

---

1. **half a pss. of eight and a dram:** Presumably, colonial money, probably silver, in the form of coins, in drams—a unit of weight.

TUESDAY, OCTOBER Ye THIRD

. . . About Three afternoon went on with my Third Guide, who Rode very hard; and having crossed Providence Ferry, we come to a River wch they Generally Ride thro'. But I dare not venture; so the Post got a Ladd and Cannoo to carry me to tother side, and hee rid thro' and Led my hors. The Cannoo was very small and shallow, so that when we were in she seem'd redy to take in water, which greatly terrified mee, and caused me to be very circumspect, sitting with my hands fast on each side, my eyes stedy, not daring so much as to lodg my tongue a hair's breadth more on one side of my mouth then tother, nor so much as think on Lott's wife,[2] for a wry thought would have oversett our wherey[3] But was soon put out of this pain, by feeling the Cannoo on shore. . . . Rewarding my sculler,[4] [we] again mounted and made the best of our way forwards.

. . . wee rode on Very deliberatly . . . when we entered a Thickett of Trees and Shrubbs, and I perceived by the Hors's going, we were on the descent of a Hill, wch, as wee come neerer the bottom, 'twas totaly dark wth the Trees that surrounded it. But I knew by the Going of the Hors wee had entered the water, wch my Guide told mee was the Hazzardos River he had told me off; and hee, Riding up close to my Side, Bid me not fear—we should be over Imediatly. I now ralyed all the Courage I was mistriss of, Knowing that I must either Venture my fate of drowning, or be left like ye Children in the wood. So, as the Post bid me, I gave Reins to my Nagg; and sitting as Stedy as Just before in the Cannoo, in a few minutes got safe to the other side, which hee told mee was the Narragansett country.

. . . I was very civilly Received, and courteously entertained, in a clean comfortable House. . . .

WEDNESDAY, OCTOBr 4TH

About four in the morning, we set out for Kingston (for so was the Town called) with a french Docter in our company. Hee and ye Post put on very furiously, so that I could not keep up with them, only as now and then they'd stop till they see mee. This Rode was poorly furnished wth accommodations for Travellers, so that we were forced to ride 22 miles by the post's account, but neerer thirty by mine, before we could bait[5] so much as our Horses. . . .

FRIDAY, OCTOBr 6th

I got up very early, in Order to hire somebody to go with mee to New Haven, being in Great parplexity at the thoughts of proceeding alone; which my most

2. **Lott's wife:** Lott's wife was a figure from the Bible who, in the midst of escaping from a burning city, famously turned for one last look (she had been told not to) and was turned immediately into a pillar of salt.
3. **oversett our wherey:** Overturned our craft.
4. **sculler:** The person who rowed her across the river.
5. **bait:** To feed and water (a horse or other animal) usually on a long journey.

hospitable entertainer observing, himselfe went, and soon return'd wth a young Gentleman of the town, who he could confide in to Go with mee; and about eight this morning wth Mr. Joshua Wheeler my new Guide, takeing leave of this worthy Gentleman, Wee advanced on towards Seabrook. The Rodes all along this way are very bad, Incumbred wth Rocks and mountainos passages, wch were very disagreeable to my tired carcass; but we went on with a moderate pace wch made ye Journy more pleasent. . . .

SATURDAY, OCT. 7th

. . . about two a clock afternoon we arrived at New Haven, where I was received with all Posible Respects and vivility. Here I discharged Mr. Wheeler with a reward to his satisfaction, and took some time to rest after so long and toilsome a Journey. . . .

They [the people of New Haven] are Govern'd by the same Laws as wee in Boston, (or little differing,) thr'out this whole Colony of Connecticot, And much the same way of Church Government, and many of them good, Sociable people, and I hope Religious too: but a little too much Independant in their principalls, and, as I have been told, were formerly in their Zeal very Riggid in their Administrations towards such as their Lawes made Offenders, even to a harmless Kiss or Innocent merriment among Young people. Whipping being a frequent and counted an easy Punishment, about wch as other Crimes, the Judges were absolute in their Sentances. . . .

Their Diversions in this part of the Country are on Lecture days and Training days[6] mostly: on the former there is Riding from town to town.

And on training dayes The Youth divert themselves by Shooting at the Target, as they call it, (but it very much resembles a pillory,) where hee that hitts neerest the white has some yards of Red Ribbin presented him, wch being tied to his hattband, the two ends streeming down his back, he is Led away in Triumph, wth great applause, as the winners of the Olympiack Games. They generally marry very young: the males oftener as I am told under twentie than above; they generally make public wedings. . . . Just before Joyning hands, the Bridegroom quitts the place, who is soon followed by the Bridesmen, and as it were, dragg'd back to duty—being the reverse to ye former practice among us, to steal ms Pride. . . .

There are every where in the Towns as I passed, a Number of Indians the Natives of the Country, and are the most salvage of all the salvages of that kind that I had ever Seen: little or no care taken (as I heard upon enquire) to make them otherwise. They have in some places Landes of their owne, and Govern'd by Law's of their own making; they marry many wives and at pleasure put them away, and on the ye least dislike or fickle humour, on either side, saying *stand away* to one another is a sufficient Divorce. And indeed those uncomely *Stand aways* are too much in Vougue among the English in this (Indulgent Colony) as

6. **Lecture days and Training days:** *Lecture days* were days on which traveling lecturers would come to town to speak on a topic; *training days* refers to special days set aside for local militias to assemble for drills, including using guns and marching in formation.

their Records plentifully prove, and that on very trivial matters, of which some have been told me, but are not proper to be Related by a Female pen, tho some of that foolish sex have had too large a share in the story. . . .

Their Cheif Red Letter day is St. Election,[7] wch is annualy Observed according to Charter, to choose their Govenr: a blessing they can never be thankfull enough for, as they will find, if ever it be their hard fortune to loos it. The present Govenor in Conecticott is the Honble John Winthrop Esq. A Gentleman of an Ancient and Honourable Family, whose Father was Govenor here sometimes before, and his Grand father had bin Govr of the Massachusetts. This gentleman is a very curteous and afable person, much Given to Hospitality, and has by his Good services Gain'd the affections of the people as much as any who had bin before him in that post.

DECr 6TH

. . . Dec. 6th we set out from New Haven. . . .

The Cittie of New York is a pleasant, well compacted place, situated on a Commodius River wch is a fine harbour for shipping. The Buildings Brick Generaly, very stately and high, though not altogether like ours in Boston. The Bricks in some of the Houses are of divers Coullers and laid in Checkers, being glazed look very agreeable. The inside of them are neat to admiration. . . .

They are Generaly of the Church of England and have a New England Gentleman for their minister, and a very fine church set out with all Customary requisites. There are also a Dutch and divers conventicles[8] as they call them, viz. Baptist, Quakers, &c. They are not strict in keeping the Sabbath as in Boston and other places where I had bin, But seem to deal with great exactness as farr as I see or Deall with. They are sociable to one another and Curteos and Civill to strangers and fare well in their houses. The English go very fashionable in their dress. But the Dutch, especially the middling sort, differ from our women, in their habitt go loose, wear French muches wch are like a Capp and a head band in one, leaving their ears bare, which are sett out wth Jewells of a large size and many in number. And their fingers hoop't with Rings, some with large stones in them of many Coullers as were their pendants in their ears, which You should see very old women wear as well as Young. . . .

Having here transacted the affair I went upon and some other that fell in the way, after about a fortnight's stay there I left New-York with no Little regrett, and Thursday, Dec. 21, set out for New Haven wth my Kinsman Trowbridge. . . .

JANUARY 6th [1705]

Being now well Recruited and fitt for business I discoursed the persons I was concerned with, that we might finnish in order to my return to Boston. . . . I

---

7. Red letter day refers to the practice of marking the dates of church festivals and saints' days on calendars in red.
8. **conventicles:** A religious congregation or meeting, especially one held in secret or in opposition to an established church.

stayed a day here Longer than I intended by the Commands of the Honble Govenor Winthrop to stay and take a supper with him whose wonderful civility I may not omitt. . . . the next day being March 3d we got safe home to Boston, where I found my aged and tender mother and my Dear and only Child in good health with open arms redy to receive me, and my Kind relations and friends flocking in to welcome mee and hear the story of my transactions and travails I having this day bin five months from home and now I cannot fully express my Joy and Satisfaction. But desire sincearly to adore my Great Benefactor for thus graciously carying forth and returning in safety his unworthy handmaid.

8

Leaving an Abusive Husband
Abigail Abbot Bailey

Memoirs of Mrs. Abigail Bailey, *originally published in 1815, is the first American autobiography detailing family violence and abuse. Abigail Abbot Bailey (1746–1815), a profoundly religious woman after her conversion to Christianity at the age of eighteen, claimed that "God gave me a heart to resolve never to be obstinate, or disobedient to my husband; but to be always kind, obedient, and obliging in all things not contrary to the word of God." However, her marriage to Asa Bailey, which lasted twenty-six years and included the birth of seventeen children, continuously and severely tested this belief. Within a month of the wedding, Asa began physically abusing Abigail so that at times she feared "that he wanted to kill" her. Then within three years he had committed adultery with a servant. A few years later he attempted to rape another servant girl but was repulsed and brought into court, only to be released for lack of evidence. After Asa committed incest with their sixteen-year-old daughter, Abigail finally began a painful effort to end the marriage. Seeking to avoid the attendant division of property, Asa persuaded Abigail to accompany him to upstate New York, where he abandoned her far from her family, church friends, and their children. She made a torturous journey alone back to their home in New Hampshire. Then her brothers accompanied her to a justice of the peace, enabling her to have Asa arrested and forcing him into a property settlement and an uncontested "bill of divorcement."*

Bailey based her Memoirs *in part on the diaries she kept throughout much of her marriage, writings largely given over to religious devotions and musings. The minister who edited the manuscript recommended it to "the intelligent reader" who would find "strikingly exhibited" there "the dreadful depravity of fallen man; the abomination of intrigue and deceit; the horrid cruelty, of which man is capable; the hardness of the way of transgressors; . . . and the wisdom of God in turning headlong the devices of the crafty." The modern reader will note as well how difficult it was for a woman of the late eighteenth century to achieve any control over a dreadful situation. As Ann Taves, a*

Ann Taves, ed., *Religion and Domestic Violence in Early New England: The Memoirs of Abigail Abbot Bailey* (Bloomington: Indiana University Press, 1989), 56–58, 68–72, 75–83.

modern scholar of the Memoirs, *writes: "Given the difficulty of obtaining a divorce in practice, if not in theory, in late-eighteenth-century New Hampshire, it is perhaps more surprising that Abigail extricated herself from her marriage at all than that it took her four and a half years to do so."*

QUESTIONS TO CONSIDER

1. Given the laws and customs of the era, did Abigail Abbot Bailey act as assertively as she could in dealing with her husband's transgressions?
2. What role did religion play in Bailey's life, and how did it influence the way she responded to her domestic situation?
3. What similarities or differences do you see between the situation of the Bailey family and current examples of domestic violence and abuse?

I Abigail Bailey (daughter of Deacon James Abbot of Newbury, Coos, who moved thither from Concord, N.H. A.D. 1763) do now undertake to record some of the dealings of the allwise God with me, in events, which I am sure I ought solemnly to remember, as long as I live.

I shall first, in few words, record the merciful dealings of my heavenly Father, in casting my lot, not only under the gospel, but in a family, where I was ever treated with the greatest kindness by my tender parents; and particularly with the most religious attention from my very pious mother; and where I was ever treated with the greatest tenderness by my brothers and sisters. I can truly say, it was seldom that an angry word was ever spoken in my father's family — by parents, brothers, or sisters — against me, from my infancy, and during my continuance in my father's house. So that I passed the morning of my days in peace and contentment.

I was married to Asa Bailey, just after having entered the 22nd year of my age. I now left my dear parents; — hoping to find in my husband a true hearted and constant friend. My desires and hopes were, that we might live together in peace and friendship; seeking each other's true happiness till death. I did earnestly look to God for his blessing upon this solemn undertaking; — sensible, that "Except the Lord build the house, they labor in vain that build it." As, while I lived with my parents, I esteemed it my happiness to be in subjection to them; so now I thought it must be a still greater benefit to be under the aid of a judicious companion, who would rule well his own house. . . .

Relative to my new companion, though I had found no evidence that he was a subject of true religion; yet I did hope and expect, from my acquaintance with him, that he would wish for good regulations in his family, and would have its external order accord with the word of God. But I met with sore disappointment, — I soon found that my new friend was naturally of a hard, uneven, rash temper; and was capable of being very unreasonable. My conviction of this was indeed grievous, and caused me many a sorrowful hour. For such were my feelings and habits, that I knew not how to endure a hard word, or a frowning look from any one; much less from a companion. I now began to learn, with trembling, that it was the sovereign pleasure of the allwise God to try me with afflictions in

that relation, from which I had hoped to receive the greatest of my earthly comforts. I had placed my highest worldly happiness in the love, tenderness, and
peace of relatives and friends. But before one month, from my marriage day,
had passed, I learned that I must expect hard and cruel treatment in my new
habitation, and from my new friend. . . .

I think God gave me a heart to resolve never to be obstinate, or disobedient
to my husband; but to be always kind, obedient, and obliging in all things not
contrary to the word of God. I thought if Mr. B. were sometimes unreasonable,
I would be reasonable, and would rather suffer wrong than do wrong. And as I
hoped Mr. B. would kindly overlook my infirmities and failings, with which I
was conscious I should abound; so I felt a forgiving spirit towards him. Many
times his treatment would grieve my heart. But I never was suffered to my
knowledge, to return any wickedness in my conduct towards him; nor ever to
indulge a revengeful feeling or ill will. For some years I thought his repeated
instances of hard treatment of me arose,—not from any settled ill will, or real
want of kind affection toward me;—but from the usual depravity of the human
heart; and from a want of self-government. I still confided in him, as my real
friend, and loved him with increasing affection. . . .

[Her husband is on two occasions unfaithful with servants. He repents both
times, but her confidence in him has been eroded.]

Now, alas! I must begin the sad detail of events, the most distressing; and
which awfully verified my most fearful apprehensions; and convinced me, that
all my trials of life hitherto, were as nothing. . . .

[Her husband concocts a pretext to go away for a lengthy period with a
teenage daughter.]

But alas! words fail to set forth the things which followed! All this pretended *plan* was but a specious cover to infernal designs. . . .

I have already related that Mr. B. said he would take one of our sons, and
one daughter, to wait on him in his distant tour, before he would take all the
family. After he had talked of this for a few days, he said he had altered his plan;
he would leave his son, and take only his daughter: he would hire what men's
help he needed: his daughter must go and cook for him. He now commenced a
new series of conduct in relation to this daughter, whom he selected to go with
him, in order (as he pretended) to render himself pleasing and familiar to her;
so that she might be willing to go with him, and feel happy: for though, as a father, he had a right to command her to go, yet (he said) he would so conduct
toward her, as to make her cheerful and well pleased to go with him. A great
part of the time he now spent in the room where she was spinning; and seemed
shy of me, and of the rest of the family. He seemed to have forgotten his age,
his honor, and all decency, as well as all virtue. He would spend his time with
this daughter, in telling idle stories, and foolish riddles, and singing songs to
her, and sometimes before the small children, when they were in that room. He

thus pursued a course of conduct, which had the most direct tendency to corrupt young and tender minds, and lead them the greatest distance from every serious subject. He would try to make his daughter tell stories with him; wishing to make her free and sociable, and to erase from her mind all that fear and reserve, which he had ever taught his children to feel toward him. He had ever been sovereign, severe and hard with his children, and they stood in the greatest fear of him. His whole conduct, toward this daughter especially, was now changed, and became most disagreeable.

For a considerable time I was wholly at a loss what to think of his conduct, or what his wish or intentions could be. Had such conduct appeared toward any young woman beside his own young daughter, I should have had no question what he intended: but as it now was, I was loth to indulge the least suspicion of base design. His daily conduct forced a conviction upon my alarmed and tortured mind, that his designs were the most vile. All his tender affections were withdrawn from the wife of his youth, the mother of his children. My room was deserted, and left lonely. His care for the rest of his family seemed abandoned, as well as all his attention to his large circle of worldly business. Every thing must lie neglected, while this one daughter engrossed all his attention.

Though all the conduct of Mr. B. from day to day, seemed to demonstrate to my apprehension, that he was determined, and was continually plotting, to ruin this poor young daughter, yet it was so intolerably crossing to every feeling of my soul to admit such a thought, that I strove with all my might to banish it from my mind, and to disbelieve the possibility of such a thing. . . . And such were my infirmities, weakness and fears, (my circumstances being very difficult) that I did not dare to hint any thing of my fears to him, or to any creature. This may to some appear strange; but with me it was then a reality. I labored to divert his mind from his follies, and to turn his attention to things of the greatest importance. But I had the mortification to find that my endeavors were unsuccessful.

I soon perceived that his strange conduct toward this daughter was to her very disagreeable. And she shewed as much unwillingness to be in the room with him, as she dared. I often saw her cheeks bedewed with tears, on account of his new and astonishing behaviour. But as his will had ever been the law of the family, she saw no way to deliver herself from her cruel father. Such were her fears of him, that she did not dare to talk with me, or any other person, upon her situation: for he was exceedingly jealous of my conversing with her, and cautioning her. If I ever dropped words, which I hoped would put her upon her guard, or inquired the cause of her troubles, or what business her father had so much with her? if I was ever so cautious, he would find it out, and be very angry. He watched her and me most narrowly; and by his subtle questions with her, he would find out what I had said, during his absence. He would make her think I had informed him what I had said, and then would be very angry with me: so that at times I feared for my life. I queried with myself which way I could turn. How could I caution a young daughter in such a case? My thoughts flew to God for relief, that the Father of mercies would protect a poor helpless creature marked out for a prey; and turn the heart of a cruel father from every wicked purpose. . . .

The black cloud, rising like a storm of hail, had rolled on, and had gathered over my head. I clearly saw that Mr. B. entertained the most vile intentions relative to his own daughter. Whatever difficulty attended the obtaining of legal proof, yet no remaining doubt existed in my mind, relative to the existence of his wickedness: and I had no doubt remaining of the violence, which he had used; and that hence arose his rage against her. It must have drawn tears of anguish from the eyes of the hardest mortals, to see the barbarous corrections, which he, from time to time, inflicted on this poor young creature; and for no just cause. Sometimes he corrected her with a rod; and sometimes with a beach stick, large enough for the driving of a team; and with such sternness and anger sparkling in his eyes, that his visage seemed to resemble an infernal; declaring, that if she attempted to run from him again, she should never want but one correction more; for he would whip her to death! This his conduct could be for no common disobedience; for she had ever been most obedient to him in all lawful commands. It seemed as though the poor girl must now be destroyed under his furious hand. She was abashed, and could look no one in the face. . . .

None can describe the anguish of my heart on the beholding of such scenes. How pitiful must be the case of a poor young female, to be subjected to such barbarous treatment by her own father; so that she knew of no way of redress!

It may appear surprising that such wickedness was not checked by legal restraints. But great difficulties attend in such a case. While I was fully convinced of the wickedness, yet I knew not that I could make legal proof. I could not prevail upon this daughter to make known to me her troubles; or to testify against the author of them. Fear, shame, youthful inexperience, and the terrible peculiarities of her case, all conspired to close her mouth against affording me, or any one, proper information. My soul was moved with pity for her wretched case: and yet I cannot say I did not feel a degree of resentment, that she would not, as she ought, expose the wickedness of her father, that she might be relieved from him, and he brought to due punishment. But no doubt his intrigues, insinuations, commands, threats, and parental influence, led her to feel that it was in vain for her to seek redress.

My circumstances, and peculiar bodily infirmities [pregnancy], at that time, were such as to entitle a woman to the tenderest affection and sympathies of a companion. On this account, and as Mr. B. was exceeding stern, and angry with me for entertaining hard thoughts of him, I felt unable to do any thing more for the relief of my poor daughter. My hope in God was my only support. And I did abundantly and earnestly commit my cause to him. I felt confident that he would, in his own time, and as his infinite wisdom should determine, grant relief. . . .

. . . I took an opportunity with Mr. B. alone to have solemn conversation. My health being now restored, I thought it high time, and had determined, to adopt a new mode of treatment with Mr. B. I calmly introduced the subject, and told him, plainly and solemnly, all my views of his wicked conduct, in which he had long lived with his daughter. He flew into a passion, was high, and seemed to imagine, he could at once frighten me out of my object. But I was carried equally above fear, and above temper. Of this I soon convinced him, I let him know, that the business I now had taken in hand was of too serious a nature, and too interesting, to be thus disposed of, or dismissed with a few angry words. I told him I should no longer be turned off in this manner; but should pursue my object with firmness, and with whatever wisdom and ability God might give me; and that God would plead my cause, and prosper my present undertaking, as he should see best. I reminded Mr. B. of my long and unusually distressing illness; how he had treated me in it; how wicked and cruel he had been to the wife of his youth; how unable I had been to check him in that awful wickedness, which I knew he had pursued; that all my inexpressible griefs and solemn entreaties had been by him trampled under foot.

I therefore had not known what to do better than to wait on God as I had done, to afford me strength and opportunity to introduce the means of his effectual control. This time I told him had arrived. And now, if God spared my life, (I told Mr. B.) he should find a new leaf turned over;—and that I would not suffer him to go on any longer as he had done. I would now soon adopt measures to put a stop to his abominable wickedness and cruelties. For this could and ought to be done. And if I did it not, I should be a partaker of his sins, and should aid in bringing down the curse of God upon our family.

By this time Mr. B. had become silent. He appeared struck with some degree of fear. He, by and by, asked me what I intended or expected to do, to bring about such a revolution as I had intimated? whether I knew what an awful crime I had laid to his charge? which he said could not be proved. He wished to know whether I had considered how difficult it would be for me to do any such thing against him? as I was under his legal control; and he could overrule all my plans as he pleased. I told him, I well knew I had been placed under his lawful government and authority, and likewise under his care and protection. And most delightful would it have been to me, to have been able quietly and safely to remain there as long as I lived. Gladly would I have remained a kind faithful, obedient wife to him, as I had ever been. But I told Mr. B. he *knew* he had violated his marriage covenant; and hence had forfeited all legal and just right and authority over me; and I should convince him that I well knew it. I told him I was not in any passion. I acted on principle, and from long and mature consideration. And though it had ever been my greatest care and pleasure (among my earthly comforts) to obey and please him; yet by his most wicked and cruel conduct, he had compelled me to undertake this most undesirable business—of stopping him in his mad career; and that I now felt strength, courage and zeal to pursue my resolution. And if my life was spared, he would find that I should bring something to pass, and probably more than he now apprehended.

As to what I could prove against him I told Mr. B. he knew not how much evidence I had of his unnatural crimes, of which I had accused him, and of which *he knew he was guilty.* I asked him why he should not expect that I should institute a process against him, for that most horrid conduct, which he had long allowed himself to pursue, and with the most indecent and astonishing boldness?

I told him I well knew that he was naturally a man of sense; and that his conscience now fully approved of my conduct.

Mr. B. seeing me thus bold and determinate, soon changed his countenance and conduct. He appeared panic-struck; and he soon became mild, sociable and pleasant. He now made an attempt, with all his usual subtlety, and flatteries to induce me to relinquish my design. He pretended to deny the charge of incest. But I told him I had no confidence in his denial of it; it was therefore in vain! Upon this he said, he really did not blame, or think hard of me, for believing him guilty of this sin. He said, he knew he had behaved foolishly; and had given me full reason to be jealous of him; and he repeated that he did not at all think hard of me for entertaining the views which I had of him. He then took the Bible, and said, he would lay his hand on it, and swear that he was not guilty of the crime laid to his charge. Knowing what I did, I was surprised and disgusted at this impious attempt. I stepped towards him, and in a resolute and solemn manner begged of him to forbear! assuring him, that such an oath could not undo or alter real facts, of which he was conscious. And this proceeding, I assured him, would be so far from giving me any satisfaction, that it would greatly increase the distress of my soul for him in his wickedness. Upon this he forbore, and laid his Bible aside.

Mr. B. now said, he was very sorry he had given me so much reason to think such things of him; and that he had so far destroyed my confidence in him as a man of truth. He then begged of me to forgive all that was past; and he promised that he would ever be kind and faithful to me in future, and never more give me reason to complain of him for any such conduct. I told him, if I had but evidence of his real reformation, I could readily forgive him as a fellow creature, and could plead with God to forgive him. But as to my living with him in the most endearing relation any longer, after such horrid crimes, I did not see that I *could*, or *ought* to do it! He then anxiously made some remarks upon the consequences of my refusing to remain his wife, and seeking a separation from him. These he seemed unable to endure. I remarked, that I well knew it was no small thing for a husband and wife to part, and their family of children to be broken up; that such a separation could not be rendered expedient or lawful, without great sin indeed: and that I would not be the cause of it, and of breaking up our family, for *all the world*. But, said I, you have done all in your power to bring about such a separation, and to ruin and destroy our family. And I meet it as my duty now to do all in my power to save them from further destruction. . . .

But God, in his infinite wisdom, did not see fit that my peculiar trials should end thus. A long and most insupportable series of afflictions still awaited me, to be occasioned by this most perfidious of men.

I again clearly perceived that the same wicked passions, as before, were in operation in Mr. B.'s heart. Alas, "Can the Ethiopian change his skin?" Upon a certain sabbath, I went to meeting. Mr. B. did not go. Before I reached home at night, I met with evidence, which convinced me, that the same horrid conduct had on this holy day been repeated in my family! I rode up to the door. Mr. B. stood waiting for me. He seemed very kind, and was coming to take me tenderly from my horse. I leaped from my saddle, before he had opportunity to reach me. My heart was disgusted at the proffer of his deceitful help. I said nothing upon the dreadful subject this day. Some broken stories of the children corroborated the information I had received. But Mr. B. probably pleased himself with the idea that all was concealed, and he was safe.

The next day, I took him alone, and told him of what he had again been guilty, even after all his vows, and fair promises of fidelity. He started, and seemed very angry, that I should think such a thing [of] him. I told him I charged him only with facts; and hence I was not worthy of his censure! He asked how I knew any such thing? I replied, that the thing was true; and he knew it! And I felt myself under no obligations to inform him how I came by the knowledge of it. . . .

I told him he had truly been a wonder to me[;] I had looked upon him with astonishment. He was naturally, I added, a man of sense; he was a man of much knowledge; — had acquired property; and had been a man of considerable note. And that he should thus degrade and ruin himself, soul and body, and destroy a large promising family, as he had done, it was indeed most astonishing! I reminded him that he had been much in good company; and many gentlemen had honored him with their friendly attention. I asked, if any sum of money would induce him to be willing that those gentlemen should know that of him, which I knew? And, that though he seemed to be too willing to throw himself away, as though he were of no worth, I assured him, I did yet set something more by myself, than to be viewed as capable of conniving at such detestable conduct.

Mr. B. replied, that if I had made up my mind no longer to live with him, I need not be at any trouble to obtain a legal separation. For he would depart to some distant country, where I should be troubled with him no more. I remarked, that when Abraham's wife was dead, he wished, however well he had loved her, to have her now buried out of his sight. And, though I could by no means compare him to the pious Sarah; yet, if true virtue and friendship in my husband were dead, I did truly wish him to be removed from my sight. And that true virtue and friendship were indeed dead in him, I thought I had the most melancholy and incontestable evidence.

Our unhappy daughter now became eighteen years of age, and thus legally free from her father. She immediately left us, and returned no more. As she was going, I had solemn conversation with her relative to her father's conduct. She gave me to understand that it had been most abominable. But I could not induce her to consent to become an evidence against him. I plead with her the honor and safety of our family; the safety of her young sisters; and her own duty; but she appeared overwhelmed with shame and grief; and nothing effectual could yet be done.

I hence saw, that in relation to commencing a legal process, God's time seemed not yet to have arrived. I must still wait and look to him to open the path of my duty.

FOR CRITICAL THINKING

1. What role did social class play in determining Abigail Bailey's and Sarah Kemble Knight's different opportunities in life?
2. Sarah Kemble Knight mentions different divorce laws in Connecticut and Dutch customs in New York. How might the differences between colonies have affected the status of women?
3. How might these two women have viewed modern feminism differently?

9

Testimony of Pueblo Indians
Pedro Naranjo and Josephe

Once Cortés conquered Tenochtitlán in 1521, the Spanish quickly gained control over the entire Aztec empire. Indians accustomed to tribute and forced labor simply adapted to new masters. But as Spanish soldiers, settlers, and missionaries moved northward in search of precious metals and outposts to secure their empire from European and Indian enemies, they found that the methods that had worked farther south failed among the more independent tribes that had never been conquered by their Aztec predecessors. Franciscan and Jesuit missionaries struggled mightily to convert Native Americans as settlement inched northward; by 1670, about twenty-eight hundred Spaniards populated the valley of the Rio Grande.

The country was generally poor, punctuated only by an occasional silver mine; the population lived largely by farming and raising livestock. Needed supplies from Mexico arrived infrequently and at great cost. Governors and missionaries battled for preeminence, while settlers, there at the king's command, were disgruntled. And the Indians, however sincere their conversion to Catholicism, were at the bottom of society bearing the brunt of these harsh circumstances. Nor were the old religions dead. The valley was a true frontier with Apache, Hopi, and Navaho, all beyond Spanish power, threatening the Pueblo Indians while providing a powerful example of freedom.

The uprising of the Pueblo Indians in 1680 drove the Spanish out of Santa Fe and all the surrounding settlements. Four hundred Spaniards died during the conflict, and the rest retreated south to El Paso. Efforts at reconquest in 1681 had only temporary success. A number of the converted Indians who made peace at La Isleta moved south for Spanish protection against their tribal enemies. But others remained independent and returned to the practice of their native religions. In the 1690s, a new Spanish commander, Don Diego de Vargas, through skillful diplomacy and a few carefully limited military campaigns, brought most of the Pueblo tribes back under Spanish rule. In the meantime, however, the Indian capture of Spanish horses had begun a momentous transformation. Within a generation, this superweapon of the age had spread far northward among the Indians. When it met the other superweapon—the rifle—carried westward by English and French frontiersmen and traders, the Plains Indian brave who has dominated the American imagination was born.

Pedro Naranjo and Josephe were captured by the Spanish during the Pueblo rebellion and brought before a royal court in 1681. While Pedro was quite contrite in his testimony to the court regarding his admitted role in the revolt, Josephe seized the opportunity to tell of the colonists' cruelty.

Charles Wilson Hackett, *Revolt of the Pueblo Indians of New Mexico and Otermín's Attempted Reconquest, 1680–1682* (Albuquerque: University of New Mexico Press, 1942), 238–42, 245–49.

1. How did Pedro Naranjo explain the revolt? To what extent do you think he was tailoring his answer to his Spanish questioners?
2. How did Josephe explain the revolt? What differences do you notice between his account and Pedro Naranjo's?
3. What according to Josephe were the strategic objectives of the leaders of the revolt? How did they inspire the Pueblo Indians to revolt?

DECLARATION OF PEDRO NARANJO OF THE QUERES NATION

December 19, 1681

In the said plaza de armas on the said day, month, and year, for the prosecution of the judicial proceedings of this case his lordship caused to appear before him an Indian prisoner named Pedro Naranjo, a native of the pueblo of San Felipe, of the Queres nation, who was captured in the advance and attack upon the pueblo of La Isleta. He makes himself understood very well in the Castilian language and speaks his mother tongue and the Tegua. He took the oath in due legal form in the name of God, our Lord, and a sign of the cross. . . .

Asked whether he knows the reason or motives which the Indians of this kingdom had for rebelling, forsaking the law of God and obedience to his Majesty, and committing such grave and atrocious crimes, and who were the leaders and principal movers, and by whom and how it was ordered; and why they burned the images, temples, crosses, rosaries, and things of divine worship, committing such atrocities as killing priests, Spaniards, women, and children, and the rest that he might know touching the question, he said that since the government of Señor General Hernando Ugarte y la Concha they have planned to rebel on various occasions through conspiracies of the Indian sorcerers, and that although in some pueblos the messages were accepted, in other parts they would not agree to it; and that it is true that during the government of the said señor general seven or eight Indians were hanged for this same cause, whereupon the unrest subsided. Some time thereafter they [the conspirators] sent from the pueblo of Los Taos through the pueblos of the custodia two deerskins with some pictures on them signifying conspiracy after their manner, in order to convoke the people to a new rebellion, and the said deerskins passed to the province of Moqui, where they refused to accept them. The pact which they had been forming ceased for the time being, but they always kept in their hearts the desire to carry it out, so as to live as they are living to-day. Finally, in the past years, at the summons of an Indian named Popé, who is said to have communication with the devil, it happened that in an estufa of the pueblo of Los Taos there appeared to the said Popé three figures of Indians who never came out of the estufa. They gave the said Popé to understand that they were going underground to the lake of Copala. He saw these figures emit fire from all the extremities of their bodies, and that one of them was called Caudi, another Tilini, and the other Tleume; and these three beings spoke to the said Popé, who was in hiding from the secretary, Francisco Xavier, who wished to punish him as a sorcerer. They told him to make a cord of maguey fiber and tie some knots in it which would signify the number of days that they must wait before the rebellion. He said that the cord was passed through all the pueblos of the kingdom so that the ones which agreed to it [the rebellion] might untie one knot in a sign of obedience, and by the other knots they would know the days which were lacking; and this was to be done on pain of death to those who refused to agree to it. As a sign of agreement and notice of having concurred in the treason and perfidy they were to send up smoke signals to that effect in each one of the pueblos singly. The said cord was taken from pueblo to pueblo by the swiftest youths under the penalty of death if they revealed the secret. Everything being thus arranged, two days before the time set for its execution, because his lordship had learned of it and had imprisoned two Indian accomplices from the pueblo of Tesuque, it was carried out prematurely that night, because it seemed to them that they were now discovered; and they killed religious, Spaniards, women, and children. This being done, it was proclaimed in all the pueblos that everyone in common should obey the commands of their father whom they did not know, which would be given through El Caydi or El Popé. This was heard by Alonso Catití, who came to the pueblo of this declarant to say that everyone must unite to go to the villa to kill the governor and the Spaniards who had remained with him, and that he who did not obey would, on their return, be beheaded; and in fear of this they agreed to it. Finally the señor governor and those who were with him escaped from the siege, and later this declarant saw that as soon as the Spaniards had left the kingdom an order came from the said Indian, Popé, in which he commanded all the Indians to break the lands and enlarge their cultivated fields, saying that now they were as they had been in ancient times, free from the labor they had performed for the religious and the Spaniards, who could not now be alive. He said that this is the legitimate cause and the reason they had for rebelling, because they had always desired to live as they had when they came out of the lake of Copala. Thus he replies to the question.

　　Asked for what reason they so blindly burned the images, temples, crosses, and other things of divine worship, he stated that the said Indian, Popé, came down in person, and with him El Saca and El Chato from the pueblo of Los Taos, and other captains and leaders and many people who were in his train, and he ordered in all the pueblos through which he passed that they instantly break up and burn the images of the holy Christ, the Virgin Mary and the other saints, the crosses, and everything pertaining to Christianity, and that they burn the temples, break up the bells, and separate from the wives whom God had given them in marriage and take those whom they desired. In order to take away their baptismal names, the water, and the holy oils, they were to plunge into the rivers and wash themselves with amole, which is a root native to the country, washing even their clothing, with the understanding that there would thus be taken from them the character of the holy sacraments. They did this, and also many other things which he does not recall, given to understand that this mandate had come from the Caydi and the other two who emitted fire from their extremities in the said estufa of Taos, and that they thereby returned to the state of their antiquity, as when they came from the lake of Copala; that this was the better life and the one they desired, because the God of the Spaniards was worth nothing and theirs was very strong, the Spaniards' God being rotten wood. These things were observed and obeyed by all except some who, moved by the zeal of Christians, opposed it, and such persons the said Popé caused to be killed immediately. He saw to it that they at once erected and rebuilt their houses of idolatry which they call estufas, and made very ugly masks in imitation of the devil in order to dance the dance of the cacina; and he said likewise that the devil had given them to understand that living thus in accordance with the law of their ancestors, they would harvest a great deal of maize, many beans, a great abundance of cotton, calabashes, and very large watermelons and cantaloupes; and that they could erect their houses and enjoy abundant health and leisure. As he has said, the people were very much pleased, living at their ease in this life of their antiquity, which was the chief cause of their falling into such laxity. Following what has already been stated, in order to terrorize them further and cause them to observe the diabolical commands, there came to them a pronouncement from the three demons already described, and from El Popé, to the effect that he who might still keep in his heart a regard for the priests, the governor, and the Spaniards would be known from his unclean face and clothes, and would be punished. And he stated that the said four persons stopped at nothing to have their commands obeyed. Thus he replies to the question.

Asked what arrangements and plans they had made for the contingency of the Spaniards' return, he said that what he knows concerning the question is that they were always saying they would have to fight to the death, for they do not wish to live in any other way than they are living at present; and the demons in the estufa of Taos had given them to understand that as soon as the Spaniards began to move toward this kingdom they would warn them so that they might unite, and none of them would be caught. He having been questioned further and repeatedly touching the case, he said that he has nothing more to say. . . . His declaration being read to him, he affirmed and ratified all of it. He declared himself to be eighty years of age, and he signed it with his lordship and the interpreters and assisting witnesses. . . .

DECLARATION OF JOSEPHE, SPANISH-SPEAKING INDIAN

December 19, 1681

In this said place and plaza de armas of this army on the 19th day of the month of December, 1681, for the said judicial proceedings of this case, his lordship caused to appear before him an Indian prisoner named Josephe, able to speak the Castilian language, a servant of Sargento Mayor Sebastián de Herrera who fled from him and went among the apostates. . . . Being asked why he fled from his master, the said Sargento Mayor Sebastián de Herrera, and went to live with the treacherous Indian apostates of New Mexico, where he has been until he came among us on the present occasion, he said that the reason why he left was that he was suffering hunger in the plaza de armas of La Toma [del Río del Norte], and a companion of his named Domingo urged this declarant to go to New Mexico for a while, so as to find out how matters stood with the Indians and to give warning to the Spaniards of any treason. They did not come with the intention of remaining always with the apostate traitors and rebels, and after they arrived they [the Indians] killed the said Domingo, his companion, because of the Pecos Indians having seen him fighting in the villa along with the Spaniards. He said that because his comrade was gone he had remained until now, when he saw the Spaniards and came to them, warning them not to be careless with the horses, because he had heard the traitors say that although the Spaniards might conclude peace with them, they would come to attack them by night and take away the horses. Thus he responds to this question.

Asked what causes or motives the said Indian rebels had for renouncing the law of God and obedience to his Majesty, and for committing so many kinds of crimes, and who were the instigators of the rebellion, and what he had heard while he was among the apostates, he said that the prime movers of the rebellion were two Indians of San Juan, one named El Popé and the other El Taqu, and another from Taos named Saca, and another from San Ildefonso named Francisco. He knows that these were the principals, and the causes they gave were alleged ill treatment and injuries received from the present secretary, Francisco Xavier, and the maestre de campo, Alonso García, and from the sargentos mayores, Luis de Quintana and Diego López, because they beat them, took away what they had, and made them work without pay. Thus he replies.

Asked why, since the said rebels had been of different minds, some believing that they should give themselves up peacefully and others opposing it, when the Spaniards arrived at the sierra of La Cieneguilla de Cochití, where the leaders of the uprising and people from all the nations were assembled, they had not attempted to give themselves up and return to the holy faith and to obedience to his Majesty—for while they had made some signs, they had done nothing definite—he said that although it is true that as soon as the Spaniards arrived some said that it was better to give up peaceably than to have war, the young men were unwilling to agree, saying that they wished to fight. In particular one Spanish-speaking Indian or coyote named Francisco, commonly called El Ollita, said that no one should surrender in peace, that all must fight, and that although some of his brothers were coming with the Spaniards, if they fought on the side of the Spaniards he would kill them, and if they came over to the side of the Indians he would not harm them. Whereupon everyone was disturbed, and there having arrived at this juncture Don Luis Tupatú, governor of the pueblo of Los Pecuríes, while they were thus consulting, news came to the place where the junta was being held from another Indian named Alonso Catití, a leader of the uprising, believed to be a coyote, in which he sent to notify the people that he had already planned to deceive the Spaniards with feigned peace. He had arranged to send to the pueblo of Cochití all the prettiest, most pleasing, and neatest Indian women so that, under pretense of coming down to prepare food for the Spaniards, they could provoke them to lewdness, and that night while they were with them, the said coyote Catití would come down with all the men of the Queres and Jemez nations, only the said Catití attempting to speak with the said Spaniards, and at a shout from him they would all rush down to kill the said Spaniards; and he gave orders that all the rest who were in the other junta where the said Don Luis and El Ollita were present, should at the same time attack the horse drove, so as to finish that too. This declarant being present during all these proceedings, and feeling compassion because of the treason they were plotting, he determined to come to warn the Spaniards, as he did, whereupon they put themselves under arms and the said Indians again went up to the heights of the sierra, and the Spaniards withdrew. Thus he replies to the question. . . .

. . . He said that what he has stated in his declaration is the truth and what he knows, under charge of his oath, which he affirms and ratifies, this, his said declaration, being read to him. He did not sign because of not knowing how, nor does he know his age. Apparently he is about twenty years old. . . .

10

The African Slave Trade
Olaudah Equiano

The Life of Olaudah Equiano, or Gustavus Vassa, the African, Written by Himself (1789) *is one of the most important eyewitness accounts of the African slave trade. While scholars have long agreed on the horrors of the trade, they have argued for more than a century over how many people were involved. Estimates range from about nine and a half million to nearly fifteen million Africans imported into the Western Hemisphere. And this does not include those who were killed while resisting capture or who died during passage.*

Equiano's book is also the pioneering African American narrative of the journey from slavery to freedom, setting many of the conventions for the more than six thousand subsequent interviews, essays, and books by which former slaves told their dramatic stories.

According to Equiano's account, Equiano (ca. 1750–1797), an Ibo prince kidnapped into slavery when he was eleven years old, was brought first to Barbados and then sent to Virginia. After service in the British navy, he was at last sold to a Quaker merchant who allowed Equiano to purchase his freedom in 1766. In later years he worked to advance the Church of England, his adopted religion, and to abolish the slave trade. Recent scholarship suggests that Equiano may have been born in South Carolina, throwing into question the reliability of his details of eighteenth-century life in West Africa. Despite this ongoing controversy, Equiano's narrative continues to fascinate and inform.

QUESTIONS TO CONSIDER

1. Describe the treatment of slaves in the slave trade, as described in the narrative.
2. What were Olaudah Equiano's greatest fears during passage?
3. Equiano asks, "Learned you this from your God, who says unto you, Do unto all men as you would men should do unto you?" How would a slave trader have answered his question?

The first object which saluted my eyes when I arrived on the [Western Africa] coast, was the sea, and a slave ship, which was then riding at anchor, and waiting for its cargo. These filled me with astonishment, which was soon converted into terror, when I was carried on board. I was immediately handled, and tossed up to see if I were sound, by some of the crew; and I was now persuaded that I had gotten into a world of bad spirits, and that they were going to kill me.

Olaudah Equiano, *The Life of Olaudah Equiano, or Gustavus Vassa, the African, Written by Himself* (New York: Isaac Knapp, 1837), 41–52.

Their complexions, too, differing so much from ours, their long hair, and the language they spoke, (which was very different from any I had ever heard) united to confirm me in this belief. Indeed, such were the horrors of my views and fears at the moment, that, if ten thousand worlds had been my own, I would have freely parted with them all to have exchanged my condition with that of the meanest slave in my own country. When I looked round the ship too, and saw a large furnace of copper boiling, and a multitude of black people of every description chained together, every one of their countenances expressing dejection and sorrow, I no longer doubted of my fate; and, quite overpowered with horror and anguish, I fell motionless on the deck and fainted. When I recovered a little, I found some black people about me, who I believed were some of those who had brought me on board, and had been receiving their pay; they talked to me in order to cheer me, but all in vain. I asked them if we were not to be eaten by those white men with horrible looks, red faces, and long hair. They told me I was not: and one of the crew brought me a small portion of spirituous liquor in a wine glass, but, being afraid of him, I would not take it out of his hand. One of the blacks, therefore, took it from him and gave it to me, and I took a little down my palate, which, instead of reviving me, as they thought it would, threw me into the greatest consternation at the strange feeling it produced, having never tasted any such liquor before. Soon after this, the blacks who brought me on board went off, and left me abandoned to despair.

I now saw myself deprived of all chance of returning to my native country, or even the least glimpse of hope of gaining the shore, which I now considered as friendly; and I even wished for my former slavery in preference to my present situation, which was filled with horrors of every kind, still heightened by my ignorance of what I was to undergo. I was not long suffered to indulge my grief; I was soon put down under the decks, and there I received such a salutation in my nostrils as I had never experienced in my life: so that, with the loathsomeness of the stench, and crying together, I became so sick and low that I was not able to eat, nor had I the least desire to taste any thing. I now wished for the last friend, death, to relieve me; but soon, to my grief, two of the white men offered me eatables; and, on my refusing to eat, one of them held me fast by the hands, and laid me across, I think the windlass, and tied my feet, while the other flogged me severely. I had never experienced any thing of this kind before, and although not being used to the water, I naturally feared that element the first time I saw it, yet, nevertheless, could I have got over the nettings, I would have jumped over the side, but I could not; and besides, the crew used to watch us very closely who were not chained down to the decks, lest we should leap into the water; and I have seen some of these poor African prisoners most severely cut, for attempting to do so, and hourly whipped for not eating. This indeed was often the case with myself. In a little time after, amongst the poor chained men, I found some of my own nation, which in a small degree gave ease to my mind. I inquired of these what was to be done with us? they gave me to understand, we were to be carried to these white people's country to work for them. I then was a little revived, and thought, if it were no worse than working, my situation was not so desperate; but still I feared I should be put to death, the white people looked and acted, as I thought, in so savage a manner; for I had never seen among any people such instances of brutal cruelty; and this not only shown towards us blacks, but also to some of the whites themselves. One white man in particular I saw, when we were permitted to be on deck, flogged so unmercifully with a large rope near the foremast, that he died in consequence of it; and they tossed him over the side as they would have done a brute. This made me fear these people the more; and I expected nothing less than to be treated in the same manner. I could not help expressing my fears and apprehensions to some of my countrymen; I asked them if these people had no country, but lived in this hollow place? (the ship) they told me they did not, but came from a distant one. "Then," said I, "how comes it in all our country we never heard of them?" They told me because they lived so very far off. I then asked where were their women? Had they any like themselves? I was told they had. "And why," said I, "do we not see them?" They answered, because they were left behind. I asked how the vessel could go? They told me they could not tell; but that there was cloth put upon the masts by the help of the ropes I saw, and then the vessel went on; and the white men had some spell or magic they put in the water when they liked, in order to stop the vessel. I was exceedingly amazed at this account, and really thought they were spirits. I therefore wished much to be from amongst them, for I expected they would sacrifice me; but my wishes were vain—for we were so quartered that it was impossible for any of us to make our escape. . . .

At last, when the ship we were in, had got in all her cargo, they made ready with many fearful noises, and we were all put under deck, so that we could not see how they managed the vessel. But this disappointment was the least of my sorrow. The stench of the hold while we were on the coast was so intolerably loathsome, that it was dangerous to remain there for any time, and some of us had been permitted to stay on the deck for the fresh air; but now that the whole ship's cargo were confined together, it became absolutely pestilential. The closeness of the place, and the heat of the climate, added to the number in the ship, which was so crowded that each had scarcely room to turn himself, almost suffocated us. This produced copious perspirations, so that the air soon became unfit for respiration, from a variety of loathsome smells, and brought on a sickness among the slaves, of which many died—thus falling victims to the improvident avarice, as I may call it, of their purchasers. This wretched situation was again aggravated by the galling of the chains, now became insupportable; and the filth of the necessary tubs, into which the children often fell, and were almost suffocated. The shrieks of the women, and the groans of the dying, rendered the whole a scene of horror almost inconceivable. Happily perhaps, for myself, I was soon reduced so low here that it was thought necessary to keep me almost always on deck; and from my extreme youth I was not put in fetters. In this situation I expected every hour to share the fate of my companions, some of whom were almost daily brought upon deck at the point of death, which I began to hope would soon put an end to my miseries. Often did I think many of the inhabitants of the deep much more happy than myself. I envied them the freedom they enjoyed, and as often wished I could change my condition for theirs. Every circumstance I met with, served only to render my state more painful, and heightened my apprehensions, and my opinion of the cruelty of the whites.

One day they had taken a number of fishes; and when they had killed and satisfied themselves with as many as they thought fit, to our astonishment who were on deck, rather than give any of them to us to eat, as we expected, they tossed the remaining fish into the sea again, although we begged and prayed for some as well as we could, but in vain; and some of my countrymen, being pressed by hunger, took an opportunity, when they thought no one saw them, of trying to get a little privately; but they were discovered, and the attempt procured them some very severe floggings. One day, when we had a smooth sea and moderate wind, two of my wearied countrymen who were chained together, (I was near them at the time,) preferring death to such a life of misery, somehow made through the nettings and jumped into the sea: immediately, another quite dejected fellow, who, on account of his illness, was suffered to be out of irons, also followed their example. . . .

During our passage, I first saw flying fishes, which surprised me very much; they used frequently to fly across the ship, and many of them fell on the deck. I also now first saw the use of the quadrant; I had often with astonishment seen the mariners make observations with it, and I could not think what it meant. They at last took notice of my surprise; and one of them, willing to increase it, as well as to gratify my curiosity, made me one day look through it. The clouds appeared to me to be land, which disappeared as they passed along. This heightened my wonder; and I was now more persuaded than ever, that I was in another world, and that every thing about me was magic. At last, we came in sight of the island of Barbados, at which the whites on board gave a great shout, and made many signs of joy to us. We did not know what to think of this; but as the vessel drew nearer, we plainly saw the harbor, and other ships of different kinds and sizes, and we soon anchored amongst them, off Bridgetown. Many merchants and planters now came on board, though it was in the evening. They put us in separate parcels, and examined us attentively. They also made us jump, and pointed to the land, signifying we were to go there. We thought by this, we should be eaten by these ugly men, as they appeared to us; and, when soon after we were all put down under the deck again, there was much dread and trembling among us, and nothing but bitter cries to be heard all the night from these apprehensions, insomuch, that at last the white people got some old slaves from the land to pacify us. They told us we were not to be eaten, but to work, and were soon to go on land, where we should see many of our country people. This report eased us much. And sure enough, soon after we were landed, there came to us Africans of all languages.

We were conducted immediately to the merchant's yard, where we were all pent up together, like so many sheep in a fold, without regard to sex or age. As every object was new to me, every thing I saw filled me with surprise. What struck me first, was, that the houses were built with bricks and stories, and in every other respect different from those I had seen in Africa; but I was still more astonished on seeing people on horseback. I did not know what this could mean; and, indeed, I thought these people were full of nothing but magical arts. While I was in this astonishment, one of my fellow-prisoners spoke to a countryman of his, about the horses, who said they were the same kind they had in their country. I understood them, though they were from a distant part of Africa; and I thought it odd I had not seen any horses there; but afterwards, when I came to converse with different Africans, I found they had many horses amongst them, and much larger than those I then saw.

We were not many days in the merchant's custody before we were sold after their usual manner, which is this:—On a signal given, (as the beat of a drum,) the buyers rush at once into the yard where the slaves are confined, and make choice of that parcel they like best. The noise and clamor with which this is attended, and the eagerness visible in the countenances of the buyers, serve not a little to increase the apprehension of terrified Africans, who may well be supposed to consider them as the ministers of that destruction to which they think themselves devoted. In this manner, without scruple, are relations and friends separated, most of them never to see each other again. I remember, in the vessel in which I was brought over, in the men's apartment, there were several brothers, who, in the sale, were sold in different lots; and it was very moving on this occasion, to see and hear their cries at parting. O, ye nominal Christians! might not an African ask you—Learned you this from your God, who says unto you, Do unto all men as you would men should do unto you? Is it not enough that we are torn from our country and friends, to toil for your luxury and lust of gain? Must every tender feeling be likewise sacrificed to your avarice? Are the dearest friends and relations, now rendered more dear by their separation from their kindred, still to be parted from each other, and thus prevented from cheering the gloom of slavery, with the small comfort of being together, and mingling their sufferings and sorrows? Why are parents to lose their children, brothers their sisters, or husbands their wives? Surely, this is a new refinement in cruelty, which, while it has no advantage to atone for it, thus aggravates distress, and adds fresh horrors even to the wretchedness of slavery.

11

On the Misfortune of Indentured Servants
Gottlieb Mittelberger

Indentured, or bonded, servants were an important source of labor in seventeenth- and eighteenth-century America. The term indentured *generally refers to immigrants who, in return for passage from Europe to America, bound themselves to work in America for a specified number of years, after which time they would become completely free. The practice was closely related to the tradition of apprenticeship, in which a youth was assigned to work for a master in a trade for a certain number of years and in return was taught the skills of that trade. Convicts were another important source of colonial labor; thousands of English criminals were sentenced to labor in the colonies for a specified period, after which they were freed.*

Many indentured servants had valuable skills that they hoped to make better use of in the New World than they had been able to do at home. Some in fact did just that, while others, as Gottlieb Mittelberger describes, did not fare well. Mittelberger came to Pennsylvania from Germany in 1750. His own fortunes were not so bleak as those of his shipmates. He served as a schoolmaster and organist in Philadelphia for three years and then returned to Germany in 1754.

QUESTIONS TO CONSIDER

1. Why did immigrants choose to endure the miseries of a transatlantic passage to come to the New World?
2. How did the treatment of indentured servants described by Gottlieb Mittelberger compare to the treatment of slaves in the slave trade described in the previous reading?
3. What happened to children whose parents died during the journey?
4. Why do you think Mittelberger returned to Germany?

Both in Rotterdam and in Amsterdam the people are packed densely, like herrings so to say, in the large sea-vessels. One person receives a place of scarcely 2 feet width and 6 feet length in the bedstead, while many a ship carries four to six hundred souls; not to mention the innumerable implements, tools, provisions, water-barrels and other things which likewise occupy much space.

Gottlieb Mittelberger, *Journey to Pennsylvania in the Year 1750 and Return to Germany in the Year 1754*, trans. Carl Theo (Philadelphia: John Joseph McVey, 1898), 19–29.

On account of contrary winds it takes the ships sometimes 2, 3 and 4 weeks to make the trip from Holland to . . . England. But when the wind is good, they get there in 8 days or even sooner. Everything is examined there and the custom-duties paid, whence it comes that the ships ride there 8, 10 to 14 days and even longer at anchor, till they have taken in their full cargoes. During that time every one is compelled to spend his last remaining money and to consume his little stock of provisions which had been reserved for the sea; so that most passengers, finding themselves on the ocean where they would be in greater need of them, must greatly suffer from hunger and want. Many suffer want already on the water between Holland and Old England.

When the ships have for the last time weighed their anchors near the city of Kaupp [Cowes] in Old England, the real misery begins with the long voyage. For from there the ships, unless they have good wind, must often sail 8, 9, 10 to 12 weeks before they reach Philadelphia. But even with the best wind the voyage lasts 7 weeks.

But during the voyage there is on board these ships terrible misery, stench, fumes, horror, vomiting, many kinds of sea-sickness, fever, dysentery, headache, heat, constipation, boils, scurvy, cancer, mouth-rot, and the like, all of which come from old and sharply salted food and meat, also from very bad and foul water, so that many die miserably.

Add to this want of provisions, hunger, thirst, frost, heat, dampness, anxiety, want, afflictions and lamentations, together with other trouble, as . . . the lice abound so frightfully, especially on sick people, that they can be scraped off the body. The misery reaches the climax when a gale rages for 2 or 3 nights and days, so that every one believes that the ship will go to the bottom with all human beings on board. In such a visitation the people cry and pray most piteously.

When in such a gale the sea rages and surges, so that the waves rise often like high mountains one above the other, and often tumble over the ship, so that one fears to go down with the ship; when the ship is constantly tossed from side to side by the storm and waves, so that no one can either walk, or sit, or lie, and the closely packed people in the berths are thereby tumbled over each other, both the sick and the well—it will be readily understood that many of these people, none of whom had been prepared for hardships, suffer so terribly from them that they do not survive it.

I myself had to pass through a severe illness at sea, and I best know how I felt at the time. These poor people often long for consolation, and I often entertained and comforted them with singing, praying and exhorting; and whenever it was possible and the winds and waves permitted it, I kept daily prayer-meetings with them on deck. Besides, I baptized five children in distress, because we had no ordained minister on board. I also held divine service every Sunday by reading sermons to the people; and when the dead were sunk in the water, I commended them and our souls to the mercy of God.

Among the healthy, impatience sometimes grows so great and cruel that one curses the other, or himself and the day of his birth, and sometimes come near killing each other. Misery and malice join each other, so that they cheat and rob one another. One always reproaches the other with having persuaded him to undertake the journey. Frequently children cry out against their parents, husbands against their wives and wives against their husbands, brothers and sisters, friends and acquaintances against each other. But most against the soul-traffickers.

Many sigh and cry: "Oh, that I were at home again, and if I had to lie in my pig-sty!" Or they say: "O God, if I only had a piece of good bread, or a good fresh drop of water." Many people whimper, sigh and cry piteously for their homes; most of them get home-sick. Many hundred people necessarily die and perish in such misery, and must be cast into the sea, which drives their relatives, or those who persuaded them to undertake the journey, to such despair that it is almost impossible to pacify and console them. . . .

No one can have an idea of the sufferings which women in confinement have to bear with their innocent children on board these ships. Few of this class escape with their lives; many a mother is cast into the water with her child as soon as she is dead. One day, just as we had a heavy gale, a woman in our ship, who was to give birth and could not give birth under the circumstances, was pushed through a loop-hole [port-hole] in the ship and dropped into the sea, because she was far in the rear of the ship and could not be brought forward.

Children from 1 to 7 years rarely survive the voyage. I witnessed . . . misery in no less than 32 children in our ship, all of whom were thrown into the sea. The parents grieve all the more since their children find no resting-place in the earth, but are devoured by the monsters of the sea.

That most of the people get sick is not surprising, because, in addition to all other trials and hardships, warm food is served only three times a week, the rations being very poor and very little. Such meals can hardly be eaten, on account of being so unclean. The water which is served out on the ships is often very black, thick and full of worms, so that one cannot drink it without loathing, even with the greatest thirst. Toward the end we were compelled to eat the ship's biscuit which had been spoiled long ago; though in a whole biscuit there was scarcely a piece the size of a dollar that had not been full of red worms and spiders' nests. . . .

At length, when, after a long and tedious voyage, the ships come in sight of land, so that the promontories can be seen, which the people were so eager and anxious to see, all creep from below on deck to see the land from afar, and they weep for joy, and pray and sing, thanking and praising God. The sight of the land makes the people on board the ship, especially the sick and the half dead, alive again, so that their hearts leap within them; they shout and rejoice, and are content to bear their misery in patience, in the hope that they may soon reach the land in safety. But alas!

When the ships have landed at Philadelphia after their long voyage, no one is permitted to leave them except those who pay for their passage or can give good security; the others, who cannot pay, must remain on board the ships till they are purchased, and are released from the ships by their purchasers. The sick always fare the worst, for the healthy are naturally preferred and purchased first; and so the sick and wretched must often remain on board in front of the city for 2 or 3 weeks, and frequently die, whereas many a one, if he could pay his debt and were permitted to leave the ship immediately, might recover and remain alive.

The sale of human beings in the market on board the ship is carried on thus: Every day Englishmen, Dutchmen, and High-German people[1] come from the city of Philadelphia and other places, in part from a great distance, say 20, 30, or 40 hours away, and go on board the newly arrived ship that has brought and offers for sale passengers from Europe, and select among the healthy persons such as they deem suitable for their business, and bargain with them how long they will serve for their passage money, which most of them are still in debt for. When they have come to an agreement, it happens that adult persons bind themselves in writing to serve 3, 4, 5, or 6 years for the amount due by them, according to their age and strength. But very young people, from 10 to 15 years, must serve till they are 21 years old.

Many parents must sell and trade away their children like so many head of cattle; for if their children take the debt upon themselves, the parents can leave the ship free and unrestrained; but as the parents often do not know where and to what people their children are going, it often happens that such parents and children, after leaving the ship, do not see each other again for many years, perhaps no more in all their lives.

It often happens that whole families, husband, wife, and children, are separated by being sold to different purchasers, especially when they have not paid any part of their passage money.

When a husband or wife has died at sea, when the ship has made more than half of her trip, the survivor must pay or serve not only for himself or herself, but also for the deceased.

When both parents have died over half-way at sea, their children, especially when they are young and have nothing to pawn or to pay, must stand for their own and their parents' passage, and serve till they are 21 years old. When one has served his or her term, he or she is entitled to a new suit of clothes at parting; and if it has been so stipulated, a man gets in addition a horse, a woman, a cow.

When a serf has an opportunity to marry in this country, he or she must pay for each year which he or she would have yet to serve, 5 to 6 pounds. But many a one who has thus purchased and paid for his bride, has subsequently repented his bargain, so that he would gladly have returned his exorbitantly dear ware, and lost the money besides.

If some one in this country runs away from his master, who has treated him harshly, he cannot get far. Good provision has been made for such cases, so that a runaway is soon recovered. He who detains or returns a deserter receives a good reward.

If such a runaway has been away from his master one day, he must serve for it as a punishment a week, for a week a month, and for a month half a year.

---

1. **High-German people:** People who had emigrated from central or southern Germany.

12

Defending Colonial Activities before Parliament
Benjamin Franklin

Benjamin Franklin, more than any other founding father, exemplifies the Enlightenment in America. A scientist, journalist, moral philosopher, and political reformer, Franklin believed in the power of human reason to understand nature and improve the lot of humankind. Among his many accomplishments were the inventions of bifocal glasses, the glass harmonica, improved navigational instruments and ships lanterns, the lightning rod, and, of course, the Franklin stove. A best-selling author and the publisher of America's first bilingual newspaper (in English and German), Franklin had the added distinction of being the only man to sign all three fundamental U.S. documents: the Declaration of Independence, the Constitution, and the Bill of Rights. He served as chief negotiator of the Treaty of Paris, which ended America's war for independence; governor of Pennsylvania; and president of the Pennsylvania Abolition Society.

Born in 1706, the tenth son of a Boston soap and candle maker, Franklin ventured to Philadelphia as a teenager and settled there permanently, making his fortune through publishing and other commercial endeavors. In 1764 he traveled to London to petition King George to convert Pennsylvania from a proprietary Penn family holding to a publicly administered royal colony. While Franklin was in London, the British parliament passed the Stamp Act of 1765 to fund the militarization of the western frontier of British North America, which was facing threats from Native Americans and the French crown. Franklin at first supported the Stamp Act, but after discovering how deeply hated it was in Pennsylvania, soon argued against "taxation without representation."

The following exchange was first published in London in 1766 as a pamphlet titled "The Examination of Doctor Franklin." Owing to the secrecy of the session of Parliament, the pamphlet gave no hint about who had printed the piece or where the examination had taken place, but later editions described it as having transpired "before an august assembly," understood to be the British parliament. The pamphlet was reprinted in 1766 in Philadelphia, New York, Boston, New London, and other American cities and was much in demand across the colonies. Though some have argued that the questions put to Franklin had been prepared and rehearsed beforehand, one of Franklin's biographers noted that "it does not appear that such prearrangements went further than that certain friendly interrogators had discussed the topics with him, so as to be familiar

William Jennings Bryan, ed., *The World's Famous Orations* (New York: Funk and Wagnalls, 1906), Vol. II, 248–54.

with his views. Every lawyer does this with his witnesses. Nor can it be supposed that the admirable replies which he made to the enemies of America were otherwise than strictly impromptu."

QUESTIONS TO CONSIDER

1. How representative of American colonial opinion is Benjamin Franklin when he says that Americans will "wear their old cloaths over again, till they can make new ones"?
2. What does Franklin mean when he describes trade with Indians as "not an American interest"?
3. Why does Franklin say that Americans "consider themselves as a part of the British empire"?

Q: Are not the Colonies, from their circumstances, very able to pay the stamp duty?

A: In my opinion, there is not gold and silver enough in the Colonies to pay the stamp duty for one year.

Q: Don't you know that the money arising from the stamps was all to be laid out in America?

A: I know it is appropriated by the act to the American service; but it will be spent in the conquered Colonies, where the soldiers are, not in the Colonies that pay it. . . .

Q: Do you think it right that America should be protected by this country, and pay no part of the expence?

A: That is not the case. The Colonies raised, cloathed and paid, during the last war, near 25000 men, and spent many millions.

Q: Were you not reimbursed by parliament?

A: We were only reimbursed what, in your opinion, we had advanced beyond our proportion, or beyond what might reasonably be expected from us; and it was a very small part of what we spent. Pennsylvania, in particular, disbursed about 500,000 Pounds, and the reimbursements, in the whole, did not exceed 60,000 Pounds. . . .

Q: Do not you think the people of America would submit to pay the stamp duty, if it was moderated?

A: No, never, unless compelled by force of arms. . . .

Q: What was the temper of America towards Great-Britain before the year 1763?

A: The best in the world. They submitted willingly to the government of the Crown, and paid, in all their courts, obedience to acts of parliament. Numerous as the people are in the several old provinces, they cost you nothing in forts, citadels, garrisons or armies, to keep them in subjection. They were governed by this country at the expence only of a little pen, ink and paper. They were led by a thread. They had not only a respect, but an affection, for Great-Britain, for its laws, its customs and manners, and even a fondness for its fashions, that greatly increased the commerce. Natives of Britain were always treated with particular regard; to be an old England-man was, of itself, a character of some respect, and gave a kind of rank among us.

Q: And what is their temper now?

A: O, very much altered.

Q: Did you ever hear the authority of parliament to make laws for America questioned till lately?

A: The authority of parliament was allowed to be valid in all laws, except such as should lay internal taxes. It was never disputed in laying duties to regulate commerce. . . .

Q: In what light did the people of America use to consider the parliament of Great-Britain?

A: They considered the parliament as the great bulwark and security of their liberties and privileges, and always spoke of it with the utmost respect and veneration. Arbitrary ministers, they thought, might possibly, at times, attempt to oppress them; but they relied on it, that the parliament, on application, would always give redress. They remembered, with gratitude, a strong instance of this, when a bill was brought into parliament, with a clause to make royal instructions laws in the Colonies, which the house of commons would not pass, and it was thrown out.

Q: And have they not still the same respect for parliament?

A: No; it is greatly lessened.

Q: To what causes is that owing?

A: To a concurrence of causes; the restraints lately laid on their trade, by which the bringing of foreign gold and silver into the Colonies was prevented; the prohibition of making paper money among themselves; and then demanding a new and heavy tax by stamps; taking away, at the same time, trials by juries, and refusing to receive and hear their humble petitions.

Q: Don't you think they would submit to the stamp-act, if it was modified, the obnoxious parts taken out, and the duty reduced to some particulars, of small moment?

A: No; they will never submit to it. . . .

Q: Was it an opinion in America before 1763, that the parliament had no right to lay taxes and duties there?

A: I never heard any objection to the right of laying duties to regulate commerce; but a right to lay internal taxes was never supposed to be in parliament, as we are not represented there.

Q: On what do you found your opinion, that the people in America made any such distinction?

A: I know that whenever the subject has occurred in conversation where I have been present, it has appeared to be the opinion of every one, that we could not be taxed in a parliament where we were not represented. But the payment of duties laid by act of parliament, as regulations of commerce, was never disputed.

Q: But can you name any act of assembly, or public act of any of your governments, that made such distinction?

A: I do not know that there was any; I think there was never an occasion to make any such act, till now that you have attempted to tax us; that has occasioned resolutions of assembly, declaring the distinction, in which I think every assembly on the continent, and every member in every assembly, have been unanimous. . . .

Q: You say the Colonies have always submitted to external taxes, and object to the right of parliament only in laying internal taxes; now can you shew that there is any kind of difference between the two taxes to the Colony on which they may be laid?

A: I think the difference is very great. An external tax is a duty laid on commodities imported; that duty is added to the first cost, and other charges on the commodity, and when it is offered to sale, makes a part of the price. If the people do not like it at that price, they refuse it; they are not obliged to pay it. But an internal tax is forced from the people without their consent, if not laid by their own representatives. The stamp-act says, we shall have no commerce, make no exchange of property with each other, neither purchase nor grant, nor recover debts; we shall neither marry, nor make our wills, unless we pay such and such sums, and thus it is intended to extort our money from us, or ruin us by the consequences of refusing to pay it.

Q: But supposing the external tax or duty to be laid on the necessaries of life imported into your Colony, will not that be the same thing in its effects as an internal tax?

A: I do not know a single article imported into the Northern Colonies, but what they can either do without, or make themselves.

Q: Don't you think cloth from England absolutely necessary to them?

A: No, by no means absolutely necessary; with industry and good management, they may very well supply themselves with all they want.

Q: Will it not take a long time to establish that manufacture among them? And must they not in the mean while suffer greatly?

A: I think not. They have made a surprising progress already. And I am of opinion, that before their old clothes are worn out, they will have new ones of their own making.

Q: Can they possibly find wool enough in North-America?

A: They have taken steps to increase the wool. They entered into general combinations to eat no more lamb, and very few lambs were killed last year. This course persisted in, will soon make a prodigious difference in the quantity of wool. And the establishing of great manufactories, like those in the clothing towns here, is not necessary, as it is where the business is to be carried on for the purposes of trade. The people will all spin, and work for themselves, in their own houses. . . .

Q: Considering the resolutions of parliament, as to the right, do you think, if the stamp-act is repealed, that the North Americans will be satisfied?

A: I believe they will.

Q: Why do you think so?

A: I think the resolutions of right will give them very little concern, if they are never attempted to be carried into practice. The Colonies will probably consider themselves in the same situation, in that respect, with Ireland; they know you claim the same right with regard to Ireland, but you never exercise it. And they may believe you never will exercise it in the Colonies, any more than in Ireland, unless on some very extraordinary occasion.

Q: But who are to be the judges of that extraordinary occasion? Is it not the parliament?

A: Though the parliament may judge of the occasion, the people will think it can never exercise such right, till representatives from the Colonies are admitted into parliament, and that whenever the occasion arises, representatives will be ordered. . . .

Q: Can any thing less than a military force carry the stamp-act into execution?

A: I do not see how a military force can be applied to that purpose.

Q: Why may it not?

A: Suppose a military force sent into America, they will find nobody in arms; what are they then to do? They cannot force a man to take stamps who chooses to do without them. They will not find a rebellion; they may indeed make one.

Q: If the act is not repealed, what do you think will be the consequences?

A: A total loss of the respect and affection the people of America bear to this country, and of all the commerce that depends on that respect and affection.

Q: How can the commerce be affected?

A: You will find, that if the act is not repealed, they will take very little of your manufactures in a short time.

Q: Is it in their power to do without them?

A: I think they may very well do without them.

Q: Is it their interest not to take them?

A: The goods they take from Britain are either necessaries, mere conveniences, or superfluities. The first, as cloth, &c. with a little industry they can make at home; the second they can do without, till they are able to provide them among themselves; and the last, which are much the greatest part, they will strike off immediately. They are mere articles of fashion, purchased and consumed, because the fashion in a respected country, but will now be detested and rejected. The people have already struck off, by general agreement, the use of all goods fashionable in mournings, and many thousand pounds worth are sent back as unsaleable. . . .

Q: Then no regulation with a tax would be submitted to?

A: Their opinion is, that when aids to the Crown are wanted, they are to be asked of the several assemblies, according to the old established usage, who will, as they always have done, grant them freely. And that their money ought not to be given away without their consent, by persons at a distance, unacquainted with their circumstances and abilities. The granting aids to the Crown, is the only means they have of recommending themselves to their sovereign, and they think it extremely hard and unjust, that a body of men, in which they have no representatives, should make a merit to itself of giving and granting what is not its own, but theirs, and deprive them of a right they esteem of the utmost value and importance, as it is the security of all their other rights. . . .

Q: Supposing the stamp-act continued, and enforced, do you imagine that ill humour will induce the Americans to give as much for worse manufactures of their own, and use them, preferably to better of ours?

A: Yes, I think so. People will pay as freely to gratify one passion as another, their resentment as their pride. . . .

Q: If the stamp act should be repealed, would not the Americans think they could oblige the parliament to repeal every external tax law now in force?

A: It is hard to answer questions of what people at such a distance will think.

Q: But what do you imagine they will think were the motives of repealing the act?

A: I suppose they will think that it was repealed from a conviction of its inexpediency; and they will rely upon it, that while the same inexpediency subsists, you will never attempt to make such another.

Q: What do you mean by its inexpediency?

A: I mean its inexpediency on several accounts; the poverty and inability of those who were to pay the tax; the general discontent it has occasioned; and the impracticability of enforcing it. . . .

Q: But if the legislature should think fit to ascertain its right to lay taxes, by any act laying a small tax, contrary to their opinion, would they submit to pay the tax?

A: The proceedings of the people in America have been considered too much together. The proceedings of the assemblies have been very different from those of the mobs, and should be distinguished, as having no connection with each other. The assemblies have only peaceably resolved what they take to be their rights; they have taken no measures for opposition by force; they have not built a fort, raised a man, or provided a grain of ammunition, in order to such opposition. The ringleaders of riots they think ought to be punished; they would punish them themselves, if they could. Every sober sensible man would wish to see rioters punished; as otherwise peaceable people have no security of person or estate. But as to any internal tax, how small soever, laid by the legislature here on the people there, while they have no representatives in this legislature, I think it will never be submitted to. They will oppose it to the last. They do not consider it as at all necessary for you to raise money on them by your taxes, because they are, and always have been, ready to raise money by taxes among themselves, and to grant large sums, equal to their abilities, upon requisition from the Crown. They have not only granted equal to their abilities, but, during all the last war, they granted far beyond their abilities, and beyond their proportion with this country, you yourselves being judges, to the amount of many hundred thousand pounds, and this they did freely and readily, only on a sort of promise from the secretary of state, that it should be recommended to parliament to make them compensation. It was accordingly recommended to parliament, in the most honourable manner, for them. America has been greatly misrepresented and abused here, in papers, and pamphlets, and speeches, as ungrateful, and unreasonable, and unjust, in having put this nation to immense expence for their defence, and refusing to bear any part of that expence. The Colonies raised, paid and clothed, near 25000 men during the last war, a number equal to those sent from Britain, and far beyond their proportion; they went deeply into debt in doing this, and all their taxes and estates are mortgaged, for many years to come, for discharging that debt. . . .

Q: But suppose Great-Britain should be engaged in a war in Europe, would North-America contribute to the support of it?

A: I do think they would, as far as their circumstances would permit. They consider themselves as a part of the British empire, and as having one common interest with it; they may be looked on here as foreigners, but they do not consider themselves as such. They are zealous for the honour and prosperity of this nation, and, while they are well used, will always be ready to support it, as far as their little power goes. In 1739 they were called upon to assist in the expedition against Carthagena,[1] and they sent 3000 men to join your army. It is true Carthagena is in America, but as remote from the Northern Colonies, as if it had been in Europe. They make no distinction of wars, as to their duty of assisting in them. I know the last war[2] is commonly spoke of here as entered into for the defence, or for the sake of the people of America. I think it is quite misunderstood. It began about the limits between Canada and Nova-Scotia, about territories to which the Crown indeed laid claim, but were not claimed by any British Colony; none of the lands had been granted to any Colonist; we had therefore no particular concern or interest in that dispute. As to the Ohio, the contest there began about your right of trading in the Indian country, a right you had by the treaty of Utrecht, which the French infringed; they seized the traders and their goods, which were your manufactures; they took a fort which a company of your merchants, and their factors and correspondents, had erected there, to secure that trade. Braddock[3] was sent with an army to re-take that fort (which was looked on here as another incroachment on the King's territory) and to protect your trade. It was not till after his defeat that the Colonies were attacked. They were before in perfect peace with both French and Indians; the troops were not therefore sent for their defence. The trade with the Indians, though carried on in America, is not an American interest. The people of America are chiefly farmers and planters; scarce any thing that they raise or produce is an article of commerce with the Indians. The Indian trade is a British interest; it is carried on with British manufactures, for the profit of British merchants and manufacturers; therefore the war, as it commenced for the defence of territories of the Crown, the property of no American, and for the defence of a trade purely British, was really a British war — and yet the people of America made no scruple of contributing their utmost towards carrying it on, and bringing it to a happy conclusion. . . .

Q: What used to be the pride of the Americans?

A: To indulge in the fashions and manufactures of Great-Britain.

Q: What is now their pride?

A: To wear their old cloaths over again, till they can make new ones.

1. **Carthagena:** The most important battle in The War of Jenkins' Ear between Spain and Great Britain, 1739–1748.
2. **The Last War:** The Seven Years War, known in North America as the French and Indian War.
3. **Braddock:** General Edward Braddock, commander-in-chief for the British side in North America during the beginning of the French and Indian War.

13

Assimilation and Discrimination
Jews in the Early Republic

It was not until the late nineteenth century that the United States became home to the largest Jewish population in the world. Between 1880 and 1920 more than two million European Jews escaped the rising anti-Semitic violence of Europe and made new lives in the United States. However, Jews had lived four centuries of history in America, starting around the time of Columbus's voyages, which coincided with the Inquisition's ordering all Jews to convert to Christianity or leave Spain. In fact, on Columbus's first ship were Jewish sailors, surgeons, and a representative of Queen Isabel who had converted only days before he sailed. While Jews were never large in number in colonial America, they were involved throughout the settlement of the region, developing close relationships and sharing public life with gentiles. All the while, they faced questions about what it meant to be Jewish in a society in which religion and identity were defined more by personal choice than by an exclusionary European caste system.

Rebecca Lazarus and Benjamin Nones were part of this early history of European Jews confronting the new challenges of American life. In the first selection that follows, Lazarus writes to her parents in Hamburg, Germany, about a concern familiar to Jews in America for over three centuries: assimilation. Like many Jewish immigrants to the colonies, Lazarus celebrated her freedom, but also lamented that the relative tolerance of her new home seemed to result in a loss of Jewish identity that she sees in colonial Virginia.

Benjamin Nones, a French Jew and Revolutionary War hero who served with both George Washington and Lafayette, confronted a very different challenge from that of Lazarus: anti-Semitism in response to his involvement in politics. Nones, a militant supporter of Jefferson's Republican Party, was the victim of anti-Semitic slurs published in the Philadelphia Gazette *during a negative political campaign waged by the more conservative Federalist Party. Philadelphia was probably the most important center of American Jewish life at the time and Nones responded with forcefulness and pride, demanding the right from the publisher of the* Gazette, *Caleb Wayne, to rebut his attacker publicly in print. When Wayne refused, Nones fought back in the Republican* Philadelphia Aurora, *which was friendly to both Nones's political cause and his ancestry.*

Beth S. Wenger, *The Jewish Americans: Three Centuries of Jewish Voices in America* (New York: Doubleday, 2007), 35–43.

QUESTIONS TO CONSIDER

1. Why do so many of the Jews in Rebecca Lazarus's account of life in colonial Virginia seem to be discarding their customs? How may this have differed in other colonies?
2. Benjamin Nones describes Jews as naturally Republican. What does he mean by this?
3. How are the concerns of these colonial Jews similar to or different from those of Jews and other minority religions in present-day America?
4. What might Benjamin Nones have said to Rebecca Lazarus about her fear that Jews were becoming American and losing their identity?

REBECCA LAZARUS ON THE PROBLEM OF ASSIMILATION

Petersburg, ca. 1792

Dear Parents:

I hope my letter will ease your mind. You can now be reassured and send me one of the family to Charleston, South Carolina. This is the place to which, with God's help, we will go after Passover. The whole reason why we are leaving this place is because of [its lack of] *Yehudhhkeit* [Jewishness].[1] Dear Parents, I know quite well you will not want me to bring up my children like Gentiles. Here they cannot become anything else. Jewishness is pushed aside here. There are here [in Petersburg] ten or twelve Jews, and they are not worthy of being called Jews. We have a *shohet* [slaughterer of animals and poultry] here who goes to market and buys *terefah* [nonkosher] meat and then brings it home. On Rosh Ha-Shanah and on Yom Kippur the people worshipped here without one sefer torah [pentateuchal scroll] and not one of them wore the tallit [a large prayer shawl worn in the synagogue] or the *arba kanfot* [the small set of fringe worn on the body], except Hyman and my Sammy's godfather. The latter is an old man of sixty, a man from Holland. He has been in America for thirty years already; for twenty years he was in Charleston, and he has been living here for four years. He does not want to remain here any longer and will go with us to Charleston. In that place there is a blessed community of three hundred Jews.

You can believe me that I crave to see a synagogue to which I can go. The way we live now is no life at all. We do not know what the Sabbath and the holidays are. On the Sabbath all the Jewish shops are open; and they do business on that day as they do throughout the whole week. But ours we do not allow to open. With us there is still some Sabbath. You must believe me that in our house we all live as Jews as much as we can.

As for the Gentiles [?], we have nothing to complain about. For the sake of a livelihood we do not have to leave here. Nor do we have to leave because of debts. I believe ever since Hyman has grown up that he has not had it so good. You cannot know what a wonderful country this is for the common man. One

---

1. Bracketed notes were provided by the original editor of these sources, Beth S. Wenger.

can live here peacefully. Hyman made a clock that goes very accurately, just like the one in the Buchenstrasse in Hamburg. Now you can imagine what honors Hyman has been getting here. In all Virginia there is no clock [like this one], and Virginia is the greatest province in the whole of America, and America is the largest section of the world. Now you know what sort of a country this is. It is not too long since Virginia was discovered. It is a young country. And it is amazing to see the business they do in this little Petersburg. At times as many as a thousand hogsheads of tobacco arrive at one time, and each hogshead contains 1,000 and sometimes 1,200 pounds of tobacco. The tobacco is shipped from here to the whole world.

When Judah [my brother?] comes here, he can become a watchmaker and a goldsmith, if he so desires. Here it is not like Germany where a watchmaker is not permitted to sell silverware. [The contrary is true in this country.] They do not know otherwise here. They expect a watchmaker to be a silversmith here. Hyman has more to do in making silverware than with watchmaking. He has a journeyman, a silversmith, a very good artisan, and he, Hyman, takes care of the watches, This work is well paid here, but in Charleston, it pays even better.

All the people who hear that we are leaving give us their blessings. They say that it is sinful that such blessed children should be brought up here in Petersburg. My children cannot learn anything here, nothing Jewish, nothing of general culture. My Schoene [my daughter], God bless her, is already three years old; I think it is time that she should learn something, and she has a good head to learn. I have taught her the bedtime prayers and grace after meals in just two lessons. I believe that no one among the Jews here can do as well as she. And my Sammy [born in 1790], God bless him, is already beginning to talk.

I could write more. However, I do not have any more paper.

I remain, your devoted daughter and servant, Rebecca, the wife of Hayyim, the son of Samuel the Levite, I send my family, my . . . [mother-in-law?] and all my friends and good friends, my regards.

BENJAMIN NONES FIGHTS BACK, *PHILADELPHIA AURORA*, AUGUST 11, 1800

Sir,

I HOPE, if you take the liberty of inserting calumnies against individuals, for the amusement of your readers, you will at least have so much regard to justice, as to permit the injured through the same channel that conveyed the slander, to appeal to the public in self-defence.—I expect of you therefore, to insert this reply to your ironical reporter of the proceedings at the meeting of the republican citizens of Philadelphia, contained in your gazette of the fifth instant; so far as I am concerned in that statement.—I am no enemy Mr. Wayne[2] to wit; nor do I think the political parties have much right to complain, if they enable

---

2. Caleb F. Wayne, publisher of the *Philadelphia Gazette*.

the public to laugh at each others expence, provided it be managed with the same degree of ingenuity, and some attention to truth and candour. But your reporter of the proceedings at that meeting is as destitute of truth and candour, as he is of ingenuity, and I think, I can shew, that the want of prudence of this Mr. Marplot,[3] in his slander upon me, is equally glaring with his want of wit, his want of veracity, his want of decency, and his want of humanity.

I am accused of being a *Jew*; of being a *Republican*; and of being *Poor*.

[I] *am* a Jew. I glory in belonging to that persuasion, which even its opponents, whether Christian, or Mahomedan, allow to be of divine origin—of that persuasion on which Christianity itself was originally founded, and must ultimately rest—which has preserved its faith secure and undefiled, for near three thousand years—whose votaries have never murdered each other in religious wars, or cherished the theological hatred so general, so unextinguishable among those who revile them. A persuasion, whose, patient followers, have endured for ages the pious cruelties of Pagans, and of the christians, and persevered in the unoffending practice of their rites and ceremonies, amidst poverties and privations—amidst pains, penalties, confiscations, banishments, tortures, and deaths, beyond the example of any other sect, which the page of history has hitherto recorded.

To be of such a persuasion, is to me no disgrace; though I well understand the inhuman language of bigotted contempt, in which your reporter by attempting to make me ridiculous, as a Jew, has made himself detestable, whatever religious persuasion may be dishonored by his adherence.

But I am a Jew. I am so—and so were Abraham, and Isaac, and Moses and the prophets, and so too were Christ and his apostles, I feel no disgrace in ranking with such society, however, it may be subject to the illiberal buffoonery of such men as your correspondents.

I am a *Republican*. Thank God, I have not been so heedless, and so ignorant of what has passed, and is now passing in the political world. I have not been so proud or so prejudiced as to renounce the cause for which I have *fought*, as an American throughout the whole of the revolutionary war, in the militia of Charleston, and in Polafkey's legion,[4] I fought in almost every action which took place in Carolina, and in the disastrous affair of Savannah, shared the hardships of that sanguinary day, and for three and twenty years I felt no disposition to change my political, any more than my religious principles.—And which in spite of the witling scribblers of aristocracy, I shall hold sacred until death as not to feel the ardour of republicanism.—Your correspondent, Mr. Wayne cannot have known what it is to serve his country from principle in time of danger and difficulties, the expence of his health and his peace, of his pocket and his person, as I have done; or he would not be as he is, a pert reviler of those who have done—as I do not suspect you Mr. Wayne, of being the author of the attack on me, I shall not enquire what share you or your relations had in establishing the liberties of your

---

3. **Mr. Marplot:** The reporter.
4. Brigadier General Casimir Pulaski's Legion. Nones fought with Pulaski at the Siege of Savannah in the autumn of 1779.

country. On religious grounds I am a republican. Kingly, government was first conceded to the foolish complaints of the Jewish people, as a punishment and a curse; and so it was to them until their dispersion, and so it has been to every nation, who have been as foolishly tempted to submit to it. Great Britain has a king, and her enemies need not wish her the sword, the pestilence, and the famine.

In the history of the Jews, are contained the earliest warnings against kingly government, as any one may know who has read the fable of Abimelick,[5] or the exhortations of Samuel.[6] But I do not recommend them to your reporter, Mr. Wayne. To him the language of truth and soberness would be unintelligible.

I am a Jew, and if for no other reason, for that reason am I a republican. Among the pious priesthood of church establishments, we are compassionately ranked with Turks, Infidels and Heretics. In the *monarchies* of Europe, we are hunted from society—stigmatized as unworthy of common civility, thrust out as it were from the converse of men; objects of mockery and insult to froward children, the butts of vulgar wit, and low buffoonery, such as your correspondent Mr. Wayne is not ashamed to set us an example of. Among the nations of Europe we are inhabitants every where—but Citizens no where *unless in Republics*. Here, in France, and in the Batavian[7] Republic alone, we are treated as men and as brethren. In republics we have *rights*, in monarchies we live but to experience *wrongs*. And why? Because we and our forefathers have *not* sacrificed our principles to interest, or earned an exemption from pain and poverty, by the dereliction of our religious duties, no wonder we are objects of derision to those, who have no principles, *moral or* religious, to guide their conduct.

How then can a Jew but be a Republican? in America particularly. Unfeeling & ungrateful would he be, if he were callous to the glorious and benevolent cause of the difference between his situation in this land of freedom, and among the proud and privileged law givers of Europe.

But I am *poor*, I am so, my family also is large, but soberly and decently brought up. They have not been taught to revile a christian, because his religion is not *so old* as theirs. They have not been taught to mock even at the errors of good intention, and conscientious belief.

I hope they will always leave this to men as unlike themselves, as I hope I am to your scurrilous correspondent.

I know that to purse proud aristocracy poverty is a crime, but it may sometimes be accompanied with honesty even in a Jew. I was a bankrupt some years ago. I obtained my certificate and I was discharged from my debts. Having been more successful afterwards, I called my creditors together, and eight years afterwards unsolicited I discharged all my old debts, I offered interest which was refused by my creditors, and they gave me under their hands without any solicitations of mine, as a testimonial of the fact (to use their own language) as a tribute due to my honor and honesty. This testimonial was signed by Messrs. J. Ball, W. Wister,

---

5. Abimelech was an Old Testament king who tried to steal Sarah, the wife of Abraham, the father of the Jews.
6. Samuel was the first prophet in the Old Testament and warned the Hebrews about the dangers of having a king.
7. **Batavian:** Dutch.

George Meade, J. Philips, C. G. Paleske, J. Bispham, J. Cohen, Robert Smith, J. H. Leuffer, A. Kuhn, John Stille, S. Pleasants, M. Woodhouse, Thomas Harrison, M. Boraef, E. Laskey, and Thomas Allibone, &c.

I was discharged by the insolvent act, true, because having the amount of my debts owing to me from the French Republic, the differences between France and America have prevented the recovery of what was due to me, in time to discharge what was due to my creditors. Hitherto it has been the fault of the political situation of the two countries, that my creditors are not paid; when peace shall enable me to receive what I am entitled to it will be my fault if they are not fully paid.[8]

This is a long defence Mr. Wayne, but you have called it forth, and therefore, I hope you at least will not object to it. The Public will now judge who is the proper object of ridicule and contempt, your facetious reporter, or

Your Humble Servant,
BENJAMIN NONES

8. This refers to the debts related to a failed business Nones had started.

14

Mapmaking and Colonialism in the New World
Amplissima Regionis Mississipi

Maps have always been political, and cartography, the theory and practice of making representations of Earth on a flat surface, has usually been connected to states' and to politicians' attempts to control people and space. Though maps have existed for thousands of years and were part of all ancient empires, dramatic changes occurred in mapmaking technology from the fifteenth to the seventeenth centuries that made cartography of much more direct use to both business and government.

One key part of this revolution in cartography was the Mercator projection, named for Gerardus Mercator, a Flemish mapmaker who in 1569 developed a world map that created an accurate depiction of the sea lanes that ships used for navigation. Although it badly distorted geographic land masses, making Africa roughly the same size as Greenland, the Mercator projection proved hugely important and remains popular to this day.

As maps became more useful to Europeans during the age of exploration, the newly invented printing press enabled them to be mass-produced for everyday use in exploration, commerce, and colonial expansion. Some scholars have even argued that this mapmaking revolution allowed for a new type of government that ruled over contiguous territory, rather than the traditional Old World pattern of kings and nobles claiming allegiance from confused patchworks of peoples and clans. As this style of territorial rule developed, mapmaking became an issue of war and peace. Columbus's discovery of America in 1492 and the maps he brought back set off a race by European powers to chart and claim vast sections of the New World for settlement and commerce.

The map pictured on page 88 was one of the most widely disseminated maps in colonial North America. Published by Homann Heirs, an important German mapmaking family business started by the cartographer to Emperor Charles VI, Amplissima Regionis Mississipi was based on the 1718 map "Carte de la Louisiane et du Cours du Mississipi," first drawn by Frenchman Guillaume de L'Isle and his father, Claude, from information derived from the explorations of Marquette, Joliet, La Salle, LeSueur, and others. It depicts a variety of Native American territories, the major rivers in French North America, Hernando de Soto's exploration of North America in 1539–1540, and, for the first time, an accurate representation of the mouth of the Mississippi River and its delta. It is also the first map to refer to the territory surrounding the Rio Grande as Teijas — an early variant of modern Texas. Versions of this map

Courtesy of Hargrett Rare Book and Manuscript Library/University of Georgia.

were in continuous use until 1797, and it is believed to be the oldest map that Lewis and Clark consulted in planning their expedition.

QUESTIONS TO CONSIDER

1. What landmarks are given most prominence, and what does this suggest about the priorities of the map's creators and users?
2. What does the detailed political mapping of Native American groups suggest about French colonialism in North America?
3. How might an English map of North America during this time have been different?
4. How did the mapmakers choose the images in the cartouches in the upper left and lower right corners?

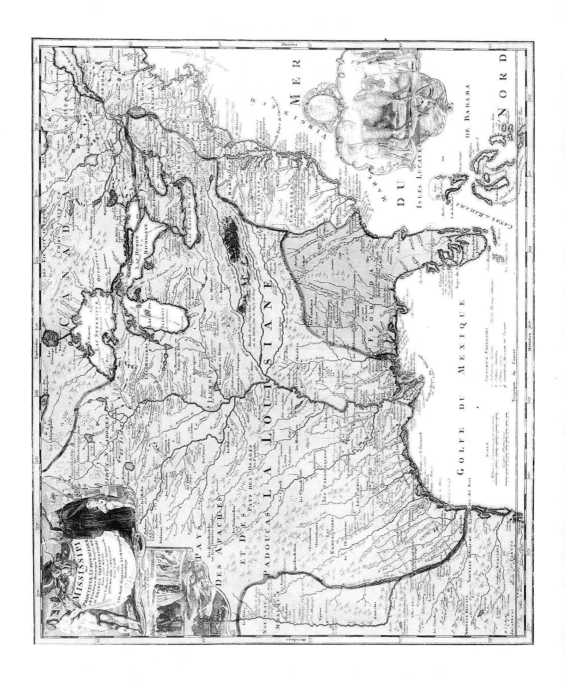

88

PART THREE

Resistance and Revolution

Struggling for Liberty

The generation that guided the colonies through the revolutionary era was welded together, despite remarkable differences among the colonies and their peoples, by a growing commitment to American nationality. That nationality was defined partly by placement in the new continent but also partly by a long-standing British political heritage, which ironically was a major ideological reason for the rupture with Great Britain.

When, after 1763, the English developed restrictive colonial policies to raise revenues for the administration of an enlarged empire that now included India and Canada, the colonists quickly perceived threats to their traditional liberties (see Document 12). Newspapers like the *Boston Gazette and Country Journal* and political leaders and pamphleteers like John Adams directly challenged Great Britain's right to legislate for the colonies, as did the growing army of Republican political cartoonists, who openly did battle with their loyalist counterparts in the popular press. Many radicals on the other side of the Atlantic were also critical of their country's governance of her North American colonies, as is evidenced by the brisk market in England for Paul Revere's engraving of the Boston Massacre. Leaders such as Captain Thomas Preston discovered how the rules of order had changed. Plain people like shoemaker George R. T. Hewes, who took part in both the Boston Massacre and the Boston Tea Party, Joseph Plumb Martin, who fought throughout the long war, and Boston merchant John Tudor developed new visions of their position in society.

To other colonists, commitment to the British tradition meant adherence to Britain. Many Americans remained loyal to the king, often at great personal cost, as Philip and Catherine Van Cortlandt's experience illustrated.

For many slaves and Native Americans, patriot success portended crushed expectations or even disaster. Slaves took desperate risks seeking freedom, often suffering when their gamble failed. Some, like Boston King, did gain their freedom by going over to the British side, but they found uncertainty and hardship after the war. Most Native American nations found their strength undermined by the long war and its freeing of the colonists from British restrictions. Those living in the border region between Canada and the United States struggled with the decision about which side to support. Most seemed to favor neutrality, hoping to be left in peace by the warring Europeans, but many openly chose sides, as evidenced by the account of Mohawk chief Major John Norton (Teyoninhokarawen), who brought his people into the War of 1812 on the side of the British king.

The American Revolution challenged long-held convictions that denied the capacity of human beings to use their reason in creating a new form of government. Women like Abigail Adams reflected this new spirit as vividly as any founding father. Such were the high stakes in the argument raging throughout the colonies over Shays's Rebellion (1786), which offered a prelude to the debates over ratification of the Constitution of the United States. At issue in both was a vision of the American Revolution as one of the climactic events of human history—a demonstration that people of virtue and reason can deliberately establish order and justice.

POINTS OF VIEW

The Boston Massacre (1770)

15

A British Officer's Description

Thomas Preston

Some historians in recent years have stressed the role of the "crowd" in the coming of the American Revolution. Anonymous colonists taking to the streets in the years after 1763 were an important part of the dynamic of revolution.

Firsthand accounts of an event do not necessarily make it easy to determine precisely what occurred. In early 1770 British troops were quartered in Boston. Many townspeople resented their presence, and on March 5 a mob of about sixty attacked a small group of soldiers. In the ensuing disturbance, some soldiers, without orders, fired on the mob, killing five people and wounding eight. The incident was taken up by anti-British radicals—the "patriots"—in Boston, who called it the "Boston Massacre." This selection is the account of the British officer who was tried for murder along with sev-

Merrill Jensen, ed., *English Historical Documents*, vol. 9 (London: Eyre and Spottiswoode, 1955), 750–53.

eral of his men. John Adams and Josiah Quincy Jr., convinced that anyone accused of a crime should have legal counsel, defended the men. Two of the soldiers were convicted of manslaughter, and the others, including Preston, were acquitted, but the "Massacre" served to inflame anti-British sentiment throughout the colonies.

QUESTIONS TO CONSIDER

1. What was Captain Preston's view of the Boston crowd?
2. Were his soldiers justified in using violence?
3. Was the outcome of the trial fair? Why or why not?

CAPTAIN THOMAS PRESTON'S ACCOUNT OF THE BOSTON MASSACRE (MARCH 13, 1770)

It is [a] matter of too great notoriety to need any proofs that the arrival of his Majesty's troops in Boston was extremely obnoxious to its inhabitants. They have ever used all means in their power to weaken the regiments, and to bring them into contempt by promoting and aiding desertions, and with impunity, even where there has been the clearest evidence of the fact, and by grossly and falsely propagating untruths concerning them. On the arrival of the 64th and 65th their ardour seemingly began to abate; it being too expensive to buy off so many, and attempts of that kind rendered too dangerous from the numbers.

And [conflict in the streets of Boston] has ever since their departure been breaking out with greater violence after their embarkation. One of their justices, most thoroughly acquainted with the people and their intentions, on the trial of a man of the 14th Regiment, openly and publicly in the hearing of great numbers of people and from the seat of justice, declared "that the soldiers must now take care of themselves, *nor trust too much to their arms,* for they were but a handful; that the inhabitants carried weapons concealed under their clothes, and would destroy them in a moment, *if they pleased."* This, considering the malicious temper of the people, was an alarming circumstance to the soldiery. Since which several disputes have happened between the townspeople and the soldiers of both regiments, the former being encouraged thereto by the countenance of even some of the magistrates, and by the protection of all the party against government. In general such disputes have been kept too secret from the officers. On the 2d instant two of the 29th going through one Gray's rope-walk, the rope-makers insultingly asked them if they would empty a vault. This unfortunately had the desired effect by provoking the soldiers, and from words they went to blows. Both parties suffered in this affray, and finally the soldiers retired to their quarters. The officers, on the first knowledge of this transaction, took every precaution in their power to prevent any ill consequence. Notwithstanding which, single quarrels could not be prevented, the inhabitants constantly provoking and abusing the soldiery. The insolence as well as utter hatred of the inhabitants to the troops increased daily, insomuch that Monday and Tuesday, the 5th and 6th instant, were privately agreed on for a general engagement, in consequence of which several of the militia came from the country armed to join their friends, menacing to destroy any who should oppose them. This plan has since been discovered.

On Monday night about 8 o'clock two soldiers were attacked and beat. But the party of the townspeople in order to carry matters to the utmost length, broke into two meeting houses and rang the alarm bells, which I supposed was for fire as usual, but was soon undeceived. About 9 some of the guard came to and informed me the town inhabitants were assembling to attack the troops, and that the bells were ringing as the signal for that purpose and not for fire, and the beacon intended to be fired to bring in the distant people of the country. This, as I was captain of the day, occasioned my repairing immediately to the main guard. On my way there I saw the people in great commotion, and heard them use the most cruel and horrid threats against the troops. In a few minutes after I reached the guard, about 100 people passed it and went towards the custom house where the king's money is lodged. They immediately surrounded the sentry posted there, and with clubs and other weapons threatened to execute their vengeance on him. I was soon informed by a townsman their intention was to carry off the soldier from his post and probably murder him. On which I desired him to return for further intelligence, and he soon came back and assured me he heard the mob declare they would murder him. This I feared might be a prelude to their plundering the king's chest. I immediately sent a non-commissioned officer and 12 men to protect both the sentry and the king's money, and very soon followed myself to prevent, if possible, all disorder, fearing lest the officer and soldiers, by the insults and provocations of the rioters, should be thrown off their guard and commit some rash act. They soon rushed through the people, and by charging their bayonets in half-circles, kept them at a little distance. Nay, so far was I from intending the death of any person that I suffered the troops to go to the spot where the unhappy affair took place without any loading in their pieces; nor did I ever give orders for loading them. This remiss conduct in me perhaps merits censure; yet it is evidence, resulting from the nature of things, which is the best and surest that can be offered, that my intention was not to act offensively, but the contrary part, and that not without compulsion. The mob still increased and were more outrageous, striking their clubs or bludgeons one against another, and calling out, come on you rascals, you bloody backs, you lobster scoundrels, fire if you dare, G—d damn you, fire and be damned, we know you dare not, and much more such language was used. At this time I was between the soldiers and the mob, parleying with, and endeavouring all in my power to persuade them to retire peaceably, but to no purpose. They advanced to the points of the bayonets, struck some of them and even the muzzles of the pieces, and seemed to be endeavoring to close with the soldiers. On which some well behaved persons asked me if the guns were charged. I replied yes. They then asked me if I intended to order the men to fire. I answered no, by no means, observing to them that I was advanced before the muzzles of the men's pieces, and must fall a sacrifice if they fired; that the soldiers were upon the half cock and charged bayonets, and my giving the word fire under those circumstances would prove me to be no officer. While I was thus speaking, one of the soldiers having received a severe blow with a stick, stepped a little on one side and instantly fired, on which turning to and asking him why he fired without orders, I was struck with a club on my arm, which for some time deprived me of the use of it, which blow had it been placed on my head, most probably would have destroyed me. On this a general attack was made on the men by a great number of heavy clubs and snowballs being thrown at them, by which all our lives were in imminent danger, some persons at the same time from behind calling out, damn your bloods—why don't you fire. Instantly three or four of the soldiers fired, one after another, and directly after three more in the same confusion and hurry. The mob then ran away, except three unhappy men who instantly expired, in which number was Mr. Gray at whose rope-walk the prior quarrels took place; one more is since dead, three others are dangerously, and four slightly wounded. The whole of this melancholy affair was transacted in almost 20 minutes. On my asking the soldiers why they fired without orders, they said they heard the word fire and supposed it came from me. This might be the case as many of the mob called out fire, fire, but I assured the men that I gave no such order; that my words were, don't fire, stop your firing. In short, it was scarcely possible for the soldiers to know who said fire, or don't fire, or stop your firing. . . .

[All was uproar and confusion, but somehow the regiment managed to retire to its barracks without immediate further incident.]

A Council was immediately called, on the breaking up of which three justices met and issued a warrant to apprehend me and eight soldiers. On hearing of this procedure I instantly went to the sheriff and surrendered myself, though for the space of 4 hours I had it in my power to have made my escape, which I most undoubtedly should have attempted and could have easily executed, had I been the least conscious of any guilt. On the examination before the justices, two witnesses swore that I gave the men orders to fire. The one testified he was within two feet of me; the other that I swore at the men for not firing at the first word. Others swore they heard me use the word "fire," but whether do or do not fire, they could not say; others that they heard the word fire, but could not say if it came from me. The next day they got 5 or 6 more to swear I gave the word to fire. So bitter and inveterate are many of the malcontents here that they are industriously using every method to fish out evidence to prove it was a concerted scheme to murder the inhabitants. Others are infusing the utmost malice and revenge into the minds of the people who are to be my jurors by false publications, votes of towns, and all other artifices. That so from a settled rancour against the officers and troops in general, the suddenness of my trial after the affair while the people's minds are all greatly inflamed, I am, though perfectly innocent, under most unhappy circumstances, having nothing in reason to expect but the loss of life in a very ignominious manner, without the interposition of his Majesty's royal goodness.

16

Colonial Accounts

George Robert Twelves Hewes, John Tudor, and the *Boston Gazette and Country Journal*

George Robert Twelves Hewes (1742–1840) was in his nineties in 1833 when he told James Hawkes the story of his experiences in revolutionary Boston. Hewes claimed not to have read any published account of the happenings there and could "therefore only give the information which I derived from the event[s] of the day." Careful checking by the distinguished labor historian Alfred F. Young has authenticated much of Hewes's account. His story provides a rare opportunity to see an ordinary citizen taking a direct part in a great historical event. Hewes also participated in the Boston Tea Party of December 16, 1773, dressing as an Indian and pitching casks of tea into the harbor. These experiences had a profound personal effect on Hewes. In the 1760s he had been an awkward young cobbler nervously deferring to his aristocratic customers. A decade later, with these experiences behind him, he would risk his employment and perhaps even a beating for his refusal to take off his hat "for any man." For Hewes, the American Revolution meant that the poor and the ordinary no longer owed the rich and powerful what in the eighteenth century was called "deference."

John Tudor (1709–1795), a Boston merchant, gives a simpler account of the massacre in his diary and captures some of the sentiment following the deaths of the colonists.

The Boston Gazette and Country Journal *was one of several struggling journals published in Boston. Ever since being threatened with taxation under the Stamp Act of 1763, colonial newspapers, particularly those in Boston, had tended to support the patriot perspective. Journalism was not yet a profession, as most newspapers were produced by printers or postmasters, and the tradition of impartial reporting was still far in the future.*

QUESTIONS TO CONSIDER

1. According to Hewes, what sparked the Boston Massacre?
2. What role did he play in the event and subsequent trial?

James Hawkes [supposed author], *A Retrospect of the Boston Tea-Party, with a Memoir of George R. T. Hewes, a Survivor of the Little Band of Patriots Who Drowned the Tea in Boston Harbour in 1773, by a Citizen of New York* (New York, 1834), 27–33, 36–41; John Tudor, *Deacon Tudor's diary; or, "Memorandums from 1709"* (Boston: Press of W. Spooner, 1896), 1, vi, 110, [vii]–xxxvii, [7]; *Boston Gazette and Country Journal*, March 12, 1770, reprinted in Merrill Jensen, ed., *English Historical Documents*, vol. 9 (London: Eyre and Spottiswoode, 1955), 745–49.

3. Tudor wrote his account at the time of the event while Hewes related his story to Hawkes six decades later. To what extent might this explain their different perspectives?
4. What political points does the *Boston Gazette and Country Journal* make about the Boston Massacre?

ACCOUNT OF GEORGE ROBERT TWELVES HEWES AS TOLD TO JAMES HAWKES

[W]hen I was at the age of twenty-six, I married the daughter of Benjamin Sumner, of Boston. At the time of our intermarriage, the age of my wife was seventeen. We lived together very happily seventy years. She died at the age of eighty-seven.

At the time when the British troops were first stationed at Boston, we had several children, the exact number I do not recollect. By our industry and mutual efforts we were improving our condition.

An account of the massacre of the citizens of Boston, in the year 1770, on the 5th of March, by some of the British troops, has been committed to the record of our history, as one of those interesting events which led to the revolutionary contest that resulted in our independence. . . . We have been informed by the historians of the revolution, that a series of provocations had excited strong prejudices, and inflamed the passion of the British soldiery against our citizens, previous to the commencement of open hostilities; and prepared their minds to burst out into acts of violence on the application of a single spark of additional excitement, and which finally resulted in the unfortunate massacre of a number of our citizens.

On my inquiring of Hewes what knowledge he had of that event, he replied, that he knew nothing from history, as he had never read any thing relating to it from any publication whatever, and can therefore only give the information which I derived from the event of the day upon which the catastrophe happened. On that day, one of the British officers applied to a barber, to be shaved and dressed; the master of the shop, whose name was Pemont, told his apprentice boy he might serve him, and receive the pay to himself, while Pemont left the shop. The boy accordingly served him, but the officer, for some reason unknown to me, went away from the shop without paying him for his service. After the officer had been gone some time, the boy went to the house where he was, with his account, to demand payment of his bill, but the sentinel, who was before the door, would not give him admittance, nor permit him to see the officer; and as some angry words were interchanged between the sentinel and the boy, a considerable number of the people from the vicinity, soon gathered at the place where they were, which was in King street, and I was soon on the ground among them. The violent agitation of the citizens, not only on account of the abuse offered to the boy, but other causes of excitement, then fresh in the recollection, was such that the sentinel began to be apprehensive of danger, and knocked at the door of the house, where the officers were, and told the servant who came to the door, that he was afraid of his life, and would quit his post unless he was protected. The officers in the house then sent a messenger to the guard-house, to require Captain Preston to come with a sufficient number of his soldiers to defend them from the threatened violence of the people. On receiving the message, he came immediately with a small guard of grenadiers, and paraded them before the custom-house, where the British officers were shut up. Captain Preston then ordered the people to disperse, but they said they would not, they were in the king's highway, and had as good a right to be there as he had. The captain of the guard then said to them, if you do not disperse, I will fire upon you, and then gave orders to his men to make ready, and immediately after gave them orders to fire. Three of our citizens fell dead on the spot, and two, who were wounded, died the next day; and nine others were also wounded. The persons who were killed I well recollect, said Hewes; they were, Gray, a rope maker, Marverick, a young man, Colwell, who was the mate of Captain Colton, Attuck[s], a mulatto, and Carr, who was an Irishman. Captain Preston then immediately fled with his grenadiers back to the guard-house. The people who were assembled on that occasion, then immediately chose a committee to report to the governor the result of Captain Preston's conduct, and to demand of him satisfaction. The governor told the committee, that if the people would be quiet that night he would give them satisfaction, so far as was in his power; the next morning Captain Preston, and those of his guard who were concerned in the massacre, were, accordingly, by order of the governor, given up, and taken into custody the next morning, and committed to prison.

It is not recollected that the offence given to the barber's boy is mentioned by the historians of the revolution; yet there can be no doubt of its correctness. The account of this single one of the exciting causes of the massacre, related by Hewes, at this time, was in answer to the question of his personal knowledge of that event.

A knowledge of the spirit of those times will easily lead us to conceive, that the manner of the British officers application to the barber, was a little too strongly tinctured with the dictatorial hauteur, to conciliate the views of equality, which at that period were supremely predominant in the minds of those of the whig party, even in his humble occupation; and that the disrespectful notice of his loyal customer, in consigning him to the attention of his apprentice boy, and abruptly leaving his shop, was intended to be treated by the officer with contempt, by so underrating the services of his apprentice, as to deem any reward for them beneath his attention. The boy too, may be supposed to have imbibed so much of the spirit which distinguished that period of our history, that he was willing to improve any occasion to contribute his share to the public excitement; to add an additional spark to the fire of political dissention which was enkindling.

When Hewes arrived at the spot where the massacre happened, it appears his attention was principally engaged by the clamours of those who were disposed to aid the boy in avenging the insult offered to him by the British officer, and probably heard nothing, at that time, of any other of the many exciting causes which led to that disastrous event, though it appeared from his general conversation, his knowledge of them was extensive and accurate.

But to pursue the destiny of Captain Preston, and the guard who fired on the citizens; in about a fortnight after, said Hewes, they were brought to trial and indicted for the crime of murder.

The soldiers were tried first, and acquitted, on the ground, that in firing upon the citizens of Boston, they only acted in proper obedience to the captain's orders. When Preston, their captain, was tried, I was called as one of the witnesses, on the part of the government, and testified, that I believed it was the same man, Captain Preston, that ordered his soldiers to make ready, who also ordered them to fire. Mr. John Adams, former president of the United States, was advocate for the prisoners, and denied the fact, that Captain Preston gave orders to his men to fire; and on his cross examination of me asked whether my position was such, that I could see the captain's lips in motion when the order to fire was given; to which I answered, that I could not. Although the evidence of Preston's having given orders to the soldiers to fire, was thought by the jury sufficient to acquit them, it was not thought to be of weight enough to convict him of a capital offence; he also was acquitted.

Although the excitement which had been occasioned by the wanton massacre of our citizens, had in some measure abated, it was never extinguished until open hostilities commenced, and we had declared our independence. The citizens of Boston continued inflexible in their demand, that every British soldier should be withdrawn from the town, and within four days after the massacre, the whole army decamped. But the measures of the British parliament, which led the American colonies to a separation from that government, were not abandoned.

JOHN TUDOR DESCRIBES THE MASSACRE IN HIS DIARY[1]

On Monday Evening the 5th current, a few minutes after 9 O'Clock a most horrid murder was committed in King Street before the Customhouse Door by eight or nine Soldiers under the Command of Captain Thomas Preston drawn of from the Main Guard on the South side of the Townhouse.

This unhappy affair began by Some Boys and young fellows throwing Snow Balls at the sentry placed at the Customhouse Door. On which eight or nine Soldiers Came to his assistance. Soon after a Number of people collected, when the Captain commanded the Soldiers to fire, which they did and three Men were Kil'd on the Spot and several Mortally Wounded, one of which died next morning. The Captain soon drew off his Soldiers up to the Main Guard, or the Consequences might have been terrible, for on the Guns firing the people were alarmed and set the Bells a Ringing as if for Fire, which drew Multitudes to the place of action. Lieutenant Governor Hutchinson, who was commander in Chief, was sent for and Came to the Council Chamber, where some of the Magistrates attended. The Governor desired the Multitude about 10 O'Clock to separate and go home peacable and he would do all in his power that Justice should be done &c. The 29 Regiment being ten under Arms on the

---

1. Spelling and punctuation have been modernized.

south side of the Townhouse, but the people insisted that the Soldiers should be ordered to their Barracks first before they would separate, Which being done the people separated about 1 O'Clock. — Captain Preston was taken up by a warrant given to the high Sheriff by Justice Dania and Tudor and came under Examination about 2 O'Clock and we sent him to Gaol soon after 3, having Evidence sufficient, to commit him, on his ordering the soldiers to fire: So about 4 O'clock the Town became quiet. The next forenoon the 8 Soldiers that fired on the inhabitants was also sent to Gaol. Tuesday A.M. the inhabitants met at Faneuil Hall and after some pertinent speeches, chose a Committee of 15 Gentlemen to wait on the Lieutenant Governor in Council to request the immediate removal of the Troops. . . .

(Thursday) Agreeable to a general request of the Inhabitants, were follow'd to the Grave (for they were all Buried in one) in succession the four Bodies of Messer's Samuel Gray, Samuel Maverick, James Caldwell, and Crispus Attucks, the unhappy victims who fell in the Bloody Massacre. On this sorrowful Occasion most of the shops and stores in Town were shut, all the Bells were order'd to toll a solemn peal in Boston, Charlesto[w]n, Cambridge, and Roxb[u]ry. The several Hearses forming a junction in King Street, the Theatre of that inhuman Tragedy, proceeded from thence thro' the main street, lengthened by an immense Concourse of people, So numerous as to be obliged to follow in Ranks of 4 and 6 abreast and brought up by a long Train of Carriages. The sorrow Visible in the Countenances, together with the peculiar solemnity, Surpass description, it was suppos'd that the Spectators and those that follow'd the corps amounted to 15,000, some supposed 20,000. Note Captain Preston was tried for his Life on the affair of the above October 24, 1770. The Trial lasted five Days, but the Jury brought him in not Guilty.

ACCOUNT IN THE *BOSTON GAZETTE*
AND COUNTRY JOURNAL

March 12, 1770

The town of Boston affords a recent and melancholy demonstration of the destructive consequences of quartering troops among citizens in a time of peace, under a pretence of supporting the laws and aiding civil authority; every considerate and unprejudiced person among us was deeply impressed with the apprehension of these consequences when it was known that a number of regiments were ordered to this town under such a pretext, but in reality to enforce oppressive measures; to awe and control the legislative as well as executive power of the province, and to quell a spirit of liberty, which however it may have been basely opposed and even ridiculed by some, would do honour to any age or country. A few persons amongst us had determined to use all their influence to procure so destructive a measure with a view to their securely enjoying the profits of an American revenue, and unhappily both for Britain and this country they found means to effect it.

It is to Governor Bernard, the commissioners, their confidants and coadjutors, that we are indebted as the procuring cause of a military power in this capital. The Boston Journal of Occurrences, as printed in Mr. Holt's *New York Gazette,* from time to time, afforded many striking instances of the distresses brought upon the inhabitants by this measure; and since those Journals have been discontinued, our troubles from that quarter have been growing upon us. We have known a party of soldiers in the face of day fire off a loaded musket upon the inhabitants, others have been pricked with bayonets, and even our magistrates assaulted and put in danger of their lives, when offenders brought before them have been rescued; and why those and other bold and base criminals have as yet escaped the punishment due to their crimes may be soon matter of enquiry by the representative body of this people. It is natural to suppose that when the inhabitants of this town saw those laws which had been enacted for their security, and which they were ambitious of holding up to the soldiery, eluded, they should more commonly resent for themselves; and accordingly it has so happened. Many have been the squabbles between them and the soldiery; but it seems their being often worsted by our youth in those encounters, has only served to irritate the former. What passed at Mr. Gray's rope-walk has already been given the public and may be said to have led the way to the late catastrophe. That the rope-walk lads, when attacked by superior numbers, should defend themselves with so much spirit and success in the club-way, was too mortifying, and perhaps it may hereafter appear that even some of their officers were unhappily affected with this circumstance. Divers stories were propagated among the soldiery that served to agitate their spirits; particularly on the Sabbath that one Chambers, a sergeant, represented as a sober man, had been missing the preceding day and must therefore have been murdered by the townsmen. An officer of distinction so far credited this report that he entered Mr. Gray's rope-walk that Sabbath; and when required of by that gentleman as soon as he could meet him, the occasion of his so doing, the officer replied that it was to look if the sergeant said to be murdered had not been hid there. This sober sergeant was found on the Monday unhurt in a house of pleasure. The evidences already collected show that many threatenings had been thrown out by the soldiery, but we do not pretend to say that there was any preconcerted plan. When the evidences are published, the world will judge. We may, however, venture to declare that it appears too probable from their conduct that some of the soldiery aimed to draw and provoke the townsmen into squabbles, and that they then intended to make use of other weapons than canes, clubs, or bludgeons.

On the evening of Monday, being the fifth current, several soldiers of the 29th Regiment were seen parading the streets with their drawn cutlasses and bayonets, abusing and wounding numbers of the inhabitants.

A few minutes after nine o'clock four youths, named Edward Archbald, William Merchant, Francis Archbald, and John Leech, jun., came down Cornhill together, and separating at Doctor Loring's corner, the two former were passing the narrow alley leading to Murray's barrack in which was a soldier brandishing a broad sword of an uncommon size against the walls, out of which he struck fire plentifully. A person of mean countenance armed with a large cudgel bore him company. Edward Archbald admonished Mr. Merchant to take care of the sword, on which the soldier turned round and struck Archbald on the arm, then pushed at Merchant and pierced through his clothes inside the arm close to the armpit and grazed the skin. Merchant then struck the soldier with a short stick he had; and the other person ran to the barrack and brought with him two soldiers, one armed with a pair of tongs, the other with a shovel. He with the tongs pursued Archbald back through the alley, collared and laid him over the head with the tongs. The noise brought people together; and John Hicks, a young lad, coming up, knocked the soldier down but let him get up again; and more lads gathering, drove them back to the barrack where the boys stood some time as it were to keep them in. In less than a minute ten or twelve of them came out with drawn cutlasses, clubs, and bayonets and set upon the unarmed boys and young folk who stood them a little while but, finding the inequality of their equipment, dispersed. On hearing the noise, one Samuel Atwood came up to see what was the matter; and entering the alley from dock square, heard the latter part of the combat; and when the boys had dispersed he met the ten or twelve soldiers aforesaid rushing down the alley towards the square and asked them if they intended to murder people? They answered Yes, by G—d, root and branch! With that one of them struck Mr. Atwood with a club which was repeated by another; and being unarmed, he turned to go off and received a wound on the left shoulder which reached the bone and gave him much pain. Retreating a few steps, Mr. Atwood met two officers and said, gentlemen, what is the matter? They answered, you'll see by and by. Immediately after, those heroes appeared in the square, asking where were the boogers? where were the cowards? But notwithstanding their fierceness to naked men, one of them advanced towards a youth who had a split of a raw stave in his hand and said, damn them, here is one of them. But the young man seeing a person near him with a drawn sword and good cane ready to support him, held up his stave in defiance; and they quietly passed by him up the little alley by Mr. Silsby's to King Street where they attacked single and unarmed persons till they raised much clamour, and then turned down Cornhill Street, insulting all they met in like manner and pursuing some to their very doors. Thirty or forty persons, mostly lads, being by this means gathered in King Street, Capt. Preston with a party of men with charged bayonets, came from the main guard to the commissioner's house, the soldiers pushing their bayonets, crying, make way! They took place by the custom house and, continuing to push to drive the people off, pricked some in several places, on which they were clamorous and, it is said, threw snow balls. On this, the Captain commanded them to fire; and more snow balls coming, he again said, damn you, fire, be the consequence what it will! One soldier then fired, and a townsman with a cudgel struck him over the hands with such force that he dropped his firelock; and, rushing forward, aimed a blow at the Captain's head which grazed his hat and fell pretty heavy upon his arm. However, the soldiers continued the fire successively till seven or eight or, as some say, eleven guns were discharged.

By this fatal maneuver three men were laid dead on the spot and two more struggling for life; but what showed a degree of cruelty unknown to British troops, at least since the house of Hanover has directed their operations, was an attempt to fire upon or push with their bayonets the persons who undertook to remove the slain and wounded!

Mr. Benjamin Leigh, now undertaker in the Delph manufactory, came up; and after some conversation with Capt. Preston relative to his conduct in this affair, advised him to draw off his men, with which he complied.

The dead are Mr. Samuel Gray, killed on the spot, the ball entering his head and beating off a large portion of his skull.

A mulatto man named Crispus Attucks, who was born in Framingham, but lately belonged to New-Providence and was here in order to go for North Carolina, also killed instantly, two balls entering his breast, one of them in special goring the right lobe of the lungs and a great part of the liver most horribly.

Mr. James Caldwell, mate of Capt. Morton's vessel, in like manner killed by two balls entering his back.

Mr. Samuel Maverick, a promising youth of seventeen years of age, son of the widow Maverick, and an apprentice to Mr. Greenwood, ivory-turner, mortally wounded; a ball went through his belly and was cut out at his back. He died the next morning.

A lad named Christopher Monk, about seventeen years of age, an apprentice to Mr. Walker, shipwright, wounded; a ball entered his back about four inches above the left kidney near the spine and was cut out of the breast on the same side. Apprehended he will die.

A lad named John Clark, about seventeen years of age, whose parents live at Medford, and an apprentice to Capt. Samuel Howard of this town, wounded; a ball entered just above his groin and came out at his hip on the opposite side. Apprehended he will die.

Mr. Edward Payne of this town, merchant, standing at his entry door received a ball in his arm which shattered some of the bones.

Mr. John Green, tailor, coming up Leverett's Lane, received a ball just under his hip and lodged in the under part of his thigh, which was extracted.

Mr. Robert Patterson, a seafaring man, who was the person that had his trousers shot through in Richardson's affair, wounded; a ball went through his right arm, and he suffered a great loss of blood.

Mr. Patrick Carr, about thirty years of age, who worked with Mr. Field, leather breeches-maker in Queen Street, wounded; a ball entered near his hip and went out at his side.

A lad named David Parker, an apprentice to Mr. Eddy, the wheelwright, wounded; a ball entered in his thigh.

The people were immediately alarmed with the report of this horrid massacre, the bells were set a-ringing, and great numbers soon assembled at the place where this tragical scene had been acted. Their feelings may be better conceived than expressed; and while some were taking care of the dead and wounded, the rest were in consultation what to do in those dreadful circumstances. But so little intimidated were they, notwithstanding their being within a few yards of the main guard and seeing the 29th Regiment under arms and drawn up in King Street, that they kept their station and appeared, as an officer of rank expressed it, ready to run upon the very muzzles of their muskets.

FOR CRITICAL THINKING

1. How does the account of the riot as reported in the *Boston Gazette and Country Journal* differ from Hewes's version? How do these accounts differ from Captain Preston's? How might the differences among these accounts be explained?

2. If you were John Adams, determined to prove that British officers and soldiers could receive a fair trial in Boston, how would you defend Captain Preston?

3. Compare the Boston Massacre with later urban riots in American history. What similarities and differences do you find?

Patriot and Loyalist Propaganda

"The Bloody Massacre" (Figure 1), Paul Revere's wood block print of 1777, depicts a conflict in the streets of Boston in that same year that led to the death of five civilians at the hands of British troops. Though to many people at the time, it might not have seemed terribly bloody or even a full-fledged massacre, it will always be remembered as the Boston Massacre, thanks, in part, to this print, which has come to represent the entire revolutionary period. In a world in which many people passed their entire lives without learning to read, such mass-produced

Figure 1. "The Bloody Massacre," engraving by Paul Revere.

political drawings were how many citizens received their news and political commentary, and developed an understanding of the world they lived in. Such visual imagery was the television and Internet of the era and, from early on, the colonial politicians knew how to exploit the medium.

In 1754, Benjamin Franklin first published the wood-block print "Join, or Die" (Figure 2) in the *Pennsylvania Gazette*. Less a political cartoon and more a recognizable graphic design or pictogram (like the heart in the ad campaign I ♥ NY), the image of a snake, believed capable of regenerating and reconstituting itself from pieces, was a call on the diffuse, disparate, and often mutually antagonistic British colonies along the eastern seaboard to unite against the French and their indigenous allies in the French and Indian War of 1754–1763. Though Franklin did not know it at the time, this was a remarkable first step down the path to revolution and eventual independence from Britain. It is probably the first popular depiction of the idea of a united British North America, encompassing the eight colonies of New England, New York, New Jersey, Pennsylvania, Maryland, Virginia, North Carolina, and South Carolina. A decade later, when the cartoon was recycled by opponents of the Stamp Act of 1765, Franklin disavowed his snake because it was being used against the British crown. Later, during the run-up to the American Revolution, it was once again as popular, this time as an image of unity and resistance to the British monarchy. Patriot Benjamin Franklin now welcomed his American snake back. Why do you think this image was so easily used both to support the British crown and to oppose it? Do you think that Benjamin Franklin was aware of the implications of a united British North America when he first drew it? What are the elements of this image that made it such effective and popular propaganda?

In February 1766, when the British parliament retreated from its hated Stamp Act of November 1765, in the face of political violence and economic boycotts across the American colonies, many people on both sides of the Atlantic

Figure 2. "Join, or Die."

started to believe that Benjamin Franklin's pieces had become a living snake, but few saw it as anything separate from the British homeland. Most struggles, like those of the Stamp Act, were phrased in terms of the right of subjects of the king to have input into issues of taxation and representation.

For many in Britain, the notion that colonies should have a vote in the British parliament was unacceptable. Franklin, who is reputed to be the author of Figure 2, continued to believe that reconciliation between the British government and its North American colonies was both possible and desirable. He, like many in British North America, believed that the growing democratic traditions and practices of Great Britain were birthrights that should unite rather than divide the two sides of the Atlantic. During the Stamp Act crisis, Franklin testified in England as the agent of Pennsylvania, Georgia, New Jersey, and Massachusetts (see Document 12). During this period he is believed to have printed cards with the image in Figure 3 and distributed them to Parliament. The banner, which reads *Date Obolum Bellisario*, means roughly "throw a coin to poor Bellisarius"[1] and shows a defenseless and dismembered Brittania incapable of reaching her spear and shield lying on the ground, the latter embossed with the British national symbol, the Union Jack. Why was Franklin comparing the British Empire to Byzantium? What does this image say about Franklin's view of the relationship between England and its colonies?

By the time of the Tea Act of 1773, relations between the British crown and its colonies were becoming increasingly strained. Several generations had already been born, grown up, and died in the colonies without ever seeing the European lands of their forebears. There was a rising sense of self-consciousness among many of them that was separate and American, and a growing unwillingness to be subject to capricious foreign rule. All the while, the crown continued to appoint colonial governors and other officials, typically born in Britain with no experience of the colony that they were sent to rule.

The famous Boston Tea Party of December 1773 excited passions on both sides of the Atlantic and spawned sympathetic actions across the colonies. The Provincial Deputies of North Carolina resolved to boycott all British tea and cloth received after September 10, 1774. The women of Edenton, North Carolina, displayed their self-conscious sense of being American when they ardently supported the boycott resolution. The women signed an agreement stating that they were "determined to give memorable proof of their patriotism" and could not be "indifferent on any occasion that appears nearly to affect the peace and happiness of our country." Shortly afterward, in October 1774, Mrs. Penelope Barker organized the Edenton Tea Party, bringing together fifty-one North Carolina women to fight against "taxation without representation."

News of the Edenton Tea Party, a political movement led by women, shocked loyalists on both sides of the Atlantic, leading to denunciations, sarcastic

---

1. **Bellisarius:** The Byzantine Empire's greatest general who nearly reunited the entire Roman Empire for his ruler, Justinian. Legend has it that when Bellisarius was later accused of plotting to take over the throne, Justinian had his eyes put out and he was reduced to begging on the street.

The Colonies Reduced.
Design'd & Engrav'd for the Political Register.

Figure 3. "The Colonies Reduced."

commentary, and public ridicule of the type exemplified by Figure 4, which was published in London in March 1775. For many conservative British, Penelope Barker became a symbol of what was wrong with the colonies. To American patriots and progressive British merchants, antimonarchists, and religious leaders, however, she was an example of how women might contribute to a just political cause. British supporters of the American cause such as London merchant William Hodgson and Presbyterian minister Thomas Wren would probably have viewed the women of Edenton positively. What behavior by the people in this image shows the view that British royalists have of colonial Americans? How does the artist use gender to argue against the patriot cause? Why do you think there is an African American woman in the background?

As tensions continued to mount in the last days before outright war, physical attacks on British officials began to occur. Figure 5 depicts the tarring and feathering of British customs commissioner John Malcolm, some four weeks after the Boston Tea Party. The patriots involved in this altercation poured boycotted tea down Malcolm's throat and threatened to hang him for his activities in support of the importation of British goods. The image was widely circulated among loyalists on both sides of the Atlantic as an example of how Americans were treating those who did not respect the boycott of British goods. What is the artist trying to say about the colonial cause by drawing this event in front of the "liberty tree"?

Figure 4. The Edenton Tea Party.

Figure 6 was also produced in England, but depicts a more sympathetic view of the struggles of Bostonians against "taxation without representation." British prime minister Lord North is pouring tea down the throat of a helpless Native American woman, whose arms are being held down by British chief justice Mansfield, while Lord Sandwich holds her legs and lasciviously looks up her skirt. Meanwhile, Britannia, bearing her shield with the Union Jack, looks

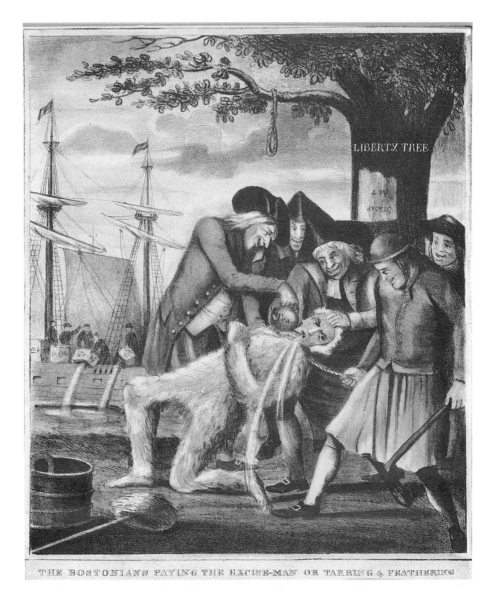

THE BOSTONIANS PAYING THE EXCISE-MAN OR TARRING & FEATHERING

Figure 5. "Bostonians Paying the Excise-Man."

away in shame, while Britain's chief rivals, Spain and France, look on in interest. A soldier stands with sword drawn in defense of these political leaders. The
Boston Port Bill, sticking out of Lord North's pocket, was passed by the British
parliament on March 30, 1774. It outlawed all use of the Port of Boston until
restitution was made for the tea that had been dumped during the Boston Tea
Party and the king was assured that order had been restored. The Boston Port
Bill crippled the economy of Boston and inspired sympathy and support across

The able Doctor, or America Swallowing the Bitter Draught.

Figure 6. "The Able Doctor, or America Swallowing the Bitter Draught."

the colonies. Though produced in Britain, this cartoon was quickly copied by patriot Paul Revere and used as a call to united action against the British king. Why has the illustrator included the figures of Spain and France in this picture? Nations are often represented by women. What effect might this depiction of the colonies as a woman have had on audiences? Why is the woman in the drawing a Native American?

FOR CRITICAL THINKING

1. What do the images in this section suggest about the role of women in the American Revolution?
2. How is visual propaganda today different or similar? How have political cartoons changed?
3. What images do you find the artists consistently using to represent different aspects of the conflict?

17

A Soldier's View of the Revolutionary War
Joseph Plumb Martin

Joseph Plumb Martin was born in western Massachusetts in 1760 and became a soldier in the Revolution before his sixteenth birthday. After serving with Connecticut troops in 1776, he enlisted as a regular in the Continental Army in April 1777 and persevered until the army was demobilized in 1783. During this period he fought with the Light Infantry as well as in the Corps of Sappers and Miners, who built fortifications and dug trenches. One of the few soldiers to serve for virtually the entire war, he repeatedly risked health and life: in the defense of New York City in 1776, at the Battle of Germantown in Pennsylvania in 1777, at Valley Forge in the winter of 1777–1778, at the Battle of Monmouth in New Jersey in 1778, and at the climactic siege of York-town in 1781.

Published in Maine in 1830, Martin's A Narrative of Some of the Adventures, Dangers, and Sufferings of a Revolutionary Soldier *is a usually good-humored, unvarnished picture of an ordinary soldier whose major concern is often his next meal or keeping warm through a cold night. Yet he expresses sharply the widely shared resentment among common soldiers toward civilian patriots "sitting still and expecting the army to do notable things while fainting from sheer starvation." And he fundamentally objects to the way his generation remembered the history of the war: "great men get great praise, little men, nothing. But it always was so and always will be." In fact, historians in the present age have at last devoted energy to recapturing the contributions of men like Joseph Plumb Martin, whose narrative offers the only detailed account historians have discovered of the wartime experience of a common Revolutionary War soldier.*

QUESTIONS TO CONSIDER

1. Why do you think Joseph Plumb Martin begins with an apology for writing his memoirs? How does he justify writing them?
2. How well did the civilian population seem to support the soldiers of the Continental Army?
3. If conditions were as bad as Martin describes them, why didn't he desert the army?

James Kirby Martin, ed., *Ordinary Courage: The Revolutionary War Adventures of Joseph Plumb Martin*, rev. ed. (St. James, NY: Brandywine Press, 1999), 1–2, 15–17, 29, 34–35, 61–64.

PREFACE

. . . I shall . . . by way of preface, inform the reader that my intention is to give a succinct account of some of my adventures, dangers, and sufferings during my several campaigns in the Revolutionary army. My readers (who, by the by, will, I hope, none of them be beyond the pale of my own neighborhood) must not expect any great transactions to be exhibited to their notice. "No alpine wonders thunder through my tale," but they are here, once for all, requested to bear it in mind, that they are not the achievements of an officer of high grade which they are perusing, but the common transactions of one of the lowest in station in an army, a private soldier.

Should the reader chance to ask himself this question (and I think it very natural for him to do so) how could any man of common sense ever spend his precious time in writing such a rhapsody of nonsense? To satisfy his inquiring mind, I would inform him, that, as the adage says, "every crow thinks her own young the whitest," so every private soldier in an army thinks his particular services as essential to carry on the war he is engaged in, as the services of the most influential general: And why not? What could officers do without such men? Nothing at all. Alexander[1] never could have conquered the world without private soldiers.

But, says the reader, this is low; the author gives us nothing but everyday occurrences; I could tell as good a story myself. Very true, Mr. Reader, everyone can tell what he has done in his lifetime, but everyone has not been a soldier, and consequently can know but little or nothing of the sufferings and fatigues incident to an army. All know everyday occurrences, but few know the hardships of the "tented field." I wish to have a better opinion of my readers, whoever they may be, than even to think that any of them would wish me to stretch the truth to furnish them with wonders that I never saw, or acts or deeds I never performed. I can give them no more than I have to give, and if they are dissatisfied after all, I must say I am sorry for them and myself too; for them, that they expect more than I can do, and myself, that I am so unlucky as not to have it in my power to please them. . . .

The critical grammarian may find enough to feed his spleen upon if he peruses the following pages; but I can inform him beforehand, I do not regard his sneers; if I cannot write grammatically, I can think, talk, and feel like other men. Besides, if the common readers can understand it, it is all I desire; and to give them an idea, though but a faint one, of what the army suffered that gained and secured our independence, is all I wish. I never studied grammar an hour in my life. When I ought to have been doing that, I was forced to be studying the rules and articles of war. . . .

A note of interrogation: Why we were made to suffer so much in so good and just a cause; and a note of admiration to all the world, that an army voluntarily engaged to serve their country, when starved, and naked, and suffering everything short of death (and thousands even that), should be able to persevere through an eight years war, and come off conquerors at last!

---

1. **Alexander:** Alexander the Great, the ancient Macedonian king who conquered territories from Greece to Egypt to India, and beyond.

But lest I should make my preface longer than my story, I will here bring it to a close.

CAMPAIGN OF 1776

I remained in New York two or three months, in which time several things occurred, but so trifling that I shall not mention them; when, sometime in the latter part of the month of August, I was ordered upon a fatigue party. We had scarcely reached the grand parade when I saw our sergeant major directing his course up Broadway toward us in rather an unusual step for him. He soon arrived and informed us, and then the commanding officer of the party, that he had orders to take off all belonging to our regiment and march us to our quarters, as the regiment was ordered to Long Island, the British having landed in force there. Although this was not unexpected to me, yet it gave me rather a disagreeable feeling, as I was pretty well assured I should have to sniff a little gunpowder. However, I kept my cogitations to myself, went to my quarters, packed up my clothes, and got myself in readiness for the expedition as soon as possible. I then went to the top of the house where I had a full view of that part of the Island; I distinctly saw the smoke of the field artillery, but the distance and the unfavorableness of the wind prevented my hearing their report, at least but faintly. The horrors of battle then presented themselves to my mind in all their hideousness; I must come to it now, thought I. Well, I will endeavor to do my duty as well as I am able and leave the event with Providence.

We were soon ordered to our regimental parade, from which, as soon as the regiment was formed, we were marched off for the ferry. At the lower end of the street were placed several casks of sea bread, . . . nearly hard enough for musket flints; the casks were unheaded and each man was allowed to take as many as he could as he marched by. As my good luck would have it, there was a momentary halt made; I improved the opportunity thus offered me, as every good soldier should upon all important occasions, to get as many of the biscuits as I possibly could; no one said anything to me, and I filled my bosom and took as many as I could hold in my hand, a dozen or more in all, and when we arrived at the ferry stairs I stowed them away in my knapsack. We quickly embarked on board the boats. As each boat started, three cheers were given by those on board, which was returned by the numerous spectators who thronged the wharves; they all wished us good luck, apparently, although it was with most of them perhaps nothing more than ceremony.

We soon landed at Brooklyn, upon the Island, marched up the ascent from the ferry to the plain. We now began to meet the wounded men, another sight I was unacquainted with, some with broken arms, some with broken legs, and some with broken heads. The sight of these a little daunted me, and made me think of home, but the sight and thought vanished together. We marched a short distance, when we halted to refresh ourselves. Whether we had any other victuals besides the hard bread I do not remember, but I remember my gnawing at them; they were hard enough to break the teeth of a rat. One of the soldiers complaining of thirst to his officer, "Look at that man," said he, pointing to me, "he is not thirsty, I will warrant it." I felt a little elevated to be styled a man.

While resting here, which was not more than 20 minutes or half an hour, the Americans and British were warmly engaged within sight of us. What were the feelings of most or all the young soldiers at this time, I know not, but I know what were mine. But let mine or theirs be what they might, I saw a lieutenant who appeared to have feelings not very enviable; whether he was actuated by fear or the canteen I cannot determine now. I thought it fear at the time, for he ran round among the men of his company, sniveling and blubbering, praying each one if he had aught against him, or if *he* had injured anyone that they would forgive him, declaring at the same time that he, from his heart, forgave them if they had offended him, and I gave him full credit for his assertion; for had he been at the gallows with a halter about his neck, he could not have shown more fear or penitence. A fine soldier you are, I thought, a fine officer, an exemplary man for young soldiers! I would have then suffered anything short of death rather than have made such an exhibition of myself. . . .

. . . A number of our sick were sent off to Norwalk in Connecticut to recruit [rest]. I was sent with them as a nurse. We were billeted among the inhabitants. I had in my ward seven or eight *sick soldiers*, who were (at least soon after their arrival there) as well in health as I was. All they wanted was a cook and something for a cook to exercise his functions upon. The inhabitants here were almost entirely what were in those days termed tories. An old lady, of whom I often procured milk, used always when I went to her house to give me a lecture on my opposition to our good King George. She had always said (she told me) that the regulars would make us fly like pigeons. . . .

Our surgeon came among us soon after this and packed us all off to camp, save two or three who were discharged. I arrived at camp with the rest, where we remained, moving from place to place as occasion required, undergoing hunger, cold, and fatigue until the 25th day of December, 1776, when I was discharged (my term of service having expired) at Philipse Manor, in the state of New York near Hudson's River.

Here ends my first campaign. I had learned something of a soldier's life, enough I thought to keep me at home for the future. Indeed, I was then fully determined to rest easy with the knowledge I had acquired in the affairs of the army. But the reader will find . . . that the ease of a winter spent at home caused me to alter my mind. I had several *kind* invitations to enlist into the standing army then about to be raised, especially a very pressing one to engage in a regiment of horse, but I concluded to try a short journey on foot first. Accordingly, I set off for my good old grandsire's, where I arrived, I think, on the 27th, two days after my discharge, and found my friends all alive and well. They appeared to be glad to see me, and I am sure I was *really* glad to see them.

CAMPAIGN OF 1777

. . . [W]e joined the grand army near Philadelphia, and the heavy baggage being sent back to the rear of the army, we were obliged to put us up huts by laying up poles and covering them with leaves, a capital shelter from winter storms. Here we continued to fast; indeed we kept a continual Lent as faithfully as ever any of the most rigorous of the Roman Catholics did. But there was this exception; we had no fish or eggs or any other substitute for our commons. Ours was a real fast and, depend upon it, we were sufficiently mortified.[2]

About this time the whole British army left the city, came out, and encamped, or rather lay, on Chestnut Hill in our immediate neighborhood. We hourly expected an attack from them; we had a commanding position and were very sensible of it. We were kept constantly on the alert, and wished nothing more than to have them engage us, for we were sure of giving them a drubbing, being in excellent fighting trim, as we were starved and as cross and ill-natured as curs. The British, however, thought better of the matter, and, after several days maneuvering on the hill, very civilly walked off into Philadelphia again. . . .

Soon after the British had quit their position on Chestnut Hill, we left this place, and after marching and countermarching back and forward some days, we crossed the Schuylkill on a cold, rainy, and snowy night upon a bridge of wagons set end to end and joined together by boards and planks. And after a few days more maneuvering we at last settled down at a place called "the Gulf" (so named on account of a remarkable chasm in the hills); and here we encamped some time, and here we had liked to have encamped forever—for starvation here *rioted* in its glory. . . .

While we lay here, there was a Continental thanksgiving ordered by Congress; and as the army had all the cause in the world to be particularly thankful, if not for being well off, at least that it was no worse, we were ordered to participate in it. We had nothing to eat for two or three days previous, except what the trees of the fields and forests afforded us. But we must now have what Congress said—a sumptuous thanksgiving to close the year of high living we had now nearly seen brought to a close. Well, to add something extraordinary to our present stock of provisions, our country, ever mindful of its suffering army, opened her sympathizing heart so wide upon this occasion as to give us something to make the world stare. And what do you think it was, reader? Guess. You cannot guess, be you as much of a Yankee as you will. I will tell you: It gave each and every man *half* a *gill* of rice and a *tablespoonful* of vinegar!!

After we had made sure of this extraordinary superabundant donation, we were ordered out to attend a meeting and hear a sermon delivered upon the happy occasion. We accordingly went, for we could not help it. . . . I remember the text, like an attentive lad at church. I can *still* remember that it was this, "And the soldiers said unto him, And what shall we do? And he said unto them, Do violence to no man, nor accuse anyone falsely." The preacher ought to have added the remainder of the sentence to have made it complete: "And be content with your wages." But that would not do, it would be too apropos; however, he heard it as soon as the service was over, it was shouted from a hundred tongues. . . .

The army was now not only starved but naked. The greatest part were not only shirtless and barefoot but destitute of all other clothing, especially blankets. I procured a small piece of raw cowhide and made myself a pair of moccasins, which kept my feet (while they lasted) from the frozen ground, although

2. A humorous reference to the Catholic tradition of fasting by eating fish and eggs in place of meat.

as I well remember the hard edges so galled my ankles while on a march that it was with much difficulty and pain that I could wear them afterwards; but the only alternative I had was to endure this inconvenience or to go barefoot, as hundreds of my companions had to, till they might be tracked by their blood upon the rough frozen ground. But hunger, nakedness, and sore shins were not the only difficulties we had at that time to encounter; we had hard duty to perform and little or no strength to perform it with.

The army continued at and near the Gulf for some days, after which we marched for the Valley Forge in order to take up our winter quarters. We were now in a truly forlorn condition—no clothing, no provisions, and as disheartened as need be. We arrived, however, at our destination a few days before Christmas. Our prospect was indeed dreary. In our miserable condition, to go into the wild woods and build us habitations to *stay* (not to *live*) in, in such a weak, starved, and naked condition, was appalling in the highest degree, especially to New Englanders, unaccustomed to such kind of hardships at home. However, there was no remedy, no alternative but this or dispersion; but dispersion, I believe, was not thought of—at least I did not think of it. We had engaged in the defense of our injured country and were willing, nay, we were determined to persevere as long as such hardships were not altogether intolerable. I had experienced what I thought sufficient of the hardships of a military life the year before (although nothing in comparison to what I had suffered the present campaign) . . . ; but we were now absolutely in danger of perishing, and that too in the midst of a plentiful country. We then had but little and often nothing to eat for days together; but now we had nothing and saw no likelihood of any betterment of our condition. Had there fallen deep snows (and it was the time of year to expect them) or even heavy and long rainstorms, the whole army must inevitably have perished. Or had the enemy, strong and well provided as he then was, thought fit to pursue us, our poor emaciated carcasses must have "strewed the plain." But a kind and holy Providence took more notice and better care of us than did the country in whose service we were wearing away our lives by piecemeal.

We arrived at the Valley Forge in the evening. It was dark; there was no water to be found, and I was perishing with thirst. I searched for water till I was weary and came to my tent without finding any; fatigue and thirst, joined with hunger, almost made me desperate. I felt at that instant as if I would have taken victuals or drink from the best friend I had on earth by force. I am not writing fiction, all are sober realities. Just after I arrived at my tent, two soldiers whom I did not know passed by; they had some water in their canteens which they told me they had found a good distance off, but could not direct me to the place as it was very dark. I tried to beg a draught of water from them, but they were as rigid as Arabs. At length I persuaded them to sell me a drink for three pence, Pennsylvania currency, which was every cent of property I could then call my own, so great was the necessity I was then reduced to.

I lay here two nights and one day and had not a morsel of anything to eat all the time, save half of a small pumpkin, which I cooked by placing it upon a rock, the skin side uppermost, and making a fire upon it. By the time it was heat[ed] through I devoured it with as keen an appetite as I should a pie made of it at some other time.

The second evening after our arrival here I was warned to be ready for a two days command. I never heard a summons to duty with so much disgust before or since as I did that; how I could endure two days more fatigue without nourishment of some sort I could not tell. . . . However, in the morning . . . I went to the parade where I found a considerable number ordered upon the same business, whatever it was. We were ordered to go to the quartermaster general and receive from him our final orders. We accordingly repaired to his quarters, which was about three miles from camp; here we understood that our destiny was to go into the country on a foraging expedition, which was nothing more nor less than to procure provisions from the inhabitants for the men in the army and forage for the poor perishing cattle belonging to it, at the point of the bayonet. We stayed at the quartermaster general's quarters till sometime in the afternoon, during which time a beef creature was butchered for us. I well remember what fine stuff it was. . . .

We were then divided into several parties and sent off upon our expedition. Our party consisted of a lieutenant, a sergeant, a corporal, and 18 privates. We marched till night when we halted, and . . . this day we arrived at Milltown, or Downingstown, a small village halfway between Philadelphia and Lancaster, which was to be our quarters for the winter. It was dark when we had finished our day's march. There was a commissary and a wagonmaster general stationed here, the commissary to take into custody the provisions and forage that we collected, and the wagonmaster general to regulate the conduct of the wagoners and direct their motions. The next day after our arrival at this place we were put into a small house in which was only one room, in the center of the village. We were immediately furnished with rations of good and wholesome beef and flour, built us up some berths to sleep in, and filled them with straw, and felt as happy as any other pigs that were no better off than ourselves. And now having got into winter quarters and ready to commence our foraging business, I shall here end my account of my second campaign.

18

Choosing Sides

Boston King

In Massachusetts and other centers of revolutionary activity, patriots enthusiastically confronted the British, young men enlisted in the Continental Army, and loyalists actively defended their king. For many, however, especially those who were uneducated or lived in the hinterlands, the decision over which side to support often hinged on such pedestrian concerns as which side of a river they lived on, who shared their property line, and where they were when war broke out. Boston King faced a more difficult choice. His decision was daunting because he was a black slave.

Both loyalists and patriots recognized the importance of blacks to the war effort. Most free blacks supported the revolutionaries, and Northern states such as Connecticut and Rhode Island, with little plantation slavery, raised all-black regiments and made widespread use of blacks in their militias. But Southern states such as Virginia, South Carolina, and Georgia were more circumspect about allowing blacks to serve in the military, fearing that it might undermine slavery.

Early in the war, the British actively encouraged slaves to desert revolutionary masters in order to expand the loyalist forces and to weaken the rebel economy. In 1775, the British governor of Virginia, Lord Dunmore, issued a proclamation promising freedom to any slave who escaped a rebel master and took up arms for the king. Many slaves heeded this call despite the dangers of escape and the terrifying threats of punishment against family and friends of runaways. In 1778, the Continental Army responded with its own policy of freeing loyalist slaves, although in practice slaves of captured masters were often resold for profit. Boston King was one of the thousands of slaves who responded to the promises of freedom by escaping to the British lines and fighting for the crown.

Born on a plantation near Charles Town (now Charleston), South Carolina, around 1760, King was raised as a "privileged" house slave. Learning to read and write and apprenticing to a carpenter as an adolescent, he had valuable skills and a freedom of movement that was rare for slaves. His fear of severe punishment after a misdeed prompted his flight to the British in his late teens. In 1782, after serving in the British army and twice escaping reenslavement, King found himself in New York, the last British stronghold,

Boston King, "Memoirs of the Life of Boston King, a Black Preacher, Written by Himself, during His Residence at Kingswood-School," <http://collections.ic.gc.ca/blackloyalists/documents/diaries/king-memoirs.htm> (1 Dec. 2002); orig. published in *Arminian [or the Methodist] Magazine* XXI (March, April, May, June 1798): 105–11, 157–61, 209–13, 261–65.

among thousands of loyalist refugees awaiting repatriation to Canada, West Florida, and Jamaica.

Ultimately, it was decided that all blacks who had come to the British lines before the signing of the provisional peace treaty of 1782 would be free, and all others would be returned to their masters. Boston and his wife, Violet King, also an escaped slave, were repatriated to Birchtown, Nova Scotia, where they joined the nucleus of Canada's first black community. Ten years later, they moved to Sierra Leone with nearly twelve hundred of their neighbors, where King started a school for natives, became a Methodist minister, and worked on his memoirs, published in 1798.

QUESTIONS TO CONSIDER

1. If you had been a slave during the American Revolution, which side would you have supported? Why?
2. What obstacles did Boston King face in his escape from slavery?
3. Why do you think King went to such lengths to explain that his decision to escape was based on his fear of severe punishment? Do you think he would have attempted escape anyway?

I was born in the Province of South Carolina, 28 miles from Charles Town. My father was stolen away from Africa when he was young. . . . My mother was employed chiefly in attending upon those that were sick, having some knowledge of the virtue of herbs, which she learned from the Indians. She likewise had the care of making the people's clothes, and on these accounts was indulged with many privileges which the rest of the slaves were not. . . .

. . . When 16 years old, I was bound apprentice to a trade. After being in the shop about two years, I had the charge of my master's[1] tools, which being very good, were often used by the men, if I happened to be out of the way: When this was the case, or any of them were lost, or misplaced, my master beat me severely, striking me upon my head, or any other part without mercy. . . . About eight months after, we were employed in building a storehouse, and nails were very dear at that time, it being in the American war, so that the workmen had their nails weighed out to them; on this account they made the younger apprentices watch the nails while they were at dinner. It being my lot one day to take care of them, which I did till an apprentice returned to his work, and then I went to dine. In the mean time he took away all the nails belonging to one of the journeymen, and he being of very violent temper, accused me to the master with stealing of them. For this offense I was beat and tortured most cruelly, and was laid up three weeks before I was able to do any work. My proprietor,[2] hearing of the bad usage I received, came to town, and severely reprimanded my master for beating me in such a manner, threatening him, that if he ever heard the like again, he would take me away and put me to another master to finish my time, and make him pay for it. This had a good effect and he behaved much

---

1. The master of his apprenticeship, who was paid by King's owner to teach him carpentry.
2. King's owner.

better to me, the two succeeding years, and I began to acquire a proper knowledge of my trade.

My master being apprehensive that Charles Town was in danger on account of the war, removed into the country, about 38 miles off. Here we built a large house for Mr. Waters, during which time the English took Charles Town. Having obtained leave one day to see my parents, who had lived about 12 miles off, and it being late before I could go, I was obliged to borrow one of Mr. Waters's horses; but a servant of my master's took the horse from me to go a little journey, and stayed two or three days longer than he ought. This involved me in the greatest perplexity, and I expected the severest punishment, because the gentleman to who the horse belonged was a very bad man, and knew not how to show mercy. To escape his cruelty, I determined to go [to] Charles Town, and throw myself into the hands of the English. They received me readily, and I began to feel the happiness, liberty, of which I knew nothing before, altho' I was grieved at first, to be obliged to leave my friends, and among strangers.

In this situation I was seized with the smallpox and suffered great hardships; for all the Blacks affected with that disease, were ordered to be carried a mile from the camp, lest the soldiers should be infected, and disabled from marching. This was a grievous circumstance to me and many others. We lay sometimes a whole day without any thing to eat or drink; but Providence sent a man, who belonged to the York volunteers whom I was acquainted with, to my relief. He brought me such things as I stood in need of; and by the blessing of the Lord I began to recover. . . .

[King continues his stint in the British army in the service of a Captain Grey.]

I tarried with Captain Grey about a year, and then left him, and came to Nelson's ferry. Here I entered into the service of the commanding officer of that place. But our situation was very precarious; and we expected to be made prisoners every day; for the Americans had 1,600 men, not far off; whereas our whole number amounted only to 250: But here were 1,200 English about 30 miles off; only we knew not how to inform them of our danger, as the Americans were in possession of the country. Our commander at length determined to send me with a letter, promising me great rewards, if I was successful in the business, I refused going on horseback, and set off on foot about 3 o'clock in the afternoon; I expected every moment to fall in with the enemy, whom I well knew would show me no mercy. I went on without interruption, till I got within six miles of my journey's end, and then was alarmed with a great noise a little before me. But I stepped out of the road, and fell flat upon my face till they were gone by. I then arose, and praised the Name of the Lord for his great mercy, and again pursued my journey, till I came to Mums-corner tavern. I knocked at the door, but they blew out the candle. I knocked again, and entreated the master to open the door. At last he came with a frightful countenance, and said "I thought it was the Americans; for they were here about an hour ago, and I thought they were returned again." I asked, how many were there? He answered, "about one hundred." I desired him to saddle his horse for me, which he did, and went with me himself. When we had gone about two miles, we were stopped by the picket-guard, till the Captain came out with 30 men: As soon as he knew that I had brought an express from Nelson's ferry, he received me with great kindness, and expressed his approbation of my courage and conduct in this dangerous business. Next morning, Colonel Small . . . sent 600 men to relieve the troops at Nelson's ferry.

Soon after I went to Charles Town, and entered on board a [man] of war. As we were going to Chesapeake Bay, we were at the taking of a rich prize. We stayed in the bay two days, and they sailed for New-York, where I went on shore. Here I endeavoured to follow my trade, but for want of tools was obliged to relinquish it, and enter into service. But the wages were so low that I was not able to keep myself in clothes, so that I was under the necessity of leaving my master and going to another. I stayed with him four months, but he never paid me, and I was obliged to leave him also, and work about the town until I was married.

A year after I was taken very ill, but the Lord raised me up again in about five weeks. I then went out in a pilotboat. We were at sea eight days, and had only provisions for five, so that we were in danger of starving. On the 9th day we were taken by an American whaleboat. I went on board them with a cheerful countenance, and asked for bread and water, and made very free with them. They carried me to Brunswick, and used me well. Notwithstanding which, my mind was fairly distressed at the thought of being again reduced to slavery, and separated from my wife and family; and at the same time it was exceeding difficult to escape from my bondage, because the river at Amboy was above a mile over, and likewise another to cross at Staten-Island.

I called to remembrance the many great deliverances the Lord had wrought for me, and besought him to save me this once, and I would serve him all the days of my life. While my mind was thus exercised, I went into the jail to see a lad whom I was acquainted with at New-York. He had been taken prisoner, and attempted to make his escape, but was caught 12 miles off: They tied him to the tail of a horse, and in this manner brought him back to Brunswick. When I saw him, his feet were fastened in the stocks, and at night both his hands. This was a terrifying sight to me, as I expected to meet with the same kind of treatment, if taken in the act of attempting to regain my liberty. I was thankful that I was not confined in a jail, and my master used me as well as I could expect; and indeed the slaves about Baltimore, Philadelphia, and New-York, have as good victuals as many of the English; for they have meat once a day, and milk for breakfast and supper; and what is better than all, many of the masters send their slaves to school at night, that they may learn to read the Scriptures. This is a privilege indeed. But alas, all these enjoyments could not satisfy me without liberty! Sometimes I thought, if it was the will of God that I should be a slave, I was ready to resign myself to his will; but at other times I could not find the least desire to content myself in slavery.

Being permitted to walk about when my work was done, I used to go to the ferry, and observed, that when it was low water the people waded across the river; tho' at the same time I saw there were guards posted at the place to prevent the escape of prisoners and slaves. As I was at prayer on Sunday evening, I thought the Lord heard me, and would mercifully deliver me. Therefore putting my confidence in him, about one o'clock in the morning I went down to the river side, and found the guards were either asleep or in the tavern. I instantly entered into the river, but when I was a little distance from the opposite shore, I heard the sentinels disputing among themselves: One said "I am sure I saw a man cross the river." Another replied, "There is no such thing." It seems they were afraid to fire at me, or make an alarm, lest they should be punished for their negligence. When I had got a little distance from the shore, I fell down upon my knees, and thanked God for the deliverance. I traveled till about five in the morning, and then concealed myself till seven o'clock at night, when I proceeded forward, thro' bushes and marshes, near the road, for fear of being discovered. When I came to the river, opposite Staten-Island, I found a boat; and altho' it was very near a whaleboat, yet I ventured into it, and cutting the rope, got safe over. The commanding officer, when informed of my case, gave me a passport, and I proceeded to New-York.

When I arrived at New-York, my friends rejoiced to see me once more restored to liberty, and joined me in praising the Lord for his mercy and goodness. But notwithstanding this great deliverance, and the promises I had made to serve God, yet my good resolutions soon vanished away like the morning dew: The love of this world extinguished my good desires, and stole away my heart from God, so that I rested in a mere form of religion for near three years. About which time, (in 1783) the horrors and devastation of war happily terminated and peace was restored between America and Great Britain, which diffused universal joy among all parties; except us, who had escaped from slavery and taken refuge in the English army; for a report prevailed at New-York, that all the slaves, in number 2000, were to be delivered up to their masters altho' some of them had been three or four years among the English. This dreadful rumour filled us all with inexpressible anguish and terror, especially when we saw our old masters coming from Virginia, North Carolina, and other parts, and seizing upon their slaves in the streets of New York, or even dragging them out of their beds. Many of the slaves had very cruel masters, so that the thoughts of returning home with them embittered life to us. For some days we lost our appetite for food, and sleep departed from our eyes.

The English had compassion upon us in the day of distress, and issued out a Proclamation, importing, That all slaves should be free, who had taken refuge in the British lines, and claimed the sanction and privileges of the Proclamations respecting the security and protection of Negroes. In consequence of this, each of us received a certificate from the commanding officer at New-York, which dispelled all our fears, and filled us with joy and gratitude. Soon after, ships were fitted out, and furnished with every necessary for conveying us to Nova Scotia. We arrived at Birch Town in the month of August, where we all safely landed. Every family had a lot of land, and we exerted all our strength in order to build comfortable huts before the cold weather set in.

19

Secret Correspondence of a Loyalist Wife
Catherine Van Cortlandt

The Revolution was also a civil war. While most white Americans favored the patriot cause, loyalists were strong in many areas and among many groups. The areas surrounding New York City and along the Hudson River were predominantly Tory, as were the eastern shore of Maryland and much of what was then the western frontier, particularly the Carolinas and Georgia. Old loyalties died hard. Benjamin Franklin's son William, as governor of New Jersey, was a prominent loyalist. George Washington, already commanding the Continental Army, still drank to the king's health daily until January 1776, when Thomas Paine's Common Sense *convinced him that the day of monarchy had passed.*

Philip Van Cortlandt of Hanover, New Jersey, retained his allegiance to the king. He escaped arrest by a patriot party in December 1776 and entered military service on the British side, receiving his commission from William Franklin. In letters sent to him by secret messenger from the patriot stronghold in which she was living, his wife, Catherine Van Cortlandt, described the family's plight. Finally, George Washington took pity on the family and gave them a pass to join Van Cortlandt in New York. The Van Cortlandts never returned to New Jersey. Like many loyalists, they migrated first to Nova Scotia and then to England.

QUESTIONS TO CONSIDER
1. Did Revolutionary War soldiers have the right to seize Catherine Van Cortlandt's provisions and destroy her property? Why or why not?
2. Why did George Washington give the family a pass to rejoin Van Cortlandt in New York?

December 15, 1776, Hanover, New Jersey

My dearest love,

You had not left us ten minutes last Sunday when a party of Light Horsemen, headed by Joseph Morris, came to our once peaceful mansion all armed, who said they had positive orders to take you, my dear Philly, prisoner to Easton, and your favourite horse Sampson to be carried to Morristown for the

---

H. O. H. Vernon-Jackson, ed., "A Loyalist's Wife: Letters of Mrs. Philip Van Cortlandt, December 1776–February 1777," *History Today* 14 (1964): 574–80.

use of General Lee from whom these cruel mandates were issued. What were my emotions on seeing these wretches alight and without ceremony enter the doors you can only conceive, you who know their base characters and how their present errand must be received by your beloved family. When these bloody-minded men came into the dining room our little flock gathered around me and with anxious eyes watched my looks, whilst I was answering questions. . . . One of them (flourishing his sword) swore bitterly that, if you was to be found alive on earth, he would take you or have your heart's blood. This was too much. They fled into their nursery, bursting into tears; screams out, "Oh my dear Pappa, they will kill him, they will kill him." One of the in-human men seemed touched and endeavoured an excuse by saying they were sent by their General and therefore were obliged to do their duty, even though against a person they formerly much esteemed, but had been represented to General Lee as one too dangerous to be permitted to stay in the country. Finding you was certainly gone . . . they went off and left me in a situation . . . scarce to be described. My first care was the nursery to comfort those innocent pledges of our mutual love. . . . Their sobbing and crying had almost overcome them; and they would not be persuaded from a belief that the wretches were gone to murder their dear Pappa. . . .

. . . The house is surrounded by eighteen or twenty armed men every night in expectation of intercepting you, as they observed that you was too much at-tached to your family to be long absent. Our dear children are again taken from school in consequence of the cruel insults they daily receive for the principles of their parents.

I now write in fear and trembling and venture this by an honest Dutch farmer who says he will deliver it into your hands.

January 20, 1777, Hanover, New Jersey

My beloved Philly,

. . . The arrival of the Rebel Troops in this neighbourhood has been severely felt by us. Parties continually passing this way were always directed by officious people to stop at our house to breakfast, dine, or stay the night; the horses from the teams were put into our barns to feed, without even the ceremony of asking liberty. During the stay of the officers of the hospital we had some protection. But immediately on their removal, several field officers from the New England line and a company of privates took possession. . . . They were the most disorderly of their species and their officers were from the dregs of the people. In-deed, two lieutenants messed and slept in the kitchen altogether, and would not be prevailed upon to leave their quarters. . . . A French general has also come on the hill at Dashwood, and daily draws his supply for his numerous cavalry from our granary and barrack.

Many of our female neighbours have been here, but I find their visits are only to gratify curiosity and to add insult to our unremitted distress. One of them who lives across the river, whose family we took so much pleasure in relieving when friendless . . . said that formerly she always respected you and loved the ground over which you walked, but now could with pleasure see your blood run down the road. . . . The pious, devout and Reverend Mr. Green is very industrious in promoting your ruin by declaring you an enemy to their cause. The farmers are forbid to sell me provisions, and the millers to grind our grain. Our woods are cut down for the use of their army, and that which you bought and left corded near the river my servants are forbid to touch, though we are in the greatest distress for the want of it. . . . Our dear children have been six weeks without any other covering to their tender feet but woollen rags sewed round them to keep them from freezing.

A few days ago, the colonel and other officers quartered here told me they expected some of their brother officers to dine and spend the evening with them. This I understood as a hint to provide accordingly, which I was determined to do to the utmost of my powers, *though from necessity*. . . . After removal of the cloth, I took the earliest opportunity . . . to absent myself; and then they set in for a drinking match, every few minutes calling aloud upon the *landlady* to replenish the decanters which were kept continually going. . . . At length, one of them [the children] observed that the Gentlemen who used to dine with Papa never did so; and if these were not his friends, why did Mamma treat them so well. . . .

A Servant came down and said the Gentlemen desired my company, as they were going to dance. This confounded me. . . . Though I was much distressed, my resolution supported me whilst I told him that the present situation of myself and children would sufficiently apologize for my refusing to partake of any scenes of mirth where my husband could not attend me. . . . Near ten o'clock . . . he returned and entreated me to honour the Company for a few minutes as a Spectator. . . . The Officers were dancing Reels with some tawdry dressed females I had never seen. . . .

February 12, 1777, Hanover, New Jersey

. . . The narrow escape of your last was something remarkable. I was sitting about the dusk of evening in my room, very disconsolate with our dear children around me, reflecting on our deplorable situation and the gloomy prospects before me, when I heard a sudden rap at the street door. . . . I went myself to see who it was, and lucky I did. A tall, thin man presented himself, and on my stooping to unbolt the door whispered, he had a letter for me. My heart fluttered. The sentry was walking before the door, and two of the Officers were coming towards me. I recollected myself and *"desired the good man to walk into my room until I could give him a little wine for the sick woman."* He took the hint, and as soon as he came to my fireside gave me a letter, the outside of which I just looked at and threw it under the head of my bed and immediately set about getting him some wine for his wife to prevent suspicion. . . . The honest man after taking a dram went away, being followed out of doors and questioned by the Officers, who had been venting, cursing, and swearing against the sentry for permitting anyone to approach the house or speak to me without their first being acquainted with it. . . . The frequent frolics of the Officers in the house, the Soldiers in the

Nursery, and Cattle constantly fed here has reduced our late Stock of plenty to a miserable pittance. The other day was almost too much for me. We had been several days without bread and were subsisting upon a half bushel of Indian meal which had been given me by a Dutch farmer I did not know, who said he had heard of our situation and would take no pay. . . . Our stock of meal had been expended five days and the Soldiers not being about, our little Sally immediately went into the Nursery, and picking up a piece of dirty bread which had been trod under their feet came running up to me, wiping it with her frock, and with joy sparkling in her eyes presented it to me crying out, "Do eat it, Mamma. 'Tis good. 'Tis charming good bread. Indeed it is. I have tasted it." This was too much.

The next day Doctor Bond . . . came to the house, and passing me suddenly went into the back room and taking from under his coat a loaf of bread he gave it to the children and before I could thank him he ran past me with his handkerchief and hat before his face. . . .

A few days after, Doctor Bond came here and with a faltering voice told me he was sent by General Washington to inform me that it was his positive orders that our house should be taken as an Hospital to innoculate his Army with the smallpox, and if I chose he would innoculate my family at the same time. . . . He . . . promised to use his influence with the General to obtain the only favour I had now to ask of him; which was, to go to my husband with my children, servants, and such effects as I could take with me. . . .

February 19, 1777, Hoboken Ferry

My beloved husband,

Doctor Bond succeeded and with orders for my removal brought me General Washington's pass which I now enclose.

To describe the scene at parting with our few though sincere friends, the destruction of our property, the insulting looks and behaviour of those who had been accessory to our ruin . . . is more than I dare attempt. At four in the afternoon, a cold, disagreeable day, we bid adieu to our home to make room for the sick of General Washington's Army and, after an unpleasant and fatiguing journey, arrived at twelve o'clock at night at the Fork of the Rivers Rockaway, Pompton and Haakinsack. A Young Woman, whose father and brother were both in the Rebel service, was much affected with my situation and endeavoured to remove me into another room. The next evening, after a most distressing ride through snow and rain . . . we arrived at Campbell's Tavern at Haakinsack, the mistress of which refused me admittance when she was informed whose family it was, alleging as an excuse that she expected a number of Officers. . . .

The town was filled with Soldiers and the night advancing . . . a person came up to me, looked me in the face, and asked me to accompany him to his Uncle's house with my whole family. On entering a room with a large fire, it had an effect on the children, whose stomachs had been empty the greatest part of the day, that caused instant puking, and was near proving fatal to them.

The next morning early, we again set off in a most uncomfortable sleet and snow. . . . Our youngest children could not pass a farm yard where they were milking cows without wishing for some. My little Willing was almost in agonies, springing in my Arms and calling for milk. I therefore rode up and requested the good man to let me have some from one of his pails. . . . The man stopped, asked who we were, and . . . swore bitterly he would not give a drop to any Tory Bitch. I offered him money, my children screamed; and, as I could not prevail, I drove on.

. . . [T]he servants . . . had been obliged to leave me soon after setting off from Haakinsack, on account of the baggage and the badness of the roads. About two hours ago, they came in and inform me that, crossing the river on the ice at the ferry, they were stopped and fired upon by a party of armed Rebels, nearly killing several of them. . . . Upon being shewn a copy of General Washington's pass, . . . they damned the General "for giving the mistress a pass" and said they were sorry they had not come a little sooner as they would have stopped the whole . . . and immediately fell to plundering chests, trunks, boxes, etc., throwing the heavy Articles into a hole in the ice, and breaking a barrel of old fashioned China into a thousand pieces. . . .

. . . [B]e not surprised, my dear Pappa, if you see your Kitty altered. Indeed, I am much altered. But I know your heart, you will not love me less, but heal with redoubled affection and tenderness the wounds received in your behalf for those principles of loyalty which alone induced you to leave to the mercy of Rebels nine innocent children and your fond and ever affectionate Wife,

C.V.C.

20

Republican Motherhood

Abigail Adams

Abigail Adams exemplified the ideal of the "Republican mother," a woman who took an active role in affairs within the narrow bounds allowed by eighteenth-century marriage while inculcating the love of virtue and country in her children.

Born Abigail Smith in Weymouth, Massachusetts, in 1744, Adams, like most young women of the era, was educated at home by her parents and relatives. John Adams, a serious young lawyer, began courting her in 1761, and three years later they wed. The couple had five children, four of whom survived into adulthood.

Abigail Adams's letters to her husband and her son John Quincy Adams, who spent much of his childhood on overseas diplomatic missions with his father, illustrate the power of her personality and the sense of authority—different from the authority accorded eighteenth-century men—that she created from the role of wife and mother. Never forgetting the sharp distinction that society made between men's responsibilities and women's, she nonetheless took clear stands on the moral and political issues of her day and molded her son into a man of virtue and patriotism according to her definitions of those traits.

QUESTIONS TO CONSIDER

1. What standards did Abigail Adams set for her son?
2. What lessons did Adams expect her son to learn from the American Revolution?
3. Compare the tone of Adams's letter to her son with that of the letter to her husband.
4. What does this famous letter ask of John Adams?

Charles Francis Adams, ed., *Letters of Mrs. Adams, the Wife of John Adams* (Boston: Wilkins, Carter, 1848), 94–96, 152–55; Charles Francis Adams, ed., *Familiar Letters of John Adams and His Wife Abigail Adams, during the Revolution* (Boston: Houghton, Mifflin, 1875), 148–50.

LETTERS TO JOHN QUINCY ADAMS

June, 1778

My Dear Son,

'Tis almost four months since you left your native land, and embarked upon the mighty waters, in quest of a foreign country. Although I have not particularly written to you since, yet you may be assured you have constantly been upon my heart and mind.

It is a very difficult task, my dear son, for a tender parent to bring her mind to part with a child of your years going to a distant land; nor could I have acquiesced in such a separation under any other care than that of the most excellent parent and guardian who accompanied you. You have arrived at years capable of improving under the advantages you will be likely to have, if you do but properly attend to them. They are talents put into your hands, of which an account will be required of you hereafter; and being possessed of one, two, or four, see to it that you double your numbers.

The most amiable and most useful disposition in a young mind is diffidence of itself; and this should lead you to seek advice and instruction from him, who is your natural guardian, and will always counsel and direct you in the best manner, both for your present and future happiness. You are in possession of a natural good understanding, and of spirits unbroken by adversity and untamed with care. Improve your understanding by acquiring useful knowledge and virtue, such as will render you an ornament to society, an honor to your country, and a blessing to your parents. Great learning and superior abilities, should you ever possess them, will be of little value and small estimation, unless virtue, honor, truth, and integrity are added to them. Adhere to those religious sentiments and principles which were early instilled into your mind, and remember that you are accountable to your Maker for all your words and actions.

You have entered early in life upon the great theatre of the world, which is full of temptations and vice of every kind. You are not wholly unacquainted with history, in which you have read of crimes which your inexperienced mind could scarcely believe credible. You have been taught to think of them with horror, and to view vice as

> a monster of so frightful mien,
> That, to be hated, needs but to be seen.

Yet you must keep a strict guard upon yourself, or the odious monster will soon lose its terror by becoming familiar to you. The modern history of our own times, furnishes as black a list of crimes, as can be paralleled in ancient times, even if we go back to Nero, Caligula, or Cæsar Borgia.[1] Young as

---

1. **Nero, Caligula, or Cæsar Borgia:** Here Adams refers to corrupt and depraved Roman emperors and an Italian Renaissance aristocrat infamous for his conniving and cruelty.

you are, the cruel war, into which we have been compelled by the haughty tyrant of Britain and the bloody emissaries of his vengeance, may stamp upon your mind this certain truth, that the welfare and prosperity of all countries, communities, and, I may add, individuals, depend upon their morals. That nation to which we were once united, as it has departed from justice, eluded and subverted the wise laws which formerly governed it, and suffered the worst of crimes to go unpunished, has lost its valor, wisdom and humanity, and, from being the dread and terror of Europe, has sunk into derision and infamy.

Be assured I am most affectionately yours,

———.

12 January, 1780

My Dear Son,

. . . These are times in which a genius would wish to live. It is not in the still calm of life, or the repose of a pacific station, that great characters are formed. Would Cicero have shone so distinguished an orator if he had not been roused, kindled, and inflamed by the tyranny of Catiline, Verres, and Mark Anthony?[2] The habits of a vigorous mind are formed in contending with difficulties. All history will convince you of this, and that wisdom and penetration are the fruit of experience, not the lessons of retirement and leisure. Great necessities call out great virtues. When a mind is raised and animated by scenes that engage the heart, then those qualities, which would otherwise lie dormant, wake into life and form the character of the hero and the statesman. War, tyranny, and desolation are the scourges of the Almighty, and ought no doubt to be deprecated. Yet it is your lot, my son, to be an eyewitness of these calamities in your own native land, and, at the same time, to owe your existence among a people who have made a glorious defence of their invaded liberties, and who, aided by a generous and powerful ally, with the blessing of Heaven, will transmit this inheritance to ages yet unborn.

Nor ought it to be one of the least of your incitements towards exerting every power and faculty of your mind, that you have a parent who has taken so large and active a share in this contest, and discharged the trust reposed in him with so much satisfaction as to be honored with the important embassy which at present calls him abroad.

The strict and inviolable regard you have ever paid to truth, gives me pleasing hopes that you will not swerve from her dictates, but add justice, fortitude, and every manly virtue which can adorn a good citizen, do honor to your country, and render your parents supremely happy, particularly your ever affectionate mother,

A. A.

---

2. **Cicero . . . Catiline, Verres, and Mark Anthony:** Here Adams refers to the famous Roman orator Cicero and the conspiracies and tyrannies instituted by Rome's strongmen.

Braintree, 26 December, 1783

My Dear Son,

The early age at which you went abroad gave you not an opportunity of becoming acquainted with your own country. Yet the revolution, in which we were engaged, held it up in so striking and important a light, that you could not avoid being in some measure irradiated with the view. The characters with which you were connected, and the conversation you continually heard, must have impressed your mind with a sense of the laws, the liberties, and the glorious privileges, which distinguish the free, sovereign, independent States of America.

Let your observations and comparisons produce in your mind an abhorrence of domination and power, the parent of slavery, ignorance, and barbarism, which places man upon a level with his fellow tenants of the woods;

> A day, an hour, of virtuous liberty
> Is worth a whole eternity of bondage.

You have seen power in its various forms, — a benign deity, when exercised in the suppression of fraud, injustice, and tyranny, but a demon, when united with unbounded ambition, — a wide-wasting fury, who has destroyed her thousands. Not an age of the world but has produced characters, to which whole human hecatombs[3] have been sacrificed.

What is the history of mighty kingdoms and nations, but a detail of the ravages and cruelties of the powerful over the weak? Yet it is instructive to trace the various causes, which produced the strength of one nation, and the decline and weakness of another; to learn by what arts one man has been able to subjugate millions of his fellow creatures, the motives which have put him upon action, and the causes of his success; — sometimes driven by ambition and a lust of power; at other times, swallowed up by religious enthusiasm, blind bigotry, and ignorant zeal; sometimes enervated with luxury and debauched by pleasure, until the most powerful nations have become a prey and been subdued by these Sirens, when neither the number of their enemies, nor the prowess of their arms, could conquer them. . . .

The history of your own country and the late revolution are striking and recent instances of the mighty things achieved by a brave, enlightened, and hardy people, determined to be free; the very yeomanry of which, in many instances, have shown themselves superior to corruption, as Britain well knows, on more occasions than the loss of her André.[4] Glory, my son, in a country which has given birth to characters, both in the civil and military departments, which may vie with the wisdom and valor of antiquity. As an immediate descendant of one of those characters, may you be led to an imitation of that disinterested patriotism and that noble love of your country, which will teach you to despise wealth, titles, pomp, and equipage, as mere external advantages, which

---

3. The ancient Greek tradition of sacrificing 100 cattle to the gods.
4. Major John André was a British officer hanged as a spy for traveling under a false identity as part of a loyalist conspiracy involving Benedict Arnold.

cannot add to the internal excellence of your mind, or compensate for the want of integrity and virtue.

May your mind be thoroughly impressed with the absolute necessity of universal virtue and goodness, as the only sure road to happiness, and may you walk therein with undeviating steps, — is the sincere and most affectionate wish of

Your mother,
A. Adams

LETTER TO JOHN ADAMS

Braintree, 31 March, 1776

I wish you would ever write me a letter half as long as I write you, and tell me, if you may, where your fleet are gone; what sort of defense Virginia can make against our common enemy; whether it is so situated as to make an able defense. Are not the gentry lords, and the common people vassals? Are they not like the uncivilized vassals Britain represents us to be? I hope their riflemen, who have shown themselves very savage and even blood-thirsty, are not a specimen of the generality of the people. I am willing to allow the colony great merit for having produced a Washington; but they have been shamefully duped by a Dunmore [British commander].

I have sometimes been ready to think that the passion for liberty cannot be equally strong in the breasts of those who have been accustomed to deprive their fellow-creatures of theirs. Of this I am certain, that it is not founded upon that generous and Christian principle of doing to others as we would that others should do unto us.

I long to hear that you have declared an independency. And, by the way, in the new code of laws which I suppose it will be necessary for you to make, I desire you would remember the ladies and be more generous and favorable to them than your ancestors. Do not put such unlimited power into the hands of the husbands. Remember, all men would be tyrants if they could. If particular care and attention is not paid to the ladies, we are determined to foment a rebellion, and will not hold ourselves bound by any laws in which we have no voice or representation.

That your sex are naturally tyrannical is a truth so thoroughly established as to admit of no dispute; but such of you as wish to be happy willingly give up the harsh title of master for the more tender and endearing one of friend. Why, then, not put it out of the power of the vicious and the lawless to use us with cruelty and indignity with impunity? Men of sense in all ages abhor those customs which treat us only as the vassals of your sex; regard us then as beings placed by Providence under your protection, and in imitation of the Supreme Being make use of that power only for our happiness.

21

Shays's Rebellion: Prelude to the Constitution
George Richards Minot

During the 1780s, political conflict splintered much of the country. For relief from the economic hardships that followed the war, farmers looked to local and state government to pass and enforce laws that favored debtors over creditors. Wealthier townspeople wanted strong government that would ensure sound money, promote trade, pay the public debt, and keep order.

Nowhere was this battle waged more fiercely than in Massachusetts. Poor harvests made it difficult for farmers to pay their debts to merchants and to meet the high taxes levied by the state to discharge its Revolutionary War obligations. Soon creditors and the state were dispossessing farmers of their land and livestock, and some were even thrown into jail for nonpayment of debt. Farmers began demanding legislation to improve their situation. They called for lower taxes, the issuance of paper money to make debt repayment easier, and "stay laws" to postpone payment to creditors. When these efforts failed, the farmers took more dramatic action, forming paramilitary units, many composed of Revolutionary War veterans. Their main target was the courts where creditors and tax collectors gathered to collect what they were owed. In an orderly, but plainly illegal manner they surrounded courthouses and stopped proceedings. Informally organized, they had few recognized leaders, but the former Revolutionary War officers among them, like Daniel Shays of Pelham, drilled the men and became at least nominal leaders of the movement.

Merchants, professionals, and government leaders were horrified by the court closings, describing the Shaysites as "the most idle, vicious and disorderly set of men" who would "plunge the community into anarchy." Boston lawyer George Richards Minot (1758–1802) shouted for "Daniel Shays's decapitation," although a year later, when he wrote the account excerpted here, he had moderated his opinion so that historians have praised the fairness of his judgments. Governor James Bowdoin called for "the most vigorous measures . . . to enforce obedience to the law," and the state legislature responded as Massachusetts organized an army under Revolutionary War general Benjamin Lincoln.

The Shaysite armies harassed merchants and tried to capture the federal arsenal at Springfield. In the end, though, General Lincoln's army of militiamen easily defeated

---

George Richards Minot, *The History of the Insurrections in Massachusetts, in the Year Seventeen Hundred and Eighty Six, and the Rebellion Consequent Thereon*, 2nd ed. (Boston: Books for Libraries Press, 1810), 108–25.

them; the rebellion dissipated, and its leaders fled the state. By the following year the economy had swung upward, and the Massachusetts government, though firmly set against the Shaysites, eased the credit squeeze by a limited issuance of paper money.

The crisis was over, but its political effect was not. The rebellion had alarmed political leaders throughout the colonies and greatly strengthened the position of those who advocated a stronger central government to control such uprisings. Shays's Rebellion was extensively debated as the Constitution was drafted and approved. The arguments over ratification in Massachusetts followed quite closely the political divisions expressed in the insurrection. Only their superior organization enabled the Federalists to achieve victory in this pivotal state by the close vote of 187 to 168.

QUESTIONS TO CONSIDER

1. What position on Shays's Rebellion does George Richards Minot take in his account?
2. What strategy did the Shaysites pursue? How aggressive do they seem? How determined were they to bring the issue to actual combat?
3. What strategy did General Benjamin Lincoln, who led the state's army, pursue? How aggressive does he seem? How determined was he to bring the issue to actual combat?
4. Why did Shays's Rebellion become an important issue throughout the colonies?

. . . General Shepard, about 4 o'clock in the afternoon of the 25th, perceived Shays advancing on the Boston road, towards the arsenal where the militia were posted, with his troops in open column. Possessed of the importance of that moment, in which the first blood should be drawn in the contest, the General sent one of his aids with two other gentlemen, several times, to know the intention of the enemy, and to warn them of their danger. The purport of their answer was, that they would have possession of the barracks; and they immediately marched onwards to within 250 yards of the arsenal. A message was again sent to inform them, that the militia were posted there by order of the Governour, and of Congress, and that if they approached nearer, they would be fired upon. To this, one of their leaders replied, that *that* was all they wanted; and they advanced one hundred yards further. Necessity now compelled General Shepard to fire, but his humanity did not desert him. He ordered the two first shots to be directed over their heads; this however, instead of retarding, quickened their approach; and the artillery was at last pointed at the centre of their column. This measure was not without its effect. A cry of murder arose from the rear of the insurgents, and their whole body was thrown into the utmost confusion. Shays attempted to display his column, but it was in vain. His troops retreated with precipitation to Ludlow, about ten miles from the place of action, leaving three of their men dead, and one wounded on the field.

The advantages which the militia had in their power, both from the disorder of this retreat, which was as injudicious as the mode of attack, and from the nature of the ground, would have enabled them to have killed the greater part of the insurgents, had a pursuit taken place. But, the object of the commander was rather to terrify, than to destroy the deluded fugitives. . . .

Notwithstanding the fatigue of a march, performed in an uncommonly severe winter, the army were ordered under arms at half past three o'clock, the same day on which they arrived. Four regiments, with four pieces of artillery, and the horse, crossed the river upon the ice, while the Hampshire troops, under the command of General Shepard, moved up the river, as well to prevent a junction of the party under Shays, who were on the east side, with those under Day, on the west, as to cut off the retreat of the latter. It was also a great object by this manœuvre, to encircle Day, with a force so evidently superior, as to prevent his people from firing, and thereby to avoid the shedding of blood. Upon the appearance of the army on the river, the guard at the ferry house turned out, but forsook the pass; and after a small shew of opposition, near the meeting house, retired in the utmost confusion. This was attended with the flight of all Day's party, who escaped to Northampton, with the loss of a very small number, that were overtaken by the light horse. The insurgent forces under Shays, made no greater opposition, on the day following. When the army approached him, he immediately began a retreat, through South-Hadley to Amherst, supplying the hunger of his men by plunder. . . .

The appearance of things was exceedingly changed by the flight of the insurgents from Springfield. . . . The apprehensions of the inhabitants had been . . . greatly raised, from the various reports of the numbers and objects of the insurgents; and more than all, from the aid which they affected to rely on, from secret, but influential characters within the state, and the discontented of neighbouring governments. From such ideas, the meeting of the two armies in full force, at Springfield was dreaded by all, in whose minds the tranquillity of the country was the primary object. But these fears wholly vanished, by the dispersing of the insurgent forces, and a security naturally arose from the flattering view of their broken and forlorn condition. . . .

The pursuit of Shays and his party, which commenced at two o'clock in the morning, was continued till the army reached Amherst, through which place, however, he passed before their arrival, on his way to Pelham, with the main body of his men. General Lincoln, finding the enemy out of his reach, directed his march to Hadley, the nearest place which could be found to afford a cover for his troops. Upon an examination of the houses at Amherst, it was discovered, that most of the male inhabitants had quitted them to follow the insurgents; and that ten sleigh loads of provisions had gone forward from the county of Berkshire for their use. Under such appearances, a strict prohibition was laid upon the remaining inhabitants, against affording any supplies to their deluded neighbours.

The morning after the arrival of the army at Hadley, information was received that a small number of General Shepard's men had been captured at Southampton, and that the enemy's party still continued there. The Brookfield volunteers, consisting of fifty men, and commanded by Colonel Baldwin, were sent in sleighs, with 100 horse, under the command of Colonel Crafts, to pursue them. They were soon found to consist of eighty men with ten sleighs, and at twelve o'clock the same night were overtaken at Middlefield. They had quartered themselves in separate places; and about one half of them, with one Luddington their captain, being lodged in a house together, were first surrounded. It was a singular circumstance, that among the government's volunteers, happened to be General Tupper, who had lately commanded a continental regiment, in which Luddington had served as a Corporal. The General, ignorant of the character of his enemy, summoned the party to surrender. How astonished was the Corporal at receiving the summons, in a voice to which he had never dared to refuse obedience! A momentary explanation took place, which but heightened the General's commands. Resistance was no longer made, the doors were opened, and a surrender was agreed to. By this time, the rest of the party had paraded under arms, at the distance of 200 yards, where they were met by a number of men prepared for their reception. Both sides were on the point of firing, but, upon an artful representation of the strength of the government's troops, the insurgents laid down their arms, and fifty-nine prisoners, with nine sleigh loads of provisions, fell into the hands of the conquerors, who returned to the army on the day following.

The whole force of the insurgents having taken post on two high hills in Pelham, called east and west hills, which were rendered difficult of access by the depth of the snow around them, General Lincoln, on the 30th of January, sent a letter directed to Captain Shays, and the officers commanding the men in arms against the government of the Commonwealth, as follows:

> Whether you are convinced or not of your error in flying to arms, I am fully persuaded that before this hour, you must have the fullest conviction upon your own minds, that you are not able to execute your original purposes.
>
> Your resources are few, your force is inconsiderable, and hourly decreasing from the disaffection of your men; you are in a post where you have neither cover nor supplies, and in a situation in which you can neither give aid to your friends, nor discomfort to the supporters of good order and government.— Under these circumstances, you cannot hesitate a moment to disband your deluded followers. If you should not, I must approach, and apprehend the most influential characters among you. Should you attempt to fire upon the troops of government, the consequences must be fatal to many of your men, the least guilty. To prevent bloodshed, you will communicate to your privates, that if they will instantly lay down their arms, surrender themselves to government, and take and subscribe the oath of allegiance to this Commonwealth, they shall be recommended to the General Court for mercy. If you should either withhold this information from them, or suffer your people to fire upon our approach, you must be answerable for all the ills which may exist in consequence thereof.

To this letter the following Answer was received.

Pelham, January 30th, 1787

To General Lincoln, commanding the government troops at Hadley.

Sir,

The people assembled in arms from the counties of Middlesex, Worcester, Hampshire and Berkshire, taking into serious consideration the purport of the flag just received, return for answer, that however unjustifiable the measures may be which the people have adopted, in having recourse to arms, various circumstances have induced them thereto. We are sensible of the embarrassments the people are under; but that virtue which truly characterizes the citizens of a republican government, hath hitherto marked our paths with a degree of innocence; and we wish and trust it will still be the case. At the same time, the people are willing to lay down their arms, on the condition of a general pardon, and return to their respective homes, as they are unwilling to stain the land, which we in the late war purchased at so dear a rate, with the blood of our brethren and neighbours. Therefore, we pray that hostilities may cease, on your part, until our united prayers may be presented to the General Court, and we receive an answer, as a person is gone for that purpose. If this request may be complied with, government shall meet with no interruption from the people, but let each army occupy the post where they now are.

DANIEL SHAYS, *Captain*

On the next day, three of the insurgent leaders came to Head Quarters with the following letter.

The Honourable General Lincoln.

Sir,

As the officers of the people, now convened in defence of their rights and privileges, have sent a petition to the General Court, for the sole purpose of accommodating our present unhappy affairs, we justly expect that hostilities may cease on both sides, until we have a return from our legislature.

Your Honour will therefore be pleased to give us an answer.

Per order of the committee for reconciliation.

FRANCIS STONE, *Chairman*
DANIEL SHAYS, *Captain*
ADAM WHEELER

Pelham, January 31, 1787

To this the following Answer was sent.

Hadley, January 31*st,* 1787

Gentlemen,

Your request is totally inadmissible, as no powers are delegated to me which would justify a delay of my operations. Hostilities I have not commenced.

I have again to warn the people in arms against government, immediately to disband, as they would avoid the ill consequences which may ensue, should they be inattentive to this caution.

B. LINCOLN

To FRANCIS STONE,
DANIEL SHAYS,
ADAM WHEELER

During these negotiations between the army and the insurgents, the time arrived for the assembling of the legislature. . . . The Court then acquainted the Governour, that they were prepared to receive his communications, and he addressed them by a speech from the chair, which contained a retrospective account of the malcontents, as to their views and proceedings, and of the measures which the government had adopted to oppose them. Vigour and energy were strongly recommended, as the proper means of crushing so unprovoked an insurrection, while a want of them might draw on the evils of a civil war. . . .

Affairs had been brought to such a crisis, that there was no room left for the legislature to waver in their opinions, or to delay their measures. The whole community were in an alarm, and the appeal to the sword was actually made. One army or the other was to be supported, and there could be no hesitation in the mind of any reasonable man, which it ought to be. On the next day, therefore, a declaration of Rebellion was unanimously passed in the Senate, and concurred by the lower House. This however was accompanied by a resolve, approving of General Lincoln's offer of clemency to the privates among the insurgents, and empowering the Governour in the name of the General Court to promise a pardon, under such disqualifications, as should afterwards be provided, to all privates and noncommissioned officers, that were in arms against the Commonwealth, unless excepted by the general officer commanding the troops, upon condition of their surrendering their arms, and taking and subscribing the oath of allegiance, within a time to be prescribed by the Governour.

On the same day, an answer was also sent to the Governour's speech. In this the Court informed his Excellency of their entire satisfaction, in the measures which he had been pleased to take for subduing a turbulent spirit, that had too long insulted the Government of the Commonwealth; and congratulated him on the success which had attended them. They earnestly intreated him still to continue them, with such further constitutional measures, as he might think necessary, to extirpate the spirit of rebellion; for the better enabling of him to do which, they thought it necessary to declare that a rebellion existed. . . . They subjoined that they would vigorously pursue every measure, which would be calculated to support the constitution, and would continue to redress any real grievances, if such should be found to exist.

22

Casting Their Lot with the British

Major John Norton (Teyoninhokarawen)

Major John Norton, or Teyoninhokarawen, was a Mohawk chief who led Native Amer-
icans living in the U.S.–Canadian border region into the War of 1812 on the side of the
British. His warriors made a key contribution to the military defeat of the U.S. Army at
Queenston Heights, Stoney Creek, and, most famously, the Siege of Detroit.

Probably born in Scotland in the 1760s to a Cherokee who had served in the
British Army and a Scottish mother, Norton himself joined the British Army as a
young man, serving in Ireland and later Canada in the 1780s. While in Canada he
rediscovered his native roots, teaching and trading among the Five Nations Iroquois,
marrying an Iroquois woman, and learning the Iroquois language and customs.

He began his Native American political career when he was adopted as nephew by
Indian leader Joseph Brant (Thayendanegea), perhaps the most famous Native Ameri-
can of his time, who had distinguished himself on the side of the British during the
American Revolution. Norton used his connections to Brant to become a chief, and after
Brant's death he was drawn back into military service in Tecumseh's war against the
Americans at the Battle of Tippecanoe in 1811. When the War of 1812 broke out the
following year, Norton traveled among his adopted people, trying to recruit them to
fight on the side of the British.

The Five Nations had been split by the outcome of the American Revolution, with
many remaining on the American side and some moving across the border to Canada.
Sitting along the U.S.–Canadian border, the Five Nations struggled with a difficult
neutrality in the War of 1812. They hoped that the white men would fight one another
to the death and leave them in peace, but they also feared that as the war dragged on,
the two powers might force them onto opposite sides of the conflict. Norton rejected this
attempt to steer a path between the two powers and argued that the biggest danger na-
tive peoples faced was in not getting into the war at the beginning and proving neces-
sary to one power.

The following passages, taken from Norton's journal, describe his failed attempts to
rally the Five Nations of the Iroquois Confederacy to the side of the British king and
the delicate discussions about how Native Americans could avoid the danger of being
dragged into fighting one another on opposite sides of the conflict. Norton did recruit
many Native American warriors to his military command, which, along with those

The Journal of Major John Norton, 1816, The Publications of the Champlain Society (Toronto: The Champlain Society, 1970), 289–95.

serving under Joseph Brant's son John, fought several successful battles against the Americans, including the Siege of Detroit, described in this passage, in which British general Isaac Brock led a dramatic victory over American general William Hull.

QUESTIONS TO CONSIDER

1. Were the Native Americans living in the border region between Canada and the United States right to remain neutral during the War of 1812?
2. How representative was John Norton's view among Native Americans that the British crown was better than the Americans?
3. What factors went into Native American decisions about which side to take in the War of 1812?

. . . In June 1812,—a Deputation of the Younger Chiefs from the Ondowaga, Onondague and Cayugwas living within the American Boundary, came to the council fire at the Grand River;—they avowed their Motive was to commune with their Brethren, that they might avoid involving themselves in the difficulties attendant on War. The Chiefs and Warriors of the Grand River assembled,—and on the first day the Ondowaga, opening the Council after the usual salutations,— Billy, as speaker for the Deputation, arose and spoke to this purport,—"Brother,— We have come from our homes to warn you, that you may preserve yourselves and families from distress. We discover that the British and the Americans are on the Eve of a War,—they are in dispute respecting some rights on the Sea, with which we are unacquainted;—should it end in a Contest, let us keep aloof:—Why should we again fight, and call upon ourselves the resentment of the Conquerors? We know that neither of these powers have any regard for us. In the former War, we espoused the cause of the King, We thought it the most honourable,—all our former Treaties having been made with his Representatives. After contending seven years without ever listening to the pacific overtures sent from the Enemy,— we found,—that Peace was concluded across the Sea, and that our Enemy claimed our Territory in consequence of the Boundary Line then acceded to. We found none to assist us to obtain Justice; We were compelled to rely on ourselves, & make the best of it. Experience has convinced us of their neglect, except when they want us. Why then should we endanger the comfort, even the existence of our families, to enjoy their smiles only for the Day in which they need us?

"The American Agent, who lives in our Neighbourhood, has told us, that the United States do not require our assistance,—that their number is endless and adequate to every emergency of War:—this entirely meets our sentiments,— We are in their power, but we do not wish to join them in War.

"Brother, — We entreat that you also sit still in your habitations, regardless of the Tempest of Battle,—you may thus escape unhurt & unobserved by the enraged Combatants.

"Let us now pledge ourselves to each other to observe a strict neutrality. We may then meet again with our hearts unclouded by disagreable circumstances— when the storm of War shall have blown over, & left the sky clear,—without a threatening Cloud. We hope our Words may penetrate your hearts,—take this Wampum,—in token of our sincerity."

Taking the Wampum, the People of the Grand River withdrew to deliberate. At this time, there was a party among the Mohawks strongly inclined to pursue the Line of conduct recommended by the Deputation from the other side, and ambitious to inculcate similar sentiments into the minds of all the people of the Grand River;—this called forth more strongly the Exertions of the firm and loyal, to render steady such as wavered from the apprehension of the great number and power of the Americans,—so strongly vaunted by themselves, and in the various Rumours circulating through Upper Canada.

It took up two days before an answer could be made for the Senecas,—in that time two of their most respectable Chiefs calling upon me, entered into conversation to this effect: "Friend,—We view you with apprehension & suspicion:—We think you so zealously disposed to serve the King that you are inclined to draw after you all these people without considering the difficulties in which you may thereby involve them. Perhaps you also imagine that we come here entirely under the Influence of the American Agent, only prepared to rehearse the Lesson he may have given us. We may both be mistaken. To convince you that we act from a disinterested Love to our people, and to ensure their welfare and preservation,—We shall lay before you the reasons which induce us to recommend a neutrality. The gloomy Day, foretold by our ancients, has at last arrived;—the Independance and Glory of the Five Nations has departed from us;—We find ourselves in the hands of two powerful Nations, who can crush us when they please. They are the same in every respect, although they are now preparing to contend. We are ignorant of the real motives which urge them to arm, but we are well assured that we have no interest therein, and that neither one nor other have any affection towards us. We know that our Blood shed in their Battles will not even ensure their compassion to our Widows and Orphans,—nor respect to our Tribes weakened in their Contests. Has not our Nation partaken in ev'ry War in which the English have been engaged,—since they first joined hands, (for then the English & Americans were one). In Standing between them and the French, many a Valiant Warrior has fallen. But although we have thus been weakened, & deprived of our Independance, it has not been by the Victories of a Conqueror;—it has been the neglect or Unkindness of our Friends. Seeing therefore, that no good can be derived from War, we think we should only seek the surest means of averting its attendant Evils;—We are of opinion that we should follow the example of some of their people,[1] who never bear arms in war, & deprecate the principle of hostility."

I answered, "What you have now said is certainly applicable to you who remain on the other side. The Americans have gained possession of all your Country, excepting the small part which you have reserved. They have enveloped you:—it is out of your power to assist us,—because in doing so,—you would hazard the Destruction of your families. You can however have no motive to assist them;—The King does not want to take your Lands nor to injure you,

1. The Quakers. [Note provided by original editor of the document.]

and the Americans will not give you more for assisting them. Even should your actions or courage merit a glorious report,—they will hardly allow you that which they bargain for themselves. It is therefore both your Interest and your Duty to remain peaceable at home.

"Our Situation is very different. You know that the preferring to live under the protection of the King, rather than fall under the power or influence of the Americans,—induced us to fix our habitations at this place. If the King is attacked, we must support him, we are sure that such conduct is honourable;—but how profitable it might be to submit to these Mighty Men without resistance, we can, by no means ascertain;—We know that We would feel it highly disgraceful, and we remember what has been the fate of those who have thought that a passive inoffensive Demeanour would be a sufficient protection. Witness the peaceable People of Conestogue butchered at Lancaster,—the harmless Moravian Delawares, murdered at their own Village on Muskingum,—and many other instances that clearly demonstrate a manly resistance to be the strongest security against armed enemies like them, who invade us with their host of new made soldiers, only confident of awing by the pomp of military parade & numbers. We know them to have always been the Enemies of the Aboriginal Nations. Last autumn, they commenced their grand Military atchievements, & marched against the Village of Tippicanoe,—astonished at the resistance of a few Warriors whom they found there, they returned home, to meditate on a more easy method of conquering."

These men spoke openly their minds. There were others, who, I discovered, had been spreading dreadful alarms of the immense preparations of the Americans,—that they would cross the Line with a great force from Detroit,—from Presqu'ile to Long Point,—from Black Rock to Fort Erie,—& that another army would invade Lower Canada, whilst the Country People in many places would espouse the Cause of the Enemy. These reports alarmed the Women, & indeed seemed to cause many others to waver: an apparent Majority however unanimously determined to give the following answer,—whilst the wavering retired.

"Brothers,—we thank you for this further proof of your affection, which you have now shewn us, in coming to forewarn us of impending danger. We lament with you the Situation in which we are now placed, by being separated. You have fallen under the power of those who were once our Enemies, and are likely to become so again;—they have encompassed you, and as we cannot extricate you from the Difficulties in which you are involved,—we recommend to you peace, & request that you restrain all your young Men from becoming subservient to the Americans;—We would be ashamed of our Tribes, should any be found among the Common Enemy of our race. They have said—that they require no assistance,—keep them to their word. In the former War they held the same Language to the Oniadas,—but when they had them in their power, they insisted on their joining,—& you know we found them in arms combined with our Enemies, and many of them have fallen by our hands.

"Brothers,—Our Forefathers, when they first took the English by the hand,—agreed to risk with them. When those who had surrounded our Villages under the name of brothers, raised their arm against our Father the King,—we all joined him because he was our father;—at the peace, we removed here to live under his protection, & if he is now attacked, we will risk with him:—We are not alarmed at the boasted numbers of the Americans,—for it is he who dwells above that will decide on our fate. We cannot lie down at ease when our Father is threatened, he has not yet given us the Hatchet,[2] but should the Enemy invade us suddenly,—we hope to find something wherewith to Strike. Brothers,—We will never consider you as belonging to them. We will caution all our Western Brethren not to hurt you, in striking at the Americans who dwell around you. May the great Spirit preserve you in peace!"

Many of these people expressed the most earnest desire that the peace might continue without interruption:—they appeared very sensible of the awkward situation in which they were placed, and notwithstanding the pacific Language of the Americans, they apprehended that they might entice some of their thoughtless young Men to join them.

A few days after the Departure of these people,—we gained notice of the Declaration of War. It was then all Bustle throughout the Country,—calling together the Militia, and making every preparation to meet the Attack expected.

The People of the grand River met again in council, although I had supposed that already they had decided on the part they would take. A small Party only repaired to Niagara, & many of these not the most steady men. General Brock however received me with that pleasing affability so natural to him, & appeared as well satisfied as if there had been with me a thousand Men. He asked me, "Can you confide in the People of the Grand River,—Do you think that they will be faithful to you, tell me without reserve:" I replied, "They are unfortunately divided into parties, and there are some plausible men, who succeed in retarding their coming forth,—but when they engage, I have no doubts they are not so depraved as to be faithless. It will be necessary however, in order to render them steady & permanently serviceable to allow them a regular stipend for their support,—otherwise want will oblige them to return to their usual occupations for the Support of their families,—their present Situation being now very different from what it was; when they possessed an extensive Country,—abounding in Game,—Wide ranges for Cattle,—& were protected from the sudden assaults of the Enemy by a desert frontier." He answered that he saw clearly the propriety of my remark, at the same time adding that he thought Goods might answer the purpose better than money.

From what passed within our observation on the opposite side of the River, it appeared that the Enemy had not as yet collected any considerable force there. With us, the Militia of the Adjacent Country had assembled & made a formidable appearance: a proportion of them, called the flank companies, were retained to do duty with the Troops, and the main body was permitted to return home, that the agriculture might not be too much neglected.

---

2. Implying that they had not yet been called upon to take up arms. [Note provided by original editor of the document.]

At this time, the Commander on the American side, wrote a Letter to General Brock, intimating that some Chiefs of the Ondowaga desiring to communicate with their Brethren on the Canadian Shore, had required him to ask permission for them to come over to meet them:—he acceded to their proposition and requested me to meet them, with some Chiefs, at Queenstown, as it would not be prudent to admit them into the Country, where they might have ascertained the Quality and Quantity of our force.

At Queenstown we met the Senecas or Ondowaga. The principal Man is named Arosa,—(one of his Ancestors of the same name was a celebrated Warrior in the French War, remarkable for his fidelity to the English, by whom he was called *Silver Heels*). They were saluted with much cordiality;—they seemed strongly impressed with the importance of their Mission, and after having been seated for a few minutes, Arosa stood forth, holding some Wampum in his hand,—he thus began,—"Brothers,—feeling that tender anxiety for your Welfare which should always influence people of the same blood and kindred,—we have come to you to explain the sentiments of our hearts. It was our intention to have abode with you some days, to gratify our Eyes with a Sight of our Brethren, but the gathering Clouds of War, covering the Earth with the Gloom of darkness, forbid us passing this place:—We, shall therefore deliver immediately what moves within our Breasts.

"Brothers,—our hearts overflow with Tenderness when we look upon you. We lament that you are on the Eve of being plunged into the Miseries of War, and we beseech you to avert them by remaining peaceably at home, unmindful of the Din of arms. We know that War is destructive;—its conclusion may be ruinous, & it is well ascertained that misery is its constant attendant.

"Brothers,—the People of the great King are our old friends, & the Americans are our Neighbours. We grieve to see them prepare to imbrue their hands in the blood of each other. We have determined not to interfere, for how could we spill the Blood of the English or of our Brethren? We entreat you therefore to imitate our Determination;—for, remember, we are in the power of the Americans, & perhaps when you shall have spread Destruction through their Ranks, they will change their Language, and insist upon us to join them:—they may compel our young Men to fight against their kindred,—and like devoted animals,—we shall be brought to destroy each other."

After deliberating a few minutes, an Onondaga Chief arose,—& as speaker for the people of the Grand River, answered in their behalf: "Brothers,—we have heard your Words with pleasure, because we know they proceed from the Goodness of your heart. We regret that we are separated, for if we had been living together, we would have been of one mind.

"Brothers,—you know that we removed from the Country of our ancestors when overhung by the power of the Americans,—in order to place ourselves under the protection of the King. He does not desire to invade the Americans, but if they follow us here to attack our Father, we cannot be passive Spectators,—we must share the same fate with him. We shall participate in the Shout of Victory,—or in the Grave,—whichever He who rules may allot us. Brothers, we commend your resolution not to join in the approaching contest,—you can have no Interest therein;—but we regret that we shall be separated. May He to whom we look for aid protect you!"

Arosa stood forth again, and spoke thus: "Brothers,—We see our Words have no Effect,—but we are easy,—We have done what we judged our Duty, & we perceive you have made your Election. Therefore we shall yet further exhort you;—As you will join with Europeans in their Wars, imitate their Example, in humanely treating your Prisoners:—Let the Warriors rage only be felt in combat, by his armed opponents;—Let the unoffending cultivator of the Ground, and his helpless family, never be alarmed by your onset, nor injured by your depredation: And you,—Teyoninhoharawen[3]—we exhort you, that, as the Five Nations listen to your Words, you will help them, & endeavour to make them happy in the favour of the Great King, and should you pass thro' the Chance of War, be to them a protector. May he who dwells above the Clouds avert ev'ry Evil from your heads, & lead you by the Hand!"

He ended,—bidding us Adieu in a Manner truly affecting, while every feature expressed the Sensibility of his heart, & they recrossed the River. . . .

---

3. Spellings were often inconsistent in the eighteenth and nineteenth centuries, and different versions of the same name were not uncommon, especially with unfamiliar Indian names, hence "Teyoninhoharawen" here instead of "Teyoninhokarawen."

PART FOUR

Defining America

The Expanding Nation

W hen the turmoil resulting from the American Revolution and the ratification of the Constitution finally subsided in the 1790s, thirteen colonies
had been forged into a new nation. Covering more than a thousand miles of the
Atlantic coast, from Maine to Georgia, the United States of America already
was populated by millions of people who spoke over a dozen European languages and countless Native American tongues. Divided between the mercan-
tile, agricultural-industrial North and the plantation South, with its upcountry
hinterlands, the one bond that seemed to unite people was their shared desire
for land and the opportunity for a better life.

For almost two hundred years, American society had been confined to the
corridor between the Atlantic Ocean and the Appalachian Mountains. Native
Americans and conflict among European powers discouraged settlers from
pushing westward. Then, after about 1795, with Native Americans having been
defeated or assimilated during the Revolution and the price of good eastern
land climbing, a sizable white migration began. Thomas Jefferson's purchase of
the vast Louisiana Territory in 1803 and his sponsorship of the expedition by
Meriwether Lewis and William Clark quickened this movement, as did rising
world prices for agricultural products.

A transportation revolution further encouraged the migration: turnpikes began to replace stump-filled rutted paths; steamboats overtook sailing ships and
river rafts; and man-made waterways, like the Erie Canal, became the great en-
gines of growth and development during the first half of the nineteenth century.
They provided the first economical means of moving bulky products from western farms to the markets of the eastern states and giving the fledgling government experience at administrating people, places, and things on a grand scale.
First opened for use in 1825, the Erie Canal would eventually fade in favor of the
railroad, the great catalyst of growth in the second half of the nineteenth century. In 1828, construction began on the first westward railroad, the Baltimore

and Ohio, and four decades later, in 1869, the last spike was hammered into the transcontinental railroad at Promontory, Utah.

By the 1840s, the land seemed to have tilted permanently, shaking its human burden westward in a long, rough tumble toward the Pacific. But the improved life people sought in the West was far more than one of simple economic gain: evangelical preachers such as James McGready, father of the camp meeting, crisscrossed the Western territories spreading their message, while believers such as Priscilla Merriman Evans and her husband trekked heroically to reach their Mormon Zion in the wilderness. Despite the rise of a "Second Great Awakening," the United States remained a country where the religious and the secular militantly competed for the nation's soul. Even an anti-Christian provocateur like Elihu Palmer could find a place to preach his brand of militant rationalist deism. Europeans were fascinated by this dynamic mix of civilization and expanding frontier and the chaotic and diverse new culture that it was creating. Alexis de Tocqueville and Frances Trollope are only two of the many Europeans who made their name by traveling the United States and writing about what they had seen.

But the new Westerners were not entering empty territory. Native Americans had been forced westward for generations by white settlement, but in 1838 the U.S. Army made over fifteen thousand Cherokee Indians march from Georgia to Oklahoma. John Ross's letter presents a native view of these events. The relocation of the Cherokee put them into competition with other groups already living in the West, including other Native Americans in the Western territories, and the Spanish and their heirs, the *Mexicanos, Californios,* and *Tejanos,* who owned much of the land and resources in those territories. Shifting political alliances, religious and cultural differences, and mutual suspicions were everyday realities for most settlers pushing westward, as described by an officer of the "Army of the West" in his account of the taking of New Mexican villages.

When Mexico and the United States finally went to war over Texas and the Southwest in 1846, it was not a surprise to most Mexicans in the West, who like Guadalupe Vallejo, Prudencia Higuera, Amalia Sibrian, and Brigida Briones saw a steady stream of land-hungry settlers permanently changing the sleepy world of *Alta California* and other parts of the northern Mexican frontier. In fact, the conflicts with Mexico determined the future of nearly a million square miles of what is now Texas, New Mexico, Arizona, Nevada, California, Utah, and parts of Colorado, Wyoming, Kansas, and Oklahoma. Finally, when gold was discovered in California in 1848, it sealed the fate of the West as part of the United States. California was fast-tracked to statehood in 1850 as a rush of miners and entrepreneurs from China, South America, Europe, and the eastern states accelerated settlement, forcing decisions about the future of these new territories that soon led to the Civil War.

23

The Great Revival of 1800
James McGready

Evangelicalism, the highly emotional proselytizing religion so characteristic of American Protestantism, began in the 1730s and 1740s with the visits to the colonies of the English preacher George Whitefield. The meetings Whitefield held triggered what became known as the Great Awakening. Thousands responded to the dynamic preaching of Whitefield and the ministers he inspired with dramatic accounts of religious conversion. The Revolutionary War and the rise of the Enlightenment greatly weakened enthusiastic religion, but at the turn of the nineteenth century revivalism once again burst forth, giving rise to a religious movement still vibrant in America today. To the surprise of religious leaders, who had worried about the religious state of the rude, unchurched Western frontier, the new inspiration came from the settlements that were farthest west — in Kentucky.

Kentucky's Presbyterian and Methodist ministers revolted against the "formality and deadness" of their churches and, encouraging direct displays of religious fervor, provoked emotional scenes in which, according to one observer, the floors of churches were "covered with the slain; their screams for mercy pierced the heavens." Word spread, and people traveled from considerable distances to gather at these services. With churches too small to hold them and distant travelers not wishing to return home after only a few hours of worship, services were held out of doors, and many camped out for several days. In this way the camp meeting was born. In 1800, a meeting was announced for August 6 at Cane Ridge, Kentucky. Word flew about the hollows and cabins, and a crowd estimated at over twenty thousand people (nearly ten percent of the state's population) gathered for the largest religious service ever experienced up to that time in the United States.

Western evangelists traveled almost endlessly across sparsely settled territory preaching their highly emotional and individualistic religion during the first decades of the nineteenth century. Their creeds emphasized the importance of personal morality, civic virtue, and education. Their contribution to the characteristic culture of the American Middle West soon provided a model for much of American life. In this reading you will see the great revivals through the eyes of Kentucky Presbyterian minister James McGready (1760–1817), writing to a friend. McGready was widely credited with being the father of camp meetings.

Posthumous Works of the Reverend and Pious James M'Gready, Minister of the Gospel, in Henderson, Kentucky, ed. the Reverend James Smith in Two Volumes (Louisville, Ky.: W. W. Worsley, 1831).

QUESTIONS TO CONSIDER

1. What similarities and differences do you see between camp meetings and contemporary religious gatherings?
2. Why did whole families travel great distances to attend these events?
3. How might more traditional religious leaders have viewed camp meetings? Why do you think the "Rev. J. B." came and "involved our infant churches in confusion, disputation, &c."?

Logan County, Kentucky,

October 23, 1801.

But I promised to give you a short statement of our blessed revival; on which you will at once say, the Lord has done great things for us in the wilderness, and the solitary place has been made glad: the desert has rejoiced and blossomed as the rose. . . .

A woman, who had been a professor,[1] in full communion with the church, found her old hope false and delusive—she was struck with deep conviction, and in a few days was filled with joy and peace in believing. She immediately visited her friends and relatives, from house to house, and warned them of their danger in a most solemn, faithful manner, and plead with them to repent and seek religion. This, as a mean, was accompanied with the divine blessing to the awakening of many. About this time the ears of all in that congregation seemed to be open to receive the word preached, and almost every sermon was accompanied with the power of God, to the awakening of sinners. During the summer about ten persons in the congregation were brought to Christ. In the fall of the year a general deadness seemed to creep on apace. Conviction and conversion work, in a great measure, ceased; and no visible alteration for the better took place, until the summer of 1798, at the administration of the sacrament of the supper, which was in July. On Monday the Lord graciously poured out his *Spirit*; a very general awakening took place—perhaps but few families in the congregation could be found who, less or more, were not struck with an awful sense of their lost estate.[2] During the week following but few persons attended to worldly business, their attention to the business of their souls was so great. On the first Sabbath of September, the sacrament was administered at Muddy River (one of my congregations). At this meeting the Lord graciously poured forth his spirit, to the awakening of many careless sinners. Through these two congregations already mentioned, and through Red River, my other congregation, awakening work went on with power under every sermon. The people seemed to hear, as for eternity. In every house, and almost in every company, the whole conversation with people, was about the state of their souls. About this time the Rev. J. B. came here, and found a Mr. R. to join him. In a little time he involved our infant churches in confusion, disputation, &c. Opposed the doctrines preached here; ridiculed the whole work of the revival; formed a considerable party, &c.

---

1. **professor:** One who professes or declares a particular faith.
2. **lost estate:** Sinful condition.

&c. In a few weeks this seemed to have put a final stop to the whole work, and our infant congregation remained in a state of deadness and darkness from the fall, through the winter, and until the month of July, 1799, at the administration of the sacrament at Red River. This was a very solemn time throughout. On Monday the power of God seemed to fill the congregation; the boldest, daring sinners in the country covered their faces and wept bitterly. After the congregation was dismissed, a large number of people stayed about the doors, unwilling to go away. Some of the ministers proposed to me to collect the people in the meeting-house again, and perform prayer with them; accordingly we went in, and joined in prayer and exhortation. The mighty power of God came amongst us like a shower from the everlasting hills—God's people were quickened and comforted; yea, some of them were filled with joy unspeakable, and full of glory. Sinners were powerfully alarmed, and some precious souls were brought to feel the pardoning love of Jesus.

At Gasper river (at this time under the care of Mr. Rankin, a precious instrument in the hand of God) the sacrament was administered in August. This was one of the days of the Son of Man, indeed, especially on Monday. I preached a plain gospel sermon on Heb. 11 and 16. The better country. A great solemnity continued during the sermon. After sermon Mr. Rankin gave a solemn exhortation—the congregation was then dismissed; but the people all kept their seats for a considerable space, whilst awful solemnity appeared in the countenances of a large majority. Presently several persons under deep convictions broke forth into a loud outcry—many fell to the ground, lay powerless, groaning, praying and crying for mercy. As I passed through the multitude, a woman, lying in awful distress, called me to her. Said she, "I lived in your congregation in Carolina; I was a professor, and often went to the communion; but I was deceived; I have no religion; I am going to hell." In another place an old, gray-headed man lay in an agony of distress, addressing his weeping wife and children in such language as this: "We are all going to hell together; we have lived prayerless, ungodly lives; the work of our souls is yet to begin; we must get religion, or we will all be damned." . . .

. . . But the year 1800 exceeds all that my eyes ever beheld upon earth. All that I have related is only, as it were, an introduction. Although many souls in these congregations, during the three preceding years, have been savingly converted, and now give living evidences of their union to Christ; yet all that work is only like a few drops before a mighty rain, when compared with the wonders of Almighty Grace, that took place in the year 1800.

In June the sacrament was administered at Red River. This was the greatest time we had ever seen before. On Monday multitudes were struck down under awful conviction; the cries of the distressed filled the whole house. There you might see profane swearers, and sabbath-breakers pricked to the heart, and crying out, "what shall we do to be saved?" There frolickers and dancers crying for mercy. There you might see little children of 10, 11 and 12 years of age, praying and crying for redemption, in the blood of Jesus, in agonies of distress. During this sacrament, and until the Tuesday following, ten persons, we believe, were savingly brought home to Christ.

In July the sacrament was administered in Gasper River Congregation. Here multitudes crowded from all parts of the country to see a strange work, from the distance of forty, fifty, and even a hundred miles; whole families came in their wagons; between twenty and thirty wagons were brought to the place, loaded with people, and their provisions, in order to encamp at the meeting-house. On Friday nothing more appeared, during the day, than a decent solemnity. On Saturday matters continued in the same way, until in the evening. Two pious women were sitting together, conversing about their exercises; which conversation seemed to affect some of the by-standers; instantly the divine flame spread through the whole multitude. Presently you might have seen sinners lying powerless in every part of the house, praying and crying for mercy. Ministers and private Christians were kept busy during the night conversing with the distressed. This night a goodly number of awakened souls were delivered by sweet believing views of the glory, fulness, and sufficiency of Christ, to save to the uttermost. Amongst these were some little children—a striking proof of the religion of Jesus. Of many instances to which I have been an eye-witness, I shall only mention one, viz. A little girl. I stood by her whilst she lay across her mother's lap almost in despair. I was conversing with her when the first gleam of light broke in upon her mind—She started to her feet, and in an ecstacy of joy, she cried out, "O he is willing, he is willing—he is come, he is come—O what a sweet Christ he is—O what a precious Christ he is—O what a fulness I see in him—O what a beauty I see in him—O why was it that I never could believe! That I never could come to Christ before, when Christ was so willing to save me?" . . . Then turning round, she addressed sinners, and told them of the glory, willingness and preciousness of Christ, and plead with them to repent; and all this in language so heavenly, and, at the same time, so rational and scriptural, that I was filled with astonishment. But were I to write you every particular of this kind that I have been an eye and ear witness to, during the two past years, it would fill many sheets of paper.

At this sacrament a great many people from Cumberland, particularly from *Shiloh* Congregation, came with great curiosity to see the work, yet prepossessed with strong prejudices against it; about five of whom, I trust, were savingly and powerfully converted before they left the place. A circumstance worthy of observation, they were sober professors in full communion. It was truly affecting to see them lying powerless, crying for mercy, and speaking to their friends and relations, in such language as this: "O, we despised the work that we heard of in *Logan*; but, O, we were deceived—I have no religion; I know now there is a reality in these things: three days ago I would have despised any person that would have behaved as I am doing now; but, O, I feel the very pains of hell in my soul." This was the language of a precious soul, just before the hour of deliverance came. When they went home, their conversation to their friends and neighbors, was the means of commencing a glorious work that has overspread all the Cumberland settlements to the conversion of hundreds of precious souls. The work continued night and day at this sacrament, whilst the vast multitude continued upon the ground until Tuesday morning. According to the best computation, we believe that forty-five souls were brought to Christ on this occasion.

Muddy River Sacrament, in all its circumstances, was equal, and in some respects superior, to that at Gasper River. This sacrament was in August. We believe about fifty persons, at this time, obtained religion.

At Ridge Sacrament, in Cumberland, the second Sabbath in September, about forty-five souls, we believe, obtained religion. At Shiloh Sacrament, the third Sabbath in September, about seventy persons. At Mr. Craighead's Sacrament, in October, about forty persons. At the Clay-Lick Sacrament, *congregation*, in Logan County, in October, eight persons. At Little Muddy-Creek Sacrament, in November, about twelve. At Montgomery's Meeting-house, in Cumberland, about forty. At Hopewell Sacrament, in Cumberland, in November, about twenty persons. To mention the circumstances of more private occasions, common-days preaching, and societies, would swell a letter to a volume.

The present year has been a blessed season likewise; yet not equal to last year in conversion work. I shall just give you a list of our Sacraments, and the number, we believe, experienced religion at each, during the present year, 1801.

[McGready went on to mention several different sacraments, held at different places, and the number that he hoped obtained true religion, amounting to 144 persons in total. He then went on to finish the letter.]

I would just remark that, among the great numbers in our country that professed to obtain religion, I scarcely know an instance of any that gave a comfortable ground of hope to the people of God, that they had religion, and have been admitted to the privileges of the church, that have, in any degree, disgraced their profession, or given us any ground to doubt their religion.

Were I to mention to you the rapid progress of this work, in vacant congregations, carried on by the means of a few supplies, and by praying societies — such as at Stone's-River, Cedar-Creek, Goose-Creek, the Red-Banks, the Forentain-Head, and many other places — it would be more than time, or the bounds of a letter would admit of. Mr. M'G. and myself administered the sacrament at the Red-Banks, on the Ohio, about a month ago — a vacant congregation, nearly a hundred miles distant from any regular organized society, formerly a place famed for wickedness, and a perfect synagogue of Satan. I visited them twice at an early period; Mr. R. twice, and Mr. H. once. These supplies the Lord blessed, as a means to start his work; and their praying societies were attended with the power of God, to the conversion of almost whole families. When we administered the sacrament amongst them, they appeared to be the most blessed little society I ever saw. I ordained ten elders among them, all precious Christians; three of which, two years ago, were professed deists, now living monuments of Almighty Grace.

The original is signed,
JAMES M'GREADY.

24

An American Deist
Elihu Palmer

A recent poll found that seventy-eight percent of Americans believe in angels, and church attendance rates are five times as high in the United States as they are in Europe. Indeed, the United States has had religious awakenings throughout its history, and right now is experiencing controversy over evangelical politics, creationism in schools, and global religious proselytizing. Yet, the United States has also been one of the great cradles of Enlightenment humanism, rationalism, progressivism, and scientific inquiry. Thomas Jefferson, Tom Paine, and Benjamin Franklin are probably the three founding fathers who were most famous for their commitment to this rationalist revolution. The religious view that all three upheld was deism, the belief that God created a self-sustaining universe that can be known through the observation and scientific study of the principles of nature — which they often likened to the interconnected movements of a clock. They believed that the received revelation, miraculous occurrence, and other examples of personal relations between God and mankind that are the basis of most organized religions are fraud or delusion.

Elihu Palmer, the author of this selection, was a deist leader and activist. Born in Connecticut in 1764, he studied at Dartmouth College and became a Baptist minister in Philadelphia, but was expelled from his ministry in 1781 when he started preaching scientific rationalism. Palmer believed that humans, as a part of nature, were essentially good, but had been saddled with corrupt institutions. He saw the American Revolution as the start of a new era when reason would free humankind from these despotic institutions and the superstitions and traditions that supported them. He believed it was his deist duty to help make this happen through education and the promotion of scientific understanding of the natural world.

Placing an advertisement in the National Gazette *in 1792 for a public lecture "against the divinity of Jesus Christ," which he believed to be a superstitious belief, Palmer suddenly found himself the target of mob violence and was forced to flee Philadelphia. He moved to New York and practiced law for a time until a bout with yellow fever left him blind. He devoted the rest of his life to deism, founding the Deistic Society of the State of New York, publishing a deist journal, and writing* Principles of Nature, *a book that he believed formed the core of an American deism. An excerpt follows.*

Elihu Palmer and Peter Annet, *Principles of Nature; or, a Development of the Moral Causes of Happiness and Misery among the Human Species* (London: John Cahuac, 1819).

QUESTIONS TO CONSIDER

1. Elihu Palmer has been called America's first atheist. Judging from this reading, do you agree or disagree?
2. What does Palmer mean by the "double despotism of Church and State"? What does he mean by the "Empire of Reason"?
3. Why was Palmer so concerned to create a religion that seems to oppose religion?
4. Several of the early presidents of the United States identified themselves as deists. Do you think it is possible that there could be a deist president today? Why or why not?

CHAPTER XXV. COMMENCEMENT OF THE NINETEENTH CENTURY; CHRISTIANITY; DEISM; REASON; SCIENCE; VIRTUE; HAPPINESS.

The nineteenth century opens to the human race with prospects of a most extraordinary and astonishing nature. It is impossible, at this moment, for the human mind to contemplate the past, and anticipate the future, without yielding to the mingled emotions of regret and joy; without perceiving itself to be alternately agitated with sentiments of misery and happiness. The commencement of a new century necessarily revives the idea of a recursive view of those great events which have had the most powerful influence, and produced the most important changes in the condition of human society. The history of mankind has, in general, consisted either of uninteresting details, or a frightful picture of universal carnage and military ferocity. During the last century, however, something more valuable and important has been combined with a mass of historic matter, and amidst the unjust and destructive wars which the poison of monarchy is still generating in the very bosom of the community, there is to be seen a splendid display of those philosophic principles which sustained the universe, and of those moral axioms which are essentially interwoven with intelligent life, and by which it is rendered susceptible of universal amelioration; of those political laws whose essence is at war with tyranny, and whose final effects will shake to the centre the thrones of the earth.

It has been during the last century that these things have been accomplished; the force of intellectual powers has been applied to the development of principle, and the combination of human labours already constitutes a colossus, against which the storms of unequal and aristocratic governments may dash in vain. The art of printing is so universally known, or rather the knowledge of it is diffused in so many countries, that it will henceforth be impossible to destroy it. The present moment exhibits the most astonishing effects of this powerful invention in the hands of nations, by that universal diffusion of principle and collision of thought, which are the most substantial guarantee of the future scientific progress of the human race. An effectual stand has been made, and resuscitated nations at this moment bid defiance to the double despotism of church and state.

The nineteenth century opens with lessons awfully impressive upon kings and tyrants; with lessons, the truth of which has already penetrated into the sacred recesses of ecclesiastical wickedness and spiritual domination in high places. America, France, Switzerland, Italy, Holland, Germany, and England, are in a high state of intellectual fermentation; if the government in some of these countries acts in opposition to the spirit of improvement, this circumstance will constitute only a partial drawback on the rapidity of the progress; the general agitation is national, the power of thought has become vastly impulsive in all these countries. The printing-press is operating, and if it be in some measure restrained, it will, nevertheless, gradually undermine, and eventually subvert the thrones of civil despots, and teach the hierarchy of every country, that the time is fast approaching in which, if they pretend to speak in the name of Heaven, they must exhibit unequivocal proofs of their celestial authority; it is this pretended intercourse with Heaven that has subverted every thing rational upon earth. Upon this subject, and in describing the fatal effects of fanaticism, the following passage from an original and eccentric writer ought to be quoted. The passage exhibits in strong colours the indiscriminate folly and mad enthusiasm of which ignorant and uninstructed man is susceptible.

"It has been the constant practice for moral doctors or teachers to pretend to a new faculty of mind, called inspiration, or communication with supernatural power; this is practiced by priests in all parts of the world, from the Lapland Magi to the civilized Pope, and if it was not an insult to good sense, to attempt, with argument, the refutation of such absurdity, I would observe, that inspiration, in proportion as it approaches and identifies with Deity, the common source, the diversity of its streams or opinion is augmented; the inspired Catholic abhors the inspired Protestant, this the inspired Jew, the Jew the inspired Mahometan, and when these bedlamites break loose, their victims burn each other at opposite piles, despising that inspiration in others which they rage with themselves. . . ."

. . . [S]ome portion of society has once more obtained a true idea of the religion of nature, or of that which may be denominated pure and simple Deism.

It is this religion which, at the present period of the world, creates, such frightful apprehensions in the household of faith, and threatens to shake to the centre the chief corner stone on which the Church is built. These apprehensions are daily disclosed by Christian professors, and they depict in such strong colours the fatal effects of Deism, that ignorant fanaticism believes it to be an immoral monster, stalking with gigantic strides over the whole civilized world, for the detestable purpose of producing universal disorder, and subverting all the sound principles of social and intelligent existence. Such are the horrid ideas which the enemies of this pure and holy religion are every where propagating amongst their credulous and deluded followers. This circumstance renders it necessary, that the true idea of Deism be fairly stated, that it may be clearly understood by those whose minds have hitherto been darkened by the mysteries of faith.

Deism declares to intelligent man the existence of one perfect God, Creator and Preserver of the Universe; that the laws by which he governs the world are like himself immutable, and, of course, that violations of these laws, or miraculous interference in the movements of nature, must be necessarily excluded from the grand system of universal existence; that the Creator is justly entitled to the adoration of every intellectual agent throughout the regions of infinite space; and that he alone is entitled to it, having no co-partners who have a right to share with him the homage of the intelligent world. Deism also declares, that the practice of a pure, natural, and uncorrupted virtue, is the essential duty, and constitutes the highest dignity of man; that the powers of man are competent to all the great purposes of human existence; that science, virtue, and happiness, are the great objects which ought to awake the mental energies, and draw forth the moral affections of the human race.

These are some of the outlines of pure Deism, which Christian superstition so dreadfully abhors, and whose votaries she would willingly consign to endless torture. But it is built upon a substantial foundation, and will triumphantly diffuse happiness among the nations of the earth, for ages after Christian superstition and fanaticism have ceased to spread desolation and carnage through the fair creation of God.

In surveying the history of man, it is clearly discovered, that the miseries and misfortunes of his existence are, in a high degree, the result of his ignorance and his vices. Ignorance renders him savage and ferocious; while science pours into his mind the benign sentiments of humanity, and gives a new colouring to his moral existence. Reason, which every kind of supernatural theology abhors; reason, which is the glory of our nature, is destined eventually, in the progress of future ages, to overturn the empire of superstition, and erect upon its ruins a fabric, against which the storms of despotism may beat in vain, against which superstition may reek her vengeance without effect, from which she will be obliged to retire in agonizing tortures.

It has been the opinion of some honest and intelligent minds, that the power of intellect is inadequate to the moral and political emancipation of man. This opinion, though sometimes it is found to be operative upon benevolent hearts, seems, however, to be at war with the intellectual structure of our existence, and the facts furnished by modern history. In the great question which relates to human improvement, the cause which is productive of thought, cannot, in any high degree, be included as influencing the final decision. It is probable, however, that the opinion which refers intellect to organic material combination would favour most an unlimited improvement of the human species. If thought be an effect of matter finely organized, and delicately constructed, the best method of augmenting its power would be, to preserve the whole human system in the most pure, regular, and natural mode of operation. Parents and instructors, in this respect, are capable of doing great injury, or of producing most important benefits to future ages.

The science of the world has been, in some measure, diminished by the propagation of an opinion, that there are only a few human beings who are possessed of what is called genius, to the exclusion of all the rest. This looks too much like mystery, and seems to include in it the idea that man is sent from heaven, to occupy for a short time a miserable and material tenement, and then return to its native home. It ought to be recollected that earth is the abode of man, and that of this the materials of his existence are composed, all are confined to this place of residence, and to the amelioration of sensitive and intelligent life all his labours ought to be directed. He should learn to respect, and not despise his reason. He should learn to consider moral virtue as the greatest good, as the most substantial joy of his existence. In order, however, to be eminently good, a full scope must be given to the operation of intellectual powers, and man must feel an unqualified confidence in his own energies.

The double despotism of Church and state has borne so hard upon human existence, that man is sunk beneath its dreadful weight; but resuscitated nations are about to teach kings and tyrants a lesson awfully impressive, in regard to the destiny which awaits the aggregate injustice of the world. The period is at hand, in which kings and thrones, and priests and hierarchies, and the long catalogue of mischiefs which they have produced, shall be swept away from the face of the earth, and buried in the grave of everlasting destruction. Then will the era of human felicity, in which the heart of unfortunate man shall be consoled; then will appear the moment of national consolation, and universal freedom; then the empire of reason, of science, and of virtue, will extend over the whole earth, and man, emancipated from the barbarous despotism of antiquity, will assume to himself his true predicament in nature, and become a standing evidence of the divinity of thought and the unlimited power of human reason.

25

Religion in America
Frances Trollope

*Throughout their history, Americans have read with interest and sometimes bemuse-
ment foreigners' descriptions of their land and culture. Travel writers and social commentators from abroad like Alexis de Tocqueville, Harriet Martineau, Charles Dickens,
and Hector de Crevecoeur, to name a few, were often disdainful of America's frontier violence, anti-intellectualism, and race relations, and harbored European upper-class opinions about American religion, manners, and cuisine. Yet they often portrayed the country
based on their own larger-than-life romantic fantasies about a land of extremes and con-
trasts. One of their favorite subjects was religion in America. Though visiting clergymen
provide far more reasoned accounts of the camp meetings of the nineteenth-century's
"great awakening," there is no account more vivid and compelling than that of novelist
Frances Trollope.*

*Trollope was born in 1779 in Bristol, England, and in her twenties moved to Lon-
don and married barrister Thomas Anthony Trollope, eventually giving birth to six
children. In 1827, after financial failures brought the family to near ruin, Trollope
took three of her children and moved to America to open a department store in Cincinnati. That business was also a failure and after three and a half years she returned to
England, where she wrote* Domestic Manners of the Americans, *based on the diaries
she had kept while in Cincinnati. It was an instant hit and in 1832, at the age of fifty-
three, she became a best-selling author.*

*Trollope, who was also the mother of British novelist Anthony Trollope, was open
about her dislike of Americans, writing, "I do not like their principles, I do not like
their manners, I do not like their opinions." She went on to write dozens of successful social reform novels and continues to be a controversial figure, who, like many other outside commentators, provides a vivid and unsettling view of who and what America was,
as a nation and a people.*

QUESTIONS TO CONSIDER
1. Why is Trollope at this camp meeting and how do you imagine revivalists are viewing her?
2. What is Trollope's attitude toward the goings-on at the camp meetings?
   Describe the tone of her descriptions.
3. How do you think Trollope's writings on camp meetings would be received by a contemporary American audience?

Frances Trollope, *Domestic Manners of the Americans*, vol. 1 (New York: Dodd, Mead, 1901), 232–44.

It was in the course of this summer that I found the opportunity I had long wished for, of attending a camp-meeting, and I gladly accepted the invitation of an English lady and gentleman to accompany them in their carriage to the spot where it is held; this was in a wild district on the confines of Indiana.

The prospect of passing a night in the back woods of Indiana was by no means agreeable, but I screwed my courage to the proper pitch, and set forth determined to see with my own eyes, and hear with my own ears, what a camp-meeting really was. I had heard it said that being at a camp-meeting was like standing at the gate of heaven, and seeing it opening before you; I had heard said that being at a camp-meeting was like finding yourself within the gates of hell; in either case there must be something to gratify curiosity, and compensate one for the fatigue of a long rumbling ride and a sleepless night.

We reached the ground about an hour before midnight, and the approach to it was highly picturesque. The spot chosen was the verge of an unbroken forest, where a space of about twenty acres appeared to have been partially cleared for the purpose. Tents of different sizes were pitched very near together in a circle round the cleared space; behind them were ranged an exterior circle of carriages of every description, and at the back of each were fastened the horses which had drawn them thither. Through this triple circle of defence we distinguished numerous fires burning brightly within it; and still more numerous lights flickering from the trees that were left in the enclosure. The moon was in meridian splendour above our heads.

We left the carriage to the care of a servant, who was to prepare a bed in it for Mrs. B. and me, and entered the inner circle. The first glance reminded me of Vauxhall,[1] from the effect of the lights among the trees, and the moving crowd below them; but the second shewed a scene totally unlike any thing I had ever witnessed. Four high frames, constructed in the form of altars, were placed at the four comers of the enclosure; on these were supported layers of earth and sod, on which burned immense fires of blazing pine-wood. On one side a rude platform was erected to accommodate the preachers, fifteen of whom attended this meeting, and with very short intervals for necessary refreshment and private devotion, preached in rotation, day and night, from Tuesday to Saturday.

When we arrived, the preachers were silent; but we heard issuing from nearly every tent mingled sounds of praying, preaching, singing, and lamentation. The curtains in front of each tent were dropped, and the faint light that gleamed through the white drapery, backed as it was by the dark forest, had a beautiful and mysterious effect, that set the imagination at work; and had the sounds which vibrated around us been less discordant, harsh, and unnatural, I should have enjoyed it; but listening at the corner of a tent, which poured forth more than its proportion of clamour, in a few moments chased every feeling derived from imagination, and furnished realities that could neither be mistaken or forgotten.

Great numbers of persons were walking about the ground, who appeared like ourselves to be present only as spectators; some of these very unceremoni-

---

1. **Vauxhall:** One of the leading neighborhoods in London for public gathering and entertainment in the first half of the nineteenth century.

ously contrived to raise the drapery of this tent, at one corner, so as to afford us a perfect view of the interior.

The floor was covered with straw, which round the sides was heaped in masses, that might serve as seats, but which at that moment were used to support the heads and the arms of the close-packed circle of men and women who kneeled on the floor.

Out of about thirty persons thus placed, perhaps half a dozen were men. One of these, a handsome looking youth of eighteen or twenty, kneeled just below the opening through which I looked. His arm was encircling the neck of a young girl who knelt beside him with her hair hanging dishevelled upon her shoulders, and her features working with the most violent agitation; soon after they both fell forward on the straw, as if unable to endure in any other attitude the burning eloquence of a tall grim figure in black, who, standing erect in the centre, was uttering with incredible vehemence an oration that seemed to hover between praying and preaching; his arms hung stiff and immoveable by his side, and he looked like an ill-constructed machine, set in action by a movement so violent, as to threaten its own destruction, so jerkingly, painfully, yet rapidly, did his words tumble out; the kneeling circle ceasing not to call in every variety of tone, on the name of Jesus; accompanied with sobs, groans, and a sort of low howling inexpressibly painful to listen to. But my attention was speedily withdrawn from the preacher, and the circle round him, by a figure which knelt alone at some distance; it was a living image of Scott's Macbriar,[2] as young, as wild, and as terrible. His thin arms tossed above his head, had forced themselves so far out of the sleeves, that they were bare to the elbow; his large eyes glared frightfully, and he continued to scream without an instant's intermission the word "Glory!" with a violence that seemed to swell every vein to bursting. It was too dreadful to look upon long, and we turned away shuddering.

We made the circuit of the tents, pausing where attention was particularly excited by sounds more vehement than ordinary. We contrived to look into many; all were strewed with straw, and the distorted figures that we saw kneeling, sitting, and lying amongst it, joined to the woeful and convulsive cries, gave to each, the air of a cell in Bedlam.[3]

One tent was occupied exclusively by Negroes. They were all full-dressed, and looked exactly as if they were performing a scene on the stage. One woman wore a dress of pink gauze trimmed with silver lace; another was dressed in pale yellow silk; one or two had splendid turbans; and all wore a profusion of ornaments. The men were in snow white pantaloons, with gay coloured linen jackets. One of these, a youth of coal-black comeliness, was preaching with the most violent gesticulations, frequently springing high from the ground, and clapping his hands over his head. Could our missionary societies have heard the trash he uttered, by way of an address to the Deity, they might perhaps have doubted whether his conversion had much enlightened his mind.

---

2. **Scott's MacBriar:** The zealous young preacher who dies in rapture after being tortured in Sir Walter Scott's 1816 novel *Old Mortality*.
3. **Bedlam:** Famous lunatic asylum in London.

At midnight a horn sounded through the camp, which, we were told, was to call the people from private to public worship; and we presently saw them flocking from all sides to the front of the preachers' stand. Mrs. B. and I contrived to place ourselves with our backs supported against the lower part of this structure, and we were thus enabled to witness the scene which followed without personal danger. There were about two thousand persons assembled.

One of the preachers began in a low nasal tone, and, like all other Methodist preachers, assured us of the enormous depravity of man as he comes from the hands of his Maker, and of his perfect sanctification after he had wrestled sufficiently with the Lord to get hold of him, *et caetera*. The admiration of the crowd was evinced by almost constant cries of "Amen! Amen!" "Jesus! Jesus!" "Glory! Glory!" and the like. But this comparative tranquility did not last long: the preacher told them that "this night was the time fixed upon for anxious sinners to wrestle with the Lord;" that he and his brethren "were at hand to help them," and that such as needed their help were to come forward into "the pen." . . .

"The pen" was the space immediately below the preachers' stand; we were therefore placed on the edge of it, and were enabled to see and hear all that took place in the very centre of this extraordinary exhibition.

The crowd fell back at the mention of the pen, and for some minutes there was a vacant space before us. The preachers came down from their stand and placed themselves in the midst of it, beginning to sing a hymn, calling upon the penitents to come forth. As they sung they kept turning themselves round to every part of the crowd, and, by degrees, the voices of the whole multitude joined in chorus. This was the only moment at which I perceived any thing like the solemn and beautiful effect, which I had heard ascribed to this woodland worship. It is certain that the combined voices of such a multitude, heard at dead of night, from the depths of their eternal forests, the many fair young faces turned upward, and looking paler and lovelier as they met the moon-beams, the dark figures of the officials in the middle of the circle, the lurid glare thrown by the altar-fires on the woods beyond, did altogether produce a fine and solemn effect, that I shall not easily forget; but ere I had well enjoyed it, the scene changed, and sublimity gave place to horror and disgust.

. . . [A]bove a hundred persons, nearly all females, came forward, uttering howlings and groans, so terrible that I shall never cease to shudder when I recall them. They appeared to drag each other forward, and on the word being given, "let us pray," they all fell on their knees; but this posture was soon changed for others that permitted greater scope for the convulsive movements of their limbs; and they were soon all lying on the ground in an indescribable confusion of heads and legs. They threw about their limbs with such incessant and violent motion, that I was every instant expecting some serious accident to occur.

But how am I to describe the sound that proceeded from this strange mass of human beings? I know no words which can convey an idea of it. Hysterical sobbings, convulsive groans, shrieks and screams the most appalling, burst forth on all sides. I felt sick with horror. As if their hoarse and over-strained voices failed to make noise enough, they soon began to clap their hands violently. . . .

Many of these wretched creatures were beautiful young females. The preachers moved about among them, at once exciting and soothing their agonies. I heard the muttered "Sister! dear sister!" I saw the insidious lips approach the cheeks of the unhappy girls; I heard the murmured confessions of the poor victims, and I watched their tormentors, breathing into their ears consolations that tinged the pale cheek with red. Had I been a man, I am sure I should have been guilty of some rash act of interference; nor do I believe that such a scene could have been acted in the presence of Englishmen without instant punishment being inflicted; not to mention the salutary discipline of the tread-mill, which, beyond all question, would, in England, have been applied to check so turbulent and so vicious a scene.

After the first wild burst that followed their prostration, the moanings, in many instances, became loudly articulate; and I then experienced a strange vibration between tragic and comic feeling.

A very pretty girl, who was kneeling in the attitude of Canova's Magdalene[4] immediately before us, amongst an immense quantity of jargon, broke out thus: "Woe! woe to the backsliders! hear it, hear it Jesus! when I was fifteen my mother died, and I backslided, oh Jesus, I backslided! take me home to my mother, Jesus! take me home to her, for I am weary! Oh John Mitchel! John Mitchel!" and after sobbing piteously behind her raised hands, she lifted her sweet face again, which was as pale as death, and said, "Shall I sit on the sunny bank of salvation with my mother? my own dear mother? oh Jesus, take me home, take me home!"

Who could refuse a tear to this earnest wish for death in one so young and so lovely? But I saw her, ere I left the ground, with her hand fast locked, and her head supported by a man who looked very much as Don Juan[5] might, when sent back to earth as too bad for the regions below.

One woman near us continued to "call on the Lord," as it is termed, in the loudest possible tone, and without a moment's interval, for the two hours that we kept our dreadful station. She became frightfully hoarse, and her face so red as to make me expect she would burst a blood-vessel. Among the rest of her rant, she said, "I will hold fast to Jesus, I never will let him go; if they take me to hell, I will still hold him fast, fast, fast!"

The stunning noise was sometimes varied by the preachers beginning to sing; but the convulsive movements of the poor maniacs only became more violent. At length the atrocious wickedness of this horrible scene increased to a degree of grossness, that drove us from our station; we returned to the carriage at about three o'clock in the morning, and passed the remainder of the night in listening to the ever increasing tumult at the pen. To sleep was impossible. At daybreak the horn again sounded, to send them to private devotion; and in about an hour afterwards I saw the whole camp as joyously and eagerly employed as if the

---

4. Italian painter Antonio Canova's famous painting of Mary Magdalene, repentant prostitute from the Bible.
5. **Don Juan:** A notorious ladies' man.

night had been passed in dancing; and I marked many a fair but pale face, that I recognised as a demoniac of the night, simpering beside a swain, to whom she carefully administered hot coffee and eggs. The preaching saint and the howling sinner seemed alike to relish this mode of recruiting their strength. . . .

For Critical Thinking

1. How do the different audiences that these three authors are writing for affect what they have to say about religion in America?
2. Which of these three perspectives is the most relevant to contemporary American religious life? Why?
3. What vision do you think each of these authors has for the relationship between religion, politics, and everyday life?

26

Crossing the Continent

Meriwether Lewis and William Clark

The most famous expedition in American history was the brainchild of Thomas Jefferson. For years Jefferson had dreamed that a party of explorers could search out a passage to the Pacific; win the allegiance of the native inhabitants to the new Republic; and study the geography, plants, and minerals of a vast and unknown territory.

Meriwether Lewis (1774–1809) and William Clark (1770–1838) were two young men willing to follow Jefferson's dream. Their expedition from St. Louis to the mouth of the Columbia River and back is one of the great adventure stories of our history. The journals and notebooks that members of the party kept have been invaluable to historians, geographers, anthropologists, botanists, and zoologists.

The selections here begin with Lewis and Clark's accounts of an episode in May 1805, in which one of the expedition's interpreters, French Canadian trapper Toussaint de Charbonneau (husband of Lewis and Clark's guide, Sacajawea), nearly capsizes a canoe carrying valuable materials. A few months later, the expedition crosses the Great Divide—the peak of the Rocky Mountains where the rivers flow either to the east or the west—in one of the most difficult parts of their journey. There, the expedition meets up with a party of Shoshone, Sacajawea's native nation from which she was separated as a small child, led by her long-lost brother Cameahwait. The reader can see their careful search for information about the best route west and their close observation of Native American ways.

QUESTIONS TO CONSIDER

1. What happens with the near-capsizing of the perogue (canoe)? What can we glean about Charbonneau and Sacajawea from Lewis and Clark's accounts of this incident?
2. Imagine you are Cameahwait, one of the chiefs that Meriwether Lewis writes about. How would you describe this historic meeting with representatives of the U.S. government in Washington, D.C.?
3. What was Lewis's strategy for gaining support from the chiefs?
4. Why is Lewis writing about the sexual mores of the Shoshonees? How are they different from those he is used to?
5. Why does Lewis write about the Spanish?

Bernard DeVoto, ed., *The Journals of Lewis and Clark* (Boston: Houghton Mifflin Co., 1953), 202–6, 207–11, 213–14.

MERIWETHER LEWIS

Tuesday May 14th 1805

. . . we had been halted by an occurrence, which I have now to recappitulate, and which altho' happily passed without ruinous injury, I cannot recollect but with the utmost trepidation and horror; this is the upseting and narrow escape of the white perogue. It happened unfortunately for us this evening that Charbono was at the helm of this Perogue, in stead of Drewyer, who had previously steered her; Charbono cannot swim and is perhaps the most timid waterman in the world; perhaps it was equally unluckey that Capt. C. and myself were both on shore at that moment, a circumstance which rarely happened; and tho' we were on the shore opposite to the perogue, were too far distant to be heard or to do more than remain spectators of her fate; in this perogue [blank with apparent erasures] were embarked, our papers, Instruments, books medicine, a great part of our merchandize and in short almost every article indispensibly necessary to further the views, or insure the success of the enterprise in which we are now launched to the distance of 2200 miles. surfice it to say, that the Perogue was under sail when a sudon squawl of wind struck her obliquely, and turned her considerably, the steersman allarmed, in stead of puting her before the wind, lufted her up into it, the wind was so violent that it drew the brace of the squarsail out of the hand of the man who was attending it, and instantly upset the perogue and would have turned her completely topsaturva, had it not have been from the resistance mad by the oarning against the water; in this situation Capt. C and myself both fired our guns to attract the attention if possible of the crew and ordered the halyards to be cut and the sail hawled in, but they did not hear us; such was their confusion and consternation at this moment, that they suffered the perogue to lye on her side for half a minute before they took the sail in, the perogue then wrighted but had filled within an inch of the gunwals; Charbono still crying to his god for mercy, had not yet recollected the rudder, nor could the repeated orders of the Bowsman, Cruzat, bring him to his recollection untill he threatend to shoot him instantly if he did not take hold of the rudder and do his duty, the waves by this time were runing very high, but the fortitude resolution and good conduct of Cruzat saved her; he ordered 2 of the men to throw out the water with some kettles that fortunately were convenient, while himself and two others rowed her as[h]ore, where she arrived scarcely above the water; we now took every article out of her and lay them to drane as well as we could for the evening, baled out the canoe and secured her; there were two other men beside Charbono on board who could not swim, and who of course must also have perished had the perogue gone to the bottom. while the perogue lay on her side, finding I could not be heard, I for a moment forgot my own situation, and involluntarily droped my gun, threw aside my shot pouch and was in the act of unbuttoning my coat, before I recollected the folly of the attempt I was about to make, which was to throw myself into the river and indevour to swim to the perogue; the perogue was three hundred yard distant the waves so high that a perogue could scarcely live in any situation, the water excessively could, and the stream rappid; had I undertaken this project therefore, there was a hundred to one but what I should have paid the forfit of my life for the madness of my project, but this had the perogue been lost, I should have valued but little.—After having all matters arranged for the evening as well as the nature of circumstances would permit, we thought it a proper occasion to console ourselves and cheer the sperits of our men and accordingly took a drink of grog and gave each man a gill of sperits.

WILLIAM CLARK

14th of May Tuesday 1805

A verry Clear Cold morning a white frost & some fog on the river the Thermomtr Stood at 32 above 0, wind from the S. W. we proceeded on verry well untill about 6 oClock a Squawl of wind Struck our Sale broad Side and turned the perogue nearly over, and in this Situation the Perogue remained untill the Sale was Cut down in which time She nearly filed with water—the articles which floated out was nearly all caught by the Squar who was in the rear. This accident had like to have cost us deerly; for in this perogue were embarked our papers, Instruments, books, medicine, a great proportion of our merchandize, and in short almost every article indispensibly necessary to further the views, or insure the success of the enterprize in which, we are now launched to the distance of 2,200 miles. it happened unfortunately that Capt. Lewis and myself were both on shore at the time of this occurrence, a circumstance which seldom took place; and tho' we were on the shore opposit to the perogue were too far distant to be heard or do more than remain spectators of her fate; we discharged our guns with the hope of attracting the attention of the crew and ordered the sail to be taken in but such was their consternation and confusion at the instant that they did not hear us. when however they at length took in the sail and the perogue wrighted; the bowsman Cruzatte by repeated threats so far brought Charbono the Sternman to his recollection that he did his duty while two hands bailed the perogue and Cruzatte and two others rowed her on shore were she arrived scarcely above the water. we owe the preservation of the perogue to the resolution and fortitude of Cruzatte. . . .

MERIWETHER LEWIS

Thursday May 16th

The morning was fair and the day proved favorable to our operations; by 4 oClock in the evening our Instruments, Medicine, merchandize provision &c, were perfectly dryed, repacked and put on board the perogue. the loss we sustained was not so great as we had at first apprehended; our medicine sustained the greatest injury, several articles of which were intirely spoiled, and many others considerably injured; the ballance of our losses consisted of some gardin seeds, a small quantity of gunpowder, and a few culinary articles which fell overboard and sunk, the Indian woman to whom I ascribe equal fortitude and resolution, with any person onboard at the time of the accedent, caught and preserved most of the light articles which were washed overboard all matters being now arranged for our departure we lost no time in seting out; proceeded on tolerably well about seven miles and encamped on the Stard. side. . . .

MERIWETHER LEWIS

Saturday August 17th 1805.

we made them [the Indians] sensible of their dependance on the will of our government for every species of merchandize as well for their defence & comfort; and apprized them of the strength of our government and it's friendly dispositions towards them. we also gave them as a reason why we wished to pe[ne]trate the country as far as the ocean to the west of them was to examine and find out a more direct way to bring merchandize to them. that as no trade could by carryed on with them before our return to our homes that it was mutually advantageous to them as well as to ourselves that they should render us such aids as they had in their power to furnish in order to haisten our voyage and of course our return home. that such were their horses to transport our baggage without which we could not subsist, and that a pilot to conduct us through the mountains was also necessary if we could not decend the river by water. but that we did not ask either their horses or their services without giving a satisfactory compensation in return. that at present we wished them to collect as many horses as were necessary to transport our baggage to their village on the Columbia where we would then trade with them at our leasure for such horses as they could spare us.

the chief thanked us for friendship towards himself and nation & declared his wish to serve us in every rispect. that he was sorry to find that it must yet be some time before they could be furnished with firearms but said they could live as they had done heretofore until we brought them as we had promised. he said they had not horses enough with them at present to remove our baggage to their village over the mountain, but that he would return tomorrow and encourage his people to come over with their horses and that he would bring his own and assist us. this was complying with all we wished at present.

we next enquired who were chiefs among them. Cameahwait pointed out two others whom he said were Chiefs. we gave him a medal of the small size with the likeness of Mr. Jefferson the President of the U' States in releif on one side and clasp hands with a pipe and tomahawk in the other, to the other Chiefs we gave each a small medal which were struck in the Presidency of George Washing[ton] Esqr. we also gave small medals of the last discription two young men whom the 1st Chief informed us were good young men and much rispected among them. we gave the 1st Chief an uniform coat shirt a pair of scarlet legings a carrot of tobacco and some small articles to each of the others we gave a shi[r]t leging[s] handkerchief a knife some tobacco and a few small articles we also distributed a good quantity paint mockerson awles knives beads looking-glasses &c among the other Indians and gave them a plentifull meal of lyed corn which was the first they had ever eaten in their lives. they were much pleased with it. every article about us appeared to excite astonishment in there minds; the appearance of the men, their arms, the canoes, our manner of work-ing them, the b[l]ack man york and the sagacity of my dog were equally objects of admiration. I also shot my air-gun which was so perfectly incomprehensible that they immediately denominated it the great medicine.

Capt. Clark and myself now concerted measures for our future operations, and it was mutually agreed that he should set out tomorrow morning with eleven men furnished with axes and other necessary tools for making canoes, their arms accoutrements and as much of their baggage as they could carry. also to take the indians, C[h]arbono and the indian woman with him; that on his arrival at the Shoshone camp he was to leave Charbono and the Indian woman to haisten the return of the Indians with their horses to this place, and to proceede himself with the eleven men down the Columbia in order to examine the river and if he found it navigable and could obtain timber to set about making canoes immedi-ately. In the mean time I was to bring the party and baggage to the Shoshone Camp, calculating that by the time I should reach that place that he would have suf-ficiently informed himself with rispect to the state of the river &c. as to determine us whether to prosicute our journey from thence by land or water. in the former case we should want all the horses which we could perchase, and in the latter only to hire the Indians to transport our baggage to the place at which we made the canoes.

Sunday August 18th 1805.

This morning while Capt. Clark was busily engaged in preparing for his rout, I exposed some articles to barter with the Indians for horses as I wished a few at this moment to releive the men who were going with Capt Clark from the labour of carrying their baggage, and also one to keep here in order to pack the meat to camp which the hunters might kill. I soon obtained three very good horses. for which I gave an uniform coat, a pair of legings, a few handkerchiefs, three knives and some other small articles the whole of which did not cost more than about 20$ in the U' States. the Indians seemed quite as well pleased with their bargin as I was. the men also purchased one for an old checked shirt a pair of old legings and a knife. two of those I purchased Capt. C. took on with him. at 10 A.M. Capt. Clark departed with his detachment and all the Indians except 2 men and 2 women who remained with us. . . .

Monday August 19th 1805.

The Shoshonees may be estimated at about 100 warriors, and about three times that number of women and children[1] they have more children among them than I expected to have seen among a people who procure subsistence with such difficulty. there are but few very old persons, nor did they appear to treat those with much tenderness or rispect. The man is the sole propryetor of his wives and daughters, and can barter or dispose of either as he thinks proper. a plural-ity of wives is common among them, but these are not generally sisters as with

1. Lewis's figures refer to this band only.

the Minnitares & Mandans but are purchased of different fathers. The father frequently disposes of his infant daughters in marriage to men who are grown or to men who have sons for whom they think proper to provide wives. the compensation given in such cases usually consists of horses or mules which the father receives at the time of contract and converts to his own uce. the girl remains with her parents untill she is conceived to have obtained the age of puberty which with them is considered to be about the age of 13 or 14 years. the female at this age is surrendered to her soveriegn lord and husband agreeably to contract, and with her is frequently restored by the father quite as much as he received in the first instance in payment for his daughter; but this is discretionary with the father. Sah-car-gar-we-ah had been thus disposed of before she was taken by the Minnetares, or had arrived to the years of puberty. the husband was yet living with this band. he was more than double her age and had two other wives. he claimed her as his wife but said that as she had had a child by another man, who was Charbono, that he did not want her.

They seldom correct their children particularly the boys who soon become masters of their own acts. they give as a reason that it cows and breaks the sperit of the boy to whip him, and that he never recovers his independence of mind after he is grown. They treat their women but with little rispect, and compel them to perform every species of drudgery. they collect the wild fruits and roots, attend to the horses or assist in that duty, cook, dress the skins and make all their apparel, collect wood and make their fires, arrange and form their lodges, and when they travel pack the horses and take charge of all the baggage; in short the man dose little else except attend his horses hunt and fish. the man considers himself degraded if he is compelled to walk any distance; and if he is so unfortunately poor as only to possess two horses he rides the best himself and leavs the woman or women if he has more than one, to transport their baggage and children on the other, and to walk if the horse is unable to carry the additional weight of their persons. the chastity of their women is not held in high estimation, and the husband will for a trifle barter the companion of his bead for a night or longer if he conceives the reward adiquate; tho' they are not so importunate that we should caress their women as the siouxs were. and some of their women appear to be held more sacred than in any nation we have seen. I have requested the men to give them no cause of jealousy by having connection with their women without their knowledge, which with them, strange as it may seem is considered as disgracefull to the husband as clandestine connections of a similar kind are among civilized nations. to prevent this mutual exchange of good officies altogether I know it impossible to effect, particularly on the part of our young men whom some months abstanence have made very polite to those tawney damsels. no evil has yet resulted and I hope will not from these connections.

notwithstanding the late loss of horses which this people sustained by the Minnetares the stock of the band may be very safely estimated at seven hundred of which they are perhaps about 40 coalts and half that number of mules. their arms offensive and defensive consist in the bow and arrows shield, some lances, and a weapon called by the Cippeways who formerly used it, the pog-gar'-

mag-gon' [war club]. in fishing they employ wairs, gigs, and fishing hooks. the salmon is the principal object of their pursuit. they snair wolves and foxes.

I was anxious to learn whether these people had the venerial, and made the enquiry through the interpreter and his wife; the information was that they sometimes had it but I could not learn their remedy; they most usually die with it's effects. this seems a strong proof that these disorders bothe ganaraehah and Louis Venerae[2] are native disorders of America. tho' these people have suffered much by the small pox which is known to be imported and perhaps those other disorders might have been contracted from other indian tribes who by a round of communications might have obtained from the Europeans since it was introduced into that quarter of the globe. but so much detached on the other ha[n]d from all communication with the whites that I think it most probable that those disorders are original with them. . . .

I now prevailed on the Chief to instruct me with rispect to the geography of his country. this he undertook very cheerfully, by delineating the rivers on the ground. but I soon found that his information fell far short of my expectation or wishes. he drew the river on which we now are [the Lemhi] to which he placed two branches just above us, which he shewed me from the openings of the mountains were in view; he next made it discharge itself into a large river which flowed from the S.W. about ten miles below us [the Salmon], then continued this joint stream in the same direction of this valley or N.W. for one days march and then enclined it to the West for 2 more days march. here we placed a number of heaps of sand on each side which he informed me represented the vast mountains of rock eternally covered with snow through which the river passed. that the perpendicular and even juting rocks so closely hemned in the river that there was no possibil[it]y of passing along the shore; that the bed of the river was obstructed by sharp pointed rocks and the rapidity of the stream such that the whole surface of the river was beat into perfect foam as far as the eye could reach. that the mountains were also inaccessible to man or horse. he said that this being the state of the country in that direction that himself nor none of his nation had ever been further down the river than these mountains.

in this manner I spend the day smoking with them and acquiring what information I could with respect to their country. they informed me that they could pass to the Spaniards by the way of the yellowstone river in 10 days. I can discover that these people are by no means friendly to the Spaniards. their complaint is, that the Spaniards will not let them have fire arms and ammunition, that they put them off by telling them that if they suffer them to have guns they will kill each other, thus leaving them defenceless and an easy prey to their bloodthirsty neighbours to the East of them, who being in possession of fire arms hunt them up and murder them without rispect to sex or age and plunder them of their horses on all occasions. they told me that to avoid their enemies

2. **ganaraehah and Louis Venerae:** Gonorrhea and syphilis.

who were eternally harrassing them that they were obliged to remain in the interior of these mountains at least two thirds of the year where the[y] suffered as we then saw great heardships for the want of food sometimes living for weeks without meat and only a little fish roots and berries. but this added Câmeahwait, with his ferce eyes and lank jaws grown meager for the want of food, would not be the case if we had guns, we could then live in the country of buffaloe and eat as our enimies do and not be compelled to hide ourselves in these mountains and live on roots and berries as the bear do. we do not fear our enimies when placed on an equal footing with them. I told them that the Minnetares Mandans . . . had promised us to desist from making war on them & that we would indevour to find the means of making the Minnetares of fort d[e] Prarie or as they call them Pahkees desist from waging war against them also. that after our finally returning to our homes towards the rising sun whitemen would come to them with an abundance of guns and every other article necessary to their defence and comfort, and that they would be enabled to supply themselves with these articles on reasonable terms in exchange for the skins of the beaver Otter and Ermin so abundant in their country. they expressed great pleasure at this information and said they had been long anxious to see the whitemen that traded guns; and that we might rest assured of their friendship and that they would do whatever we wished them.

27

The Trail of Tears

John Ross

John Ross (1790–1866), of mixed Cherokee and European ancestry, epitomized the "civilized," literate, and prosperous Native American gentleman farmer of the antebellum South. He fought as an officer under Andrew Jackson against the Creek Indians at Horseshoe Bend and owned a three-hundred-acre plantation and more than twenty slaves. In the years after the War of 1812, the prosperous and rapidly expanding Georgia settler society came into conflict with an equally prosperous and growing Cherokee nation over land. The Cherokee were considered a "civilized tribe" and had developed a representative democratic government based on the U.S. Constitution; built their own schools, roads, and churches; and created an alphabet for use in the fledgling Cherokee press.

The young, educated, and diplomatically astute Ross was pushed forward by older chiefs to represent the growing Cherokee nation to the leaders in Washington. In 1818 Ross was named president of the Cherokee National Committee, and in 1827 upon the death of his mentor, Pathkiller, Ross became the Principal Chief of the United Cherokee Nation, a position he would be elected to ten times during the following forty years.

In 1828 the state of Georgia subjected the Cherokee to direct control, in the hopes of precipitating their removal to less-productive lands in the West. Ross led a legal battle against Georgia and its ally, President Andrew Jackson. He brought his case to Congress and the Supreme Court, but in 1835, a few hundred Cherokee, who had lost faith in Ross's tactics, signed a treaty authorizing removal behind the backs of the roughly 17,000 Cherokee who had elected Ross to represent them. Ratification of the removal act passed in the Senate by one vote and the U.S. Army general responsible resigned his commission in protest, but the removal proceeded according to Andrew Jackson's will.

In 1838 the U.S. Army began what would be called the Trail of Tears, the forced march of the Cherokee to Oklahoma. Thousands died from winter cold and the brutal indifference of the army. In response, Ross convinced the government to allow him to manage his people's journey west. His own wife, Quatie, a full-blooded Cherokee, died during the journey.

QUESTIONS TO CONSIDER

1. How did John Ross argue the case against the removal of the Cherokee in the *Memorial and Petition* submitted to the Senate and House of

Gary E. Moulton, ed., *The Papers of Chief John Ross: Volume I, 1807–1839* (Tulsa: University of Oklahoma Press, 1985), 169–75.

Representatives? What are the chief points he made? How persuasive is his argument?

2. What were the main problems facing Ross in carrying out the removal of his people to the West?

TO THE SENATE AND
HOUSE OF REPRESENTATIVES

Washington City February 22ed 1837

The memorial and petition of the undersigned, a delegation appointed by the Cherokee nation in full council respectfully showeth:

That the Cherokee Nation deeply sensible of the evils under which they are now laboring and the still more frightful miseries which they have too much reason to apprehend, have in the most formal and solemn manner known to them, assembled in General Council to deliberate upon their existing relations with the Government of the United States, and to lay their case with respectful deference before your honorable bodies.

Invested with full powers to conclude an arrangement upon all the matters which interest them we have arrived at the seat of Government, and, in accordance with our usual forms of proceeding have notified the Honorable the Secretary of War [Benjamin F. Butler] that we had reached this place and, through him, solicited an interview with the Executive [Andrew Jackson]. This request has not yet been granted, nor has it to this day received an official answer, but we have reason to apprehend from circumstances which have reached us that we shall be denied this application, and are thus compelled in the discharge of our duty to our constituents, to submit to your Honorable bodies the memorial of which we are the bearers.

On former occasions we have in much detail laid before you the prominent facts of our case. We have reminded you of our long and intimate connexion with the United States, of the scenes of peril and difficulty which we have shared in common; of the friendship which had so long been generously proffered and affectionately and gratefully accepted; of the aids which were supplied us in promoting our advancement in the arts of civilized life, of the political principles which we had imbibed, of the religious faith we have been taught.

We have called your attention to the progress which under your auspices we have made, of the improvements which have marked our social and individual states; our lands brought into cultivation, our natural resources developed, our farms, workshops and factories, approximating in character and value to those of our brethren whose example we had diligently imitated.

A smooth and beautiful prospect of future advancement was opened before us. Our people had abandoned the pursuits, the habits and the tastes of the savage, and had put on the vestments of civilization, of intelligence and of a pure religion. The progress we had made furnished us with the most assured hopes of continued improvement, and we indulged in the anticipation that the time was not far distant when we should be recognised, on the footing of equality by the brethren from whom we had received all which we were now taught to prize.

This promise of golden sunshine is now overspread. Clouds and darkness have obscured its brilliancy. The winds are beginning to mutter their awful forebodings, the tempest is gathering thick and heavy over our heads, and threatens to burst upon us with terrific energy and overwhelming ruin.

In this season of calamity, where can we turn with hope or confidence? On all former occasions of peril or of doubt the Government of the United States spread over us its broad and paternal shield. It invited us to seek an asylum and a protection under its mighty arm. It assisted us with its encouragement and advice, it soothed us with its consoling assurances, it inspired us with hope and gave us a feeling of confidence and security.

But alas! this our long-cherished friend seems now to be alienated from us: this our father has raised his arm to inflict the hostile blow; this strength so long our protection is now exerted against us, and on the wide scene of existence no human aid is left us. Unless you avert your arm we are destroyed. Unless your feelings of affection and compassion are once more awakened towards your destitute and despairing children our annihilation is complete.

It is a natural inquiry among all who commiserate our situation what are the causes which have led to this disastrous revolution, to this entire change of relations? By what agency have such results been accomplished?

We have asked, and we reiterate the question how have we offended? Show us in what manner we have, however unwittingly, inflicted upon you a wrong, you shall yourselves be the judges of the extent and manner of compensation. Show us the offence which has awakened your feelings of justice against us and we will submit to that measure of punishment which you shall tell us we have merited. We cannot bring to our recollections anything we have done or anything we have omitted calculated to awaken your resentment against us.

But we are told a treaty has been made and all that is required at our hands is to comply with its stipulations. Will the faithful historian, who shall hereafter record our lamentable fate, say—the Cherokee Nation executed a treaty by which they freely and absolutely ceded the country in which they were born and educated, the property they had been industriously accumulating and improving, and, abandoning the high road to which they had been advancing from savagism had precipitated themselves into worse than their pristine degradation, will not the reader of such a narrative require the most ample proof before he will credit such a story? Will he not inquire where was the kind and parental guardian who had heretofore aided the weak, assisted the forlorn, instructed the ignorant and elevated the depressed? Where was the Government of the United States with its vigilant care over the Indian when such a bargain was made? How will he be surprised at hearing that the United States was a party to the transaction—that the authority of that Government, and the representatives of that people, which had for years been employed in leading the Cherokees from ignorance to light, from barbarism to civilization, from paganism to christianity, who had taught them new habits and new hopes was the very party which was about to appropriate to itself the fruits of the Indian's industry, the birth places of his children and the graves of his ancestors.

If such a recital could command credence must it not be on the ground that experience had shown the utter failure of all the efforts and the disappointment of all the hopes of the philanthropist and the Christian? That the natives of this favored spot of God's creation were incapable of improvement and unsusceptible of education and that they in wilful blindness, spurning the blessings which had been proffered and urged upon them would pertinaciously prefer the degradation from which it had been attempted to lead them and the barbarism from which it had been sought to elevate them?

How will his astonishment be augmented when he learns that the Cherokee people almost to a man denied the existence and the obligation of the alleged compact—that they proclaimed it to have been based in fraud and concocted in perfidy—that no authority was ever given to those who undertook in their names and on their behalf to negotiate it; that it was repudiated with unexampled unanimity when it was brought to their knowledge; that they denied that it conferred any rights or imposed any obligations.

Yet such must be the story which the faithful historian must record. In the name of the whole Cherokee people we protest against this unhallowed and unauthorized and unacknowledged compact. We deny its binding force. We recognise none of its stipulations. If contrary to every principle of justice it is to be enforced upon us, we shall at least be free from the disgrace of self humiliation. We hold the solemn disavowal of its provisions by eighteen thousand of our people.

We, the regularly commissioned delegation of the Cherokee Nation in the face of Heaven and appealing to the Searcher of all hearts for the truth of our statements ask you to listen to our remonstrances. We implore you to examine into the truth of our allegations. We refer you to your own records, to your own agents, to men deservedly enjoying your esteem and confidence as our witnesses, and we proffer ourselves ready if you will direct the inquiry to establish the truth of what we aver. If we fail to substantiate our statements overwhelm us with ignominy and disgrace. Cast us off from you forever. If however on the other hand every allegation we make shall be sustained by the most convincing and abundant proof, need we make further or stronger appeals than the simple facts of the case will themselves furnish, to secure your friendship, your sympathy and your justice.

We will not and we cannot believe after the long connexion that has subsisted between us, after all that has been done and all that has been promised that our whole nation will be forcibly ejected from their native land and from their social hearths without the pretence of crime, without charge, without evidence, without trial: that we shall be exiled from all that we hold dear and venerable and sacred, and driven into a remote, a strange and a sterile region, without even the imputation of guilt. We will not believe that this will be done by our ancient allies, our friends, our brethren. Yet between this and the abrogation to the pretended treaty there is no medium. Such an instrument so obtained, so contaminated cannot cover the real nature of the acts which it is invoked to sanction. If power is to be exerted let it come unveiled. We shall but submit and die.

Jno Ross

TO MATTHEW ARBUCKLE[1]

Illinois [Cherokee Nation] Apl 23rd 1839

Sir

From the many complaints which are daily made to me by Cherokees who have been recently removed into this country, of their sufferings, from the want of being properly subsisted with provisions, I am constrained to address you this hasty letter. It is reported that, apart from the scantiness of the ration allowed under the contract made on the part of the United States Government with [James] Glasgow & [James] Harrison, many inconveniences have been experienced by the Cherokee people, from the irregularity of proceedings on the part of those employed for carrying out the contract.

It has also been stated that the contractors were only required to furnish "one pound of fresh beef, three half pints of corn & four qts. of salt to every 100 lbs. of beef—or, if they (the contractors) choose they might furnish in lieu of the beef, 3/4 lb. salt pork or bacon provided the Indians will receive it." The beef being poor & not considered wholesome this season of the year, the Cherokees have generally objected to and refused receiving it and have insisted on being furnished with Salt Pork or Bacon in lieu of the beef, but it seems that the contractors do not choose and have refused to comply with the demand; saying that they were only bound to furnish Beef rations. Yet they would commute the ration by paying in money one dollar pr. month for the same. Thus the Cherokees are placed in a situation by compulsion to accept of either the beef or the money offered or to go unsupplied altogether. Here I must beg leave to remark, that previous to the removal of the Cherokees from the East to the West, the subject of providing subsistence for them after their arrival in this country was fully discussed with Major Genl. [Winfield] Scott who communicated with the War Deptmt. in reference to it. And we were afterwards informed by that distinguished officer that the Hon. Secry. of War [Joel R. Poinsett] had decided that the Cherokees should at least for a time be subsisted with provisions in kind, until they could provide for themselves, and then such an arrangement as would be most satisfactory to them should be made with them through Capt. Collins. Now Sir, it is evident from the exorbitant prices of meat and bread stuffs in this country that the Cherokees who have thus been forced to receive commutation in money from the contractors at the rate stated will soon be found in a starving condition—instead of being provided with subsistence as was anticipated and promised them. If the articles of agreement entered

---

1. **Matthew Arbuckle:** Brigadier General Arbuckle was area commander in the Indian Territory.

into with the contractors are to be construed so as to leave it wholly optional with them whether to furnish Salt Pork or Bacon in lieu of Beef, then it is obvious that there were no practical advantage for the interest of the Cherokees to have inserted any clause in that instrument in regard to Salt Pork or Bacon — for its effect has only been and will continue to be to mislead the mind of the people. And how it can be reconciled with the obligations imposed by the contract for the contractors to adopt the mode of commuting the subsistence rations they have engaged to furnish the Cherokees with and that too by a rate fixed by themselves, is a mystery which the Cherokees cannot understand — for it is not pretended that such a right or discretion has ever been given to them by the contract with the agents or the U.S. Govt. for subsisting the Cherokees. Nor can the sacred principle of justice sanction such a course under existing circumstances. Confiding however in the fair intentions of the Government towards them on this subject, the Cherokees still believe that the Hon. Secry. of War will when deemed expedient commute their rations at a rate at least equal to any sum fully ample to purchase provisions with for their comfortable subsistence — and that no sum less will be offered than what others would engage to supply the same for. I beg leave herewith to lay before you copies of sundry letters which I have just received from several leading men on behalf of the Cherokees on this very unpleasant subject. And in conclusion will further remark, that the health and existence of the whole Cherokee people who have recently been removed to this distant country demands a speedy remedy for the inconveniences and evils complained of, & unless a change of the quantity and the kind of rations as well as of the mode of issuing the same, be made from that which has heretofore been granted and observed, the Cherokees must inevitably suffer. Therefore to avoid hunger & starvation they are reduced to the necessity of calling upon you and other officers as the proper representatives of the U.S. Govt. in this matter, to take immediate steps as will ensure the immediate subsistence of the Cherokees who have recently been removed here, with ample and wholesome provisions, until such other arrangements, as may be most satisfactory to them, can be made for subsisting themselves &c. When every thing in reference to the late removal of the Cherokee nation from the East to the West is considered, and seen that it has been consummated through the military authority of the U.S. Govt. I trust you will pardon me for addressing this communication to you, especially when you are assured that the Cherokee people have been taught to expect that justice and protection would be extended to them through the Commanding General in this Hemisphere.

Jno Ross

28

Pulling a Handcart to the Mormon Zion
Priscilla Merriman Evans

*Many of the men and women who settled the Far West often endured extraordinary phys-
ical hardships and dangers to reach their destinations. The Mormon pioneers who walked
from Iowa City, Iowa, to Salt Lake City, Utah, pulling handcarts made of hickory were
driven by both economic and religious motives. The handcart immigrants were poor: if
they could have afforded to migrate any other way, they would have. They spoke one or
more of several languages—German, Welsh, Danish, Swedish—as well as English.
And they did not all have so successful a journey as the pregnant Mrs. Thomas D. Evans.
With her one-legged husband, Priscilla Merriman Evans walked the one thousand miles
in five months, arriving in Salt Lake City in October 1856, comfortably ahead of the winter weather. In two parties later that year, hundreds died in winter blizzards.*

*Nine more handcart companies reached the Mormon Zion in the five years after
the Evanses' journey. All received rich welcomes with prayers and hymns. Priscilla
Merriman Evans concluded her narrative by saying that she always "thanked the Lord
for a contented mind, a home and something to eat."*

QUESTIONS TO CONSIDER

1. Why did Priscilla Merriman Evans become a Mormon and choose to
   emigrate?
2. What were the principal difficulties of the trip to Utah?
3. What rewards did Evans find in "Zion"?

I, Priscilla Merriman Evans, born May 4, 1835 at Mounton New Marbeth,
Pembrokeshire, Wales, am the daughter of Joseph and Ann James Merriman.
About 1839, father moved his family from Mounton up to Tenby, about ten
miles distant. Our family consisted of father, mother, Sarah, aged six, and myself, aged four. Tenby was a beautiful place, as are all those Celtic Islands, with
remains of old castles, vine- and moss-covered walls, gone to ruin since the time
of the Conqueror. . . .

Besides reading, writing, spelling, and arithmetic, we were taught sewing
and sampler making. The sampler work was done in cross stitch, worked in

---

Kate B. Carter, comp., *Heart Throbs of the West*, vol. 9 (Salt Lake City: International Society Daughters of Utah Pioneers), 8–13.

bright colors, on canvas made for that purpose. . . . We were also taught the Bible. I was greatly interested in school, but was taken out at eleven years of age, owing to the illness in our family. I was a natural student, and greatly desired to continue my studies, but mother's health was very poor, so I was taken out to help with the work. . . .

[When] Mother died on the eighth of November 1851 . . . the responsibility of the family rested on my young shoulders. . . . After the death of my mother we were very lonely, and one evening I accompanied my father to the house of a friend. When we reached there, we learned that they were holding a cottage meeting. Two Mormon Elders were the speakers, and I was very much interested in the principles they advocated. I could see that my father was very worried, and would have taken me away, had he known how. When he became aware that I believed in the Gospel as taught by the Elders, I asked him if he had ever heard of the restored Gospel. He replied, "Oh, yes, I have heard of Old Joe Smith, and his Golden Bible." When my father argued against the principles taught by the Elders, I said, "If the Bible is true, then Mormonism is true."

My father was very much opposed to my joining the Church . . . as he thought the Saints were too slow to associate with. . . . But I had found the truth and was baptized into the Church of Jesus Christ of Latter-day Saints in Tenby, February 26, 1852. My sister Sarah took turns with me going out every Sunday. She would go where she pleased on Sunday, while I would walk seven miles to Stepaside and attend the Mormon meeting. My father was very much displeased with me going out every Sunday. He forbade me to read the Church literature, and threatened to burn all I brought home. At the time I had a Book of Mormon borrowed from a friend, and when Father found out I had it, he began looking for it. It was in plain sight, among other books in the book case. I saw him handling it with the other books, and I sent up a silent prayer that he might not notice it, which he did not, although it was before him in plain sight. I do not think my father was as bitter against the principles of the Gospel as he seemed to be, for many times when the Elders were persecuted, he defended them, and gave them food and shelter. But he could not bear the idea of my joining them and leaving home.

About this time, Thomas D. Evans, a young Mormon Elder, was sent up from Merthyr Tydfil, Wales, as a missionary to Pembrokeshire. He was a fine speaker, and had a fine tenor voice, and I used to like to go around with the missionaries and help with the singing. Elder Evans and I seemed to be congenial from our first meeting, and we were soon engaged. He was traveling and preaching the restored Gospel without purse or script. Perhaps his mission will be better understood if I give a little account: [his father had died] and left his mother a widow with eight children, Thomas D. being four years old and the youngest. He was placed in a large forge of two-thousand men at the age of seven years to learn the profession of Iron Roller. At nine years of age, he had the misfortune to lose his left leg at the knee. He went through the courses and graduated as an Iron Roller. When I think of [when they met in 1852] it seems that we had put the world aside, and were not thinking of our worldly pleasures, and what our next dress would be. We had no dancing in those days, but we were happy in the enjoyment of the spirit of the Gospel. . . .

I was familiar with the Bible doctrine, and when I heard the Elders explain it, it seemed as though I had always known it, and it sounded like music in my ears. We had the spirit of gathering and were busy making preparations to emigrate.

About that time the Principle of Plurality of Wives was preached to the world, and it caused quite a commotion in our branch. One of the girls came to me with tears in her eyes and said, "Is it true that Brigham Young has nine wives? I can't stand that, Oh, I can't stand it!" I asked her how long it had been since I had heard her testify that she knew the Church was true, and I said if it was then, it is true now. I told her I did not see anything for her to cry about. After I talked to her awhile, she dried her eyes and completed her arrangements to get married and emigrate. She came with us. My promised husband and I went to Merthyr to visit his Mother, brothers, sisters, and friends, preparatory to emigrating. His family did all in their power to persuade him to remain with them. They were all well off, and his brothers said they would send him to school, support his wife, and pay all of his expenses but all to no avail. He bade them all goodbye, and returned to Tenby.

I think I would have had a harder time getting away, had it not been that my father was going to be married again, and I do not suppose the lady cared to have in the home, the grown daughter who had taken the place of the mother for so many years.

Elder Thomas D. Evans, my promised husband, and I walked the ten miles from Tenby to Pembroke, where we got our license and were married, and walked back to Tenby. We were married on the third of April, 1856. On our return from Pembroke we found a few of our friends awaiting us with supper ready. We visited our friends and relatives and made our preparations to emigrate to Zion. We took a tug from Pembroke to Liverpool, where we set sail on the 17th of April, 1856, on the sailing vessel S.S. *Curling.* Captain Curling said he would prefer to take a load of Saints than others, as he always felt safe with Saints on board. We learned that the next trip across the water that he was loaded with gentiles and his vessel sank with all on board. We were on the sea five weeks; we lived on the ship's rations. I was sick all the way. [Priscilla was then pregnant with their first child.]

We landed in Boston on May 23rd, then travelled in cattle cars . . . to Iowa City. We remained in Iowa City three weeks, waiting for our carts to be made. We were offered many inducements to stay there. My husband was offered ten dollars a day to work at his trade of Iron Roller, but money was no inducement to us, for we were anxious to get to Zion. We learned afterwards that many who stayed there apostatized[1] or died of cholera.

When the carts were ready we started on a three-hundred-mile walk to Winterquarters on the Missouri River. There were a great many who made fun of us as we walked, pulling our carts, but the weather was fine and the roads were excellent and although I was sick and we were tired out at night, we still thought, "This is a glorious way to come to Zion."

---

1. **apostatized:** Having abandoned their faith.

We began our journey of one thousand miles on foot with a handcart for each family, some families consisting of man and wife, and some had quite large families. There were five mule teams to haul the tents and surplus flour. Each handcart had one hundred pounds of flour, that was to be divided and [more got] from the wagons as required. At first we had a little coffee and bacon, but that was soon gone and we had no use for any cooking utensils but a frying pan. The flour was self-raising and we took water and baked a little cake; that was all we had to eat.

After months of travelling we were put on half rations and at one time, before help came, we were out of flour for two days. We washed out the flour sacks to make a little gravy.

There were in our tent my husband with one leg, two blind men . . . a man with one arm, and a widow with five children. The widow, her children, and myself were the only ones who could not talk Welsh. My husband was commissary for our tent, and he cut his own rations short many times to help little children who had to walk and did not have enough to eat to keep up their strength.

The tent was our covering, and the overcoat spread on the bare ground with the shawl over us was our bed. My feather bed, and bedding, pillows, all our good clothing, my husband's church books, which he had collected through six years of missionary work, with some genealogy he had collected, all had to be left in a storehouse. We were promised that they would come to us with the next emigration in the spring, but we never did receive them. It was reported that the storehouse burned down, so that was a dreadful loss to us.

Edward Bunker was the Captain of our Company. His orders of the day were, "If any are sick among you, and are not able to walk, you must help them along, or pull them on your carts." No one rode in the wagons. Strong men would help the weaker ones, until they themselves were worn out, and some died from the struggle and want of food, and were buried along the wayside. It was heart rending for parents to move on and leave their loved ones to such a fate, as they were so helpless, and had no material for coffins. Children and young folks, too, had to move on and leave father or mother or both.

Sometimes a bunch of buffaloes would come and the carts would stop until they passed. Had we been prepared with guns and ammunition, like people who came in wagons, we might have had meat, and would not have come to near starving. President Young[2] ordered extra cattle sent along to be killed to help the sick and weak, but they were never used for that purpose. One incident happened which came near being serious. Some Indians came to our camp and my husband told an Indian who admired me that he could have me for a pony. He was always getting off jokes. He thought no more about it, but in a day or two, here came the Indian with the pony, and wanted his pretty little squaw. It was no joke with him. I never was so frightened in all my life. There was no place to hide, and we did not know what to do. The Captain was called, and they had some difficulty in settling with the Indian without trouble.

---

2. **President Young:** Brigham Young, president of the Church of Jesus Christ of Latter-day Saints from 1847–1877.

In crossing rivers, the weak women and the children were carried over the deep places, and they waded the others. We were much more fortunate than those who came later, as they had snow and freezing weather. Many lost limbs, and many froze to death. President Young advised them to start earlier, but they got started too late. My husband, in walking from twenty to twenty-five miles per day [had pain] where the knee rested on the pad: the friction caused it to gather and break and was most painful. But he had to endure it, or remain behind, as he was never asked to ride in a wagon.

We reached Salt Lake City on October 2, 1856, tired, weary, with bleeding feet, our clothing worn out and so weak we were nearly starved, but thankful to our Heavenly Father for bringing us to Zion. William R. Jones met us on the Public Square in Salt Lake City and brought us to his home in Spanish Fork. I think we were over three days coming from Salt Lake City to Spanish Fork by ox team, but what a change to ride in a wagon after walking 1330 miles from Iowa City to Salt Lake City!

We stayed in the home of an ex-bishop, Stephen Markham. His home was a dugout. It was a very large room built half underground. His family consisted of three wives, and seven children. . . . There was a large fireplace in one end with bars, hooks, frying pans, and bake ovens, where they did the cooking for the large family, and boiled, fried, baked, and heated their water for washing.

There was a long table in one corner, and pole bedsteads fastened to the walls in the three other corners. They were laced back and forth with rawhide cut in strips, and made a nice springy bed. There were three trundle beds, made like shallow boxes, with wooden wheels, which rolled under the mother's bed in the daytime to utilize space. There was a dirt roof, and the dirt floor was kept hard and smooth by sprinkling and sweeping. The bed ticks were filled with straw. . . .

Aunt Mary [Markham] put her two children . . . in the foot of her bed and gave us the trundle bed. . . . How delightful to sleep on a bed again, after sleeping on the ground for so many months with our clothes on. We had not slept in a bed since we left the ship *Sam Curling.*

On the 31st of December, 1856, our first daughter was born. . . . My baby's wardrobe was rather meager: I made one night gown from her father's white shirt, another out of a factory lining of an oilcloth sack. Mrs. Markham gave me a square of homemade linsey for a shoulder blanket, and a neighbor gave me some old underwear, that I worked up into little things. They told me I could have an old pair of jean pants left at the adobe yard. I washed them and made them into petticoats. I walked down to the Indian farm and traded a gold pen for four yards of calico that made her two dresses.

One day my husband went down in the field to cut some willows to burn. The ax slipped and cut his good knee cap. It was with difficulty that he crawled to the house. He was very weak from the loss of blood. My baby was but a few days old, and the three of us had to occupy the trundle bed for awhile.

Wood and timber were about thirty miles up in the canyon, and when the men went after timber to burn, they went in crowds, armed, for they never knew when they would be attacked by Indians. Adobe houses were cheaper than log or frame, as timber was so far away. Many of the people who had lived in the dugouts after coming from Palmyra got into houses before the next winter. They exchanged work with each other, and in that way got along fine. Mr. Markham had an upright saw, run by water. The next spring they got timber from the canyon, and my husband helped Mr. Markham put up a three-roomed house and worked at farming.

He worked for William Markham a year, for which he received two acres of land. I helped in the house, for which, besides the land, we got our board and keep. The next Spring we went to work for ourselves. We saved our two acres of wheat, and made adobes for a two-roomed house, and paid a man in adobes for laying it up. It had a dirt roof. He got timber from Mr. Markham to finish the doors, windows, floors, shelves, and to make furniture. My husband made me a good big bedstead and laced it with rawhides. There were benches and the frames of chairs with the rawhide seat, with the hair left on; a table, shelves in the wall on either side of the fireplace, which was fitted with iron bars and hooks to hang kettles on to boil, frying pans and bake oven. A tick for a bed had to be pieced out of all kinds of scraps, as there were no stores, and everything was on a trade basis.

If one neighbor had something they could get along without, they would exchange it for something they could use. We were lucky to get factory, or sheeting to put up to the windows instead of glass. We raised a good crop of wheat that fall, for which we traded one bushel for two bushels of potatoes. We also exchanged for molasses and vegetables. We had no tea, coffee, meat, or grease of any kind for seasoning. No sugar, milk, or butter. In 1855–1856 the grasshoppers and crickets took the crops and the cattle nearly all died. They were dragged down in the field west [and left to die].

We bought a lot on Main Street, and my husband gave his parents our first little home with five acres of land. They had a good ox team, two cows, a new wagon, and they soon got pigs, chickens and a few sheep. It wasn't long before they were well off. . . .

It was indeed comfortable to be in a good house with a shingled roof and good floors. He set out an orchard of all kinds of fruit; also currents and goose-berries, planted lucern[3] . . . in a patch by itself for cows and pigs. We had a nice garden spot, and we soon had butter, milk, eggs, and meat. We raised our bread, potatoes, and vegetables. While our fruit trees were growing is when the saleratus[4] helped. When I had the babies all about the same size, I could not get out to gather saleratus as others did; so we went with team and wagon, pans, buckets, old brooms, and sacks down on the alkali land, between Spanish Fork and Springville. The smallest children were put under the wagon on a quilt, and the rest of us swept and filled the sacks, and the happiest time was when we were headed for home. The canyon wind seemed always to blow and our faces, hands and eyes were sore for some time after. We took our saleratus over to

---

3. **lucern:** Alfalfa.
4. **saleratus:** A form of baking soda.

Provo, where they had some kind of refining machinery where it was made into soda for bread. It was also used extensively in soap making. We got our pay in merchandise. . . .

. . . My husband had poor luck farming. His farm was in the low land, near the river where the sugar factory now stands. Sometimes it would be high water, sometimes grasshoppers or crickets would take his crop; so he got discouraged with farming, sold his farm and put up a store. We had just got well started in the business and had got a bill of goods, when in the spring of 1875 my husband was called on another mission to England.

Before starting on his mission he sold his team and all available property, also mortgaged our home, for although he was called to travel without purse or scrip,[5] he had to raise enough money to pay his passage and his expenses to his field of labor in Europe. He had too tender a heart for a merchant; he simply could not say no when people came to him with pitiful stories of sickness and privation. He would give them credit, and the consequence was that when he was suddenly called on a mission, the goods were gone and there were hundreds of dollars coming to us from the people, some of which we never got. Everything was left in my hands.

On the 24th of October 1875, after my husband's departure, our daughter Ada was born. . . . I nursed her, along with my little granddaughter Maud, as twins, kept all the books and accounts . . . and was sustained as President and Secretary of the Relief Society Teachers, which office I held through many reorganizations.

During my husband's absence, we had considerable sickness. My little daughter, Mary, came near dying with scarlet fever. To help out, our eldest daughter, Emma, got a position as clerk in the Co-op store. I appreciated that action of the Board very much, as before that time they had not been employing lady clerks and she was the first girl to work in the store. . . .

In 1877, my twelfth child was born. . . . I have had seven daughters and five sons. . . .

My husband's health was not good after his return from his mission. He had pneumonia twice. We sold our home on Main Street, paid off the mortgage and put up a little house on the five acres of land we had given his parents. They had left it to us when they died. We have some of our children as near neighbors and are quite comfortable in our new home.

5. **scrip:** Any paper substitute for money that is not the legal tender of a state.

29

How the West Was Won

An Officer of the "Army of the West"

The Mexican-American War of 1846–1848 was seen by many in the United States as being part of what had been called "our manifest destiny to overspread and to possess the whole of the continent" in an 1845 editorial in John L. O'Sullivan's U.S. Magazine and Democratic Review. *Yet when the Mexican and U.S. governments signed the Treaty of Guadalupe Hidalgo in February 1848, few Americans had a strong understanding of what they had won in the West.*

The Southwest remained something of a mystery to most Americans before, during, and after the war. No one was sure who the eighty thousand former Mexicans inhabiting these lands were, how they felt about becoming Americans, and whether they could ever be fully assimilated. There had always been a smattering of English-speaking Protestants in the West, but most residents there spoke Spanish, adhered in various degrees to Catholicism, and saw themselves as Mexican. Neither the Spanish-colonial government nor the new independent Mexican government had ever successfully tamed this northern frontier or fully integrated its settlers, who received little protection from the Native Americans who raided their towns and livestock and traded stolen animals with the Anglos for guns.

Despite their different language and religion, many Mexicans in the West were clearly amenable to the possibility that American rule might have benefits. Unlike the war being waged in the heart of Mexico by generals Taylor and Scott, the war of the West was won as much by diplomacy and persuasion as it was by military valor. Nevertheless, the conquest of the West had its share of conflicts, such as the rebellion at Taos, New Mexico, and the battles of Los Angeles and Sacramento. This account is by an unnamed officer who participated in the taking of Santa Fe by the U.S. Army. The village of San Miguel, which he mentions, is about one-third of the way from Las Vegas to Santa Fe.

QUESTIONS TO CONSIDER
1. If you were a Spanish-speaking inhabitant of New Mexico, which side of the war would you have supported?
2. What accounted for the different reactions by Spanish-speaking villagers to the arrival of the U.S. Army?

"Diary of an Officer of the 'Army of the West' " in "War with Mexico," *Niles' National Register*, October 10, 1846, 89–91.

3. What stereotypes or assumptions did this author hold regarding the Spanish-speaking inhabitants?

Thursday, August 13.—Started at 12 M., Col. Doniphan's regiment in sight as we left the camp. We soon met the spy company, (Capt. Bent,) who, with his small party, had captured four Mexicans, well mounted and armed. They summoned him and his party to surrender, but the captain told them that he thought their safest plan was to surrender to him.—They prudently consented to do so. They acknowledged themselves sent to ascertain who we were.— They were made prisoners.

One of the Mexicans who was taken day before yesterday, was disarmed and sent forward to his village, distant twenty-four miles, with letters and proclamations. He promised to meet us to-morrow. At eight miles, we came to the establishment of a Mr. Wells, an American. He had an abundance of horses, mules, and cattle. With him was another American, who had been sent from Santa Fe by an American merchant of that place, to inform Gen. Kearney that the Mexicans were 10,000 strong and had determined to meet us fifteen miles this side of Santa Fe, at a deep ravine which they were fortifying. He stated, as his opinion, that not more than 2,000 would be well armed; and also, that they had four pieces of cannon.

The Americans at Santa Fe and other towns are very much alarmed for their safety. The Mexicans tell them, that if defeated, they will return to the towns and villages and take full vengeance on them. . . .

Saturday, Aug. 15.— . . . News reached the general late last night, that we would have a fight to-day in one of the mountain gorges, and our movement has been in a strict military manner. When passing through these narrow defiles, (where an enemy would be most formidable) the word, "draw sabre," was given and passed through at a fast trot. But no enemy has been seen. The infantry passed over the mountain to take them in rear. We passed through several other villages, where the general assembled the inhabitants and proceeded as with the first [telling them that he came by order of the government of the United States to take possession of New Mexico and to extend the laws of the United States over them]. The two last appeared to be happy to be recognized as citizens of the United States, and were seen to embrace each other in token of their joy at the change of government. At the last one, they brought forward their wives to receive the congratulations of the general, (whose manner on such occasions is most happy,) and it was evident that his words had gladdened their hearts, for they smiled upon him in a manner which woman alone knows how to do. We encamped at 4 P.M., in poor grass, having marched seventeen miles.—Captain Cook met us to-day, from Santa Fe, and says Governor Armijo[1] will meet us with an army. He had been kindly treated while in Santa Fe, and smoked a "segarito" from the fair lips of the ladies.

---

1. **Governor Armijo:** General Manuel Armijo was the de facto governor (top official reporting to the governor of Chihuahua) of New Mexico from January 1824 to August 1846.

The villages we have passed to-day are built of sun-burnt bricks. The houses have flat roofs covered with earth, and are dry, and comfortable, from the absence of rain or moisture. Each one has a church, and a grave yard with high walls of sun-burnt brick. There is more intelligence among them than I expected to find, and with a good government and protection from the Indians, they will become a happy people.

The Eutaws have recently stolen their stock and carried off several children. Well may they hail this revolution as a blessing. One of the Alcaldes[2] said to-day, that God ruled the destinies of men, and that as we had come with a strong army among them to change their form of government, it must be right, and he submitted cheerfully. Major Swords and Lieutenant Gillman brought us the mail to the 19th of July, and many a heart was made glad by tidings from wives, mothers, children, and dearly beloved ones. There are plenty of cattle, sheep, and goats in the country, and we shall fare well enough.

Sunday, August 16. Started at the usual hour, and at seven miles came to the village of St. Miguel, built like the others, of sun-burned brick, and with flat roofs. After much delay the Alcalde and Padre were found, and presented to General Kearney, but it was evident that they did not relish an interview with him. This village contains a respectable church and about two or three hundred houses. The general expressed a wish to ascend one of the houses, with the priest and Alcalde, and to address the people of the town, informing them of the object of his mission. After many evasions, delays, and useless speeches, the Padre made a speech, stating that "he was a *Mexican*, but should obey the laws that were placed over him for *the time*, but if the general should point all his cannon at his breast, he could not consent to go up there and address the people."

The general very mildly told him, through the interpreter, Mr. Robideau, that he had not come to injure him, nor did he wish him to address the people. He only wished him to go up there and hear him (the general) address them. The Padre still fought shy, and commenced a long speech which the general interrupted, and told him, he had no time to listen to "useless remarks," and repeated that he only wanted him to go up and listen to his speech. He consented. The general made pretty much the same remarks to the Alcalde and people, that he had made to the people of the other villages. He assured them that he had an ample force and would have possession of the country against all opposition, but gave them assurances of the friendship and protection of the United States. He stated to them that this had never been given them by the government of Mexico, but the United States were able and would certainly protect them, not only in their persons, property, and religion, but against the cruel invasion of the Indians. That they saw but a small part of the force that was at his disposal. Many more troops were near him on another road (some of which he showed them a mile or two distant) and that another army would, probably, be through their village in three weeks. After this, he said, "Mr. Alcalde, are you willing to take the oath of allegiance to the United States." He replied that "he would prefer waiting till the general had taken possession of the capital." The

2. **Alcaldes:** Mayors.

general told him, "it was sufficient for him to know that he had possession of his village." He then consented and with the usual formalities, he said, "You swear that you will bear true allegiance to the government of the United States of America." The Alcalde said, "provided I can be protected in my religion." The general said, "I swear you shall be." He then continued, "and that you will defend her against all her enemies and opposers, in the name of the Father, Son, and Holy Ghost—Amen."

The general then said, "I continue you as the Alcalde of this village, and require you, the inhabitants of this village to obey him as such. Your laws will be continued for the present, but as soon as I have time to examine them, if any change can be made that will be for your benefit, it shall be done." After shaking hands with them he left. The Padre then invited him to his house, and gave him and his staff refreshments; and after sundry hugs, jokes, and professions of friendship, with an expression from the general, that, "the better they became acquainted the better friends they would be," and an invitation to the Padre to visit him at Santa Fe (which he promised), we left the village. The Padre was evidently the ruling spirit of the village, and the Alcalde was under great restraint by his presence. The visit to the priest, and the frank and friendly manner of the general had the desired effect, and I believe they parted the best of friends, and have no doubt that the inhabitants of St. Miguel will soon be as good democrats as can be found in Missouri.

The Alcalde informed the general that 400 men left the village to join the Mexican army, but that two hundred had returned home.

Soon after leaving this village an express arrived from Santa Fe, informing the general that a large force would oppose his march 15 miles from that place, in a deep ravine. It was headed by an individual known as Salazar. That Gen. Armijo refused to command them, and said he would defend the town. The same information was soon after brought by Puebla Indians, who said there was a large force of their people among the Mexicans, armed with bows and arrows; that their people had been forced into the service, and their chiefs would not permit them to take their guns.

As it is not more than two days march to Santa Fe, if we have to fight it will probably be to-morrow.—Marched 17 miles.

Monday, Aug. 17.—Started at the usual time. Our picket guard took a prisoner, the son of the noted Salazar, well remembered by the Texan prisoners for his cruelties to them. He stated that the Mexican army had left the cannon and gone home. The general told him he would keep him a prisoner, and if he found that he had told him falsely, he would hang him. We soon met others from Santa Fe, who congratulated the general on his arrival in the country, and their deliverance from the tyrannical rule of Armijo.

They further said, that Armijo had taken one hundred dragoons and his cannon, and gone this morning towards Chihuahua. We passed to-day the ruins of the ancient town of Pecos. I visited it with some Mexicans, and an interpreter, who gave me a full account of it. It was said to have been built long before the conquest. It stands on an eminence. The dwellings were built of small stones and mud; some of the buildings are still so far perfect as to show three full stories. There were four rooms under ground, fifteen feet deep and twenty-five feet across in a circular form. In one of these rooms, burned the "holy fire," which was kindled many centuries before the conquest; and when the Pecos Indians were converted to the Catholic faith they still continued their own religious rites, and among them the "sacred fire," which never ceased to burn till seven years since, when the village was broken up. The population is probably one thousand. The church is large, and although in ruins, was evidently a fine building. It was built after the conquest. The eastern roof of the main building is still good—it is filled with birds. As we came in front of it the Mexicans took off their hats, and on entering the building we did the same.

The general learned to-day that Salazar had been in command at the cannon, and that he had passed around us and gone to St. Miguel, the town we passed yesterday. The general sent him word that he had his son a prisoner, and would treat him well, if the father remained peaceable, but if he took up arms, or excited the people to resistance, he would hang him.

We encamped at 3 P.M., on the Pecos creek, in excellent grass, where there was a beautiful farm well watered—distance to-day fifteen and three quarter miles.

An abundance of vegetables have been brought into camp this evening, and we have fared better than since we left Missouri. Bread, coffee, and bacon are excellent articles of food, when accompanied with other little "fixings" which ladies can only provide us with, but of themselves, after a few weeks, campaigners become a little tired.

An American gentleman has just arrived in camp from Santa Fe; he left at 12 M. to-day, and says that after the governor's abdication, the Alcaldes held a meeting, and *gravely* discussed the propriety of tearing down the churches to prevent their being converted into barracks, and that the American citizens interfered and assured them that they had nothing to fear on that subject; and thereby saved the churches. A lady also sent for him this morning, and asked him if he did not think it advisable for her to leave the town, with her daughters, to save them from dishonor. He advised her by all means to remain at home, and assured her that she and her daughters were in no danger from the approach of the army.

Most of the respectable people of the town have left, and many country people are going to town for protection.

Tuesday, August 18. — Started as usual and at six miles came to the cannon, where the Mexican army under Armijo had been assembled. There had been 3,000 troops there, but it seems that the nearer we approach them, the fewer they became, and when we passed through they had all gone. The position they chose was near the lower end, and it was one of great strength. The passage was not more than forty feet wide—in front they had made an obstruction with timber, and beyond this, at 300 yards distance, was an eminence in the road, on which their cannon had been placed; and it was thought by us, that their position was equal to 5,000 men. We reached the hill which overlooks Santa Fe at 5 P.M. Major Clark's artillery was put into line, and the mounted troops and infantry were marched through the town to the Palace (as it is called) on the public square, whether [*sic*, where] the general and his staff dismounted, and were received by the acting governor and other dignitaries and conducted to a large room.

30

Life in California before the Gold Discovery
Guadalupe Vallejo et al.

People often say that California could be the fifth wealthiest nation on Earth, but it was once just an isolated part of the Mexican northern frontier. The few Americans who journeyed there before the completion of the transcontinental railroad in 1868 faced many weeks at sea traveling around the southern tip of South America. The Spanish began to settle California in 1769 in response to a growing Russian presence near what is now San Francisco. They converted natives; built four presidios *(forts) at San Diego, Monterey, San Francisco, and Santa Barbara; and set up a system of missions and civil pueblos (towns), but California was still a distant outpost.*

Like the Spanish-speaking Tejanos *who were born and raised in Texas, the ranchers and their servants in* Alta California *had little connection to the government in Mexico City. At independence in 1821, they ceased to be Spanish, but remained isolated from Mexico, calling themselves* Californios. *Also like the Tejanos, they watched as the 1820s, 1830s, and 1840s brought a steady stream of English-speaking settlers into their lives.*

When the United States declared war on Mexico in May 1846, it was uncertain whether the Californios *would side with the United States, with Mexico, or would try to create their own* Republica de California. *Jose Castro, their Mexico City–appointed governor, issued an edict proclaiming all land acquisitions by settlers who were not naturalized Mexicans to be null and void. Anglo settlers organized an armed resistance, and on June 9, 1846, took Mexican general Mariano Vallejo prisoner, lowered the Mexican flag at the center of town, and raised the "Bear Flag," proclaiming a "California Republic."*

The U.S. Army, which had been hoping to win over the Californios *and avoid war in the West, was forced to back "the Bears," as they came to be known. The California Republic lasted for only a month, not enough time to create the kind of nationalist identity the Texans formed with their Alamo martyrs; founding fathers; national congress; and diverse Spanish, English, Mexican, French, and Native American citizenry.*

The Mexican War ended in 1848 with the Treaty of Guadalupe Hidalgo. Mexico lost most of what is now the western United States, but the treaty guaranteed linguistic, cultural, and property rights for Mexicans within this vast territory. Few of these property rights were respected, and Mexicans, Chicanos, and Anglos in the western states continue to debate over linguistic and cultural issues. However, California has remained

---

"Life in California before the Gold Discovery," *The Century Magazine*, December 1890, 183, 189, 192–93, 464–76.

a meeting ground for Latino and Anglo peoples and cultures. The May 2005 election of Antonio Villaraigosa as mayor of Los Angeles brought comparisons to earlier periods in the history of that city, which had had Latino mayors until 1872.

The following documents are from aging Californios, remembering life before the 1846 "Bear Flag Revolt" and the 1849 gold rush brought tens of thousands of immigrants to California. The first account is by Guadalupe Vallejo, who was the nephew of the general taken prisoner by "the Bears." The subsequent three accounts are by daughters of some of the important Mexican ranching families, many of whom lost land, animals, and social status to the newly arrived Anglo settlers.

QUESTIONS TO CONSIDER

1. How did the changes brought about by the gold rush and by becoming part of the United States affect what these *Californios* wrote and what they remembered about life in Mexican California?
2. How did these *Californios* feel about the arrival of Americans?
3. Some time in the late nineteenth century, *Californios* seem to have disappeared as a group. What might have happened to them?

GUADALUPE VALLEJO

Ranch and Mission Days in Alta California

It seems to me that there never was a more peaceful or happy people on the face of the earth than the Spanish, Mexican, and Indian population of Alta California before the American conquest. We were the pioneers of the Pacific coast, building towns and Missions while General Washington was carrying on the war of the Revolution, and we often talk together of the days when a few hundred large Spanish ranches and Mission tracts occupied the whole country from the Pacific to the San Joaquin. No class of American citizens is more loyal than the Spanish Californians, but we shall always be especially proud of the traditions and memories of the long pastoral age before 1840. Indeed, our social life still tends to keep alive a spirit of love for the simple, homely, outdoor life of our Spanish ancestors on this coast, and we try, as best we may, to honor the founders of our ancient families, and the saints and heroes of our history since the days when Father Junípero planted the cross at Monterey.

The leading features of old Spanish life at the Missions, and on the large ranches of the last century, have been described in many books of travel, and with many contradictions. I shall confine myself to those details and illustrations of the past that no modern writer can possibly obtain except vaguely, from hearsay, since they exist in no manuscript, but only in the memories of a generation that is fast passing away. My mother has told me much, and I am still more indebted to my illustrious uncle, General Vallejo, of Sonoma, many of whose recollections are incorporated in this article.

When I was a child there were fewer than fifty Spanish families in the region about the bay of San Francisco, and these were closely connected by ties of blood or intermarriage. My father and his brother, the late General Vallejo, saw, and were a part of, the most important events in the history of Spanish California, the revolution and the conquest. My grandfather, Don Ygnacio Vallejo, was equally prominent in his day, in the exploration and settlement of the province. The traditions and records of the family thus cover the entire period of the annals of early California, from San Diego to Sonoma.

What I wish to do is to tell, as plainly and carefully as possible, how the Spanish settlers lived, and what they did in the old days. The story will be partly about the Missions, and partly about the great ranches. . . .

A number of trappers and hunters came into Southern California and settled down in various towns. There was a party of Kentuckians, beaver-trappers, who went along the Gila and Colorado rivers about 1827, and then south into Baja California to the Mission of Santa Catalina. Then they came to San Diego, where the whole country was much excited over their hunter clothes, their rifles, their traps, and the strange stories they told of the deserts, and fierce Indians, and things that no one in California had ever seen. Captain Paty was the oldest man of the party, and he was ill and worn out. All the San Diego people were very kind to the Americans. It is said that the other Missions, such as San Gabriel, sent and desired the privilege of caring for some of them. Captain Paty grew worse, so he sent for one of the fathers and said he wished to become a Catholic, because, he added, it must be a good religion, for it made everybody so good to him. Don Pio Pico and Doña Victoria Dominguez de Estudillo were his sponsors. After Captain Paty's death the Americans went to Los Angeles, where they all married Spanish ladies, were given lands, built houses, planted vineyards, and became important people. Pryor repaired the church silver, and was called "Miguel el Platero."[1] Laughlin was always so merry that he was named "Ricardo el Buen Mozo."[2] They all had Spanish names given them besides their own. One of them was a blacksmith, and as iron was very scarce he made pruning shears for the vineyards out of the old beaver traps.

On Christmas night, 1828, a ship was wrecked near Los Angeles, and twenty-eight men escaped. Everybody wanted to care for them, and they were given a great Christmas dinner, and offered money and lands. Some of them staid, and some went to other Missions and towns. One of them who staid was a German, John Gronigen, and he was named "Juan Domingo," or, because he was lame, "Juan Cojo."[3] Another, named Prentice, came from Connecticut, and he was a famous fisherman and otter hunter. After 1828 a good many other Americans came in and settled down quietly to cultivate the soil, and some of them became very rich. They had grants from the governor, just the same as the Spanish people.

It is necessary, for the truth of the account, to mention the evil behavior of many Americans before, as well as after, the conquest. At the Mission San José there is a small creek, and two very large sycamores once grew at the Spanish ford, so that it was called *la aliso*.[4] A squatter named Fallon, who lived near the

---

1. **Miguel el Platero:** Miguel the Silversmith.
2. **Ricardo el Buen Mozo:** Ricardo the Good Guy.
3. **Juan Cojo:** Limping Juan.
4. *la aliso:* The alder.

crossing, cut down these for firewood, though there were many trees in the canon. The Spanish people begged him to leave them, for the shade and beauty, but he did not care for that. This was a little thing, but much that happened was after such pattern, or far worse.

In those times one of the leading American squatters came to my father, Don J. J. Vallejo, and said: "There is a large piece of your land where the cattle run loose, and your vaqueros[5] have gone to the gold mines. I will fence the field for you at my expense if you will give me half." He liked the idea, and assented, but when the tract was inclosed the American had it entered as government land in his own name, and kept all of it. In many similar cases American settlers in their dealings with the rancheros took advantage of laws which they understood, but which were new to the Spaniards, and so robbed the latter of their lands. Notes and bonds were considered unnecessary by a Spanish gentleman in a business transaction, as his word was always sufficient security.

Perhaps the most exasperating feature of the coming-in of the Americans was owing to the mines, which drew away most of the servants, so that our cattle were stolen by thousands. Men who are now prosperous farmers and merchants were guilty of shooting and selling Spanish beef "without looking at the brand," as the phrase went. My father had about ten thousand head of cattle, and some he was able to send back into the hills until there were better laws and officers, but he lost the larger part. . . .

PRUDENCIA HIGUERA

Trading with the Americans

In the autumn of 1840 my father lived near what is now called Pinole Point, in Contra Costa County, California. I was then about twelve years old, and I remember the time because it was then that we saw the first American vessel that traded along the shores of San Pablo Bay. One afternoon a horseman from the Peraltas, where Oakland now stands, came to our ranch, and told my father that a great ship, a ship "with two sticks in the center," was about to sail from Yerba Buena into San Pablo and Suisun, to buy hides and tallow.

The next morning my father gave orders, and my brothers, with the peons, went on horseback into the mountains and smaller valleys to round up all the best cattle. They drove them to the beach, killed them there, and salted the hides. They tried out the tallow in some iron kettles that my father had bought from one of the Vallejos, but as we did not have any barrels, we followed the common plan in those days. We cast the tallow in round pits about the size of a cheese, dug in the black adobe and plastered smooth with clay. Before the melted tallow was poured into the pit an oaken staff was thrust down in the center, so that by the two ends of it the heavy cake could be carried more easily. By working very hard we had a large number of hides and many pounds of tallow ready on the beach when the ship appeared far out in the bay and cast anchor near another point two or three miles away. The captain soon came to our

5. **vaqueros:** Cowboys.

landing with a small boat and two sailors, one of whom was a Frenchman who knew Spanish very well, and who acted as interpreter. The captain looked over the hides, and then asked my father to get into the boat and go to the vessel. Mother was much afraid to let him go, as we all thought the Americans were not to be trusted unless we knew them well. We feared they would carry my father off and keep him a prisoner. Father said, however, that it was all right; he went and put on his best clothes, gay with silver braid, and we all cried, and kissed him good-by, while mother clung about his neck and said we might never see him again. Then the captain told her: "If you are afraid, I will have the sailors take him to the vessel, while I stay here until he comes back. He ought to see all the goods I have, or he will not know what to buy." After a little my mother let him go with the captain, and we stood on the beach to see them off. Mother then came back, and had us all kneel down and pray for father's safe return. Then we felt safe.

He came back the next day, bringing four boat-loads of cloth, axes, shoes, fish-lines, and many new things. There were two grindstones and some cheap jewelry. My brother had traded some deerskins for a gun and four tooth-brushes, the first ones I had ever seen. I remember that we children rubbed them on our teeth till the blood came, and then concluded that after all we liked best the bits of pounded willow root that we had used for brushes before. After the captain had carried all the hides and tallow to his ship he came back, very much pleased with his bargain, and gave my father, as a present, a little keg of what he called Boston rum. We put it away for sick people.

After the ship sailed my mother and sisters began to cut out new dresses, which the Indian women sewed. On one of mine mother put some big brass buttons about an inch across, with eagles on them. How proud I was! I used to rub them hard every day to make them shine, using the tooth-brush and some of the pounded egg-shell that my sisters and all the Spanish ladies kept in a box to put on their faces on great occasions. . . .

AMALIA SIBRIAN

A Spanish Girl's Journey from Monterey to Los Angeles

Early in the winter of 1829 my father, who had long expected an appointment under the governor, received a letter from Los Angeles saying that his papers were in the hands of the authorities there, and would only be delivered in person. He decided to take my mother and myself with him and go overland, without waiting for the yearly vessel from Yerba Buena which would soon be due at Monterey, where we were staying. It was nearly Christmas when we began the journey. Word was sent ahead by a man on horseback to some of the smaller ranches at which we meant to stop, so that we were expected. A young American who had reached the coast with letters from the city of Mexico heard of our plans, and came to my father to ask if he might travel with us to Los Angeles, which was easily arranged. He did not know a word of Spanish, and I have often laughed at some of his experiences on the road, owing to his ignorance of our ways and speech. At one house the señora gave him some fruit, whereupon he handed her two reals, which she let fall on the floor in surprise, while the old don, her husband, fell upon his knees and said in Spanish, "Give us no money, no money at all; everything is free in a gentleman's house!" A young lady who was present exclaimed in great scorn, "*Los Engleses pagor por todos!*" ("The English pay for everything.") I afterward told the American what they had said, and explained the matter as well as I could, but he thought it a foolish thing that no one, not even servants, would take money for services. We several times met grown people, and heads of families, who had never heard any language except Spanish, and who did not know, in fact, that any other language existed. They were really afraid of our American, and once I was asked if there were any other people like him.

Our route took us up the Salinas Valley and over the mountains to the coast valleys and the Missions. At San Miguel we found everything prepared for a jubilee over the prosperous year. The men walked about and fired off their carbines and home-made fire works, while the padres' servant swung a burning oaken brand in the air, and lighted a few rockets. Inside the church the Indian choir was singing. We saw it all, until about ten o'clock that night; then the alcalde[6] of the village came with fresh horses, and we went on, as it was very pleasant traveling.

The young American picked up some words in Spanish; he could say "*Gracios,*" "*Si, señor,*" and a few other phrases. One day we passed a very ugly Indian woman, and he asked me how to ask her how old she was. Out of mischief I whispered, "*Yo te amor,*"[7] which he said at once, and she, poor creature, immediately rose from her seat on the ground and replied, "*Gracios, Señor, pero soy indio*" ("but I am an Indian"), which gave us sport till long after. The next day our companion gave me a lesson in English by way of revenge. It was the day before Christmas, and we had reached San Buenaventura. It was a holiday for every one. After mass all the men and boys assembled on horseback in front of the church, with the padre and the alcalde at their head. They rode about in circles like a circus, fired guns, beat drums, and shouted. I thought it was very fine, and by signs I asked my American friend how he liked it, and he answered, "Damfools!" with such energy that I supposed they were words of praise. Indeed, I used the bad words as very proper English for a year or two, until I learned better, when I was of course much mortified.

When near Los Angeles we had the nearest approach to an adventure of our whole journey. We spent the night at a ranch-house. As I was the young lady of the party, the hostess gave up her own private room to me. At the end of it was an alcove with a window, and in front of the window stood a shrine, with wax figures of the holy Virgin and the child Christ. Before them were vases, and fresh wild-flowers from the hills—the golden poppies, the first blue "baby eyes," and the white "star-flowers," that bloom at Christmas time.

To judge from appearances the only shrine to which our host was devoted was the cockpit, for the courtyard of the adobe was fairly lined with rows of the "blooded birds" so popular at that time with many wealthy rancheros, each one

6. **alcalde:** Mayor.
7. *Yo te amor:* I love you.

tied to a stake by his leg, and being trained for the battlefield. The young American, who, like many other foreigners, took up with our bad customs more easily than with our good ones, was greatly delighted when he saw the rows of fighting cocks in the yard. He offered to buy one, but the owner thought them too precious to sell. At last, by signs, he wagered a dollar on the homeliest of the lot. The host, accepting the wager, released his favorite. Instead of fighting, the two birds went through the window into the room I had occupied, and that with such force that there was a crash, and a mixture of feathers, wax saints, and flowers on the floor. Our host turned pale, and rushed in to disentangle his pets, while the American jumped up and down on a porch, shouting, "*Bueno! bueno!*" The birds were now fighting in earnest, but the host separated them, gave them to a servant, mounted the saddled horse which always stood ready, day or night, and, with a faint "*Adios*" to me, disappeared. He knew what he was about, as events proved, for the rage of his wife when she saw the broken shrine was something terrible. The moment she came on the scene she cried out, "Where is he?" and going into the inner courtyard she began to release the game-cocks, which hastened to hide in the nearest shelter. The next morning, when we took our departure, the master of the house had not yet returned, and the mistress was endeavoring to restore the shrine.

BRIGIDA BRIONES

A Glimpse of Domestic Life in 1827

The ladies of Monterey in 1827 were rarely seen in the street, except very early in the morning on their way to church. We used to go there attended by our servants, who carried small mats for us to kneel upon, as there were no seats. A tasteful little rug was considered an indispensable part of our belongings, and every young lady embroidered her own. The church floors were cold, hard, and damp, and even the poorer classes managed to use mats of some kind, usually of tule woven by the Indians.

The dress worn in the mornings at church was not very becoming; the *rebozo*[8] and the petticoat being black, always of cheap stuff, and made up in much the same way. All classes wore the same; the padres told us that we must never forget that all ranks of men and women were equal in the presence of the Creator, and so at the morning service it was the custom to wear no finery whatever. One mass was celebrated before sunrise, for those whose duties compelled them to be at work early; later masses took place every hour of the morning. Every woman in Monterey went daily to church, but the men were content to go once a week.

For home wear and for company we had many expensive dresses, some of silk, or of velvet, others of laces, often of our own making, which were much liked. In some families were imported laces that were very old and valuable. The rivalry between beauties of high rank was as great as it could be in any

8. *rebozo:* Shawl.

country, and much of it turned upon attire, so that those who had small means often underwent many privations in order to equal the splendor of the rich.

Owing to the unsettled state of affairs for a generation in Mexico and in all the provinces, and the great difficulty of obtaining teachers, most of the girls of the time had scanty educations. Some of my playmates could speak English well, and quite a number knew something of French. One of the gallants of the time said that "dancing, music, religion, and amiability" were the orthodox occupations of the ladies of Alta California. Visitors from other countries have said many charming things about the manners, good health, and comeliness of these ladies, but it is hardly right for any of us to praise ourselves. The ladies of the province were born and educated here; here they lived and died, in complete ignorance of the world outside. We were in many ways like grown-up children.

Our servants were faithful, agreeable, and easy to manage. They often slept on mats on the earthen floor, or, in the summer time, in the courtyards. When they waited on us at meals we often let them hold conversations with us, and laugh without restraint. As we used to say, a good servant knew when to be silent and when to put in his *cuchara* (or spoon).

31

Miners during the California Gold Rush

Daguerreotype by
Joseph B. Starkweather

The United States was a sparsely populated and largely rural country in the nineteenth century, with large amounts of uncultivated land and frequent labor shortages in its growing industrial sector. For this reason, through most of the nineteenth century, no significant legal restrictions prevented immigrants from simply coming and staying. In fact, some states and companies advertised in Europe to attract immigrants. All this changed with the California gold rush and the arrival of the Chinese on the West Coast.

The nineteenth century was a time of movement and migration. Throughout the world, political change and agricultural crises drove people to cross continents and oceans looking for higher wages and new economic opportunities, and the discovery of gold in California in late 1848 brought tens of thousands of migrants from all over the United States and the far corners of the world. In a matter of months, California had more immigrants than anywhere else in the United States. Until 1860, leaving China was a violation of imperial law that was punishable by death. However, one of the first forty-niners (named after 1849, the first full year of the gold rush) to strike it rich was a Chinese prospector named Chum Ming, whose tale of overnight wealth inspired thousands of Chinese to bribe ship captains and port officials to let them escape a country that had been defeated by the British in the Opium Wars and was declining into political and economic crisis.

Once in California, Chinese immigrants faced a cold welcome. In 1850, nativist attempts to exclude immigrant prospectors yielded the California Foreigner Miners License Law. In a multiethnic state, with little formal record keeping and a population composed of Spanish-speaking Californios, multilingual Native Americans, migrants from eastern states (many of whom were foreign born), and a dizzying array of people who fit into several of these categories, it was often difficult to determine who was foreign and who was not. However, one thing everyone agreed on was that the Chinese were foreigners and they wound up paying nearly eighty-five percent of all the license fees collected by the state of California.

As initial gold fever dissipated with the exhaustion of surface gold and prospecting fees cut into Chinese miners' incomes, those who stayed in California went in search of other work or started small businesses in the booming San Francisco–area economy.

Head of Auburn Ravine, 1852. Courtesy of the California History Room, California State Library, Sacramento, California.

Despite much prejudice, they were tolerated as long as the economy was growing and there were jobs for all. A change in Chinese law that enabled migration to the United States, along with the need for laborers to construct the transcontinental railroad in 1864, brought many more Chinese to America and opened opportunities for Chinese businesses and jobs in the shadow of the Central Pacific Railroad, which at one time had roughly ten thousand Chinese in its employ.

The following image is from a daguerreotype made by Joseph B. Starkweather in 1852 at the head of Auburn Ravine in California. It depicts white and Chinese miners standing next to a sluice box, which was used to sort gold from rock and dirt by means of running water.

QUESTIONS TO CONSIDER

1. Many historians have stressed the tremendous isolation that Chinese Americans lived under in their first one hundred years in the United States. In what ways does this photograph confirm or contradict this view?

2. Do you think these "forty-niners" are prospecting together or separately? What evidence can you find to support your view?

3. How might ethnicity have been important in deciding how these miners shared the sluice, the work, and the gold?

Miners during the California gold rush, daguerreotype by Joseph B. Starkweather.

PART FIVE

An Age of Reform

Rearranging Social Patterns

During the second quarter of the nineteenth century, new social forces swept through the American villages, farms, and regions that had once existed in near isolation, disrupting traditional ways of work and life. The transportation revolution overcame barriers of distance, as highways, canals, steamships, and railroads linked and transformed established communities and existing markets. Farmers and craftspeople, inventors and factory owners, learned new ways to shape and dominate the physical world. Enterprises like the Lowell Mills introduced new methods of work as well as novel forms of social organization that changed the lives of workers like Mary Paul. The growing public school system inculcated common ideas and goals in young American minds, while evangelical Protestantism labored to purify souls.

The numerous reform movements of the time also represented a determination to perfect the republic of the founding fathers and, if possible, the lands beyond the nation's borders. In their search for social perfection, a few reformers questioned the foundations of capitalism. Some turned to religious or social experiments designed to reshape society. Most aimed at correcting specific problems. Reformers sometimes disagreed on goals and methods because they responded to contradictory moods: some feared what they saw as disorder in society, loss of community, and declining morality; others acted on an optimistic faith in the ultimate perfectibility of the world in general and American society in particular.

As the nation slid toward Civil War, however, the crusade against slavery came to dominate American reform. Slaves themselves generated much of the heat that ignited the fierce controversy. Nat Turner's rebellion in 1831 ushered in an angrier era. Henry "Box" Brown was a slave who executed one of the most famous escapes from slavery in history. He wrote an account of his life under slavery, and publicized the abolitionist cause as an entertainer and entrepreneur. Ex-slave Harriet Jacobs described her sexual exploitation at the hands of her owners. Such testimonies provided the growing abolition movement with support for its arguments against the institution of slavery. White reformers like William Lloyd Garrison, whose newspaper the *Liberator* began publication in the same year as Nat Turner's rebellion, made Southern leaders fearful of economic disaster by insisting on immediate abolition. As antislavery sentiment grew in the North, images of slaves and of the institution of slavery assumed an increasingly stark character, as the visual portfolio "Slavery and Freedom" (pages 251–60) illustrates. By 1856, Americans like John Brown were already taking up arms in Kansas over the question of slavery and freedom. And most of the early leaders of the women's rights movement had their first taste of organizing, petitioning, and public speaking in the antislavery movement. From this beginning, Elizabeth Cady Stanton, Susan B. Anthony, and others pioneered a women's rights movement that over many years would markedly affect the lives of American women.

POINTS OF VIEW
Nat Turner's Rebellion (1831)

32

A Slave Insurrection
Nat Turner

Slave owners, especially those in areas with large slave populations, lived in dread of uprisings. Rebellions in 1739 in South Carolina, in 1800 in Virginia, in 1811 in Louisiana, and in 1822 in South Carolina kept such fears alive. Nat Turner (1800–1831), a slave in Southampton County, Virginia, led the most sensational rebellion in 1831. Beginning on August 21, Turner's rebellion lasted only five days, but it claimed the lives of at least fifty whites. In response, terrified white Southerners gunned down slaves and free blacks and increased restrictions on slaves' education, marriage, and freedom to gather together. The rebellion also dealt a serious blow to any chance of the South's voluntarily emancipating its slaves.

The Confessions of Nat Turner was published in 1832 by Thomas R. Gray, who interviewed Turner shortly before he was tried and executed. Gray had interviewed several other slaves who had been involved in the uprisings and he was clearly aware of the great commercial potential for a Turner manuscript. He personally believed that

The Confessions of Nat Turner, Leader of the Late Insurrection in Southampton, Virginia, as Fully and Voluntarily Made to Thomas R. Gray (1832; New York, 1964), 5–17.

Turner was a dangerous fanatic and may have shaped the account in a sensational manner to make the manuscript more saleable.

QUESTIONS TO CONSIDER

1. What was Nat Turner's revelation? What purpose did he consider himself destined to fulfill?
2. How well planned was the rebellion? Why did it fail?
3. What did Turner and his compatriots expect to achieve by their rebellion?
4. Historians have speculated about which parts of the text are authentically Turner's and which parts represent the voice of Thomas Gray. Can you identify any differences?

Agreeable to his own appointment, on the evening he was committed to prison, with permission of the jailer, I visited Nat on Tuesday the first of November, when, without being questioned at all, he commenced his narrative in the following words:

Sir,

You have asked me to give a history of the motives which induced me to undertake the late insurrection, as you call it. To do so I must go back to the days of my infancy, and even before I was born. I was thirty-one years of age the second of October last, and born the property of Benjamin Turner, of this county. In my childhood a circumstance occurred which made an indelible impression on my mind, and laid the groundwork of that enthusiasm which has terminated so fatally to many both white and black, and for which I am about to atone at the gallows. It is here necessary to relate this circumstance—trifling as it may seem, it was the commencement of that belief which has grown with time, and even now, sir, in this dungeon, helpless and forsaken as I am, I cannot divest myself of. Being at play with other children, when three or four years old, I was telling them something, which my mother overhearing, said it had happened before I was born. I stuck to my story, however, and related some things which went in her opinion to confirm it. Others being called on were greatly astonished, knowing that these things had happened, and caused them to say in my hearing, I surely would be a prophet, as the Lord had shown me things that had happened before my birth. And my father and mother strengthened me in this my first impression, saying in my presence, I was intended for some great purpose, which they had always thought from certain marks on my head and breast.

My grandmother, who was very religious, and to whom I was much attached—my master, who belonged to the church, and other religious persons who visited the house, and whom I often saw at prayers, noticing the singularity of my manners, I suppose, and my uncommon intelligence for a child, remarked I had too much sense to be raised—and if I was, I would never be of any service to any one—as a slave. The manner in which I learned to read and write, not only had great influence on my own mind, as I acquired it with the most perfect ease, so much so that I have no recollection whatever of learning the alphabet—but to the astonishment of the family, one day, when a book was shown me to keep me from crying, I began spelling the names of different objects—this was a source of wonder to all in the neighborhood, particularly the blacks—and this learning was constantly improved at all opportunities. When I got large enough to go to work, while employed, I was reflecting on many things that would present themselves to my imagination. I was not addicted to stealing in my youth, nor have never been. Yet such was the confidence of the Negroes in the neighborhood, even at this early period of my life, in my superior judgment, that they would often carry me with them when they were going on any roguery, to plan for them. Growing up among them, with this confidence in my superior judgment, and when this, in their opinions, was perfected by divine inspiration, from the circumstances already alluded to in my infancy, and which belief was ever afterward zealously inculcated by the austerity of my life and manners, which became the subject of remark by white and black. By this time, having arrived to man's estate, and hearing the Scriptures commented on at meetings, I was struck with that particular passage which says: "Seek ye the kingdom of Heaven and all things shall be added unto you." I reflected much on this passage, and prayed daily for light on this subject. As I was praying one day at my plough, the spirit spoke to me, saying "Seek ye the kingdom of Heaven and all things shall be added unto you." *Question*—What do you mean by the Spirit? *Answer*—The Spirit that spoke to the prophets in former days—and I was greatly astonished, and for two years prayed continually, whenever my duty would permit—and then again I had the same revelation, which fully confirmed me in the impression that I was ordained for some great purpose in the hands of the Almighty. Several years rolled round, in which many events occurred to strengthen me in this my belief. . . . I began to direct my attention to this great object, to fulfill the purpose for which, by this time, I felt assured I was intended. Knowing the influence I had obtained over the minds of my fellow servants, (not by the means of conjuring and such like tricks—for to them I always spoke of such things with contempt) but by the communion of the Spirit whose revelations I often communicated to them, and they believed and said my wisdom came from God.

And on the twelfth of May 1828, I heard a loud noise in the heavens, and the Spirit instantly appeared to me and said the Serpent was loosened, and Christ had laid down the yoke he had borne for the sins of men, and that I should take it on and fight against the Serpent, for the time was fast approaching, when the first should be last and the last should be first. *Question*—Do you not find yourself mistaken now? *Answer*—Was not Christ crucified? And by signs in the heavens that it would make known to me when I should commence the great work—and until the first sign appeared, I should conceal it from the knowledge of men—and on the appearance of the sign (the eclipse of the sun last February), I should arise and prepare myself, and slay my enemies with their own weapons. And immediately on the sign appearing in the heavens, the seal was removed from my lips, and I communicated the great work laid out for me to do, to four in whom I had the greatest confidence (Henry, Hark, Nelson, and Sam). It was intended by us to have begun the work of death on the fourth of July last. Many were the plans formed and rejected by us, and it affected my mind to such a degree that I fell sick, and the time passed without our coming to any determination how to commence — still forming new schemes and rejecting them when the sign appeared again, which determined me not to wait longer.

Since the commencement of 1830, I had been living with Mr. Joseph Travis, who was to me a kind master, and placed the greatest confidence in me; in fact, I had no cause to complain of his treatment to me. On Saturday evening, the twentieth of August, it was agreed between Henry, Hark, and myself to prepare a dinner the next day for the men we expected, and then to concert a plan, as we had not yet determined on any. Hark on the following morning brought a pig, and Henry brandy, and being joined by Sam, Nelson, Will, and Jack, they prepared in the woods a dinner, where, about three o'clock, I joined them. . . .

I saluted them on coming up, and asked Will how came he there; he answered his life was worth no more than others, and his liberty as dear to him. I asked him if he thought to obtain it? He said he would or lose his life. This was enough to put him in full confidence. Jack, I knew, was only a tool in the hands of Hark. It was quickly agreed we should commence at home (Mr. J. Travis') on that night, and until we had armed and equipped ourselves, and gathered sufficient force, neither age nor sex was to be spared (which was invariably adhered to). We remained at the feast until about two hours in the night, when we went to the house and found Austin; they all went to the cider press and drank, except myself. On returning to the house, Hark went to the door with an ax, for the purpose of breaking it open, as we knew we were strong enough to murder the family, if they were awakened by the noise; but reflecting that it might create an alarm in the neighborhood, we determined to enter the house secretly, and murder them while sleeping. Hark got a ladder and set it against the chimney, on which I ascended, and hoisting a window, entered and came down stairs, unbarred the door, and removed the guns from their places. It was then observed that I must spill the first blood. On which armed with a hatchet, and accompanied by Will, I entered my master's chamber; it being dark, I could not give a death blow, the hatchet glanced from his head, he sprang from the bed and called his wife, it was his last word. Will laid him dead, with a blow of his ax, and Mrs. Travis shared the same fate, as she lay in bed. The murder of this family, five in number, was the work of a moment, not one of them awoke; there was a little infant sleeping in a cradle, that was forgotten, until we had left the house and gone some distance, when Henry and Will returned and killed it. We got here four guns that would shoot, and several old muskets, with a pound or two of powder. We remained some time at the barn, where we paraded; I formed them in a line as soldiers, and after carrying them through all the maneuvers I was master of, marched them off to Mr. Salathul Francis', about six hundred yards distant. Sam and Will went to the door and knocked. Mr. Francis asked who was there, Sam replied it was him, and he had a letter for him, on which he got up and came to the door; they immediately seized him, and dragging him out a little from the door, he was dispatched by repeated blows on the head; there was no other white person in the family. We started from there for Mrs. Reese's, maintaining the most perfect silence on our march, where finding the door unlocked, we entered, and murdered Mrs. Reese in her bed, while sleeping; her son awoke, but it was only to sleep the sleep of death, he had only time to say who is that, and he was no more. From Mrs. Reese's we went to Mrs. Turner's, a mile distant, which we reached about sunrise on Monday morning. Henry, Austin, and Sam went to the still, where, finding Mr. Pebbles, Austin shot him, and the rest of us went to the house; as we approached, the family discovered us, and shut the door. Vain hope! Will, with one stroke of his ax, opened it, and we entered and found Mrs. Turner and Mrs. Newsome in the middle of a room almost frightened to death. Will immediately killed Mrs. Turner, with one blow of his ax. I took Mrs. Newsome by the hand, and with the sword I had when I was apprehended, I struck her several blows over the head, but not being able to kill her, as the sword was dull. Will turning around and discovering it, dispatched her also. A general destruction of property and search for money and ammunition always succeeded the murders. By this time my company amounted to fifteen, and nine men mounted, who started for Mrs. Whitehead's (the other six were to go through a byway to Mr. Bryant's and re-join us at Mrs. Whitehead's). . . . As we pushed on to the house, I discovered someone running round the garden, and thinking it was some of the white family, I pursued them, but finding it was a servant girl belonging to the house, I returned to commence the work of death, but they whom I left had not been idle; all the family were already murdered, but Mrs. Whitehead and her daughter Margaret. As I came round to the door I saw Will pulling Mrs. Whitehead out of the house, and at the step he nearly severed her head from her body, with his broad ax. Miss Margaret, when I discovered her had concealed herself in the corner, formed by the projection of the cellar cap from the house; on my approach she fled, but was soon overtaken, and after repeated blows with a sword, I killed her by a blow on the head with a fence rail. By this time, the six who had gone by Mr. Bryant's rejoined us, and informed me they had done the work of death assigned them. We again divided, part going to Mr. Richard Porter's and from thence to Nathaniel Francis', the others to Mr. Howell Harris', and Mr. T. Doyle's. On my reaching Mr. Porter's, he had escaped with his family. I understood there that the alarm had already spread.

I proceeded to Mr. Levi Waller's, two or three miles distant. I took my station in the rear, and as it was my object to carry terror and devastation wherever we went, I placed fifteen or twenty of the best armed and most to be relied on in front, who generally approached the houses as fast as their horses could run; this was for two purposes, to prevent their escape and strike terror to the inhabitants—on this account I never got to the houses, after leaving Mrs. Whitehead's, until the murders were committed, except in one case. I sometimes got in sight in time to see the work of death completed, viewed the mangled bodies as they lay, in silent satisfaction, and immediately started in quest of other victims. Having murdered Mrs. Waller and ten children, we started for Mr. William Williams'—having killed him and two little boys that were there; while engaged in this, Mrs. Williams fled and got some distance from the house, but she was pursued, overtaken, and compelled to get up behind one of the company, who brought her back, and after showing her the mangled body of her lifeless husband, she was told to get down and lay by his side, where she was shot dead. I then started for Mr. Jacob Williams', where the family were murdered. Here we found a young man named Drury, who had come on business with Mr. Williams. He was pursued, overtaken, and shot. Mrs. Vaughan's was the next place we visited—and after murdering the family here, I determined on starting for Jerusalem. Our number amounted now to fifty or sixty, all mounted and armed with guns, axes, swords, and clubs. On reaching Mr. James W. Parker's gate, immediately on the road leading to Jerusalem, and about three miles distant, it was proposed to me to call there, but I objected, as I knew he was gone to Jerusalem, and my object was to reach there as soon as possible; but some of the men having relations at Mr. Parker's it was agreed that they might call and get his people. I remained at the gate on the road, with seven or eight; the others going across the field to the house, about half a mile off. After waiting some time for them, I became impatient, and started to the house for them, and on our return we were met by a party of white men, who had pursued our blood-stained track and who had fired on those at the gate and dispersed them, which I knew nothing of, not having been at that time rejoined by any of them. Immediately on discovering the whites, I order my men to halt and form, as they appeared to be alarmed. The white men, eighteen in number, approached us in about one hundred yards, when one of them fired.

I then ordered my men to fire and rush on them; the few remaining stood their ground until we approached within fifty yards, when they fired and retreated. We pursued and overtook some of them who we thought we left dead; after pursuing them about two hundred yards, and rising a little hill, I discovered they were met by another party, and had halted, and were reloading their guns, thinking that those who retreated first, and the party who fired on us at fifty or sixty yards distant, had all only fallen back to meet others with ammunition. As I saw them reloading their guns, and more coming up than I saw at first, and several of my bravest men being wounded, the others became panic struck and squandered over the field; the white men pursued and fired on us several times. Hark had his horse shot under him, and I caught another for him as it was running by me; five or six of my men were wounded, but none left on the field; finding myself defeated here I instantly determined to go through a private way, and cross the Nottoway River at the Cypress Bridge, three miles below Jerusalem, and attack that place in the rear, as I expected they would look for me on the other road, and I had a great desire to get there to procure arms and ammunition. After going a short distance in this private way, accompanied by about twenty men, I overtook two or three who told me the others were dispersed in every direction. After trying in vain to collect a sufficient force to proceed to Jerusalem, I determined to return, as I was sure they would make back to their old neighborhood, where they would rejoin me, make new recruits, and come down again. On my way back, I called at Mrs. Thomas's, Mrs. Spencer's, and several other places. The white families having fled, we found no more victims to gratify our thirst for blood, we stopped at Major Ridley's quarter for the night, and being joined by four of his men, with the recruits made since my defeat, we mustered now about forty strong. After placing out sentinels, I laid down to sleep, but was quickly roused by a great racket. Starting up, I found some mounted, and others in great confusion; one of the sentinels having given the alarm that we were about to be attacked, I ordered some to ride round and reconnoiter, and on their return the others being more alarmed, not knowing who they were, fled in different ways, so that I was reduced to about twenty again; with this I determined to attempt to recruit, and proceed on to rally in the neighborhood I had left. Dr. Blunt's was the nearest house, which we reached just before day; on riding up the yard, Hark fired a gun. We expected Dr. Blunt and his family were at Major Ridley's, as I knew there was a company of men there; the gun was fired to ascertain if any of the family were at home; we were immediately fired upon and retreated leaving several of my men. I do not know what became of them, as I never saw them afterward. Pursuing our course back, and coming in sight of Captain Harris's, where we had been the day before, we discovered a party of white men at the house, on which all deserted me but two (Jacob and Nat), we concealed ourselves in the woods until near night, when I sent them in search of Henry, Sam, Nelson, and Hark, and directed them to rally all they could at the place we had had our dinner the Sunday before, where they would find me, and I accordingly returned there as soon as it was dark, and remained until Wednesday evening, when discovering white men riding around the place as though they were looking for someone, and none of my men joining me, I concluded Jacob and Nat had been taken, and compelled to betray me. On this I gave up all hope for the present; and on Thursday night, after having supplied myself with provisions from Mr. Travis's, I scratched a hole under a pile of fence rails in a field, where I concealed myself for six weeks, never leaving my hiding place but for a few minutes in the dead of night to get water, which was very near; thinking by this time I could venture out, I began to go about in the night and eavesdrop the houses in the neighborhood; pursuing this course for about a fortnight and gathering little or no intelligence, afraid of speaking to any human being, and returning every morning to my cave before the dawn of day. I know not how long I might have led this life, if accident had not betrayed me, a dog in the neighborhood passing by my hiding place one night while I was out was attracted by some meat I had in my cave, and crawled in and stole it, and was coming out just as I returned. A few nights after, two Negroes having started to go hunting with the same dog, and passed that way, the dog came again to the place, and having just gone out to walk about, discovered me and barked, on which, thinking myself discovered, I spoke to them to beg concealment. On making myself known, they fled from me. Knowing then they would betray me, I immediately left my hiding place, and was pursued almost incessantly until I was taken a fortnight afterward by Mr. Benjamin Phipps, in a little hole I had dug out with my sword, for the purpose of concealment, under the top of a fallen tree. On Mr. Phipps discovering the place of my concealment, he cocked his gun and aimed at me. I requested him not to shoot, and I would give up, upon which he demanded my sword. I delivered it to him, and he brought me to prison. During the time I was pursued, I had many hair breadth escapes, which your time will not permit you to relate. I am here loaded with chains, and willing to suffer the fate that awaits me.

[Gray:] I here proceeded to make some inquiries of him, after assuring him of the certain death that awaited him, and that concealment would only bring destruction of the innocent as well as guilty, of his own color, if he knew of any extensive or concerted plan. His answer was, I do not. When I questioned him as to the insurrection in North Carolina happening about the same time, he denied any knowledge of it.

33

Who Is to Blame?

William Lloyd Garrison et al.

Nat Turner's rebellion occurred just when slavery was under attack from other quarters. In 1829, a free black man named David Walker published his incendiary Walker's Appeal in Four Articles, Together with a Preamble to the Colored Citizens of the World, But in Particular and Very Expressly to Those of the United States of America, *which quoted the Declaration of Independence in justification of a slave insurrection. Then William Lloyd Garrison (1805–1879), who would also cite the Declaration of Independence, broke with the tradition among white abolitionists of calling for gradual emancipation. From the first issue of the* Liberator, *published in Boston on January 1, 1831, Garrison demanded the immediate and unconditional abolition of slavery.*

The Southern states reacted viscerally to Nat Turner's rebellion. In the immediate hysteria, slaves and free blacks were gunned down. The ongoing debate in Virginia over gradual emancipation ended. Instead, the Southern states moved toward strengthening the slave system by restricting the rights of free blacks as well as the right of owners to free slaves, augmenting the patrols that constricted the mobility of the slave population, setting limits on black religious meetings, and ensuring that marriage did not restrict the slave trade. And they moved on many fronts to close the South to antislavery propaganda, touching off a national debate by forbidding the federal postal service from delivering antislavery writings such as the Liberator *in Southern states.*

QUESTIONS TO CONSIDER
1. Did William Lloyd Garrison approve of Nat Turner's rebellion? How did he explain its occurrence and what comparisons did he draw to explain it to his readers?
2. Did John Hampden Pleasants, editor of the Richmond *Constitutional Whig*, approve of the treatment of blacks in the wake of the rebellion? How did he explain its occurrence?

William E. Cain, ed., *William Lloyd Garrison and the Fight against Slavery* (Boston: Bedford/St. Martin's, 1995), 80; *Constitutional Whig*, Richmond, Virginia, September 3, 1831; the original of Floyd's letter to Hamilton can be found in the Manuscript Division of the Library of Congress.

3. How did Virginia governor John Floyd explain the rebellion? What did he propose to avoid further uprisings?

WILLIAM LLOYD GARRISON

The Liberator, *September 3, 1831*

What we have so long predicted,—at the peril of being stigmatized as an alarmist and declaimer,—has commenced its fulfilment. The first step of the earthquake, which is ultimately to shake down the fabric of oppression, leaving not one stone upon another, has been made. The first drops of blood, which are but the prelude to a deluge from the gathering clouds, have fallen. The first flash of the lightning, which is to smite and consume, has been felt. The first wailings of a bereavement, which is to clothe the earth in sackcloth, have broken upon our ears. . . .

You have seen, it is to be feared, but the beginning of sorrows. All the blood which has been shed will be required at your hands. At your hands alone? No—but at the hands of the people of New-England and of all the free states. The crime of oppression is national. The south is only the agent in this guilty traffic. But, remember! the same causes are at work which must inevitably produce the same effects; and when the contest shall have again begun, it must be again a war of extermination. In the present instance, no quarters have been asked or given.

But we have killed and routed them now—we can do it again and again— we are invincible! A dastardly triumph, well becoming a nation of oppressors. Detestable complacency, that can think, without emotion, of the extermination of the blacks! We have the power to kill *all*—let us, therefore, continue to apply the whip and forge new fetters!

In his fury against the revolters, who will remember their wrongs? What will it avail them, though the catalogue of their sufferings, dripping with warm blood fresh from their lacerated bodies, be held up to extenuate their conduct? It is enough that the victims were black—that circumstance makes them less precious than the dogs which have been slain in our streets! They were black— brutes, pretending to be men—legions of curses upon their memories! They were black—God made them to serve us!

Ye patriotic hypocrites! ye panegyrists[1] of Frenchmen, Greeks, and Poles! ye fustian[2] declaimers for liberty! ye valiant sticklers for equal rights among yourselves! ye haters of aristocracy! ye assailants of monarchies! ye republican nullifiers! ye treasonable disunionists! be dumb! Cast no reproach upon the conduct of the slaves, but let your lips and cheeks wear the blisters of condemnation!

Ye accuse the pacific friends of emancipation of instigating the slaves to revolt. Take back the charge as a foul slander. The slaves need no incentives at our hands. They will find them in their stripes—in their emaciated bodies—in their ceaseless toil—in their ignorant minds—in every field, in every valley, on

1. **panegyrists:** People who celebrate a person, group, or deed.
2. **fustian:** Pretentious, pompous.

every hill-top and mountain, wherever you and your fathers have fought for liberty—in your speeches, your conversations, your celebrations, your pamphlets, your newspapers—voices in the air, sounds from across the ocean, invitations to resistance above, below, around them! What more do they need? Surrounded by such influences, and smarting under their newly made wounds, is it wonderful[3] that they should rise to contend—as other "heroes" have contended—for their lost rights? It is *not* wonderful.

In all that we have written, is there aught to justify the excesses of the slaves? No. Nevertheless, they deserve no more censure than the Greeks in destroying the Turks, or the Poles in exterminating the Russians, or our fathers in slaughtering the British. Dreadful, indeed, is the standard erected by worldly patriotism!

For ourselves, we are horror-struck at the late tidings. We have exerted our utmost efforts to avert the calamity. We have warned our countrymen of the danger of persisting in their unrighteous conduct. We have preached to the slaves the pacific precepts of Jesus Christ. We have appealed to christians, philanthropists and patriots, for their assistance to accomplish the great work of national redemption through the agency of moral power—of public opinion—of individual duty. How have we been received? We have been threatened, proscribed, vilified and imprisoned—a laughing-stock and a reproach. Do we falter, in view of these things? Let time answer. If we have been hitherto urgent, and bold, and denunciatory in our efforts,—hereafter we shall grow vehement and active with the increase of danger. We shall cry, in trumpet tones, night and day,—Wo to this guilty land, unless she speedily repent of her evil doings! The blood of millions of her sons cries aloud for redress! IMMEDIATE EMANCIPATION can alone save her from the vengeance of Heaven, and cancel the debt of ages!

JOHN HAMPDEN PLEASANTS

Constitutional Whig, *September 3, 1831*

We have been astonished since our return from Southampton (whither we went with Capt. Harrison's Troop of Horse) in reading over the mass of exchange papers accumulated in our absence, to see the number of false, absurd, and idle rumors, circulated by the Press, touching the insurrection in that county. Editors seem to have applied themselves to the task of alarming the public mind as much as possible by persuading the slaves to entertain a high opinion of their strength and consequences. While truth is always the best policy, and best remedy, the exaggerations to which we have alluded are calculated to give the slaves false conceptions of their numbers and capacity, by exhibiting the terror and confusion of the whites, and to induce them to think that practicable, which they see is so much feared by their superiors.

We have little to say of the Southampton Tragedy beyond what is already known. The origin of the conspiracy, the prime agents, its extent and ultimate

---

3. **wonderful:** Worthy of being wondered at; surprising.

direction, is matter of conjecture.—The universal opinion in that part of the country is that Nat, a slave, a preacher, and a pretended prophet was the first [blurred word], the actual leader, and the most remorseless of the executioners. According to the evidence of a negro boy whom they carried along to hold their horses, Nat commenced the scene of murder at the first house (Travis') with his own hand. Having called upon two others to make good their valiant boasting, so often repeated, of what they would do, and these shrinking from the requisition, Nat proceeded to dispatch one of the family with his own hand. Animated by the example and exhortations of their leader, having a taste of blood and convinced that they had now gone too far to recede, his followers dismissed their doubts and became as ferocious as their leader wished them. To follow the [blurred word] capture of Travis' house early that day, to their dispersion at Parker's cornfield early in the afternoon, when they had traversed near 20 miles, murdered 63 whites, and approached within 3 or 4 miles of the Village of Jerusalem; the immediate object of their movement—to describe the scenes at each house, the circumstances of the murders, the hair breadth escapes of the few who were lucky enough to escape—would prove as interesting as heart rending. Many of the details have reached us but not in so authentic a shape as to justify their publication, nor have we the time or space. Let a few suffice. Of the event at Dr. Blount's we had a narrative from the gallant old gentleman himself, and his son, a lad about 15, distinguished for his gallantry and modesty, and whom we take leave to recommend to Gen. Jackson, for a warrant in the Navy or at West Point. The Doctor had received information of the insurrection, and that his house would be attacked a short time before the attack was made. Crippled with the gout, and indisposed to leave, he decided to defend his home. His force was his son, overseer and three other white men. Luckily there were six guns, and plenty of powder and shot in the house. These were barely loaded, his force posted, and the instructions given, when the negroes from 15 to 30 strong, rode up about day break. The Doctor's orders were that each man should be particular in his aim and should fire one at a time; he himself reserved one gun, resolved if the house was forced to sell his life as dearly as he could. The remaining five fired in succession upon the assailants, at the distance of fifteen or twenty steps. The blacks, upon the fifth fire, retreated, leaving one killed (we believe) and one wounded (a fellow named Hark,) and were pursued by the Doctor's negroes with shouts and execrations. Had the shot been larger, more execution doubtless would have been done.

Mrs. Vaughan's was among the last houses attacked. A venerable negro woman described the scene which she had witnessed with great emphasis: it was near noon and her mistress was making some preparations in the porch for dinner, when happening to look towards the road she discerned a dust and wondered what it could mean. In a second, the negroes mounted and armed, rushed into view, and making an exclamation indicative of her horror and agony, Mrs. Vaughan ran into the house.—The negroes dismounted and ran around the house, pointing their guns at the doors and windows. Mrs. Vaughan appeared at a window, and begged for her life, inviting them to take everything she had. The prayer was answered by one of them firing at her, which was followed by another, and a fatal, shot. In the meantime, Miss Vaughan, who was upstairs, and unappraised of the terrible advent until she heard the noise of the attack, rushed down, and begging for her life, was shot as she ran a few steps from the door. A son of Mrs. Vaughan, about 15, was at the still house, when hearing a gun and conjecturing, it is supposed, that his brother had come from Jerusalem, approached the house and was shot as he got over the fence. It is difficult for the imagination to conceive a situation so truly and horribly awful, as that in which these unfortunate ladies were placed. Alone, unprotected, and unconscious of danger, to find themselves without a moment's notice for escape or defence, in the power of a band of ruffians, from whom instant death was the least they could expect! In a most lively and picturesque manner, did the old negress describe the horrors of the scene; the blacks riding up with imprecations, the looks of her mistress, white as a sheet, her prayers for her life, and the actions of the scoundrels environing the house and pointing their guns at the doors and windows, ready to fire as occasion offered. When the work was done they called for drink, and food, and becoming nice, damned the brandy as vile stuff.

The scene at Vaughan's may suffice to give an idea of what was done at the other houses. A bloodier and more accursed tragedy was never acted, even by the agency of the tomahawk and scalping knife. Interesting details will no doubt be evolved in the progress of the trials and made known to the public.

It is with pain we speak of another feature of the Southampton Rebellion; for we have been most unwilling to have our sympathies for the sufferers diminished or affected by their misconduct. We allude to the slaughter of many blacks, without trial, and under circumstances of great barbarity. How many have thus been put into death (generally by decapitation or shooting) reports vary; probably however some five and twenty and from that to 40; possibly a yet larger number. To the great honor of General Eppes, he used every precaution in his power, and we hope and believe with success, to put a stop to the disgraceful procedure.—We met with one individual of intelligence, who stated that he himself had killed between 10 and 15. He justified himself on the grounds of the barbarities committed on the whites. . . .

The numbers engaged in the insurrection are variously reported. They probably did not exceed 40 or 50, and were fluctuating from desertions and new recruits. About fifty are in Southampton jail, some of them on suspicion only.— We trust and believe that the intelligent magistracy of the county, will have the firmness to oppose the popular passions, should it be disposed to involve the innocent with the guilty, and to take suspicion for proof.

The presence of the troops from Norfolk and Richmond alone prevented retaliation from being carried much farther.

At the date of Capt. Harrison's departure from Jerusalem, Gen. Nat had not been taken. On that morning, however, Dred, another insurgent chief, was brought prisoner to Jerusalem, having surrendered himself to his master, in the apprehension, no doubt, of starving in the swamps or being shot by the numerous parties of local militia, who were in pursuit. Nat had not certainly been heard from since the skirmish in Parker's cornfield, which was in fact, the termination of the insurrection; the negroes after that dispersing themselves, and making no further attempt. He is represented as a shrewd fellow, reads, writes, and preaches;

and by various artifices had acquired great influence over the minds of the wretched beings whom he has led into destruction. It is supposed that he induced them to believe that there were only 80,000 whites in the country, who, being exterminated, the blacks might take possession. Various of his tricks to acquire and preserve influence had been mentioned, but they are not worth repeating. If there was any ulterior purpose, he probably alone knows it. For our own part, we still believe there was none; and if he be the intelligent man represented, we are incapable of conceiving the arguments by which he persuaded his own mind of the feasibility of his attempt, or how it could possibly end but in certain destruction. We therefore incline to the belief that he acted upon no higher principle than the impulse of revenge against the whites, as the enslavers of himself and his race; that, being a fanatic, he possibly persuaded himself that Heaven would interfere; and that he may have convinced himself, as he certainly did his deluded followers to some extent, that the appearance of the sun some weeks ago, prognosticated something favorable to their cause. We are inclined to think that the solar phenomenon exercised considerable influence in promoting the insurrection; calculated as it was to impress the imaginations of the ignorant.

A more important inquiry remains—whether the conspiracy was circumscribed to the neighborhood in which it broke out, or had its ramifications through other counties. We, at first, adopted the first opinion; but there are several circumstances which favor the latter. We understand that the confessions of all the prisoners go to show that the insurrection broke out too soon, as it is supposed, in consequence of the last day of July being a Sunday, and not, as the negroes in Southampton believed, the Saturday before. The report is that the rising was fixed for the fourth Sunday in August, and that they supposing Sunday, the 31st of July to be the first Sunday in August, they were betrayed into considering the 3d Sunday as the 4th. This is the popular impression founded upon confessions, upon the indications of an intention of the negroes in Nansemond and other places to unite, and upon the allegation that Gen. Nat extended his preaching excursions to Petersburg and this city; allegations which we, however, disbelieve. It is more than probable, nevertheless, that the mischief was concerted and concocted under the cloak of religion. The trials which are now proceeding in Southampton, Sussex, and elsewhere, will develop all the truth. We suspect the truth will turn out to be that the conspiracy was confined to Southampton, and that the idea of its extensiveness originated in the panic which seized upon the South East of Virginia.

GOVERNOR JOHN FLOYD OF VIRGINIA

Letter to Governor James Hamilton Jr. of South Carolina

Richmond
November 19, 1831

Sir:

I received your letter yesterday and with great pleasure will give you my impressions freely—

I will notice this affair in my annual message, but here only give a very careless history of it, as it appeared to the public—

I am fully persuaded, the spirit of insubordination which has, and still manifests itself in Virginia, had its origin among, and eminated from, the Yankee population, upon their *first* arrival amongst us, but mostly especially the Yankee pedlers and traders.

The course has been by no means a direct one—they began first, by making them religious—their conversations were of that character—telling the blacks, God was no respecter of persons—the black man was as good as the white—that all men were born free and equal—that they cannot serve two masters—that the white people rebelled against England to obtain freedom, so have the blacks a right to do.

In the mean time, I am sure without any purpose of this kind, the preachers, principally Northern—were very assidious in operating upon our population, day and night, they were at work—and religion became, and is, the fashion of the times—finally our females and of the most respectable were persuaded that it was piety to teach negroes to read and write, to the end that they might read the *Scriptures*—many of them became tutoresses in Sunday schools and, pious distributors of tracts, from the New York Tract Society.

At this point, more active operations commenced—our magistrates and laws became more inactive—large assemblages of negroes were suffered to take place for religious purposes—Then commenced the efforts of the black preachers, often from the pulpits these pamphlets and papers were read—followed by the incendiary publications of Walker,[4] Garrison and Knapp[5] of Boston, these too with songs and hymns of a similar character were circulated, read and commented upon—We resting in apathetic security until the Southampton affair.

From all that has come to my knowledge during and since this affair—I am fully convinced that every black preacher in the whole country east of the Blue Ridge was in the secret, that the plans as published by those Northern presses were adopted and acted upon by them—that their congregations, as they were called knew nothing of this intended rebellion, except a few leading and intelligent men, who may have been head men in the Church—*the mass* were prepared by making them aspire to an equal station by such conversations as I have related as the first step.

I am informed that they had settled the form of government to be that of white people, whom they intended to cut off to a man—with the difference that the preachers were to be their Governors, Generals and Judges. I feel fully justified to myself, in believing the Northern incendiaries, tracts, Sunday Schools, religion and reading and writing has accomplished this end.

I shall in my annual message recommend that laws be passed—To confine the Slaves to the estates of their masters—prohibit negroes from preaching—absolutely to drive from this State all free negroes—and to substitute the surplus

---

4. **Walker:** David Walker, a free black man whose published writing justified slave insurrection.
5. **Knapp:** Isaac Knapp, abolitionist editor and associate of William Lloyd Garrison.

revenue in our Treasury annually for slaves, to work for a time upon our Rail Roads etc etc and these sent out of the country, preparatory, or rather as the first step to emancipation—This last point will of course be tenderly and cautiously managed and will be urged or delayed as your State and Georgia may be disposed to co-operate.

In relation to the extent of this insurrection I think it greater than will ever appear—the facts will as now considered, appear to be these—It commenced with Nat and nine others on Sunday night—two o'clock, we date it, Monday morning before day and ceased by the dispersion of the negroes on Tuesday morning at ten o'clock—During this time the negroes had murdered sixty one persons, and traversed a distance of twenty miles, and increased to about seventy slave men—they spared but one family and that one was so wretched as to be in all respects upon a par with them—all died bravely indicating no reluctance to loose [sic] their lives in such a cause.

> I am Sir,
> with consideration and respect
> Your obt Sevnt
> John Floyd

His Excy
James Hamilton, Jr.
Governor of South Carolina

FOR CRITICAL THINKING

1. Examine the language of *The Confessions of Nat Turner.* Can you identify parts that seem to be the language expected of a Virginia lawyer like Thomas Gray and parts that you might imagine to be Nat Turner's own words?

2. Compose a defense of his actions as you think Nat Turner might have presented it.

3. Why did many people link Turner's rebellion with the writings of William Lloyd Garrison? What does that say about their view of the slaves? What was Garrison's response to this linking?

4. Compose a possible reply from South Carolina governor James Hamilton Jr. to Governor Floyd's letter.

34

The Lowell Textile Workers
Mary Paul

Traditionally, improvements in agricultural techniques have lowered food prices for con-
sumers, making each new generation of family-farmers more vulnerable to financial
downturns. Nineteenth-century America was no exception, with countless stories of young
men seeking their fortune out West or in the big city. What is often forgotten is that many
young women also left family farms, because declining incomes, a dearth of marriageable
young men, and little cultural stimulation drove them to work in factories like the one
owned by Francis Cabot Lowell, where fifteen-year-old Mary Paul started work in 1845.

Lowell, a New England industrialist, pioneered the celebrated Lowell–Waltham
system in Massachusetts in the 1820s, which recruited young farm women to his textile
factories, while guaranteeing their families that their moral conduct would be upheld.
"Lowell girls," as they were called, were paid much lower wages than were men, but
were provided accommodation in carefully chaperoned boardinghouses and required to
attend church as part of the conditions of their employment.

Lowell became fabulously wealthy from his experiment, helping to fuel the pre–Civil
War cloth boom in New England and the industrialization of America. Women workers
like Mary Paul typically felt liberated by the freedom of making their own income and
living independently, but often became disillusioned by the seventy-three-hour average
working week, overcrowded boardinghouses, and strict rules.

In the 1830s, Lowell reduced wages in response to growing competition from France
and England. The Lowell girls fought back, becoming some of America's first and most
militant labor leaders. They organized strikes in 1834 and 1836 and founded the Fac-
tory Girls Association and the Lowell Female Labor Reform Association. They gained
great community support and contributed to the success of the ten-hour workday move-
ment. However, they struggled with their lack of voting rights, the expectation that they
would marry and leave their jobs, and Lowell's ability to recruit new girls from the
countryside. The struggle between Lowell and "his girls" was ended by the Irish potato
famine of the 1840s, when hundreds of thousands of starving families arrived in New
England and filled Lowell's factories with a new and lower-paid workforce.

Some of the Lowell women made names for themselves in public life, such as Har-
riet Robinson, who had started factory work at ten and went on to become an important
abolitionist, author, and suffragist. However, most, like Mary Paul, found their satis-
factions in private life. Paul, who started at Lowell as a fifteen-year-old from Vermont,

Thomas Dublin, ed., *Farm to Factory: Women's Letters, 1830–1860*, Second Edition (New York: Columbia University Press, 1981), 137–46.

eight years later sought a better life in a utopian commune run by followers of Charles Fourier, who advocated a society organized into small, self-sustaining communal groups. She later left the commune and married the son of her former Lowell boardinghouse manager. We know that she bore two children, but thereafter she disappears from the historical record.

QUESTIONS TO CONSIDER

1. What factors influenced the decision of women like Mary Paul to move to Lowell to work in the mills?
2. What made communes like the Phalanx popular?
3. In what ways did the Lowell system advance women's rights? In what ways did the system set them back?

[Mary Paul wrote this first letter when she was still working as a domestic servant for a Vermont family.]

[*Woodstock, Vt.*] Saturday, Sept. 13th 1845

Dear Father

I received your letter this afternoon by Wm Griffith. . . .

I am very glad you sent my shoes. They fit very well indeed they [are] large enough.

I want you to consent to let me go to Lowell if you can. I think it would be much better for me than to stay about here. I could earn more to begin with than I can any where about here. I am in need of clothes which I cannot get if I stay about here and for that reason I want to go to Lowell or some other place. We all think that if I could go with some steady girl that I might do well. I want you to think of it and make up your mind. Mercy Jane Griffith is going to start in four or five weeks. Aunt Miller and Aunt Sarah think it would be a good chance for me to go if you would consent—which I want you to do if possible. I want to see you and talk with you about it.

Aunt Sarah gains slowly.

Mary

[This next letter was written from the Lowell mills, where Mary Paul was now employed.]

Lowell Dec 21st 1845

Dear Father,

I received your letter on Thursday the 14th with much pleasure. I am well which is one comfort. My health and life are spared while others are cut off. Last Thursday one girl fell down and broke her neck which caused instant death. She was going in or coming out of the mill and slipped down it being very icy. The same day a man was killed by the car [the railroad cars next to the factory].[1] Another had nearly all of her ribs broken. Another was nearly killed by falling down and having a bale of cotton fall on him. Last Tuesday we were paid. In all I had six dollars sixty cents paid $4.68 for board. With the rest I got me a pair of rubbers and a pair of 50.cts shoes. Next payment I am to have a dollar a week beside my board. We have not had much snow the deepest being not more than 4 inches. It has been very warm for winter. Perhaps you would like something about our regulations about going in and coming out of the mill. At 5 o'clock the bell rings for the folks to get up and get breakfast. At half past six it rings for the girls to get up and at seven they are called into the mill. At half past twelve we have dinner are called back at one and stay till half past seven. I get along very well with my work. I can doff [remove full bobbins of yarn and replace them with empty ones] as fast as any girl in our room. The usual time for learning is six months but I think I shall have frames before I shall have been in three as I get along so fast. I think that the factory is the best place for me and if any girl wants employment I advise them to come to Lowell. Tell Harriet that though she does not hear from me she is not forgotten. I have little time to devote to writing that I cannot write all I want to. There are half a dozen letters which I ought to write today but I have not time. Tell Harriet I send my love to her and all of the girls. Give my love to Mrs. Clement. Tell Henry this will answer for him and you too for this time.

> This from
> Mary S Paul

Lowell April 12 1846

Dear Father

I received your letter with much pleasure but was sorry to hear you had been lame. I had waited for a long time to hear from you but no letter came last Sunday so I thought I would write again which I did and was going to send it to the [post] office Monday but at noon I received a letter from William and so I did not send it at all. Last Friday I received a letter from you. You wanted to know what I am doing. I am at work in a spinning room and tending four sides of warp which is one girls work. The overseer tells me that he never had a girl get along better than I do and that he will do the best he can by me. I stand it well, though they tell me that I am growing very poor. I was paid nine shillings [about $1.50] a week last payment [exclusive of room and board] and am to have more this one though we have been out considerable for backwater [flooding that blocked the waterwheel providing the mill's power] which will take off a good deal. The Agent promises to pay us nearly as much as we should have made but I do not think that he will. The payment was up last night and we are to be paid this week. I have a very good boarding place have enough to eat and that

---

1. Bracketed notes were provided by the original editor of these sources, Thomas Dublin.

which is good enough. The girls are all kind and obliging. The girls that I room with are all from Vermont and good girls too. Now I will tell you about our rules at the boarding house. We have none in particular except that we have to go to bed about 10 o'clock. At half past four in the morning the bell rings for us to get up and at five for us to go into the mill. At seven we are called out to breakfast are allowed half an hour between bells and the same at noon till the first of May when we have three quarters [of an hour] until the first of September. We have dinner at half past 12 and supper at seven. If Julius should go to Boston tell him to come this way and see me. He must come to the Lawrence Counting room and call for me. He can ask someone to show him where the Lawrence is. I hope he will not fail to go. . . .

> Yours affectionately,
> Mary S Paul

[Between the following letter and the last, Mary Paul had left Lowell and then returned.]

Lowell Nov 5th 1848

Dear Father,

Doubtless you have been looking for a letter from me all the week past. I would have written but wished to find whether I should be able to stand it—to do the work that I am now doing. I was unable to get my old place in the cloth room on the Suffolk or on any other corporation. . . . So I went to my old overseer on the Tremont Cor[poration]. I had no idea that he would want one, but he *did*, and I went to work last Tuesday—warping—the same work I used to do.

It is *very* hard indeed and sometimes I think I shall not be able to endure it. I never worked so hard in my life but perhaps I shall get used to it. I shall try to do so for there is no other work I can do unless I spin, and that I shall not undertake on any account. I presume you have heard before this that the wages are to be reduced on the 20th of this month. It is *true* and there seems to be a good deal of excitement on the subject but I cannot tell what will be the consequence. . . . The companies claim they are losing immense sums every *day* and therefore are obliged to lessen the wages, but this seems perfectly absurd to me for they are constantly making *repairs* and it seems to me that this would not be if there were really any danger of their being obliged to *stop* the mills.

It is very difficult for anyone to get into the mill on any corporation. All seem to be very full of help. I expect to be paid about two dollars a week [exclusive of room and board] but it will be dearly earned. I cannot tell how it is but never since I have worked in the mill have I been so tired as I have for the last week but it may be owing to the long rest I have had for the last six months. . . . But enough of this. The Whigs of Lowell had a great time on the night of the 3rd. They had an immense procession of men on foot bearing *torches* and *banners* got up for the occasion. The houses were illuminated (Whigs' houses) and by the way I should think the whole of *Lowell* were Whigs. I went out to see the illuminations and they truly did look splendid. The Merrimack house was illuminated from attic to cellar. Every pane of glass in the house had a half candle to it and there were many others lighted in the same way. One entire block of the Merrimack Cor[poration] with the exception of one tenement which doubtless was occupied by a free soiler[2] who would not illuminate on any account whatever.

(Monday Eve) I have been to work today and think I shall manage to get along with the work. I am not so tired as I was last week. I have not yet found out what wages I shall get but presume they will be about $2.00 per week exclusive of board. I think of nothing further to write excepting I wish you to prevail on *Henry* to write me, also tell *Olive* to write and *Eveline* when she comes. . . .

Write soon. Yours affectionately,
Mary S Paul

Brattleboro Nov. 27, 1853

Dear father,

I think I will write you a few words tonight as you may be wishing to hear from me. . . .

I have a plan for myself which I am going to lay before you and to see what you think of it. When I was in Manchester last spring my friend Carrie and her husband were talking of going to New Jersey to live and proposed that I should go with them. They have decided to go and are going in a few weeks, maybe as soon as Jan. though they may not go until April or May. I have been thinking of it all summer and have told them I will go if you do not object. I can hardly get *my own* consent to go any farther away from you, though I know that in reality a few miles cannot make much difference. The name of the town is Atlantic. . . . about 40 miles from New York City. The people among whom they are going are Associationists. The name will give you something of an idea of their principles. There [are] about 125 persons in all that live there, and the association is called the "North American Phalanx."[3] I presume that you may have heard of it. You have if you read the "Tribune." The editor Mr "Greely" is an Associationist and a shareholder in the "Phalanx," but he does not live there. The advantage that will arise from my going there will be that I can get better pay without working as hard as at any other place. The price for work there being 9 cts an hour and the number of hours for a days work, *ten* besides I should not be confined to one kind of work but could do almost anything, could have the privilege of doing anything that is done there—*Housework* if I choose and that without degrading myself, which is more than I could do anywhere else. That is, in the opinion of most people, a very foolish and wrong idea by the way, but one that has so much weight with girls, that they would live on 25 cts per week at sewing, or school teaching rather than work at housework. I would do it myself although I

2. **Free soiler:** Member of a political party that opposed the extension of slavery to the territories.
3. **North American Phalanx:** *Phalanx* was the name given to the communities inspired by the French reformer Charles Fourier. Fourier's disciples often called themselves Associationists.

think it foolish. This all comes from the way servants are *treated*, and I cannot see why girls should be blamed after all, for not wishing to "work out" as it is called. At the "Phalanx" it is different. All work there, and all are paid alike. Both men and women have the same pay for the same work. There is no such word as aristocracy unless there is real (not pretended) superiority, that will make itself felt, if not acknowledged, everywhere. The members can live as cheaply as they choose and pay only for what they eat, and no profit on that, most of the provision being raised on the grounds. One can join them with or without funds, and can leave at any time they choose. Frank has been there this Fall and was very much pleased with what he saw there and thought that it would be the best thing for Carrie and me to do with ourselves. A woman gets much better pay there than elsewhere, though it is not so with a man, though he is not meanly paid by any means. There is more equality in such things according to the work not the sex. You know that men often get more than double the pay for doing the same work that women do. . . . Another advantage from living there is this, the members can have privileges of *Education* free of expense to themselves alone, the extent of this education must of course depend on the *means* of the society. If I could see you I could give you a better idea. That I can possibly do by writing, but you will know something by this, enough to form an opinion perhaps and I wish you to let me know what you think of my plans. . . . I hope sometime to be able to do something for you sometime and sometimes feel ashamed that I have not before this. I am not one of the *smart* kind, and never had a passion for laying up money. . . . One thing more, I have never had good pay. I am getting along slowly on coats, and shall do better as I get used to the business. I can work at my trade if I wish at the Phalanx. . . .

    Affectionately yours,
    Mary S Paul

North American Phalanx, N.J.
Sunday morn May 7th 1854

Dear father

    I feel that you must be anxious to hear from me, and so will write a few lines that you may know I am here safe and well. . . .
    By the way it is spring here, peach trees are out of blossom, cherry & apple trees are in full glory. As far as I can see from the window, at which I am writing, nothing but immense orchards of peach, cherries, & apple trees present themselves to view. I never saw *orchards* before, but I have got a long way from my story. I'll go back. We arrived here a good deal *wet* & were kindly received, had been expected for a long time they told us. . . . Our things which should have been here with us did not come until Monday afterward, and then not all of them. We have been very busy all the week putting things to rights. Have not done much work beside our own. I have worked about two hours each day for the Phalanx, three quarters in sweeping, one and a quarter in the dining hall, clearing & laying the tables. Tomorrow I am going to begin sewing which will add three hours each

day to my work. On ironing days I shall iron one, two, or three days just as I like. I must prepare to go to my dinner now. We have one hour, from 12 to 1, for dinner, breakfast from 5 1/2 to 7, teas from 6 1/2 to 7 1/2. After dinner from one till quarter past two I do my work in the dining hall. Three o'clock, I have come back to finish my letter. I cannot tell you anything definite now about matters and things because I dont know about them myself. I shall write you again as soon as I can & then I will tell you more about ways here. The place is very pleasant and the people remarkably kind. Upon the whole I think that I may like it very well after I get used to the strange ways. . . .

    Yours truly,
    Mary S Paul

Phalanx New Jersey March 3 [18]55

My dear father

    I have been wishing to write to you for some time but was prevented by the state of affairs here, at least I did not wish to write until I had something definite to say respecting my prospects here. . . . I think I wrote you early in the winter that the loss of the mill [to a fire] involved the Association in difficulties from which it would be hard to extricate it. The fear seemed to pass away and many seemed to think the foundations were too firm to be shaken even by an enormous debt, but it seems we were wrong for this Association is most certainly in the very last stage. . . . I do not know how long I can stay here but will not leave until I am obliged to. The life here has many attractions & advantages which no other life can have, and as imperfect as it is I have already seen enough to convince me that the Association is the true life. And although all the attempts that have ever yet been made toward it have been failures, inasmuch as they have passed away (but they have all left their mark) my faith in the principles is as strong as ever, stronger if possible. There is a better day coming for the world. "We may not live to see the day but the Earth shall glisten in the ray of the good time coming." Don't be worried about me father, for I am certainly more comfortable here than I could be anywhere else. I suppose when I leave here I shall have to take up sewing again as that seems to be the only thing open to me. I flatter myself that I had fairly escaped from the confinement of the needle, but I shall have to return to it after all. Well I expect it will all be for the best. . . . Give my love to everybody that cares for me and accept the same for yourself from

    Your affectionate daughter
    Mary S Paul

A Family Torn Apart by Slavery
Henry "Box" Brown

Henry "Box" Brown was born a slave on a plantation in Virginia sometime around 1815. When he was fifteen, the death of his master broke up his family and he and his sister Martha were sold to a slave owner in Richmond, Virginia. There, his sister did domestic work and he worked for wages in his new master's tobacco factory.

Richmond gave him a clear view of the increasingly turbulent and contradictory world of American slavery. He worked for wages with 150 other African Americans, some of whom were free and some of whom were slaves, tendering most of their wages to their masters. Soon after arriving in Richmond, he witnessed the spectacle of whites fleeing in terror of their own slaves, soldiers patrolling the streets, and armed mobs killing and torturing blacks during the great Nat Turner's slave uprising of 1831.

In Richmond, Brown became a respected member of the community, marrying, fathering three children, saving for old age, and developing a network of both white and black friends. Despite Brown's remarkable privileges as an employed "town slave," he discovered, in 1849, how little control he had over his life when his master sold his wife and children away from him. The account that follows charts his failed attempts to preserve an ordinary life and keep his family together within the "peculiar institution" of slavery. With his family gone and his life in shambles, there was nothing left tying the resourceful Brown to slavery. Enlisting the help of friends, he climbed into a wooden box and mailed himself to freedom in Philadelphia.

In addition to planning and executing the most famous escape in the history of American slavery, Brown was a gifted self-promoter and entrepreneur. Claiming the name "Box," he published his narrative, from which this account is taken and went on the antislavery lecture circuit, giving speeches, reenacting his escape, and displaying a giant painted canvas panorama called The Mirror of Slavery, *which depicted American history from a black perspective. Brown was such an accomplished showman that he came under criticism from antislavery activists for putting his commercial interests ahead of the abolitionist movement.*

After the U.S. government passed the Fugitive Slave Act in 1850, Brown was almost captured in Rhode Island by bounty hunters. He fled to England, where he had a brief but successful career as an antislavery entertainer: singing, lecturing, selling lithographs of himself, and even having himself shipped in a box from Bradford to Leeds.

Henry Box Brown, *Narrative of the Life of Henry Box Brown Written by Himself* (Oxford: Oxford University Press, 1851), 20–50.

Little is known about Brown's later years, but it is believed that he married an English-woman and settled in Wales.

QUESTIONS TO CONSIDER
1. In what way was Box Brown's life different from the lives of slaves in the countryside?
2. What does Brown's account say about the negotiations that went on between masters and slaves?
3. What are Brown's views of religion?

I had now been about two years in Richmond city, and not having, during that time, seen, and very seldom heard from, my mother, my feelings were very much tried by the separation which I had thus to endure. I missed severely her welcome smile when I returned from my daily task; no one seemed at that time to sympathise with me, and I began to feel, indeed, that I really was alone in the world; and worse than all, I could console myself with no hope, not even the most distant, that I should ever see my beloved parents again. . . .

I now began to think of entering the matrimonial state; and with that view I had formed an acquaintance with a young woman named Nancy, who was a slave belonging to a Mr. Leigh a clerk in the Bank, and, like many more slaveholders, professing to be a very pious man. We had made it up to get married, but it was necessary in the first place, to obtain our masters' permission, as we could do nothing without their consent.

I therefore went to Mr. Leigh, and made known to him my wishes, when he told me he never meant to sell Nancy, and if my master would agree never to sell me, I might marry her. He promised faithfully that he would not sell her, and pretended to entertain an extreme horror of separating families. He gave me a note to my master, and after they had discussed the matter over, I was allowed to marry the object of my choice. . . .

From the apparent sincerity of his promises to us, we felt confident that he would not separate us. We had not, however, been married above twelve months, when his conscientious scruples vanished, and he sold my wife to a Mr. Joseph H. Colquitt, a saddler, living in the city of Richmond, and a member of Dr. Plummer's church there. This Mr. Colquitt was an exceedingly cruel man, and he had a wife who was, if possible, still more cruel. She was very contrary and hard to be pleased she used to abuse my wife very much, not because she did not do her duty, but because, it was said, her manners were too refined for a slave. At this time my wife had a child and this vexed Mrs. Colquitt very much; she could not bear to see her nursing her baby and used to wish some great calamity to happen to my wife. Eventually she was so much displeased with my wife that she induced Mr. Colquitt to sell her to one Philip M. Tabb, Jr. for the sum of 450 dollars; but coming to see the value of her more clearly after she tried to do without her, she could not rest till she got Mr. Colquitt to repurchase her from Mr. Tabb, which he did in about four months after he had sold her, for 500 dollars, being 50 more than he had sold her for.

Shortly after this Mr. Colquitt was taken sick. . . . He proceeded to sell my wife to one Samuel Cottrell, who wished to purchase her. Cottrell was a saddler and had a shop in Richmond. This man came to me one day and told me that Mr. Colquitt was going to sell my wife, and stated that he wanted a woman to wait upon his wife, and he thought my wife would precisely suit her; but he said her master asked 650 dollars for her and her children, and he had only 600 that he could conveniently spare but if I would let him have fifty, to make up the price, he would prevent her from being sold away from me. I was, however, a little suspicious about being fooled out of my money, and I asked him if I did advance the money what security I could have that he would not sell my wife as the others had done; but he said to me "do you think if you allow me to have that money, that I could have the heart to sell your wife to any other person but yourself, and particularly knowing that your wife is my sister and you my brother in the Lord; while all of us are members of the church? *Oh! no*, I never could have the heart to do such a deed as that."

After he had shown off his religion in this manner, and lavished it upon me, I thought I would let him have the money, not that I had implicit faith in his promise, but that I knew he could purchase her if he wished whether I were to assist him or not, and I thought by thus bringing him under an obligation to me it might at least be somewhat to the advantage of my wife and to me; so I gave him the 50 dollars and he went off and bought my wife and children:—and that very same day he came to me and told me, that my wife and children were now his property, and that I must hire a house for them and he would allow them to live there if I would furnish them with everything they wanted, and pay him 50 dollars, a year; "if you dont do this," he said, "I will sell her as soon as I can get a buyer for her." I was struck with astonishment to think that this man, in one day, could exhibit himself in two such different characters. A few hours ago filled with expressions of love and kindness, and now a monster tyrant, making light of the most social ties and imposing such terms as he chose on those whom, but a little before, had begged to conform to his will.

Now, being a slave, I had no power to hire a house, and what this might have resulted in I do not know, if I had not met with a friend in the time of need, in the person of James C. A. Smith, Jr. He was a free man and I went to him and told him my tale and asked him to go and hire a house for me, to put my wife and children into; which he immediately did. He hired one at 72 dollars per annum, and stood master of it for me; and, notwithstanding the fearful liabilities under which I lay, I now began to feel a little easier, and might, perhaps, have managed to live in a kind of a way if we had been let alone here. But Mr. S. Cottrell had not yet done with robbing us; he no sooner saw that we were thus comfortably situated, than he said my wife must do some of his washing. I still had to pay the house hire, and the hire of my wife; to find her and the children with everything they required, and she had to do his washing beside. Still we felt ourselves more comfortable than we had ever been before. In this way, we went on for some time: I paid him the hire of my wife regularly, whenever he called for it—whether it was due or not—but he seemed still bent on robbing me more thoroughly than he had the previous day; for one pleasant morning, in the month of August, 1848, when my wife and children, and myself, were sitting at table, about to eat our breakfast, Mr. Cottrell called, and said, he wanted some money today, as he had a demand for a large amount. I said to him, you know I have no money to spare, because it takes nearly all that I make for myself, to pay my wife's hire, the rent of my house, my own ties to my master, and to keep ourselves in meat and clothes; and if at any time, I have made anything more than that, I have paid it to you in advance, and what more can I do? Mr. Cottrell, however said, "I want money, and money I will have."

I could make him no answer; he then went away. I then said to my wife, "I wonder what Mr. Cottrell means by saying I want money and money I will have," my poor wife burst into tears and said perhaps he will sell one of our little children, and our hearts were so full that neither of us could eat any breakfast, and after mutually embracing each other, as it might be our last meeting, and fondly pressing our little darlings to our bosoms, I left the house and went off to my daily labour followed by my little children who called after me to come back soon. I felt that life had joys worth living for if I could only be allowed to enjoy them, but my heart was filled with deep anguish from the awful calamity, which I was thus obliged to contemplate, as not only a possible but a highly probable occurrence. . . .

I had not been many hours at my work, when I was informed that my wife and children were taken from their home, sent to the auction mart and sold, and then lay in prison ready to start away the next day for North Carolina with the man who had purchased them. I cannot express, in language, what were my feelings on this occasion. My master treated me kindly but he still retained me in a state of slavery. His kindness however did not keep me from feeling the smart of this awful deprivation. I had left my wife and children at home in the morning as well situated as slaves could be; I was not anticipating their loss, not on account of the feigned piety of their owner, for I had long ago learned to look through such hollow pretences in those who held slaves, but because of the obligation to me for money I had advanced to him, *on the expressed condition that he should not sell her to any person but myself*; such, however was the case. . . . I went to my *Christian* master and informed him how I was served, but he shoved me away from him as if I was not human. I could not rest with this however, I went to him a second time and implored him to be kind enough to buy my wife and to save me from so much trouble of mind; still he was inexorable and only answered me by telling me to go to my work and not bother him any more. I went to him a *third* time, which would be about ten o'clock and told him how Cottrell had robbed me, as this scoundrel was not satisfied with selling my wife and children, but he had no sooner got them out of the town than he took everything which he could find in my house and carried it off to be sold; the things which he then took had cost me nearly three hundred dollars. I begged master to write Cottrell and make him give me up my things, but his answer was Mr. Cottrell is a gentleman I am afraid to meddle with his business. . . . I went sorrowfully back to my own deserted home, and found that what I had heard was quite true; not only had my wife and children been taken away, but every article of furniture had also been removed to the auction mart to be sold.

I then made inquiry as to where my things had been put; and having found this out went to the sheriff's office and informed him, that the things Mr. Cottrell had brought to be sold did not belong to him, but that they were mine, and I hoped he would return them to me. I was then told by the sheriff that Mr. Cottrell had left the things to be sold in order to pay himself a debt of seventeen dollars and twenty-one cents, which he said if I would pay he would let me take away the things. I then went to my good friend Doctor Smith who was always ready and willing to do what he could for me, and having got the money, I paid it to the sheriff and took away the things which I was obliged to do that night, as far as I was able, and what were left I removed in the morning. When I was taking home the last of my things I met Mr. Cottrell, and two of his Christian brethren, in the street. He stopped me and said he had heard I had been to the sheriff's office and got away my things. Yes I said I have been and got away *my things* but I could not get away *my wife and children* whom you have put beyond my power to redeem. He then began to give me a round of abuse, while his two Christian friends stood by and heard him, but they did not seem to be the least offended at the terrible barbarity which was there placed before them.

I now left Mr. Cottrell and his friends, and going home, endeavoured to court a little rest by lying down in a position so as to induce sleep. I had borne too heavy a load of grief on my mind to admit of me even closing my eyes for an hour during the whole night. Many schemes for effecting the redemption of my family passed through my mind, but when the morning's sun arose I found myself on my way towards my master's house, to make another attempt to induce him to purchase my wife. But although I besought him, with tears in my eyes, I did not succeed in making the least impression on his obdurate heart, and he utterly refused to advance the smallest portion of the 5000 dollars I had paid him in order to relieve my sufferings, and yet he was a church member of considerable standing in Richmond. He even told me that I could get another wife and so I need not trouble myself about that one; but I told him those that God had joined together let no man put asunder, and that I did not want another wife, but my own whom I had loved so long. The mentioning of the passage of scripture seemed to give him much offence for he instantly drove me from his house saying he did not wish to hear that!

My agony was now complete, she with whom I had travelled the journey of life *in chains*, for the space of twelve years, and the dear little pledges God had given us I could see plainly must now be separated from me for ever, and I must continue, desolate and alone, to drag my chains through the world.

O dear, I thought shall my wife and children no more greet my sight with their cheerful looks and happy smiles! for far away in the North Carolina swamps are they henceforth to toil beneath the scorching rays of a hot sun deprived of a husband's and a father's care! Can I endure such agony—shall I stay behind while they are thus driven with the tyrant's rod? I must stay, I am a slave, the law of men gives me no power to ameliorate my condition; it shuts up every avenue of hope; but, thanks be to God, their is a law of heaven which senates' laws cannot control!

While I was thus musing I received a message, that if I wished to see my wife and children, and bid them the last farewell, I could do so, by taking my stand on the street where they were all to pass on their way for North Carolina. . . .

These beings were marched with ropes about their necks, and staples on their arms, and, although in that respect the scene was no very novel one to me, yet the peculiarity of my own circumstances made it assume the appearance of unusual horror. This train of beings was accompanied by a number of wagons loaded with little children of many different families, which as they appeared rent the air with their shrieks and cries and vain endeavours to resist the separation which was thus forced upon them, and the cords with which they were thus bound; but what should I now see in the very foremost wagon but a little child looking towards me and pitifully calling, father! father! This was my eldest child, and I was obliged to look upon it for the last time that I should, perhaps, ever see it again in life. . . .

Thus passed my child from my presence—it was my own child—I loved it with all the fondness of a father; but things were so ordered that I could only say, farewell, and leave it to pass in its chains while I looked for the approach of another gang in which my wife was also loaded with chains. My eye soon caught her precious face, but, gracious heavens! that glance of agony may God spare me from ever again enduring! My wife, under the influence of her feelings, jumped aside; I seized hold of her hand while my mind felt unutterable things, and my tongue was only able to say, we shall meet in heaven! I went with her for about four miles hand in hand, but both our hearts were so overpowered with feeling that we could say nothing, and when at last we were obliged to part, the look of mutual love which we exchanged was all the token which we could give each other that we should yet meet in heaven.

I now began to get weary of my bonds; and earnestly panted after liberty. I felt convinced that I should be acting in accordance with the will of God, if I could snap in sunder those bonds by which I was held body and soul as the property of a fellow man. I looked forward to the good time which every day I more and more firmly believed would yet come, when I should walk the face of the earth in full possession of all that freedom which the finger of God had so clearly written on the constitutions of man, and which was common to the human race; but of which, by the cruel hand of tyranny, I, and millions of my fellow-men, had been robbed.

36

Life of a Female Slave

Harriet Jacobs

Harriet Jacobs's Incidents in the Life of a Slave Girl *is only now emerging as the classic narrative of a woman slave, a work to rank with the several autobiographies of Frederick Douglass. Published under a pseudonym in 1861, edited by a white abolitionist, and borrowing form and rhetoric from sentimental novels such as Harriet Beecher Stowe's* Uncle Tom's Cabin, *the work remained suspect for 120 years. Only in 1981, when Jean Fagan Yellin published documentary evidence of Jacobs's authorship (*American Literature, *November 1981: 479–86), did recognition come that this is a major work of African American literature, as well as an essential document for the history of slavery. Her bold discussion of sexual relations between the races prepared her audience in the North for the images of slave and slaveholder families such as those of Figures 8 and 9 in the visual portfolio "Slavery and Freedom" (page 256).*

Jacobs (1813–1897), writing under the pseudonym of Linda Brent, emerges as a remarkably determined woman. To prevent the permanent enslavement of her children, she hid for seven years in the attic of her grandmother's house, a tiny space only three feet high, while deceiving her master into thinking she had escaped to the North by smuggling out letters to be mailed from New York City and Boston. Finally she and then her children escaped from slave territory to discover the ambiguities of freedom in the so-called free states.

QUESTIONS TO CONSIDER

1. What does Harriet Jacobs's account of her experience add to our picture of slavery?
2. Does she see herself as a victim? What does she emphasize about her reaction to the position her master placed her in?
3. How do you think readers of the time reacted to her tale of the experiences of young female slaves?

THE TRIALS OF GIRLHOOD

During the first years of my service in Dr. Flint's family, I was accustomed to share some indulgences with the children of my mistress. Though this seemed to me no more than right, I was grateful for it, and tried to merit the kindness by

---

Harriet Jacobs, *Incidents in the Life of a Slave Girl* (Boston, 1861), 44–49, 51–55, 57–67, 82–89.

the faithful discharge of my duties. But I now entered on my fifteenth year—a sad epoch in the life of a slave girl. My master began to whisper foul words in my ear. Young as I was, I could not remain ignorant of their import. I tried to treat them with indifference or contempt. The master's age, my extreme youth, and the fear that his conduct would be reported to my grandmother, made me bear this treatment for many months. He was a crafty man, and resorted to many means to accomplish his purposes. Sometimes he had stormy, terrific ways, that made his victims tremble; sometimes he assumed a gentleness that he thought must surely subdue. Of the two, I preferred his stormy moods, although they left me trembling. He tried his utmost to corrupt the pure principles my grandmother had instilled. He peopled my young mind with unclean images, such as only a vile monster could think of. I turned from him with disgust and hatred. But he was my master. I was compelled to live under the same roof with him—where I saw a man forty years my senior daily violating the most sacred commandments of nature. He told me I was his property; that I must be subject to his will in all things. My soul revolted against the mean tyranny. But where could I turn for protection? No matter whether the slave girl be as black as ebony or as fair as her mistress. In either case, there is no shadow of law to protect her from insult, from violence, or even from death; all these are inflicted by fiends who bear the shape of men. The mistress, who ought to protect the helpless victim, has no other feelings towards her but those of jealousy and rage. The degradation, the wrongs, the vices, that grow out of slavery, are more than I can describe. . . .

Every where the years bring to all enough of sin and sorrow; but in slavery the very dawn of life is darkened by these shadows. Even the little child, who is accustomed to wait on her mistress and her children, will learn, before she is twelve years old, why it is that her mistress hates such and such a one among the slaves. Perhaps the child's own mother is among those hated ones. She listens to violent outbreaks of jealous passion, and cannot help understanding what is the cause. She will become prematurely knowing in evil things. Soon she will learn to tremble when she hears her master's footfall. She will be compelled to realize that she is no longer a child. If God has bestowed beauty upon her; it will prove her greatest curse. That which commands admiration in the white woman only hastens the degradation of the female slave. I know that some are too much brutalized by slavery to feel the humiliation of their position; but many slaves feel it most acutely, and shrink from the memory of it. I cannot tell how much I suffered in the presence of these wrongs, nor how I am still pained by the retrospect. My master met me at every turn, reminding me that I belonged to him, and swearing by heaven and earth that he would compel me to submit to him. If I went out for a breath of fresh air, after a day of unwearied toil, his footsteps dogged me. If I knelt by my mother's grave, his dark shadow fell on me even there. The light heart which nature had given me became heavy with sad forebodings. The other slaves in my master's house noticed the change. Many of them pitied me; but none dared to ask the cause. They had no need to inquire. They knew too well the guilty practices under that roof; and they were aware that to speak of them was an offence that never went unpunished.

I longed for some one to confide in. I would have given the world to have laid my head on my grandmother's faithful bosom, and told her all my troubles. But Dr. Flint swore he would kill me, if I was not as silent as the grave. Then, although my grandmother was all in all to me, I feared her as well as loved her. I had been accustomed to look up to her with a respect bordering upon awe. I was very young, and felt shamefaced about telling her such impure things, especially as I knew her to be very strict on such subjects. Moreover, she was a woman of a high spirit. She was usually very quiet in her demeanor; but if her indignation was once roused, it was not very easily quelled. I had been told that she once chased a white gentleman with a loaded pistol, because he insulted one of her daughters. I dreaded the consequences of a violent outbreak; and both pride and fear kept me silent. But though I did not confide in my grandmother, and even evaded her vigilant watchfulness and inquiry, her presence in the neighborhood was some protection to me. Though she had been a slave, Dr. Flint was afraid of her. He dreaded her scorching rebukes. Moreover, she was known and patronized by many people; and he did not wish to have his villany made public. It was lucky for me that I did not live on a distant plantation, but in a town not so large that the inhabitants were ignorant of each other's affairs. Bad as are the laws and customs in a slaveholding community, the doctor, as a professional man, deemed it prudent to keep up some outward show of decency. . . .

I once saw two beautiful children playing together. One was a fair white child; the other was her slave; and also her sister. When I saw them embracing each other, and heard their joyous laughter, I turned sadly away from the lovely sight. I foresaw the inevitable blight that would fall on the little slave's heart. I knew how soon her laughter would be changed to sighs. The fair child grew up to be a still fairer woman. From childhood to womanhood her pathway was blooming with flowers, and overarched by a sunny sky. Scarcely one day of her life had been clouded when the sun rose on her happy bridal morning.

How had those years dealt with her slave sister, the little playmate of her childhood? She, also, was very beautiful; but the flowers and sunshine of love were not for her. She drank the cup of sin, and shame, and misery, whereof her persecuted race are compelled to drink.

In view of these things, why are ye silent, ye free men and women of the north? Why do your tongues falter in maintenance of the right? Would that I had more ability! But my heart is so full, and my pen is so weak! There are noble men and women who plead for us, striving to help those who cannot help themselves. God bless them! God give them strength and courage to go on! God bless those, every where, who are laboring to advance the cause of humanity!

THE JEALOUS MISTRESS

I would ten thousand times rather that my children should be the half-starved paupers of Ireland than to be the most pampered among the slaves of America. I would rather drudge out my life on a cotton plantation, till the grave opened to give me rest, than to live with an unprincipled master and a jealous mistress.

The felon's home in a penitentiary is preferable. He may repent, and turn from the error of his ways, and so find peace; but it is not so with a favorite slave. She is not allowed to have any pride of character. It is deemed a crime in her to wish to be virtuous. . . .

I had entered my sixteenth year, and every day it became more apparent that my presence was intolerable to Mrs. Flint. Angry words frequently passed between her and her husband. He had never punished me himself, and he would not allow any body else to punish me. In that respect, she was never satisfied; but, in her angry moods, no terms were too vile for her to bestow upon me. Yet I, whom she detested so bitterly, had far more pity for her than he had, whose duty it was to make her life happy. I never wronged her, or wished to wrong her; and one word of kindness from her would have brought me to her feet.

After repeated quarrels between the doctor and his wife, he announced his intention to take his youngest daughter, then four years old, to sleep in his apartment. It was necessary that a servant should sleep in the same room, to be on hand if the child stirred. I was selected for that office, and informed for what purpose that arrangement had been made. By managing to keep within sight of people, as much as possible, during the daytime, I had hitherto succeeded in eluding my master, though a razor was often held to my throat to force me to change this line of policy. At night I slept by the side of my great aunt, where I felt safe. He was too prudent to come into her room. She was an old woman, and had been in the family many years. Moreover, as a married man, and a professional man, he deemed it necessary to save appearances in some degree. But he resolved to remove the obstacle in the way of his scheme; and he thought he had planned it so that he should evade suspicion. He was well aware how much I prized my refuge by the side of my old aunt, and he determined to dispossess me of it. The first night the doctor had the little child in his room alone. The next morning, I was ordered to take my station as nurse the following night. A kind Providence interposed in my favor. During the day Mrs. Flint heard of this new arrangement, and a storm followed. I rejoiced to hear it rage. . . .

The secrets of slavery are concealed like those of the Inquisition. My master was, to my knowledge, the father of eleven slaves. But did the mothers dare to tell who was the father of their children? Did the other slaves dare to allude to it, except in whispers among themselves? No, indeed! They knew too well the terrible consequences. . . .

Southern women often marry a man knowing that he is the father of many little slaves. They do not trouble themselves about it. They regard such children as property, as marketable as the pigs on the plantation; and it is seldom that they do not make them aware of this by passing them into the slave-trader's hands as soon as possible, and thus getting them out of their sight. I am glad to say there are some honorable exceptions.

I have myself known two southern wives who exhorted their husbands to free those slaves towards whom they stood in a "parental relation;" and their request was granted. These husbands blushed before the superior nobleness of their wives' natures. Though they had only counselled them to do that which it was their duty to do, it commanded their respect, and rendered their conduct more exemplary. Concealment was at an end, and confidence took the place of distrust.

Though this bad institution deadens the moral sense, even in white women, to a fearful extent, it is not altogether extinct. I have heard southern ladies say of Mr. Such a one, "He not only thinks it no disgrace to be the father of those little niggers, but he is not ashamed to call himself their master. I declare, such things ought not to be tolerated in any decent society!"

A PERILOUS PASSAGE
IN THE SLAVE GIRL'S LIFE

Dr. Flint contrived a new plan. He seemed to have an idea that my fear of my mistress was his greatest obstacle. In the blandest tones, he told me that he was going to build a small house for me, in a secluded place, four miles away from the town. I shuddered; but I was constrained to listen, while he talked of his intention to give me a home of my own, and to make a lady of me. Hitherto, I had escaped my dreaded fate, by being in the midst of people. My grandmother had already had high words with my master about me. She had told him pretty plainly what she thought of his character, and there was considerable gossip in the neighborhood about our affairs, to which the open-mouthed jealousy of Mrs. Flint contributed not a little. When my master said he was going to build a house for me, and that he could do it with little trouble and expense, I was in hopes something would happen to frustrate his scheme; but I soon heard that the house was actually begun. I vowed before my Maker that I would never enter it. I had rather toil on the plantation from dawn till dark; I had rather live and die in jail, than drag on, from day to day, through such a living death. I was determined that the master, whom I so hated and loathed, who had blighted the prospects of my youth, and made my life a desert, should not, after my long struggle with him, succeed at last in trampling his victim under his feet. I would do any thing, every thing, for the sake of defeating him. What *could* I do? I thought and thought, till I became desperate, and made a plunge into the abyss.

And now, reader, I come to a period in my unhappy life, which I would gladly forget if I could. The remembrance fills me with sorrow and shame. It pains me to tell you of it; but I have promised to tell you the truth, and I will do it honestly, let it cost me what it may. I will not try to screen myself behind the plea of compulsion from a master; for it was not so. Neither can I plead ignorance or thoughtlessness. For years, my master had done his utmost to pollute my mind with foul images, and to destroy the pure principles inculcated by my grandmother, and the good mistress of my childhood. The influences of slavery had had the same effect on me that they had on other young girls; they had made me prematurely knowing, concerning the evil ways of the world. I knew what I did, and I did it with deliberate calculation.

But, O, ye happy women, whose purity has been sheltered from childhood, who have been free to choose the objects of your affection, whose homes are protected by law, do not judge the poor desolate slave girl too severely! If slavery had been abolished, I, also, could have married the man of my choice; I could have had a home shielded by the laws; and I should have been spared the painful task of confessing what I am now about to relate; but all my prospects had been blighted by slavery. I wanted to keep myself pure; and, under the most adverse circumstances, I tried hard to preserve my self-respect; but I was struggling alone in the powerful grasp of the demon Slavery; and the monster proved too strong for me. I felt as if I was forsaken by God and man; as if all my efforts must be frustrated; and I became reckless in my despair.

I have told you that Dr. Flint's persecutions and his wife's jealousy had given rise to some gossip in the neighborhood. Among others, it chanced that a white unmarried gentleman had obtained some knowledge of the circumstances in which I was placed. He knew my grandmother, and often spoke to me in the street. He became interested for me, and asked questions about my master, which I answered in part. He expressed a great deal of sympathy, and a wish to aid me. He constantly sought opportunities to see me, and wrote to me frequently. I was a poor slave girl, only fifteen years old.

So much attention from a superior person was, of course, flattering; for human nature is the same in all. I also felt grateful for his sympathy, and encouraged by his kind words. It seemed to me a great thing to have such a friend. By degrees, a more tender feeling crept into my heart. He was an educated and eloquent gentleman; too eloquent, alas, for the poor slave girl who trusted in him. Of course I saw whither all this was tending. I knew the impassable gulf between us; but to be an object of interest to a man who is not married, and who is not her master, is agreeable to the pride and feelings of a slave, if her miserable situation has left her any pride or sentiment. It seems less degrading to give one's self, than to submit to compulsion. There is something akin to freedom in having a lover who has no control over you, except that which he gains by kindness and attachment. A master may treat you as rudely as he pleases, and you dare not speak; moreover, the wrong does not seem so great with an unmarried man, as with one who has a wife to be made unhappy. There may be sophistry in all this; but the condition of a slave confuses all principles of morality, and, in fact, renders the practice of them impossible.

When I found that my master had actually begun to build the lonely cottage, other feelings mixed with those I have described. Revenge, and calculations of interest, were added to flattered vanity and sincere gratitude for kindness. I knew nothing would enrage Dr. Flint so much as to know that I favored another; and it was something to triumph over my tyrant even in that small way. I thought he would revenge himself by selling me, and I was sure my friend, Mr. Sands, would buy me. He was a man of more generosity and feeling than my master, and I thought my freedom could be easily obtained from him. The crisis of my fate now came so near that I was desperate. I shuddered to think of being the mother of children that should be owned by my old tyrant. I knew that as soon as a new fancy took him, his victims were sold far off to get rid of them; especially if they had children. I had seen several women sold, with his babies at the breast. He never allowed his offspring by slaves to remain long in sight of himself and his wife. Of a man who was not my master I could ask to have my children well supported; and in this case, I felt confident I should obtain the boon. I also felt quite sure that they would be made free. With all these thoughts revolving in my mind, and seeing no other way of escaping the doom I so much dreaded, I made a headlong plunge. Pity me, and pardon me, O virtuous reader! You never knew what it is to be a slave; to be entirely unprotected by law or custom; to have the laws reduce you to the condition of a chattel, entirely subject to the will of another. You never exhausted your ingenuity in avoiding the snares, and eluding the power of a hated tyrant; you never shuddered at the sound of his footsteps, and trembled within hearing of his voice. I know I did wrong. No one can feel it more sensibly than I do. The painful and humiliating memory will haunt me to my dying day. Still, in looking back, calmly, on the events of my life, I feel that the slave woman ought not to be judged by the same standard of others.

The months passed on. I had many unhappy hours. I secretly mourned over the sorrow I was bringing on my grandmother, who had so tried to shield me from harm. I knew that I was the greatest comfort of her old age, and that it was a source of pride to her that I had not degraded myself, like most of the slaves. I wanted to confess to her that I was no longer worthy of her love; but I could not utter the dreaded words.

As for Dr. Flint, I had a feeling of satisfaction and triumph in the thought of telling *him*. From time to time he told me of his intended arrangements, and I was silent. At last, he came and told me the cottage was completed, and ordered me to go to it. I told him I would never enter it. He said, "I have heard enough of such talk as that. You shall go, if you are carried by force; and you shall remain there."

I replied, "I will never go there. In a few months I shall be a mother."

He stood and looked at me in dumb amazement, and left the house without a word. I thought I should be happy in my triumph over him. But now that the truth was out, and my relatives would hear of it, I felt wretched. Humble as were their circumstances, they had pride in my good character. Now, how could I look them in the face? My self-respect was gone! I had resolved that I would be virtuous, though I was a slave. I had said, "Let the storm beat! I will brave it till I die." And now, how humiliated I felt!

I went to my grandmother. My lips moved to make confession, but the words stuck in my throat. I sat down in the shade of a tree at her door and began to sew. I think she saw something unusual was the matter with me. The mother of slaves is very watchful. She knows there is no security for her children. After they have entered their teens she lives in daily expectation of trouble. This leads to many questions. If the girl is of a sensitive nature, timidity keeps her from answering truthfully, and this well-meant course has a tendency to drive her from maternal counsels. Presently, in came my mistress, like a mad woman, and accused me concerning her husband. My grandmother, whose suspicions had been previously awakened, believed what she said. She exclaimed, "O Linda! has it come to this? I had rather see you dead than to see you as you now are. You are a disgrace to your dead mother." She tore from my fingers my mother's wedding ring and her silver thimble. "Go away!" she exclaimed, "and never come to my house, again." Her reproaches fell so hot and heavy, that they left me no chance to answer. Bitter tears, such as the eyes never shed but once, were my only answer. I rose from my seat, but fell back again, sobbing. She did not speak to me; but the tears were running down her furrowed cheeks, and they scorched me like fire. She had always been so kind to me! *So* kind! How I longed to throw myself at her feet, and tell her all the truth! But she had ordered me to go, and never to come there again. After a few minutes, I mustered strength, and started to obey her. With what feelings did I now close that little gate, which I used to open with such an eager hand in my childhood! It closed upon me with a sound I never heard before.

Where could I go? I was afraid to return to my master's. I walked on recklessly, not caring where I went, or what would become of me. When I had gone four or five miles, fatigue compelled me to stop. I sat down on the stump of an old tree. The stars were shining through the boughs above me. How they mocked me, with their bright, calm light! The hours passed by, and as I sat there alone a chilliness and deadly sickness came over me. I sank on the ground. My mind was full of horrid thoughts. I prayed to die; but the prayer was not answered. At last, with great effort I roused myself, and walked some distance further, to the house of a woman who had been a friend of my mother. When I told her why I was there, she spoke soothingly to me; but I could not be comforted. I thought I could bear my shame if I could only be reconciled to my grandmother. I longed to open my heart to her. I thought if she could know the real state of the case, and all I had been bearing for years, she would perhaps judge me less harshly. My friend advised me to send for her. I did so; but days of agonizing suspense passed before she came. Had she utterly forsaken me? No. She came at last. I knelt before her, and told her the things that had poisoned my life; how long I had been persecuted; that I saw no way of escape; and in an hour of extremity I had become desperate. She listened in silence. I told her I would bear any thing and do any thing, if in time I had hopes of obtaining her forgiveness. I begged of her to pity me, for my dead mother's sake. And she did pity me. She did not say, "I forgive you," but she looked at me lovingly, with her eyes full of tears. She laid her old hand gently on my head, and murmured, "Poor child! Poor child!"

37

A Pioneer for Women's Rights

Elizabeth Cady Stanton

The women's movement before the Civil War was among the most intensely unpopular of all the reform efforts of that era. The ideal of domesticity, which assigned to women a separate and less-powerful role in the family than that of men, made the reformists' claims for equal rights, especially the right to vote, a violation of social convention and of the religious beliefs of many. Friendships were enormously important in providing the courage and emotional support women needed to oppose the sometimes oppressive institutions of family, religion, and politics. Elizabeth Cady Stanton (1815–1902) was inspired by Lucretia Mott, whose Quaker ministry had given her experience in public speaking that she applied to the antislavery cause. The two had met at an antislavery convention in London in 1840 and, as Stanton was to recall later, "resolved to hold a convention as soon as we returned home, and form a society to advocate the rights of women." Yet eight years elapsed before this resolve bore fruit in the Seneca Falls Woman's Rights Convention. In the interim, Stanton had settled in three different locations, bore three children (she would eventually have seven), and assumed all the other cares of a financially strapped, middle-class household.

Reflecting on the Seneca Falls convention in her autobiography, Eighty Years and More, *published in 1898 when she was eighty-three and excerpted below, Elizabeth Cady Stanton remained astonished at the avalanche of criticism and sarcasm provoked by the "Declaration of Sentiments" that the Seneca Falls participants had issued, a document modeled on the U.S. Declaration of Independence and reprinted here. Commenting on the meeting, a Philadelphia newspaper asserted, "A pretty girl is equal to ten thousand men," and sneered, "The ladies of Philadelphia . . . are resolved to maintain their rights as Wives, Belles, Virgins and Mothers, and not as Women." But the women who met at Seneca Falls in upstate New York in 1848 had succeeded in launching a women's rights movement that would continue, mainly by following Stanton's strategy of making woman suffrage the major objective until that goal was achieved in 1920 with the ratification of the Nineteenth Amendment to the Constitution.*

QUESTIONS TO CONSIDER

1. Why was Elizabeth Cady Stanton's attendance at the World's Antislavery Convention in 1840 so important to her development as a women's rights advocate?

Elizabeth Cady Stanton, *Eighty Years and More: Reminiscences, 1815–1897* (London: T. Fisher Unwin, 1898), 79–83, 143–50; Copy of the Declaration of Sentiments, courtesy of the Seneca Falls Historical Society, Seneca Falls, NY.

2. How did Stanton's life between the World's Anti-slavery Convention in 1840 and the Seneca Falls Convention of 1848 deepen her commitment to women's equal rights?
3. What was the relationship between abolitionism and the women's rights movement? Do you think that civil rights movements for women and those for African Americans are natural collaborators or competitors?
4. Viewed more than a century and a half later, what relevance do you see in the Declaration of Sentiments?

EIGHTY YEARS AND MORE

Our chief object in visiting England at this time was to attend the World's Anti-slavery Convention, to meet June 12, 1840, in Freemasons' Hall, London. Delegates from all the anti-slavery societies of civilized nations were invited, yet, when they arrived, those representing associations of women were rejected. Though women were members of the National Anti-slavery Society, accustomed to speak and vote in all its conventions, and to take an equally active part with men in the whole anti-slavery struggle, and were there as delegates from associations of men and women, as well as those distinctively of their own sex, yet all alike were rejected because they were women. Women, according to English prejudices at that time, were excluded by Scriptural texts from sharing equal dignity and authority with men in all reform associations; hence it was to English minds pre-eminently unfitting that women should be admitted as equal members to a World's Convention. The question was hotly debated through an entire day. My husband made a very eloquent speech in favor of admitting the women delegates.

When we consider . . . [the] many remarkable women . . . [who] were all compelled to listen in silence to the masculine platitudes on woman's sphere, one may form some idea of the indignation of unprejudiced friends, and especially that of such women as Lydia Maria Child, Maria Chapman, Deborah Weston, Angelina and Sarah Grimké, and Abby Kelly, who were impatiently waiting and watching on this side, in painful suspense, to hear how their delegates were received. Judging from my own feelings, the women on both sides of the Atlantic must have been humiliated and chagrined, except as these feelings were outweighed by contempt for the shallow reasoning of their opponents and their comical pose and gestures in some of the intensely earnest flights of their imagination.

The clerical portion of the convention was most violent in its opposition. The clergymen seemed to have God and his angels especially in their care and keeping, and were in agony lest the women should do or say something to shock the heavenly hosts. Their all-sustaining conceit gave them abundant assurance that their movements must necessarily be all-pleasing to the celestials whose ears were open to the proceedings of the World's Convention. . . .

One of our champions in the convention, George Bradburn, a tall thick-set man with a voice like thunder, standing head and shoulders above the clerical representatives, swept all their arguments aside by declaring with tremendous

emphasis that, if they could prove to him that the Bible taught the entire subjection of one-half of the race to the other, he should consider that the best
thing he could do for humanity would be to bring together every Bible in the
universe and make a grand bonfire of them.

It was really pitiful to hear narrow-minded bigots, pretending to be teachers and leaders of men, so cruelly remanding their own mothers, with the rest
of womankind, to absolute subjection to the ordinary masculine type of humanity. I always regretted that the women themselves had not taken part in the debate before the convention was fully organized and the question of delegates
settled. It seemed to me then, and does now, that all delegates with credentials
from recognized societies should have had a voice in the organization of the
convention, though subject to exclusion afterward. However, the women sat in
a low curtained seat like a church choir, and modestly listened to the French,
British, and American Solons[1] for twelve of the longest days in June, as did, also,
our grand Garrison and Rogers[2] in the gallery. They scorned a convention that
ignored the rights of the very women who had fought, side by side, with them
in the anti-slavery conflict. "After battling so many long years," said Garrison,
"for the liberties of African slaves, I can take no part in a convention that strikes
down the most sacred rights of all women." After coming three thousand miles
to speak on the subject nearest his heart, he nobly shared the enforced silence of
the rejected delegates. It was a great act of self-sacrifice that should never be
forgotten by women. . . .

As the convention adjourned, the remark was heard on all sides, "It is about
time some demand was made for new liberties for women." As Mrs. Mott and I
walked home, arm in arm, commenting on the incidents of the day, we resolved
to hold a convention as soon as we returned home, and form a society to advocate the rights of women. At the lodging house on Queen Street, where a large
number of delegates had apartments, the discussions were heated at every meal,
and at times so bitter that, at last, Mr. Birney packed his valise and sought more
peaceful quarters. Having strongly opposed the admission of women as delegates to the convention it was rather embarrassing to meet them, during the intervals between the various sessions, at the table and in the drawing room.

These were the first women I had ever met who believed in the equality of
the sexes and who did not believe in the popular orthodox religion. The acquaintance of Lucretia Mott, who was a broad, liberal thinker on politics, religion, and all questions of reform, opened to me a new world of thought. As we
walked about to see the sights of London, I embraced every opportunity to talk
with her. It was intensely gratifying to hear all that, through years of doubt, I
had dimly thought, so freely discussed by other women, some of them no older
than myself—women, too, of rare intelligence, cultivation, and refinement. . . .

1. **French, British, and American Solons:** Here Cady Stanton refers sarcastically to the no-
toriously sage statesman of Ancient Greece, Solon.
2. **Garrison and Rogers:** Abolitionists William Lloyd Garrison (see p. 208) and Nathaniel
P. Rogers.

In the spring of 1847 we moved to Seneca Falls. Here we spent sixteen years of our married life, and here our other children—two sons and two daughters—were born. . . .

The house we were to occupy had been closed for some years and needed many repairs, and the grounds, comprising five acres, were overgrown with weeds. My father gave me a check and said, with a smile, "You believe in woman's capacity to do and dare; now go ahead and put your place in order." After a minute survey of the premises and due consultation with one or two sons of Adam, I set the carpenters, painters, paper-hangers, and gardeners at work, built a new kitchen and woodhouse, and in one month took possession. Having left my children with my mother, there were no impediments to a full display of my executive ability. In the purchase of brick, timber, paint, etc., and in making bargains with workmen, I was in frequent consultation with Judge Sackett and Mr. Bascom. The latter was a member of the Constitutional Convention, then in session in Albany, and as he used to walk down whenever he was at home, to see how my work progressed, we had long talks, sitting on boxes in the midst of tools and shavings, on the status of women. I urged him to propose an amendment to Article II, Section 3, of the State Constitution, striking out the word "male," which limits the suffrage to men. But, while he fully agreed with all I had to say on the political equality of women, he had not the courage to make himself the laughing-stock of the convention. Whenever I cornered him on this point, manlike he turned the conversation to the painters and carpenters. However, these conversations had the effect of bringing him into the first woman's convention, where he did us good service.

In Seneca Falls my life was comparatively solitary, and the change from Boston was somewhat depressing. There, all my immediate friends were reformers, I had near neighbors, a new home with all the modern conveniences, and well-trained servants. Here our residence was on the outskirts of the town, roads very often muddy and no sidewalks most of the way, Mr. Stanton was frequently from home, I had poor servants, and an increasing number of children. To keep a house and grounds in good order, purchase every article for daily use, keep the wardrobes of half a dozen human beings in proper trim, take the children to dentists, shoemakers, and different schools, or find teachers at home, altogether made sufficient work to keep one brain busy, as well as all the hands I could impress into the service. Then, too, the novelty of housekeeping had passed away, and much that was once attractive in domestic life was now irksome. I had so many cares that the company I needed for intellectual stimulus was a trial rather than a pleasure.

There was quite an Irish settlement at a short distance, and continual complaints were coming to me that my boys threw stones at their pigs, cows, and the roofs of their houses. This involved constant diplomatic relations in the settlement of various difficulties, in which I was so successful that, at length, they constituted me a kind of umpire in all their own quarrels. If a drunken husband was pounding his wife, the children would run for me. Hastening to the scene of action, I would take Patrick by the collar, and, much to his surprise and shame, make him sit down and promise to behave himself. I never had one of them offer the least resistance, and in time they all came to regard me as one having authority. I strengthened my influence by cultivating good feeling. I lent the men papers to read, and invited their children into our grounds; giving them fruit, of which we had abundance, and my children's old clothes, books, and toys. I was their physician, also—with my box of homeopathic medicines I took charge of the men, women, and children in sickness. Thus the most amicable relations were established, and, in any emergency, these poor neighbors were good friends and always ready to serve me.

But I found police duty rather irksome, especially when called out dark nights to prevent drunken fathers from disturbing their sleeping children, or to minister to poor mothers in the pangs of maternity. Alas! alas! who can measure the mountains of sorrow and suffering endured in unwelcome motherhood in the abodes of ignorance, poverty, and vice, where terror-stricken women and children are the victims of strong men frenzied with passion and intoxicating drink?

Up to this time life had glided by with comparative ease, but now the real struggle was upon me. My duties were too numerous and varied, and none sufficiently exhilarating or intellectual to bring into play my higher faculties. I suffered with mental hunger, which, like an empty stomach, is very depressing. I had books, but no stimulating companionship. To add to my general dissatisfaction at the change from Boston, I found that Seneca Falls was a malarial region, and in due time all the children were attacked with chills and fever which, under homeopathic treatment in those days, lasted three months. The servants were afflicted in the same way. Cleanliness, order, the love of the beautiful and artistic, all faded away in the struggle to accomplish what was absolutely necessary from hour to hour. Now I understood, as I never had before, how women could sit down and rest in the midst of general disorder. Housekeeping, under such conditions, was impossible, so I packed our clothes, locked up the house, and went to that harbor of safety, [my parents'] home, as I did ever after in stress of weather.

I now fully understood the practical difficulties most women had to contend with in the isolated household, and the impossibility of woman's best development if in contact, the chief part of her life, with servants and children. Fourier's phalansterie[3] community life and co-operative households had a new significance for me. Emerson says, "A healthy discontent is the first step to progress." The general discontent I felt with woman's portion as wife, mother, housekeeper, physician, and spiritual guide, the chaotic conditions into which everything fell without her constant supervision, and the wearied, anxious look of the majority of women impressed me with a strong feeling that some active measures should be taken to remedy the wrongs of society in general, and of women in particular. My experience at the World's Anti-slavery Convention,

---

3. **phalansterie:** A community of the followers of Charles Fourier, who advocated a society organized into small, self-sustaining communal groups.

all I had read of the legal status of women, and the oppression I saw everywhere, together swept across my soul, intensified now by many personal experiences. It seemed as if all the elements had conspired to impel me to some onward step. I could not see what to do or where to begin — my only thought was a public meeting for protest and discussion.

In this tempest-tossed condition of mind I received an invitation to spend the day with Lucretia Mott, at Richard Hunt's, in Waterloo. There I met several members of different families of Friends, earnest, thoughtful women. I poured out, that day, the torrent of my long-accumulating discontent, with such vehemence and indignation that I stirred myself, as well as the rest of the party, to do and dare anything. My discontent, according to Emerson, must have been healthy, for it moved us all to prompt action, and we decided, then and there, to call a "Woman's Rights Convention." We wrote the call that evening and published it in the *Seneca County Courier* the next day, the 14th of July, 1848, giving only five days' notice, as the convention was to be held on the 19th and 20th. The call was inserted without signatures, — in fact it was a mere announcement of a meeting, — but the chief movers and managers were Lucretia Mott, Mary Ann McClintock, Jane Hunt, Martha C. Wright, and myself. The convention, which was held two days in the Methodist Church, was in every way a grand success. The house was crowded at every session, the speaking good, and a religious earnestness dignified all the proceedings.

These were the hasty initiative steps of "the most momentous reform that had yet been launched on the world — the first organized protest against the injustice which had brooded for ages over the character and destiny of one-half the race." No words could express our astonishment on finding, a few days afterward, that what seemed to us so timely, so rational, and so sacred, should be a subject for sarcasm and ridicule to the entire press of the nation. With our Declaration of Rights and Resolutions for a text, it seemed as if every man who could wield a pen prepared a homily on "woman's sphere." All the journals from Maine to Texas seemed to strive with each other to see which could make our movement appear the most ridiculous. The anti-slavery papers stood by us manfully and so did Frederick Douglass, both in the convention and in his paper, *The North Star,* but so pronounced was the popular voice against us, in the parlor, press, and pulpit, that most of the ladies who had attended the convention and signed the declaration, one by one, withdrew their names and influence and joined our persecutors. Our friends gave us the cold shoulder and felt themselves disgraced by the whole proceeding.

If I had had the slightest premonition of all that was to follow that convention, I fear I should not have had the courage to risk it, and I must confess that it was with fear and trembling that I consented to attend another, one month afterward, in Rochester. Fortunately, the first one seemed to have drawn all the fire, and of the second but little was said. But we had set the ball in motion, and now, in quick succession, conventions were held in Ohio, Indiana, Massachusetts, Pennsylvania, and in the City of New York, and have been kept up nearly every year since.

DECLARATION OF SENTIMENTS, 1848

When, in the course of human events, it becomes necessary for one portion of the family of man to assume among the people of the earth a position different from that which they have hitherto occupied, but one to which the laws of nature and of nature's God entitle them, a decent respect to the opinions of mankind requires that they should declare the causes that impel them to such a course.

We hold these truths to be self-evident: that all men and women are created equal; that they are endowed by their Creator with certain inalienable rights; that among these are life, liberty, and the pursuit of happiness; that to secure these rights governments are instituted, deriving their just powers from the consent of the governed. Whenever any form of government becomes destructive of these ends, it is the right of those who suffer from it to refuse allegiance to it, and to insist upon the institution of a new government, laying its foundation on such principles, and organizing its powers in such form, as to them shall seem most likely to effect their safety and happiness. Prudence, indeed, will dictate that governments long established should not be changed for light and transient causes; and accordingly all experience hath shown that mankind are more disposed to suffer, while evils are sufferable, than to right themselves by abolishing the forms to which they were accustomed. But when a long train of abuses and usurpations, pursuing invariably the same object evinces a design to reduce them under absolute despotism, it is their duty to throw off such government, and to provide new guards for their future security. Such has been the patient sufferance of the women under this government, and such is now the necessity which constrains them to demand the equal station to which they are entitled.

The history of mankind is a history of repeated injuries and usurpations on the part of man toward woman, having in direct object the establishment of an absolute tyranny over her. To prove this, let facts be submitted to a candid world.

He has never permitted her to exercise her inalienable right to the elective franchise.

He has compelled her to submit to laws, in the formation of which she had no voice.

He has withheld from her rights which are given to the most ignorant and degraded men—both natives and foreigners.

Having deprived her of this first right of a citizen, the elective franchise, thereby leaving her without representation in the halls of legislation, he has oppressed her on all sides.

He has made her, if married, in the eye of the law, civilly dead.

He has taken from her all right in property, even to the wages she earns.

He has made her, morally, an irresponsible being, as she can commit many crimes with impunity, provided they be done in the presence of her husband. In the covenant of marriage, she is compelled to promise obedience to her husband, he becoming to all intents and purposes, her master—the law giving him power to deprive her of her liberty, and to administer chastisement.

He has so framed the laws of divorce, as to what shall be the proper causes of divorce, and in case of separation, to whom the guardianship of the children shall be given, as to be wholly regardless of the happiness of women — the law, in all cases, going upon a false supposition of the supremacy of man, and giving all power into his hands.

After depriving her of all rights as a married woman, if single and the owner of property, he has taxed her to support a government which recognizes her only when her property can be made profitable to it.

He has monopolized nearly all the profitable employments, and from those she is permitted to follow, she receives but a scanty remuneration.

He closes against her all the avenues to wealth and distinction, which he considers most honorable to himself. As a teacher of theology, medicine, or law, she is not known.

He has denied her the facilities for obtaining a thorough education — all colleges being closed against her.

He allows her in Church as well as State, but a subordinate position, claiming Apostolic authority for her exclusion from the ministry, and, with some exceptions, from any public participation in the affairs of the Church.

He has created a false public sentiment by giving to the world a different code of morals for men and women, by which moral delinquencies which exclude women from society, are not only tolerated, but deemed of little account in man.

He has usurped the prerogative of Jehovah himself, claiming it as his right to assign for her a sphere of action, when that belongs to her conscience and to her God.

He has endeavored, in every way that he could, to destroy her confidence in her own powers, to lessen her self-respect, and to make her willing to lead a dependent and abject life.

Now, in view of this entire disfranchisement of one-half the people of this country, their social and religious degradation, — in view of the unjust laws above mentioned, and because women do feel themselves aggrieved, oppressed, and fraudulently deprived of their most sacred rights, we insist that they have immediate admission to all the rights and privileges which belong to them as citizens of these United States.

In entering upon the great work before us, we anticipate no small amount of misconception, misrepresentation, and ridicule; but we shall use every instrumentality within our power to effect our object. We shall employ agents, circulate tracts, petition the State and national Legislatures, and endeavor to enlist the pulpit and the press in our behalf. We hope this Convention will be followed by a series of Conventions, embracing every part of the country.

Firmly relying upon the final triumph of the Right and the True, we do this day affix our signatures to this declaration.

38

Taking Up Arms against Slavery

John Brown

In October 1859, fifty-nine-year-old John Brown, a white abolitionist, tanner, farmer, and failed businessman, launched the ultimate battle in his war against slavery. With five black and sixteen white followers, two of them his sons, he captured the federal arsenal at Harpers Ferry, a town then still in Virginia about sixty miles northwest of Washington, D.C., at the meeting point of the Potomac and Shenandoah rivers. Intending that slaves use arms from the arsenal to rise up and claim their freedom, he planned to set off a spreading slave rebellion that made use of weapons from other arsenals.

Utterly committed to a Christianity rooted in the Old Testament, Brown had begun his campaign of armed struggle in Kansas. In 1854, Senator Stephen A. Douglas of Illinois introduced the proposal known as the Kansas-Nebraska Act, which deepened the division between defenders and opponents of slavery. The measure created two territories and allowed the inhabitants of each to decide whether upon achieving statehood it should institute or prohibit slavery. Soon after passage of Douglas's bill, proslavery migrants from Missouri and antislavery partisans from the North were settling in Kansas, aiming to determine the future of the territory.

In Kansas, Brown and several sons participated in the guerrilla warfare over whether the territory would become a slave or a free state. Brown's murder of five men at Pottawatomie Creek in retaliation for the killing of an antislavery partisan quickened the violence that flared briefly in the territory in the mid-1850s. Later, while living in the black community at North Elba, New York, he planned the venture at Harpers Ferry.

After thirty-six hours, federal troops led by Robert E. Lee overwhelmed Brown and his remaining men at Harpers Ferry. His behavior during his trial—a statement from which is included here—and at his hanging that December, and his calm conviction in the face of death, impressed even the governor of Virginia and caught the imagination of the country as it hurtled toward a greater conflict. The raid at the little Virginia town had failed. Or had it?

When President Lincoln met Harriet Beecher Stowe, the author of the best-selling Uncle Tom's Cabin, *published in 1851, he supposedly greeted her as the little woman who had started the great war. Yet it was not only the powerful though sentiment-soaked novel but in good measure the actions of John Brown, who adopted the policy*

"John Brown Song," J. Wrigley. Publisher, of Songs, Ballads, and Toy Books &c., New York, New York. J. Wrigley "No. 964."

of "war to the knife, and the knife to the hilt," that scraped the nerves of white Southerners so raw that after Lincoln's election they seceded. And in the conflict that followed, their slave system collapsed around them.

As Brown's memory was becoming an object of Southern rage, Northern abolitionists adapted a song about a young soldier in the Massachusetts Volunteer Militia who shared Brown's name to use as their anthem, reprinted below. The music the song was set to would soon carry the words of the great "Battle Hymn of the Republic" by Julia Ward Howe. Brown, in death, provided the Union with an anthem. In his last hour, as he fearlessly neared the gallows, he had handed a soldier escorting him a note announcing as though in anticipation of his country's greatest war, "I, John Brown, am now quite certain that the sins of this guilty land will never be purged away but with blood." Ralph Waldo Emerson predicted that Brown would "make the gallows as glorious as the cross." Brown's last address to the Virginia court on November 2, 1859, is reprinted below. This section closes with two daguerreotypes taken of Brown, one in 1856 and one in 1859.

QUESTIONS TO CONSIDER

1. History has remembered John Brown's fanaticism, emotional instability, and use of violence, but he was very popular and even respected by his enemies at the time of his death. What has changed?
2. John Brown argues that if he had intervened on behalf of the rich, he would have been rewarded rather than punished for his actions. What does he mean by this?
3. Brown believed that spilling blood would be necessary to free African American slaves, and many of his contemporaries agreed. How would this view be received today?
4. Why do you think John Brown's appearance changed so dramatically from the first photo to the second?
5. In the nineteenth century, photographs were difficult to create and expensive to have made; therefore, people gave lots of thought to how they dressed and how they posed for them. What would you imagine the discussion to be between John Brown and his photographer?

LYRICS TO "JOHN BROWN'S BODY"

John Brown's body lies a mouldering in the grave,
While weep the sons of bondage, whom he ventured all to save,
But tho' he lost his life in struggling for the slave,
His soul is marching on.

Chorus — Glory, Glory Hallelujah!
　　　　Glory, Glory Hallelujah!
　　　　Glory, Glory Hallelujah!
　　　　His soul is marching on.

John Brown was a hero undaunted, true, and brave,
And Kansas knew his valor, when he fought her rights to save:
And now though the grass grows green above his grave,
His soul is marching on.   Glory, &c.

He captured Harpers Ferry with his nineteen men so few,
And he frighten'd old Virginny till she trembled through and through:
They hung him for a traitor; themselves a traitor crew,
But his soul is marching on.   Glory, &c.

John Brown was John the Baptist, of Christ we are to see,
Christ who of the bondman shall the Liberator be,
And soon throughout the sunny South, the slaves shall all be free,
For his soul is marching on.   Glory, &c.

The conflict that he heralded, he looks from heaven to view,
On the army of the Union, with his flag Red, White and Blue;
And heaven shall ring with anthems, o'er the deed they mean to do
For his soul is marching on.   Glory, &c.

Ye soldiers of Freedom, then strike, while strike ye may,
The death-blow of oppression in a better time and way;
For the dawn of old John Brown, has brightened into day,
And his soul is marching on.   Glory, &c.

LAST ADDRESS TO THE VIRGINIA COURT
ON NOVEMBER 2, 1859

I have, may it please the Court, a few words to say.

In the first place, I deny everything but what I have all along admitted, of a design on my part to free the slaves. I intended certainly to have made a clean thing of that matter, as I did last winter, when I went into Missouri and there took slaves without the snapping of a gun on either side, moved them through the country, and finally left them in Canada. I designed to have done the same thing again, on a larger scale. That was all I intended. I never did intend murder, or treason, or the destruction of property, or to excite or incite slaves to rebellion, or to make insurrection.

I have another objection; and that is, it is unjust that I should suffer such a penalty. Had I interfered in the manner which I admit, and which I admit has been fairly proved (for I admire the truthfulness and candor of the greater portion of the witnesses who have testified in this case), — had I so interfered in behalf of the rich, the powerful, the intelligent, the so-called great, or in behalf of any of their friends, — either father, mother, brother, sister, wife, or children, or any of that class, — and suffered and sacrificed what I have in this interference, it would have been all right; and every man in this court would have deemed it an act worthy of reward rather than punishment.

This court acknowledges, as I suppose, the validity of the law of God. I see a book kissed here which I suppose to be the Bible, or at least the New Testament. That teaches me that all things whatsoever I would that men should do to me, I should do even so to them. It teaches me, further to "remember them that are in bonds, as bound with them." I endeavored to act up to that instruction. I say, I am yet too young to understand that God is any respecter of persons. I believe that to have interfered as I have done—in behalf of His despised poor, was not wrong, but right. Now, if it is deemed necessary that I should forfeit my life for the furtherance of the ends of justice, and mingle my blood further with the blood of my children and with the blood of millions in this slave country whose rights are disregarded by wicked, cruel, and unjust enactments,—I submit; so let it be done!

Let me say one word further.

I feel entirely satisfied with the treatment I have received on my trial.

John Brown in 1856.

John Brown in 1859, the year he led the attack on the federal
arsenal at Harpers Ferry.

Slavery and Freedom

Visual representations of African Americans in the nineteenth century varied considerably over time and according to the presuppositions of the beholder. The growing controversy over the institution of slavery fostered new images that first appeared before the public in the 1830s. With the advent of photography in 1839, stills and daguerreotypes of slaves as well as of free blacks were developed for personal and public use. Magazines such as *Harper's Weekly* illustrated their stories with wood engravings made from photographs. Next, several commercial forms of photography evolved for sale to a mass market. One was the stereo card, a format that offered the illusion of three dimensions when two side-by-side images were seen through a viewer and that remained popular from the 1850s well into the twentieth century. Another was the *carte-de-visite*. Originally a way to produce small portraits cheaply, it soon led to the extensive sale of pictures of celebrities. About the size of the visiting card used in social life—hence their name—*cartes-de-visite* consisted of an image on a thin piece of photographic paper that was pasted to a thicker cardboard backing; messages could be inscribed on the back. Most of these texts were simple advertisements for the photographic studios, but some were used as conveyors of propaganda to represent people's political, moral, or aesthetic passions, much as we print messages on buttons, T-shirts, and bumper stickers today. People collected *cartes-de-visite* most commonly for celebrity worship, as hobbyists buy and sell sports-figure cards today.

Early photographic processes set certain limits and created specific conventions about the images produced in this era. Bulky equipment, the time required for preparation of a photosensitive surface, and lengthy exposure times gave nineteenth-century portraiture a solemn character. Movement produced a blur, so people had to set their faces into an expression that they could hold for about thirty seconds, a rather long time. Smiling and saying "cheese" belong to a much later era when cameras had become easier to use and the portrait had evolved into the "snapshot"—an image captured in an instant. Most photographs from the nineteenth century convey seriousness, with their subjects, even unwilling ones, striving for a dignified appearance.

The figures on these pages offer sharply divergent images of slavery. Children throughout the nation learned about the American South from images like the woodcut shown in Figure 1, taken from a widely used school geography

Figure 1. Unknown artist, "United States: The South," from *Malte-Brun's School Geography*, 1836.

Figure 2. Thomas M. Easterly, "Southern Man, His Two Daughters, and Nanny," St. Louis, Mo., 1848.

book of the 1830s. What impressions of the region does this woodcut convey to viewers?

Figures 2 through 6 on these pages are all daguerreotypes made for private enterprises or for personal reasons. Figure 2 is a portrait of a slaveholding family, probably done at significant expense. Why do you think the family chose to include the African American nanny? What details do you notice about costume and placement of family members, and what do you think are their significance?

Louis Agassiz, one of the leading scientists in the United States at that time, used the images in Figures 3 and 4, which he instructed a South Carolina daguerreotypist to make, to demonstrate an anthropological theory of the "separate creation" of the different races. Such public displays of non-European bodies were a common spectacle in nineteenth-century North Atlantic societies. Medical researchers combined with promoters to put on photographic as

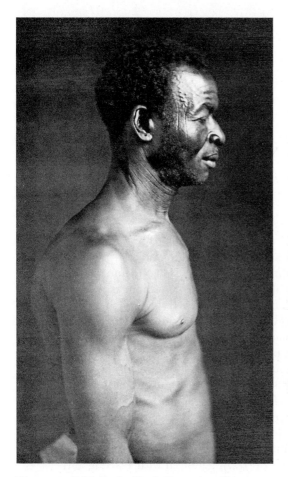 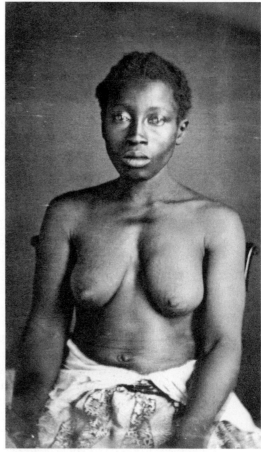

Figure 3. J. T. Zealy, "Jack (Driver), a Slave in Columbia, S.C., ' . . . from the Guinea Coast,' " 1850.

Figure 4. J. T. Zealy, "Delia, a Slave in Columbia, S.C., ' . . . Country Born of African Parents,' " 1850.

253

Figure 5. Thomas M. Easterly, "Robert J. Wilkinson, Successful Businessman," St. Louis, Mo., c. 1860.

Figure 6. Augustus Washington, "Portrait of an Unidentified Woman," Hartford, Conn., c. 1850.

well as sometimes live displays, such as the famous Hottentot Venus, South African Sara Baartman, who was "exhibited" in Europe in 1810 by British medical researchers. Images like Figures 3 and 4, which clearly violated norms of nineteenth-century public modesty, did not gain widespread condemnation for their depictions of nudity, but were the object of anger by abolitionists. Why do you think it was acceptable among "polite society" to display such nudity? What do you think the relationship was between scientific inquiry and prurient interest? Why do you think abolitionists objected so strongly to these images?

Figures 5 and 6 are representations of free African Americans who chose to be photographed at their own expense, just as middle-class whites of the period did. Figure 6, in fact, was made by Augustus Washington, an African American daguerreotypist who owned a studio in Hartford, Connecticut.

Figures 7 through 10 are all public representations of slaves from Northern sources. The photos were designed to make a particular point, as were the daguerreotypes that supposedly demonstrated racial theories for Agassiz. Figures 7 and 8 are wood engravings from *Harper's Weekly*, a journal with a strong anti-slavery bias. What is it about Figures 7 and 8 that might have promoted the anti-slavery agenda of *Harper's Weekly*? Why do you think *Harper's Weekly* chose to describe those in Figure 8 as "white and colored"? How do you think the images of light-skinned children in Figures 8 and 9 might have been viewed by Northern audiences at the time of the Civil War? The message on the back of Figure 10, a carte-de-visite portrait of Gordon, a slave who entered Union territory in 1863 and became a Union soldier, reads:

> "The Peculiar Institution" Illustrated. Copy of a photograph taken from life at Baton Rouge, La. Ap. 2, '63; the lacerated body—months after the brutal flogging had been inflicted—having healed in the manner represented. The alleged offense was a trifling one. How noble and benignant the countenance of the victim!

Does this image remind you of any modern images used in the mass media?

The images in Figures 11 and 12 were made near the end of the Civil War by men who sold their work in various formats to a mass market. Consider the

Figure 7. Unknown artist, "The Africans of the Slave Bark 'Wildfire,'" *Harper's Weekly,* June 2, 1860.

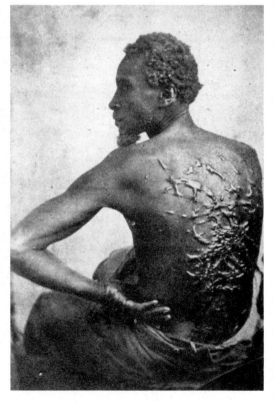

Above left: **Figure 8.** Unknown artist, "Emancipated Slaves, White and Colored," *Harper's Weekly*, January 30, 1864.

Far left: **Figure 9.** Charles Payson, "Freedom's Banner. Charley, a Slave Boy from New Orleans," 1863.

Left: **Figure 10.** McPherson & Oliver, "'The Peculiar Institution.' Gordon, Escaped from Mississippi," 1863.

ways in which these last two images suggest possible future questions that go beyond those of slavery and freedom that were posed by image makers before and during the Civil War.

Figures 13 and 14 are images from late in the Civil War and from the post-war Reconstruction era. The captions in Figure 13, along with the portrayal of both whites and freed slaves as dependent and idle, suggest some of the criticisms that *Harper's Weekly* had of the policies being pursued by the federal occupation of the Southern states immediately after the Civil War. The freed slaves in the image believe they will survive on rations and the white Southerners expect to

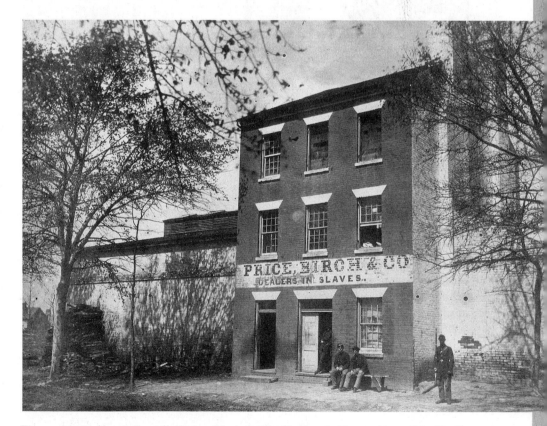

Figure 11. Andrew J. Russell, "Price, Birch & Co., Dealers in Slaves, Alexandria, Va.," 1865.

Figure 12. Brady & Co., "Interior View of the Price, Birch & Co. Slave Dealership, Alexandria, Va.," 1865.

manage the government, but nobody envisions engaging in productive labor. Figure 14 depicts a formal wedding, where bride and groom are African Americans, something that would have been uncommon and far less public in the antebellum South. Consider the ways in which these last two images suggest possible future directions for race relations in the twenty-first century.

Figure 13. Unknown artist, "Solution of the Labor Question in the South," *Harper's Weekly*, December 2, 1865.

Figure 14. Unknown artist, "The Ebony Bridal — The Wedding Ceremony," *Frank Leslie's Popular Monthly*, October 1877.

FOR CRITICAL THINKING

1. How did the image of slavery change from the schoolbook image of 1836 shown in Figure 1 to the depictions of slavery from 1865 shown in Figures 13 and 14?
2. What do the faces shown in Figures 2 through 6 tell you about slavery and freedom?
3. How do Figures 8 and 9 connect to what you know about the experiences of young female slaves?
4. Figures 7 through 10 were produced for the public from Northern sources. What message about slavery was each of these images delivering? How did the public debate over slavery influence the way African Americans were visualized in these images?
5. What effect did the Civil War and the Reconstruction era have on photographers' perceptions of African Americans?
6. What do Figures 13 and 14 suggest about the present and future of race relations in the South?

PART SIX

Civil War and Reconstruction

The Price of War

During the thirty years leading to the Civil War, the United States' early nationalism gave way to antebellum sectionalism. Settlers from the North and from the South resolutely proceeded westward, but in economic and societal matters the rapidly growing Southwest, including Alabama, Mississippi, and Louisiana, differed greatly from the new Northwest of Ohio, Illinois, and Wisconsin. Though both regions were dominated by small farms, the South also cultivated large plantations. Slaves worked vast acreage in the South, while free labor developed the North. One society produced a rural gentry, and the other cities, entrepreneurs, and lawyers; one grew conservative and fearful of change, while the other spawned liberal religions and reforms. Beneath the expansion was a national antipathy to the black race that made Southerners fearful of the abolition of slavery and committed Northerners to halting the expansion of slavery in their own society, a commitment that in parts of the North coexisted with a moral abhorrence of the institution of slavery.

The readings in this section reflect the crises the nation faced at midcentury. Union nurse Cornelia Hancock's description of the battlefield and the accounts by Union soldier Samuel Cormany and his wife, Rachel, of the battle at Gettysburg graphically illustrate the impact of war. Ellen Leonard's account of the New York antidraft riot in 1863, as well as the difficulties encountered by black soldiers when they were finally accepted into the Union Army in late 1862 expose the dilemma of conflicting visions of the goals of the war. Victory for the Union did not answer all the major questions posed by the antislavery debate and the war.

As the war wound down in 1865, the nation was fatigued, the dead could be counted in the hundreds of thousands, and nearly everybody—from the most impoverished ex-slave and poor up-country white to elite senators and internationally famous abolitionists like Frederick Douglass—understood that the war had really only resolved the question of slavery. The real struggle for what the nation's future would be had just begun.

In the months following Lee's surrender to Grant at Appomattox, the South was a landscape of abandoned fields, twisted rails, burned buildings, white men hobbling about on one leg or dangling an empty sleeve, and former slaves exploring their new freedom or searching for food, shelter, and work. The visual document of the ruins in Charleston, South Carolina (p. 322), demonstrates the extent of the destruction. Some things the war had settled: secession was impossible, slavery dead, and the South desperately impoverished, its prewar agricultural, slave-based economy gone with the wind. Other outcomes the region and the United States struggle with still. In particular, victory for the Union did not resolve questions about the role that African American men and women were to play in American life. The first attempts to secure rights for the former slaves, known as Reconstruction (1865–1876), produced the Thirteenth, Fourteenth, and Fifteenth Amendments to the Constitution, which provided the legal basis for a revolutionary change in American life. African Americans built schools, farms, homesteads, and community institutions, electing black senators and congressmen, including a majority of the Congressional representatives at various times in South Carolina, Louisiana, and Mississippi. Many white Southerners, like plantation owner Henry Ravenel, simply did not know what to make of the changes, while other white Southerners, like Caleb Forshey, had a clearer vision of what it was they were fighting for and against.

The Compromise of 1877 finally put an end to Reconstruction by removing federal troops from the South and returning land to former slave owners. Ordinary freedmen, like Felix Haywood, who had rejoiced at newly won freedoms, suddenly found themselves facing a world of Southern sharecropping where they were neither slaves nor fully free. These struggles of Reconstruction would shape race relations and the African American struggle for civil rights during much of the following century.

Winding Down the War and an Uncertain Future

39

What the Black Man Wants

Frederick Douglass

As the Civil War came to a close in early 1865, the big question facing Americans on both sides was what would happen to four million newly emancipated slaves. Where would they live and work? Who would govern them and on what terms?

General William Tecumseh Sherman began the process before the end of the war with Special Field Order No. 15, which provided black families with forty acres of abandoned plantation land along the Georgia seacoast and a U.S. Army mule. This military strategy by a general still at war who hoped to break his enemy and provide for the forty thousand freedmen following his army inspired hope among African Americans throughout the South. However, when Lincoln was assassinated three months later, the new president, Andrew Johnson, returned the land to the former owners.

Communities of freedmen often began the process of Reconstruction on their own, setting up local government and education schemes in liberated parts of the South. However, land was the crucial element. Black families often believed they were entitled to land they had worked and lived on for generations without pay. White plantation owners viewed this issue differently. Such questions were being debated in both the North and South by people from across the political spectrum, among them Frederick Douglass, a black man and escaped slave.

Born Frederick Washington Bailey in 1818 in Maryland, the son of a white man and a black slave, Douglass was taken from his mother early and passed from master to master. At twelve he was taught to read by his master's wife, an act that was prohibited by law. As a teenager, Douglass himself taught fellow slaves to read in Sunday school and organized several failed attempts at mass escapes, finally succeeding on his own at nineteen disguised as a free black sailor. He changed his name to Frederick Douglass, married Anna Murray, and settled in New Bedford, Massachusetts. There he joined the American Anti-Slavery Society, and went on to become a leading abolitionist with brilliant oratorical skills, publish his autobiography (which became an international best seller), edit his own antislavery newspaper, The North Star, *serve as an adviser to Abraham Lincoln during the war, and eventually become president of the Freedman's Savings and Trust Company during Reconstruction.*

The Life and Writings of Frederick Douglass, ed. Philip S. Foner (New York: International Publishers, 1950), Vol. 4, 157–65.

Douglass delivered the following speech on the equality of all men before the law at the Annual Meeting of the Massachusetts Anti-Slavery Society in Boston, April 1865. A few days later the Civil War officially ended and President Lincoln was assassinated. Douglass would deliver the eulogy at Lincoln's funeral, for which he received a standing ovation.

QUESTIONS TO CONSIDER

1. At the end of this speech Frederick Douglass says, "The American people have always been anxious to know what they shall do with us." He then says, "Do nothing with us!" What does he mean?
2. Douglass argues that abolitionist societies should fight for universal suffrage for African Americans. Can you imagine why societies that fought against slavery might be divided on this issue?
3. Douglass mentions the fact that women cannot vote. How do you think this might have had an impact on discussions about the vote for freed slaves?

. . . I do not know, from what has been said, that there is any difference of opinion as to the duty of abolitionists, at the present moment. How can we get up any difference at this point, or any point, where we are so united, so agreed? I went especially, however, with that word of Mr. Phillips, which is the criticism of Gen. Banks and Gen. Banks' policy.[1] I hold that that policy is our chief danger at the present moment; that it practically enslaves the Negro, and makes the Proclamation[2] of 1863 a mockery and delusion. What is freedom? It is the right to choose one's own employment. Certainly it means that, if it means anything; and when any individual or combination of individuals undertakes to decide for any man when he shall work, where he shall work, at what he shall work, and for what he shall work, he or they practically reduce him to slavery. [Applause.] He is a slave. That I understand Gen. Banks to do—to determine for the so-called freedman, when, and where, and at what, and for how much he shall work, when he shall be punished, and by whom punished. It is absolute slavery. It defeats the beneficent intention of the Government, if it has beneficent intentions, in regards to the freedom of our people.

I have had but one idea for the last three years to present to the American people, and the phraseology in which I clothe it is the old abolition phraseology. I am for the "immediate, unconditional, and universal" enfranchisement of the black man, in every State in the Union. [Loud applause.] Without this, his liberty is a mockery; without this, you might as well almost retain the old name of slavery for his condition; for in fact, if he is not the slave of the individual

1. General Banks instituted a labor policy in Louisiana that was discriminatory of blacks, claiming that it was to help prepare them to better handle freedom. Wendell Phillips, a prominent lawyer, abolitionist, and advocate for Native Americans, countered by saying, "If there is anything patent in the whole history of our thirty years' struggle, it is that the Negro no more needs to be prepared for liberty than the white man."
2. **Proclamation:** The Emancipation Proclamation.

master, he is the slave of society, and holds his liberty as a privilege, not as a right. He is at the mercy of the mob, and has no means of protecting himself.

It may be objected, however, that this pressing of the Negro's right to suffrage is premature. Let us have slavery abolished, it may be said, let us have labor organized, and then, in the natural course of events, the right of suffrage will be extended to the Negro. I do not agree with this. The constitution of the human mind is such, that if it once disregards the conviction forced upon it by a revelation of truth, it requires the exercise of a higher power to produce the same conviction afterwards. The American people are now in tears. The Shenandoah has run blood—the best blood of the North. All around Richmond, the blood of New England and of the North has been shed—of your sons, your brothers and your fathers. We all feel, in the existence of this Rebellion, that judgments terrible, wide-spread, far-reaching, overwhelming, are abroad in the land; and we feel, in view of these judgments, just now, a disposition to learn righteousness. This is the hour. Our streets are in mourning, tears are falling at every fireside, and under the chastisement of this Rebellion we have almost come up to the point of conceding this great, this all-important right of suffrage. I fear that if we fail to do it now, if abolitionists fail to press it now, we may not see, for centuries to come, the same disposition that exists at this moment. [Applause.] Hence, I say, now is the time to press this right.

It may be asked, "Why do you want it? Some men have got along very well without it. Women have not this right." Shall we justify one wrong by another? This is the sufficient answer. Shall we at this moment justify the deprivation of the Negro of the right to vote, because some one else is deprived of that privilege? I hold that women, as well as men, have the right to vote [applause], and my heart and voice go with the movement to extend suffrage to woman; but that question rests upon another basis than which our right rests. We may be asked, I say, why we want it. I will tell you why we want it. We want it because it is our right, first of all. No class of men can, without insulting their own nature, be content with any deprivation of their rights. We want it again, as a means for educating our race. Men are so constituted that they derive their conviction of their own possibilities largely by the estimate formed of them by others. If nothing is expected of a people, that people will find it difficult to contradict that expectation. By depriving us of suffrage, you affirm our incapacity to form an intelligent judgment respecting public men and public measures; you declare before the world that we are unfit to exercise the elective franchise, and by this means lead us to undervalue ourselves, to put a low estimate upon ourselves, and to feel that we have no possibilities like other men. Again, I want the elective franchise, for one, as a colored man, because ours is a peculiar government, based upon a peculiar idea, and that idea is universal suffrage. If I were in a monarchial government, or an autocratic or aristocratic government, where the few bore rule and the many were subject, there would be no special stigma resting upon me, because I did not exercise the elective franchise. It would do me no great violence. Mingling with the mass I should partake of the strength of the mass; I should be supported by the mass, and I should have the same incentives to endeavor with the mass of my fellow-men; it would be no particular burden, no particular deprivation; but here where universal suffrage is the rule, where that is the fundamental idea of the Government, to rule us out is to make us an exception, to brand us with the stigma of inferiority, and to invite to our heads the missiles of those about us; therefore, I want the franchise for the black man.

There are, however, other reasons, not derived from any consideration merely of our rights, but arising out of the conditions of the South, and of the country—considerations which have already been referred to by Mr. Phillips—considerations which must arrest the attention of statesmen. I believe that when the tall heads of this Rebellion shall have been swept down, as they will be swept down, when the Davises and Toombses and Stephenses, and others who are leading this Rebellion shall have been blotted out, there will be this rank undergrowth of treason, to which reference has been made, growing up there, and interfering with, and thwarting the quiet operation of the Federal Government in those states. You will see those traitors, handing down, from sire to son, the same malignant spirit which they have manifested and which they are now exhibiting, with malicious hearts, broad blades, and bloody hands in the field, against our sons and brothers. That spirit will still remain; and whoever sees the Federal Government extended over those Southern States will see that Government in a strange land, and not only in a strange land, but in an enemy's land. A postmaster of the United States in the South will find himself surrounded by a hostile spirit; a collector in a Southern port will find himself surrounded by a hostile spirit; a United States marshal or United States judge will be surrounded there by a hostile element. That enmity will not die out in a year, will not die out in an age. The Federal Government will be looked upon in those States precisely as the Governments of Austria and France are looked upon in Italy at the present moment. They will endeavor to circumvent, they will endeavor to destroy, the peaceful operation of this Government. Now, where will you find the strength to counterbalance this spirit, if you do not find it in the Negroes of the South? They are your friends, and have always been your friends. They were your friends even when the Government did not regard them as such. They comprehended the genius of this war before you did. . . . When Seward[3] said the status of no man in the country would be changed by the war, the Negro did not believe him. [Applause.] When our generals sent their underlings in shoulder-straps to hunt the flying Negro back from our lines into the jaws of slavery, from which he had escaped, the Negroes thought that a mistake had been made, and that the intentions of the Government had not been rightly understood by our officers in shoulder-straps, and they continued to come into our lines, threading their way through bogs and fens, over briers and thorns, fording streams, swimming rivers, bringing us tidings as to the safe path to march, and pointing out the dangers that threatened us. They are our only friends in the South, and we should be true to them in this their trial hour, and see to it that they have the elective franchise.

---

3. **Seward:** William Henry Seward (1801–1872), U.S. statesman and Secretary of State from 1861 to 1869.

I know that we are inferior to you in some things—virtually inferior. We walk about you like dwarfs among giants. Our heads are scarcely seen above the great sea of humanity. The Germans are superior to us; the Irish are superior to us; the Yankees are superior to us [Laughter]; they can do what we cannot, that is, what we have not hitherto been allowed to do. But while I make this admission, I utterly deny, that we are originally, or naturally, or practically, or in any way, or in any important sense, inferior to anybody on this globe. [Loud applause.] This charge of inferiority is an old dodge. It has been made available for oppression on many occasions. It is only about six centuries since the blue-eyed and fair-haired Anglo-Saxons were considered inferior by the haughty Normans, who once trampled upon them. If you read the history of the Norman Conquest, you will find that this proud Anglo-Saxon was once looked upon as of coarser clay than his Norman master, and might be found in the highways and byways of Old England laboring with a brass collar on his neck, and the name of his master marked upon it. You were down then! [Laughter and applause.] You are up now. I am glad you are up, and I want you to be glad to help us up also. [Applause.]

The story of our inferiority is an old dodge, as I have said; for wherever men oppress their fellows, wherever they enslave them, they will endeavor to find the needed apology for such enslavement and oppression in the character of the people oppressed and enslaved. . . . It is said that we are ignorant; I admit it. But if we know enough to be hung, we know enough to vote. If the Negro knows enough to pay taxes to support the government, he knows enough to vote; taxation and representation should go together. If he knows enough to shoulder a musket and fight for the flag, fight for the government, he knows enough to vote. If he knows as much when he is sober as an Irishman knows when drunk, he knows enough to vote, on good American principles. [Laughter and applause.] . . .

. . . But I will not dwell upon this. I put it to the American sense of honor. The honor of a nation is an important thing. It is said in the Scriptures, "What doth it profit a man if he gain the whole world, and lose his own soul?" It may be said, also, What doth it profit a nation if it gain the whole world, but lose its honor? I hold that the American government has taken upon itself a solemn obligation of honor, to see that this war—let it be long or short, let it cost much or let it cost little—that this war shall not cease until every freedman at the South has the right to vote. [Applause.] It has bound itself to it. What have you asked the black men of the South, the black men of the whole country to do? Why, you have asked them to incure the enmity of their masters, in order to befriend you and to befriend this Government. You have asked us to call down, not only upon ourselves, but upon our children's children, the deadly hate of the entire Southern people. You have called upon us to turn our backs upon our masters, to abandon their cause and espouse yours; to turn against the South and in favor of the North; to shoot down the Confederacy and uphold the flag—the American flag. You have called upon us to expose ourselves to all the subtle machinations of their malignity for all time. And now, what do you propose to do when you come to make peace? To reward your enemies, and trample in the dust your friends? Do you intend to sacrifice the very men who have come to the rescue of your banner in the South, and incurred the lasting displeasure of their masters thereby? Do you intend to sacrifice them and reward your enemies? Do you mean to give your enemies the right to vote, and take it away from your friends? . . . When this nation was in trouble, in its early struggles, it looked upon the Negro as a citizen. In 1776 he was a citizen. At the time of the formation of the Constitution the Negro had the right to vote in eleven States out of the old thirteen. In your trouble you have made us citizens. In 1812 Gen. Jackson addressed us as citizens—"fellow-citizens." He wanted us to fight. We were citizens then! And now, when you come to frame a conscription bill, the Negro is a citizen again. He has been a citizen just three times in the history of this government, and it has always been in time of trouble. In time of trouble we are citizens. Shall we be citizens in war, and aliens in peace? Would that be just?

. . . Let me not be misunderstood here. I am not asking for sympathy at the hands of abolitionists, sympathy at the hands of any. I think the American people are disposed often to be generous rather than just. I look over this country at the present time, and I see Educational Societies, Sanitary Commissions, Freedmen's Associations, and the like,—all very good: but in regard to the colored people there is always more that is benevolent, I perceive, than just, manifested towards us. What I ask for the Negro is not benevolence, not pity, not sympathy, but simply justice. [Applause.] The American people have always been anxious to know what they shall do with us. Gen. Banks was distressed with solicitude as to what he should do with the Negro. Everybody has asked the question, and they learned to ask it early of the abolitionists, "What shall we do with the Negro?" I have had but one answer from the beginning. Do nothing with us! Your doing with us has already played the mischief with us. Do nothing with us! If the apples will not remain on the tree of their own strength, if they are wormeaten at the core, if they are early ripe and disposed to fall, let them fall! I am not for tying or fastening them on the tree in any way, except by nature's plan, and if they will not stay there, let them fall. And if the Negro cannot stand on his own legs, let him fall also. All I ask is, give him a chance to stand on his own legs! Let him alone! If you see him on his way to school, let him alone, don't disturb him! If you see him going to the dinner table at a hotel, let him go! If you see him going to the ballot-box, let him alone, don't disturb him! [Applause.] If you see him going into a work-shop, just let him alone,—your interference is doing him a positive injury. Gen. Banks' "preparation" is of a piece with this attempt to prop up the Negro. Let him fall if he cannot stand alone! If the Negro cannot live by the line of eternal justice, so beautifully pictured to you in the illustration used by Mr. Phillips, the fault will not be yours, it will be his who made the Negro, and established that line for his government. [Applause.] Let him live or die by that. If you will only untie his hands, and give him a chance, I think he will live. He will work as readily for himself as the white man. A great many delusions have been swept away by this war. One was, that the Negro would not work; he has proved his ability to work. Another was, that the Negro would not fight; that he possessed only the most sheepish attributes of humanity; was a perfect lamb, or an "Uncle Tom;" disposed to take off his coat whenever required, fold his hands, and be whipped by anybody who wanted to whip him. But the war has proved that there is a great deal of human nature in the Negro, and that "he will fight," as Mr. Quincy, our President, said, in earlier days than these, "when there is reasonable probability of his whipping anybody." [Laughter and applause.]

40

A Slave Owner's Journal at the End of the Civil War

Henry William Ravenel

In a letter of August 26, 1865, Henry William Ravenel (1814–1887) summarized the immediate effects of the collapse of the Confederacy as well as anyone ever has:

> *A new era opens before us, but alas! with what great changes. Our country is in ruins, and our people reduced to poverty. . . . We had no money but Confederate and that is now worthless . . . all our securities and investments are bankrupt. . . . There is little money in the country, little cotton and other produce, so there is no business or employment for those who are anxiously seeking to make a living. . . .*

Emancipation had altered social relations; the collapse of the Confederacy and then Reconstruction were transforming Southern politics; the war and emancipation had upset every economic arrangement, making currency worthless, land unsalable, and credit — previously based on chattel mortgages on slave "property" — scarcely to be obtained.

Ravenel belonged to a prominent South Carolina slaveholding family. In addition to managing a plantation, he became an important self-trained naturalist whose studies of American fungi achieved international renown. After the war he supported his family by selling seeds and parts of his collections of fungi to collectors and later worked as a naturalist for the U.S. Department of Agriculture. After his death, Ravenel's botanical collections were sold to the British Museum.

Ravenel began his journal in 1859 and continued it to within weeks of his death in 1887. The journal shows how one thoughtful and well-placed member of the Southern elite struggled to understand the collapse of his familiar world.

QUESTIONS TO CONSIDER
1. How did Henry William Ravenel interpret the causes and outcome of the Civil War?
2. What did he expect to happen to former slaves, and how did he explain their behavior?
3. Are his reactions what you expected of a slaveholder, or do they surprise you?

Arney Robinson Childs, ed., *The Private Journal of Henry William Ravenel, 1859–1887* (Columbia: University of South Carolina Press, 1947), 202–3, 206–7, 210–21 passim, 228–29, 237, 239–40.

November [1864]

F. 18   The Augusta paper of this morning has startling intelligence from Atlanta. There is no doubt that Sherman has burned Rome, Decatur & Atlanta, & has commenced a move with 4 or 5 army corps (40 to 50,000) in the direction of Macon & Augusta. The Northern papers say his intention is to move through to Charleston & Mobile, destroy the rail road & bridges behind him & feed his army from the country. I have been apprehending just such a move since Hood's army was withdrawn. It is a bold stroke, & if successful, would bring untold evils upon us, in the destruction of property & the means of subsistance. . . .

Sunday 20   Beauregard telegraphs the people to be firm & resolute—to obstruct his [Sherman's] passage by cutting the woods in his front & flank—to destroy all provisions which cannot be carried away—to remove all negroes, horses & cattle, & leave a scene of desolation in his front, instead of in his rear as it would be if he passed. . . . Should Sherman succeed in taking Augusta, his march will be onward toward Charleston, & his track will be a scene of desolation. I await the developments of the next few days with anxiety, chiefly on account of my negroes. If I send them away & the farm & house is left without protection, my house will be robbed & despoiled of every thing, whether the enemy passes here or not. I must wait before removing them, until I am very sure the enemy will succeed in his designs upon Augusta—& then perhaps it may be too late.

M. 21   I have had a talk with my negroes on the subject, & explained to them the true state of affairs—that should the enemy pass through this place they must escape & take care of themselves for a while until the danger is passed. I am well satisfied from their assurances, that they are really alarmed at the idea of being seized & taken off by the Yankees, & that they will not desert me.

F. 25   We are now at the gloomiest period of the war which for nearly four years has afflicted our land. I cannot conceal from myself the many discouraging features of our situation & the perilous straits in which we stand. . . .

Sunday 8   Samuel Ravenel at home on furlough from Measles was here this morning. He told me that the Post Surgeon had offered Harry & himself & three other boys, exemptions on account of their age & size, & that two had accepted. He & Harry & another had declined. I was gratified to hear that our boys took such high views of their duty. Sam says they have no tents, & have to lie on the bare ground, or with such protection as a few bushes or straw can give. They do picket & *vidette* [watch] duty in sight & hearing of the enemy, see them drill & enjoy the music from their bands every day. . . .

January [1865]

Sunday 15   My claim for compensation for slave (Jim) lost in Confed. service, has passed the Legislature & $2000 are allowed. I am to send James Wilson a power of attorney to receive it. They have commenced to fortify Columbia. . . .

M. 23   Our currency still continues to depreciate, as is shown by the increasing prices of all articles. . . .

February [1865]

Sunday 19   Dr. Frank Porcher dined here today. He thinks we should remain where we are. The upper country is in danger of famine, & will soon be without salt, now the coast is given up. . . . Charleston was occupied by the enemy yesterday at 10 A.M.—Columbia has been captured. We hear of a great fire in Charleston yesterday, but no particulars yet. Exciting times!

M. 20   In a few days the last of our army will have crossed the Santee, the bridge burnt behind them—& we then become an evacuated & conquered region. We fall under Yankee rule & the laws & authority of the U. States are established during the continuance of the war. What new relations between us & our negroes will be established we cannot tell but there is no doubt it will be a radical change. I do not apprehend destructive raids, or personal violence to citizens who remain, but we will be compelled to conform to the new conditions under which we are placed, as a conquered people. I suppose all the cotton will be seized & confiscated to the use of the U. S. govt,—& probably a system of culture will be adopted & enforced the profits from which will accrue to them. I think it the duty of all slave owners & planters who remain, to be with their negroes. They have been faithful to the last, & they deserve in turn, confidence from him, protection, attention & care. . . .

T. 21   I think masters who are within these lines of the enemy, should remain on their plantations among their negroes;—the first change of conditions should not be volunteered by us. We have always believed we were right in maintaining the relation of master & slave for the good of the country & also for the benefit of the negro. If we have believed firmly in the Divine sanction which the Bible affords to this relation, we should not be the first to sever it, by abandoning them. They have grown up under us, they look to us for support, for guidance & protection—They have faithfully done their duty during this trying time, when the great temptations were offered to leave us. In the sight of God, we have a sacred duty to stand by them as long as they are faithful to us. We know that if left to themselves, they cannot maintain their happy condition. We must reward their fidelity to us by the same care & consideration we exercised when they were more useful. . . .

T. 28   David returned with a cart from PineVille last night, & said Rene told him the Yankees had been, or were, in PineVille, taking poultry & whatever they wanted. The negroes on many places have refused to go to work. . . . I have spoken to some of them here & intend to give them advice as a friend to continue on the plantation, & work—Of course there must be great care & judgement used in preserving discipline & I have advised with the overseer. I think for their own good & the good of the country, it would be best for the present organization of labor to go on, so that all may get a subsistance, the old & young, the sick & disabled, & the other non producers. . . . The freed & idle negroes who are not kept now under discipline or fear will give us trouble. I feel great anxiety for the future. . . .

March [1865]

Th. 2 Half past two o'clock A.M. Night of horrors! How can I describe the agonizing suspense of the past six hours! Thank God who has protected us all we are still alive & have lost nothing but property.—About half past 8 oclock I was standing in the back piazza, when I heard the discharge of 3 or 4 fire arms. The negroes soon came running up to inform us that the Yankees were in the negro yard. They soon after entered the house, (4 or 5 colored men) armed & demanded to see the owner of the house. I called to Pa & he walked up to the back door where they were. They told him that they had come for provisions, corn, bacon, poultry & whatever they wanted—demanded his horses & wagons, his guns, wine &c. That they had come to tell the negroes they were free & should no longer work for him. They used very threatening language with oaths & curses. They then proceeded to the stable & took my pair & Renes horse—Took the 2 sets harness & put in the horses, into the two wagons & Lequeax buggy. They then emptied the smoke house, store room & meat house, giving to the negroes what they did not want. They then took from the fowl house what poultry they wanted, took the two plantation guns, & used great threats about the wine & brandy. To our great relief they did not enter the house again, & at 1.30 A.M. drove off. They told the negroes if they worked for their master again they would shoot them when they came back. What the future is to be to us God only knows. I feel that my trust is still unshaken in his all protecting Providence. I have all confidance in the fidelity of the negroes & their attachment to us if they are not restrained from showing it. We are all up for the night as the excitement is too great to permit sleep - - - - - 9 A.M. at the usual hour this morning the house negroes came in—They seemed much distressed & said the troops told them last night if they came to the yard or did anything for us, they would shoot them—That a large troop would come today. We told them to go back & not bring trouble upon themselves, until we could see the Commanding officer. The fidelity & attachment of some who have come forward is very gratifying. The girls have been cooking our simple breakfast & we have taken our first meal under the new regime. I long for a visit from some officer in authority, that we may know our future condition & whether the negroes will be allowed to hire themselves to us or not. I know if they are not restrained there are many who would willingly & gladly help us. I had heard often of insurrectionary feelings among the negroes, but I never believed they would be brought to it of their own accord. The experience of this war, & especially of last night all tend to confirm that conviction. Even when compelled by intimidation, & fear of the consequences to their lives, many of them evince real distress, & not one has yet joined in any language or act of defiance. Their fidelity & attachment is amazing with the temptations before them. Those who were engaged in the sacking of the store room & meat house, did so stealthily & I believe not until they were commanded to help themselves.

S. 4 Inauguration of Presdt. Lincoln today for his 2d term of 4 years. Will any thing come out of it in respect to the war? The negroes are completely bewildered at the change of their condition. Many are truly distressed, some of the younger ones delirious with the prospect of good living & nothing to do. Some are willing to remain & work, but object to gang work,—all is in a chaotic state. When they were told that they were free, some said they did not wish to be free, & they were immediately silenced with threats of being shot. I fear this region will be a desolate waste in one year hence, if this state of things continue- -On Thursday night when the army was camped here, their troops were among our negroes, distributing sugar, coffee, meats & bread in pro-fusion—they killed 8 or 10 of the sheep & had them cooked in the negro yard. This was all intended as an earnest of the good things which followed their freedom. . . .

M. 6   The events of the past week have brought up vividly before us the horrors of the French Revolution—& those startling scenes which Dickens describes in his "Tale of two cities." We are in a fearful & trying crisis. If those who had unsettled the present order of things in the name of Humanity, were consistent, they would make some effort to order the freed negroes for their good, & ought to take some steps toward restoring order & recommanding & enforcing some plan by which such a large number may escape the horrors of insubordination, violence & ultimately starvation. The negroes are intoxicated with the idea of freedom. Many of them are deluded into the hope that their future is to be provided for by the U S. Govt.—& hence they do not feel the necessity of work. Many are disposed to remain, but perhaps will insist on terms which are incompatable with discipline & good management. It is a fear-ful crisis.

T. 7   No disposition evinced among the negroes to go to work. There seems to be sullenness which I dislike to see. I think those who are disposed to work or to do for us, are restrained. I hear that many of the negroes are armed with pis-tols & guns. Some were at Black Oak last night firing off pistols. This is a bad feature in this fearful period.—Oh, Humanity! what crimes are committed in thy name. One week ago we were in the midst of a peaceful, contented & or-derly population—now all is confusion, disorder, discontent, violence, anar-chy. If those who uprooted the old order of things had remained long enough to reconstruct another system in which there should be order restored, it would have been well, but they have destroyed our system & left us in the ruins— "God is our refuge & strength, a very present help in trouble"- - - -The ne-groes are rambling about the country. This morning 4 mounted on horses & mules rode through the negro yard, stopping for a while, & some have passed through in vehicles. It is said they were told to go to St Stephens for horses which the army left behind.

W. 8   We heard guns again last night, but cannot learn from the negroes who fired them. The disordered state of affairs keeps us anxious. . . . On this day a week ago the old system of slave labour was in peaceful operation. The breath of Emancipation has passed over the country, & we are now in that tran-sition state between the new & the old systems—a state of chaos & disorder. Will the negro be materially benefitted by the change? Will the condition of

ie country in its productive resources, in material prosperity be improved?
Will it be a benefit to the landed proprietors? These are questions which will
have their solution in the future. They are in the hands of that Providence
which over-ruleth all things for good. It was a strong conviction of my best
judgement that the old relation of master & slave, had received the divine sanction & was the best condition in which the two races could live together for
mutual benefit. There were many defects to be corrected & many abuses to be
remedied, which I think would have been done if we had gained our independence & were freed from outside pressure. Among these defects I will enumer-
ate the want of legislation to make the marriage contract binding—to prevent
the separation of families, & to restrain the cupidity of cruel masters. Perhaps it
is for neglecting these obligations that God has seen fit to dissolve that relation.
I believe the negro must remain in this country & that his condition although a
freed-man, must be to labour on the soil. Nothing but necessity will compel
him to labour. Now the question is, will that necessity be so strong as to compel
him to labour, which will be profitable to the landed proprietors. Will he make
as much cotton, sugar, rice & tobacco for the world as he did previously? They
will now have a choice *where* to labour. This will ensure good treatment & the
best terms. The most humane, the most energetic & the most judicious managers have the best chances in the race for success. I expect to see a revolution
in the ownership of landed estates. Those only can succeed who bring the best
capacity for the business. Time will show. . . .

Sunday 12   Some of the very peculiar traits of negro character are now exhibited. John & Solomon left Morefield on Thursday with the black troops wild
with excitement & probably drunk—In all this reign of disorder & anarchy I
have not seen or heard of any violence or even of rudeness or incivility from the
plantation negroes. Docility & submissiveness still prevail. There are two exhi-
bitions of character which have surprised us, & which were never anticipated.
1st. On many places where there was really kind treatment & mutual attachment, the exciting events of the last week or two, & the powerful temptations
brought to bear upon them, have seemed to snap the ties suddenly. Some have
left their comfortable homes & kind masters & friends, & gone off with the
army, thinking to better their conditions. We must be patient & charitable in
our opinions—They are ignorant of what they have to encounter, mere children in knowledge & experience, excitable, impulsive & have fallen under the
tempting delusions presented to them in such glowing terms—Some who are
disposed to take a proper view of their condition, & to return to work, are intimidated & kept back by threats from the more strong & overbearing. They do
not clearly comprehend this situation—they have been told they are free, &
their idea of freedom is associated with freedom from work & toil. In many
places there was bad discipline & little care for the negroes. These are generally
the foremost in all the acts of disorder,—& their example & word keep back
others. We are astonished at this defection when we do not expect it, but on re-
flection the causes at work are sufficient to account for it. 2nd. Had we been
told four years ago, that our negroes would have withstood the temptation to fi-

delity which have been constantly before them during the war, we would have doubted the possibility—& had we been told further of the events of the last two weeks, the incitements to acts of violence both by the example & the precepts of the black troops all throughout this region, we would have shuddered for the consequences. Except from the black soldiers, I have not heard of a single act of violence, or even of rude or uncivil language. Their behaviour is perfectly civil so far, & I believe, with a judicous course on the part of the whites, will continue so. This whole revolution from its commencement has developed in its progress, a course of events which no human sagacity on either side, ever foresaw. We are carried along by an inscrutable providence to the consummation of great & radical changes,—we are the actors in a Great Revolution where, not civil institutions only, but social polity, must be reconstructed & re-organized. . . .

May [1865]

May M. 1   Gen Lees surrender took place on the 9th.ult,[1] but it only reached us through our papers & the returning prisoners about a week ago. . . . [This] means the loss of our Independence for which we have been struggling for four years with immense loss of life & property. But the fate of nations is controlled & over-ruled by a wise Providence, which sees the end from the beginning, & orders all things in the highest wisdom. Whatever therefore may be the will of God regarding our destiny, I accept His decision as final & as eminently good. I have honestly believed we were right in our revolution, & would receive the divine sanction—if I have erred, I pray God to forgive me the error, & I submit with perfect satisfaction to His decree, knowing that He cannot err.

   M. 22   We begin now to realize the ruin to property which the war has entailed upon us. All classes & conditions of men will suffer who had property, except the small farmers who owned no negroes. Confederate securities, I consider a total loss. Bank stock, confederation & private bonds, are all more or less dependent for their availability upon Confed securities, & upon the value of negro property; both of which are lost. The Rail road companies are nearly all ruined by the destruction of their roads & the heavy debt they must incur to rebuild. The only money now in possession of our people is coin in small quantities which had been hoarded through the war, & some bills of the local banks. There will be but little means of increasing this amount for some time to come, as provisions are scarce, & the cotton has been mostly burnt, captured or sold. The financial prospect is a gloomy one, & there will be much distress before our conditions can improve. . . .

   M. 29   I went in to Aiken this morning & called at the hotel to inquire if any officer in Aiken was authorized to administer the Oath of Allegiance. They expected in a day or two to have it done here. It is necessary now in order to save property, have personal protection, or exercise the rights of citizenship, or any business calling. Every one who is allowed, is now taking the oath, as the

---

1. **ult:** *ultimo*, Latin for "last month"; that is, April 9.

Confederate govt. is annulled, the state govt. destroyed, & the return into the Union absolutely necessary to our condition as an organized community. As Gen. Gillmore's order based upon Chief Justice Chase's opinion announces the freedom of the negroes there is no further room to doubt that it is the settled policy of the country. I have today formally announced to my negroes the fact, & made such arrangements with each as the new relation rendered necessary. Those whose whole time we need, get at present clothes & food, house rent & medical attendance. The others work for themselves giving me a portion of their time on the farm in lieu of house rent. Old Amelia & her two grandchildren, I will spare the mockery of offering freedom to. I must support them as long as I have any thing to give.

T. 30   My negroes all express a desire to remain with me. I am gratified at the proof of their attachment. I believe it to be real & unfeigned. For the present they will remain, but in course of time we must part, as I cannot afford to keep so many, & they cannot afford to hire for what I could give them. As they have always been faithful & attached to us, & have been raised as family servants, & have all of them been in our family for several generations, there is a feeling towards them somewhat like that of a father who is about to send out his children on the world to make their way through life. Those who have brought the present change of relation upon us are ignorant of these ties. They have charged us with cruelty. They call us, man stealers, robbers, tyrants. The indignant denial of these charges & the ill feelings engendered during 30 years of angry controversy, have culminated at length in the four years war which has now ended. It has pleased God that we should fail in our efforts for independance — & with the loss of independance, we return to the Union under the dominion of the abolition sentiment. The experiment is now to be tried. The negro is not only to be emancipated, but is to become a citizen with all the right & priviledges! It produces a financial, political & social revolution at the South, fearful to contemplate in its ultimate effects. Whatever the result may be, let it be known & remembered that neither the negro slave nor his master is responsible. It has been done by those who having political power, are determined to carry into practice the sentimental philanthropy they have so long & angrily advocated. Now that is fixed. I pray God for the great issues at stake, that he may bless the effort & make it successful — make it a blessing & not a curse to the poor negro.

FOR CRITICAL THINKING

1. How might Henry Ravenel have responded to Frederick Douglass's urging that "if the Negro cannot stand on his own legs, let him fall"? Would Ravenel and Douglass have been able to find common ground on issues of slavery and Reconstruction? Why or why not?

2. Douglass's speech was intended for (and delivered to) a public audience; Ravenel's diary was a record of his private musings. How might these circumstances have affected the tone and content of these writings?

41

Three Days of Terror

Ellen Leonard

Rioting was an all too regular part of mid-nineteenth-century New York City life. Six-teen major and many lesser riots erupted in the city between 1834 and 1874. Almost any reason sufficed to bring out the clubs, guns, and paving stones: Protestants attacked Catholics, Irish Catholics fought Irish Protestants, slavery-supporting mobs roughed up abolitionists, partisans of one actor attacked the fans of another, rival fire companies and gangs started violence that simply spread. In addition, municipal government was inef-fective and corrupt; the weak and unprofessional New York police often could not main-tain order without calling out the militia; alcohol was cheap and people habitually drank to excess; and vast numbers of new immigrants and unskilled laborers lived perpetually on the edge of destitution. When the Civil War sharpened political conflicts and war-induced inflation made the living conditions of the poor even worse than usual, widespread rioting broke out in the great draft riot of 1863.

When the Civil War began, North and South fielded large armies of patriotic vol-unteers, but as the war continued, both sides turned to conscription. Only about seven percent of those whose names were drawn in draft lotteries actually served. Many simply refused or ran off to another district. And both sides allowed those drafted to hire substi-tutes to fight in their place or to pay a fee of $300 to avoid serving, arousing cries that the conflict was "a rich man's war, but a poor man's fight."

With the Union's conscription law vastly unpopular, the Democratic Party press made the draft a major issue, fanning opposition particularly among urban Irish American populations who largely opposed the war and feared black competition from freed slaves for the unskilled jobs that provided their meager livelihoods. One orator told a mass meeting in New York City that "when the President called upon them to go and carry on a war for the nigger, he would be d—— d if he believed they would go." As soon as actual conscription began taking place in July 1863, rioting broke out in sev-eral cities. Most horrific was the one in which Ellen Leonard found herself trapped from July 13 through 16 in New York City.

It remains, in fact, one of the worst riots in New York City history. Many of the federal troops usually stationed in the city were in Pennsylvania in pursuit of General Lee's retreating army after the battle of Gettysburg. Over one hundred people died, most of them rioters gunned down when troop reinforcements arrived to retake control of the streets. In addition to random looting and vandalism, the rioters lynched several

Ellen Leonard, "Three Days of Terror," *Harper's New Monthly Magazine*, January 1867, 225–33.

blacks, burned down the Colored Orphan Asylum, and attacked Republican newspapers, the homes of prominent Republicans and abolitionists, and businesses that employed blacks. Ellen Leonard's article on the riot, published in Harper's New Monthly Magazine *in 1867, offers a rare eyewitness account of an innocent visitor accidentally trapped in these dramatic and dangerous events.*

QUESTIONS TO CONSIDER

1. According to Ellen Leonard's account, what seem to have been the main motivators of the mob?
2. How much danger did the mob pose to the citizens of the city and to visitors like Ellen Leonard?
3. How did women behave during the riot? In what ways did they behave more assertively than demanded by the "separate spheres" ideology of the era?

THREE DAYS OF TERROR

On the tenth of July, 1863, my mother and myself arrived in the city of New York. We had set out on a grand tour of visitation. After vegetating year after year in a New England village, we had sallied forth in genuine country fashion to hunt up our kinsfolk in various parts of the land. We were in no hurry. We had the whole summer before us. . . . We hoped now to spend a few days quietly with my brother J., call on various friends and relatives, visit Central Park and a lion or so, shop a little, and move onward at our leisure.

But man proposes and Fate *disposes,* and nothing in New York turned out as we expected. Instead of visiting our friends and meandering leisurely about the city, we were caught in a mob and penned up in our first stopping-place. . . . The streets were dark, dirty, and crowded with ill-looking people. The whole city was enveloped in fog and gloom. The home regiments had gone to drive the rebels from Pennsylvania, and many hearts were trembling. The household which received us had its full share of anxiety. Its youngest member, a youth of seventeen, had gone with the volunteers, and other friends were in the Army of the Potomac. . . .

I [went] to Broadway. But even there I could see nothing attractive. Every thing looked hot, glaring, and artificial, and every body looked shabby, jaded, and care-worn. An overworked horse dropped dead in the street before me, and I was glad to take refuge for a time in the Astor Library.

Returning thence at mid-day I first saw signs of disturbance. A squad of policemen passed before me into Third Avenue, clerks were looking eagerly from the doors, and men whispering in knots all up and down the street; but I was too much a stranger to be certain that these appearances were unusual, though they annoyed me so much that I crossed at once to Second Avenue, along which I pursued my way peacefully, and once at home thought no more of it. We were indulging ourselves in siestas after our noonday lunch, when a great roaring suddenly burst upon our ears — a howling as of thousands of wild Indians let loose at once; and before we could look out or collect our thoughts at all the cry arose from every quarter, "The mob! the mob!" "The Irish have risen to resist the draft!"

In a second my head was out the window, and I saw it with my own eyes. We were on a cross-street between First and Second avenues. First Avenue was crowded as far as we could see it with thousands of infuriated creatures, yelling, screaming, and swearing in the most frantic manner; while crowds of women, equally ferocious, were leaning from every door and window, swinging aprons and handkerchiefs, and cheering and urging them onward. The rush and roar grew every moment more terrific. Up came fresh hordes faster and more furious; bareheaded men, with red, swollen faces, brandishing sticks and clubs, or carrying heavy poles and beams; and boys, women, and children hurrying on and joining with them in this mad chase up the avenue like a company of raging fiends. In the hurry and tumult it was impossible to distinguish individuals, but all seemed possessed alike with savage hate and fury. The most dreadful rumors flew through the street, and we heard from various sources the events of the morning. The draft had been resisted, buildings burned, twenty policemen killed, and the remainder utterly routed and discomfited; the soldiers were absent, and the mob triumphant and increasing in numbers and violence every moment.

Our neighborhood was in the greatest excitement. The whole population turned out at once, gazing with terror and consternation on the living stream passing before them, surging in countless numbers through the avenue, and hurrying up town to join those already in action. Fresh yells and shouts announced the union of forces, and bursting flames their accelerated strength and fury. The armory on Twenty-second Street was broken open, sacked, and fired, and the smoke and flames rolled up directly behind us. . . .

Bells were tolling in every quarter. The rioters were still howling in Twenty-second Street, and driving the firemen from the burning armory. The building fell and the flames sunk, and then darkness came all at once and shut out every thing. We gathered gloomily around my brother in the back-parlor. An evening paper was procured, but brought no comfort. It only showed more clearly the nature and extent of this fearful outbreak. It only told us that the whole city was as helpless and anxious as ourselves. Many were in far greater danger, for obscurity is sometimes safety; but the black, lowering night, and the disabled condition of our only male protector, oppressed us heavily. Our neighborhood was all alive. Men tramped incessantly through the street, and women chatted and scolded in the windows; children cried and cats squalled; a crazy man in the rear raved fiercely for Jeff Davis and the Southern Confederacy; but over every other sound every few moments the bells rang out the alarm of some new fire. Some were very near; some at a distance. . . .

As the clocks struck twelve a great shout startled me, and a light flamed right up before me. A huge bonfire had been kindled in the middle of the street not far below us. Wild forms were dancing about it, and piling on fresh fuel. Great logs and beams and other combustibles were dragged up and heaped upon it. Sleep, now, was of course impossible. From a seat in an upper window I saw it rise and fall, flame up and fade. . . .

[The next day] there was no milk, no ice to be had, and meat and bread were on the wane; and so I ventured out with my sister H. for supplies. We found our street full of people, excitement, and rumors. Men and boys ran past us with muskets in their hands. We heard that a fight was in progress above Twenty-second Street. The mob had seized a gun-factory and many muskets; but the police had driven them off and taken back part of their plunder. It was cheering to find that the police were still alive. . . . Men talked in low, excited tones, and seemed afraid of each other. The stores were mostly closed and business suspended. With difficulty we procured supplies of provisions and a newspaper. . . . The mob were gathering in great force in our vicinity, and things looked every moment more threatening; so we hurried home as fast as possible, and I took my post again at the window.

New and strange sights met my eyes. Such multitudes of people every where; filling street and sidewalks, crowding all the doors and windows, the balconies and roofs of the houses. Many were merely spectators; some not far distant were *actors.* In the First Avenue the crowd was now very dense and clamorous. The liquor store on the corner was thronged with villainous-looking customers, and the women who had welcomed the mob on their first appearance were again talking loudly as if urging them on to action. "Die *at home!*" was the favorite watch-word which often reached our ears. Every thing indicated that a collision was approaching. We caught, after a time, a glimpse of soldiers, and heard the welcome rattle of musketry, distant at first, then nearer and nearer. The soldiers marched to and through Twenty-second Street and turned down First Avenue. The mob yelled and howled and stood their ground. Women from the roofs threw stones and brickbats upon the soldiers. Then came the volleys; the balls leaped out and the mob gave way at once and fled in every direction. A great crowd rushed through our street, hiding in every nook and corner. We closed doors and blinds, but still peeped out of the windows. The soldiers marched slowly back up the avenue, firing along the way; crossed over into Second Avenue, marched down opposite our street and fired again. Again the mob scattered, and scampered in droves through the street. Yet another volley, and balls came tearing down the centre of our street right before us, dashing along the pavements and carrying off frames from the trees. A boy on the sidewalk opposite was struck; he fell in a pool of blood, and was carried away to die. The streets were now cleared, the crowds had vanished, the soldiers withdrew, and the mob was quelled. For two hours peace and quiet prevailed. . . .

The papers brought no encouragement. Fearful deeds of atrocity were recorded. The mob were increasing in power and audacity, and the city was still paralyzed and panic-struck. The small military force available could only protect a few important positions, leaving the greater part defenseless. Our inflammable neighborhood was wholly at the mercy of the mob. . . .

Another day had come, Wednesday, July 15th. . . . The city was not all burned down, we found. The newspapers were still alive, and insisting that more troops were on hand and the mob checked; but we saw no signs of it. The morning indeed passed more quietly. The rioters were resting from the labors of the night; but business was not resumed, and swarms of idle men still hung about the streets and stores. . . .

As night approached we heard drums beating, and gangs of rioters marched up their favorite avenue. . . . Then some one shouted, "They are coming!" and a small band of soldiers appeared marching up our street. The mob seemed to swell into vast dimensions, and densely filled the whole street before them. Hundreds hurried out on the house-tops, tore up brickbats, and hurled them with savage howls at the approaching soldiers. Shots were fired from secret ambushes, and soldiers fell before they had fired. Then they charged bravely into the mob, but their force was wholly inadequate. One small howitzer and a company of extemporized militia could do little against those raging thousands. A fierce conflict raged before our eyes. With breathless interest we watched them from door and windows. We feared the soldiers would be swallowed up and annihilated. Some now appeared in sight with a wounded officer and several wounded men, looking from side to side for shelter. Their eyes met ours with mute appeal. There was no time to be lost; the mob might any moment be upon them. There was a moment's consultation, a hasty reference to J., an unhesitating response: "Yes, by all means"; we beckoned them in, and in they came. Doors and windows were at once closed, and the house became a hospital, and seemed filled with armed men. The wounded men were carried into my brother's room; the Colonel was laid on the bed, and the others propped up with pillows. There were a few moments of great commotion and confusion. We flew for fans, ice water, and bandages. Some of the soldiers went out into the fight again, and some remained with the wounded. A surgeon, who had volunteered as a private under his old commander, dressed the wounds of the sufferers. The Colonel was severely wounded in the thigh by a slug made of a piece of lead pipe, producing a compound fracture. The wounds of two others, though less dangerous, were severe and painful.

Twilight was now upon us, and night rapidly approaching. The soldiers had been forced to retreat, leaving the mob in great force and fury. We heard them shouting and raving on the corner, and knew that we were in great danger. Already they were clamoring for the wounded soldiers who had escaped them. We thought of Colonel O'Brien's fate, and could not suppress the thought that our own house might be made the scene of a like tragedy. Could we defend ourselves if attacked? A hurried consultation was held. We had arms and ammunition, and, including J. and the slightly wounded soldiers, half a dozen men able and willing to use them. But we could not "man our lines." We were open to attack at once from the front and rear, the roof, the front basement, and the balcony above it. We might, indeed, retreat to the upper stories, barricade the stairway, and hold it against all the assailants that could crowd into the hall. But if they chose to fire the house below we could not prevent it, and then there would be no escape either for our wounded or ourselves.

The Colonel promptly decided the question; resistance was hopeless, could only make the case worse, and must not be attempted. Not only so, but all signs of the presence of soldiers must be removed. Arms, military apparel, and bloody clothing were accordingly concealed. The Colonel was conveyed to the cellar and placed on a mattress. The young soldier, next to him most severely wounded, was assisted up to the rear apartment on the upper floor and placed in charge of my mother and myself. The soldiers who had remained were then ordered to make their escape from the house as they best could, and to hasten to head-quarters with an urgent request that a force might be sent to our relief. . . .

J., with his bandaged head and disabled arm, was liable to be taken for a wounded soldier, and his wife and her sister, Mrs. P ——— , insisted that he also should betake himself to the roof. He could render no material assistance if he remained; on the other hand, his presence might precipitate a scene of violence which would not be offered to ladies alone. They did not feel that they were personally in danger — so far there was no report that the lawless violence of the rioters had been directed against women; and if he could get away he might be the means of bringing speedier relief. Very reluctantly he yielded to these considerations, and prepared to accompany the wounded soldier. The mother of the household took refuge in her room on the second-floor. To her daughter-in-law, wife of an absent son, was assigned a post of observation at a front window. The two heroic women, H. and her sister, remained below to confront the mob. . . .

In front the demonstrations were still more alarming. The rioters had taken possession of the street, stationed a guard on both avenues, and were chasing up and down for the soldiers. Then they were seen searching from house to house. . . . Then came a rush up the steps, and the bell rang violently. Not a sound was heard through the house. Again and yet again the bell rang, more and more furiously. Heart throbbed, nerves quivered, but no one stirred. Then came knocks, blows, kicks, threats, attempts to force the door. Come in they must and would; nothing could stay them.

Having gained for the retreating party all the time she could, Mrs. P ——— at length unlocked the door, opened it, passed out, and closing it behind her, stood face to face with the mob, which crowded the steps and swarmed on the sidewalk and the adjacent street. What could she do? She knew that they would come in, that they would search the house, that they would find the men; but she was determined not to give them up without an effort to save them. Possibly, in parleying with them, she might at least calm somewhat the fury of the passion that swayed that howling mob; possibly in that brutal and maddened throng there might be a few with human hearts in their bosoms to which she might find a way, win them to her side, and enlist their aid in saving the lives of the intended victims. That was her only hope.

"What do you want?" she asked, while the air was yet ringing with the cry that came up from the crowd, "The soldiers! the soldiers!" "Bring out the soldiers!" One who stood near and seemed to be a leader replied, "There were two soldiers went into this house, and we must have them. You must give them up."

"There *were* two that came in, but went out again. They are not here now."

She spoke in a low but perfectly clear and steady voice, that compelled attention, and the crowd hushed its ravings to catch her words.

"Let us see; if they are not here we will not harm you; but we must search the house."

"We can not let you in; there are only women here — some that are old and feeble, and the sight of such a crowd will frighten them to death."

"They shall not all come in," was the reply; and after some further parley it was agreed that half a dozen only should enter and make the search. The leader gave his orders, the door was opened, and the men detailed came in; but before it could be closed the mob surged up, pressed in, and filled the hall. Many of them were armed with the stolen carbines.

"Light the gas!" was the cry.

"My sister has gone for a light."

It came, and the parley was renewed. The leader again demanded the soldiers; insisted that they were there, and said it would be better for themselves if they would give them up. She persisted in the statement she had made.

"She is fooling us, and using up the time while they are getting away by the roof!" cried one, and pressing forward with his musket pointed at her, endeavored to pass her. Very deliberately she took hold of the muzzle and turned it aside, saying, "Don't do that. You know I am a woman, and it might frighten me."

The leader returned to the charge. "We know the men are here, and if you give them up to us you shall not be harmed. But if you do not, and we find them, you know what a mob is. I can not control them; your house will be burned over your heads, and I will not guarantee your lives for five minutes."

"You will not do that," was the reply. "We are not the kind of people whose houses you wish to burn. My only son works as you do, and perhaps in the same shop with some of you, for seventy cents a day."

She did not tell them that her amateur apprentice boy had left his place to go to Pennsylvania and fight their friends the rebels. A young man, whom she had noticed as one of the few of decent appearance, stepped to her side and whispered to her, advising her compliance with the demand, assuring her that the men could not be controlled. The tone more than the words indicated to her that she had made one friend; and she found another, in the same way, a moment later.

Meantime the leaders were consulting whether they should go first above or below, and decided on the latter. Stationing one man with a musket at the door, and one at the stairs, they proceeded, pioneered by H., first to the parlors, and then to the basement, thoroughly examining both. Most fortunately the sentinels were the two young men in whom Mrs. P —— felt she had found friends, and she was not slow to improve the opportunity to deepen the impression she had made. But now the crowd outside, thundering at the basement door, burst in the panels, and forcing it open, with terrible oaths and threats rushed in and filled the lower hall. Part joined the searching party, and some hurried up the first-floor. One, crowding past the sentinel, was striding up the stairs. We heard his call to his comrades, "Come on up stairs!" and our hearts sunk within us. But the sentinel's stern command, enforced by his leveled piece, brought him back.

The main party, having ransacked the basement rooms, now turned to the cellar. In a moment a loud shout announced that they had found a victim. The surgeon was dragged up, forced out at the lower door, and delivered over to the crowd outside. A blow from a bludgeon or musket felled him to the earth, inflicting a terrible wound on the head. "Hang him, hang him!" "To the post at the Twenty-second Street corner!" were the cries as they hurried him off. The search within proceeded; a moment more and they had found the Colonel. A new and fiercer shout was sent up. An order from a leader thrilled through the hall, "Come down here some of yees wid yer muskets!"

At the first cry from the cellar Mrs. P —— sprung for the basement, intending to make her way at any hazard. A sentinel stood at the head of the stairway; a stalwart brute, reeking with filth and whisky. He seized her, with both arms about her waist, with a purpose of violence quite too evident. She struggled to free herself without raising an alarm, but in vain; then a sudden and piercing shriek, which rung through the house, made him for an instant relax his hold, and, wrenching herself away, she hurried back and sought the protection of the friendly sentinel.

"He will not let me pass; I must go down."

"You must not," he replied; "it is no place for you." And then he added, looking sternly at her, "You have deceived us. You said there was no one here, and there is."

"I would have done the same thing for you if you had been wounded. Look at me; do you not believe me?"

He did look, full in her eye, for an instant; then said: "Yes, I do believe it. You have done right, and I admire your spirit."

"But I must go down. Go with me."

"No; it is no place for you."

"Then go yourself, and save his life."

And turning over his charge to the sentinel at the door, he did go. Meantime the searching party, having found the Colonel, proceeded to question him. He said he was a citizen, accidentally wounded, and had been obliged to seek refuge there.

"Why did you hide, if you are a citizen?"

Because, he said, he was afraid he should be taken for a soldier. They would not believe, but still he insisted on his statement. Then the muskets were sent for, and four pieces leveled at his head, as he lay prostrate and helpless.

"Fire, then, if you will, on a wounded man and a citizen. I shall die, any how, for my wound is a mortal one. But before you fire I wish you would send for a priest."

"What, are you a Catholic?"

"Yes."

This staggered them; and while they were hesitating the sentinel joined the group, and as soon as he looked on the Colonel exclaimed: "I know that man. I used to go to school with him. He is no soldier."

This turned the scale. The leaders were satisfied, and decided to let him go. . . .

Those of the mob who had remained above, disappointed of their prey, with oaths and execrations protested against the action of their leaders, and sent the ruffian at the head of the stairway down to see if it was all right. But the positive statements of the friendly sentinel, which Mrs. P —— had the satisfaction of hearing him rehearse, as the two met in the lower hall, disarmed even his suspicions, and the rest could do no otherwise than acquiesce. So well satisfied, indeed, were the leaders, and, as it is not unreasonable to suppose, so impressed with the resolute bearing of the two ladies, that they volunteered to station a guard before the door to prevent the annoyance of any further search. As they had found the two men who had been reported to them as having entered the house, it did not seem to occur to them that there might be still others concealed; and so they took their departure, leaving the upper stories unvisited. . . .

It was now, we thought, past midnight. We had no hope of relief, no thought or expectation but of struggling on alone hour after hour of distress and darkness; but as I was listening in my window to some unusually threatening demonstrations from the mob, I heard the distant clank of a horse's hoof on the pavement. Again and again it sounded, more and more distinctly; and then a measured tread reached my ears, the steady, resolute tramp of a trained and disciplined body. No music was ever half so beautiful! It might, it must be, our soldiers! Off I flew to spread the good news through the household, and back again to the window to hear the tramp nearer and fuller and stronger, and see a long line of muskets gleam out from the darkness, and a stalwart body of men stop at our door. "Halt!" was cried; and I rushed down stairs headlong, unlocked the door without waiting for orders, and with tears of joy and gratitude which every one can imagine and nobody describe, welcomed a band of radiant soldiers and policemen, and in the midst of them all who should appear but my brother, pale and exhausted, who had gotten off the house-top in some mysterious way and brought this gallant company to our rescue! . . .

42

The Battle of Gettysburg: At War and at Home
Samuel and Rachel Cormany

Early in May 1863 at Chancellorsville, Virginia, the Army of Northern Virginia under General Robert E. Lee won an important victory over the Union, marred only by the death of the great Confederate general Thomas "Stonewall" Jackson. Soon after Chancellorsville, with Vicksburg under siege and the possibility of a Confederate victory hanging in the balance, Lee ventured upon a brilliantly daring plan. He would invade southern Pennsylvania, taking the conflict into Union territory to the north of the nation's capital. Achievement might win independence for the Confederacy, if not by total military triumph on the field, then by a political success: a deepening of discouragement in the North that would lead to the equivalent to surrender.

By the end of June, Lee was in Pennsylvania. At about the same time, President Lincoln made George Meade commander of the Union Army of the Potomac. Meade's immediate task was to counter the Confederate advance. A triumph by Meade in the battle that followed at Gettysburg in Pennsylvania could not give the Union total victory in the war; but a defeat would come close to total victory for the Confederacy.

The great battle began on July 1. For a time, the Union was on the defensive, clinging to the slope known as Cemetery Ridge. On July 2, the scholarly Joshua Chamberlain of Maine, destined for a mild academic career later in his life, averted what could have been a decisive defeat for the Union Army. At Chamberlain's command, the Maine troops holding Little Round Top—now out of ammunition—swept down in a desperate and successful bayonet charge that preserved that point in the Union lines against a powerful Confederate assault. That same day, a handful of Minnesota troops attacked a rebel force numbering several times their own strength. Although their losses were great—they lost over four in five men—the Minnesota troops successfully beat back the Confederate soldiers. Together, the Maine and the Minnesota troops were instrumental in keeping intact the Union position on the field.

The battle at Gettysburg could have been an indecisive slaughter. But on July 3, General Lee ordered Confederate general James Longstreet to initiate an attack on the Union center. Led by Virginia general George Pickett, fourteen thousand rebel troops advanced upward on exposed ground against a combination of artillery and infantry fire far heavier than the Confederate officers had expected. The assault briefly touched the Union lines, but then wilted against impossible firepower. The heroic venture has

Franklin County: Diary of Rachel Cormany and *Franklin County: Diary of Samuel Cormany*, 1863. From *The Cormany Diaries: A Northern Family in the Civil War*, ed. James C. Mohr (Pittsburgh: University of Pittsburgh Press, 1982).

won a place of fame in American history. The repulsion of Pickett's Charge effectively ended the Confederate hope of Lee's winning at Gettysburg. Though the federal army failed to pursue the rebel troops as they retreated into Virginia, thereby conceivably losing a chance to win the whole war, Gettysburg was a heartening moment for the Union, intensified by General Ulysses S. Grant's nearly simultaneous capture of Vicksburg on the Mississippi River.

The writers of the following journal entries, Samuel and Rachel Cormany, were both witness to the Battle of Gettysburg, but in very different ways. Samuel was a soldier in battle, while Rachel remained a civilian on a "homefront" that was barely twenty-five miles away. The couple were married in 1860, after meeting at university in Ohio. Samuel was from Chambersburg, Pennsylvania, and Rachel was from Canada. They went to Canada just after their marriage. After the birth of their first child, Cora, in August 1862 they returned to Samuel's home on a farm north of Chambersburg, Pennsylvania. The next month, Samuel enlisted in the army as a second lieutenant in the sixteenth Pennsylvania Cavalry and Rachel and Cora moved into a rented space in town, where she spent the rest of the war. After the war, they moved out West to build a family farm in Missouri.

Questions to Consider

1. How did access to information shape people's experiences of the war? How does this differ from modern conflicts?
2. How important was it to soldiers to believe they had widespread civilian support?
3. How did living in the shadow of one of the bloodiest and most important battles in American history affect Rachel Cormany's everyday life? Does anything surprise you about her account?

DIARY OF SAMUEL CORMANY

June 30, 1863

Tuesday. We moved out early to within a few miles of Westminster and drew up in line for battle—our advance moved on—and the Reg't supported—met little resistance in taking the City—Took 8 prisoners.

The Regiment halted close to the City—We got some eatables—The people were ecstatic to see our troops driving out and following up the "Johnies." They did all in their power for us—The Rebs had acted awful meanly—Took everything like hats, boots, shoes, clothing &c—The streets and fence corners were strewn with their discarded old ones. Some of them, yes many, were almost able to join in the march, being so full of lice—Soon we were called on to muster for pay—still near town—and at noon took up the march Manchester—I never saw more cherries, ripe and ripening, and better crops then are to be seen hereabouts—Lieut Barnes & I got a fine supper at Mr. Bingamins—Fine ladies about. Exultant on our arrival, and almost worshipped us as their protectors—i.e., our soldiers—For the night we picketed and laid ready—I stood Post two hours—

July 1, 1863

Wednesday. I had a fine chicken breakfast—and a feast of other good things. Took up march for Hanover. Very fine rich country—and such fine water—Settlers are Old Style People. Many Dunkerds. We were given any amount to eat all along the way—The Rebs who had passed this way acted very meanly—All around—demanding setters to pay money to exempt horses from being taken and barns and houses from being burned—One old man said he paid $100 to exempt 2 horses—another paid $23 to save his horse—Still another—$100 to save his barn. We found this hideous thing to be quite common—We struck Hanover at dark. Found N.C.R.R.[1] badly torn up—During the day we heard heavy canonading—and later musketry firing—in the direction of Gettysburg. Rumor was, "Theres a Battle on at Gettysburg" and was not hard to believe—Some of our Cavalry had fought desperately here today, early—Charging into the enemy's rear and flanks—Killed some 30 rebs and hustled large forces on their way. So they had to abandon their dead and some of their wounded—We lay on arms in a field for the night—we were well fed, but awfully tired and sleepy—A shower of rain failed to awaken me—I was lying in a furrow, an old furrow. I partially awakened in the night feeling coolish on my lower side—but didn't fully awake. In the morning I discovered that water had run down the furrow—and I had "dam'd" it somewhat and so was pretty wet from below, while my poncho had kept me dry from the top—

July 2, 1863

Thursday. More or less Picket firing[2] all night—We were aroused early, and inspection showed a lot of our horses too lame and used up for good action—So first, our good mounts were formed for moving out, and were soon off—with the Brigade and took Reb. Genl. Steward by surprise on the Deardorf Farm—on right and rear of the army line—where Steward was expected to at least annoy the rear of Genl Mead—But our boys charged him—and after severe fighting dealt him an inglorious defeat and later in the day came in and lay on arms in the rear of Meads right—While our mounted men were paying attention to Genl Steward, we fellows had our horses cared for and were marched down to the right of the main line—to occupy a gap and do Sharpshooting—at long range, with our Carbines—we soon attracted attention, and later an occasional shell fell conspicuously close—but far enough to the rear of us so we suffered no serious harm. Towards noon firing became more general and in almost all directions—and we were ordered to our horses—and joined our returned heroes, and lay in readiness for any emergency—The general battle increaced in energy—and occasional fierceness—and by 2 P.M. the canonading was most terrific and continued til 5 P.M. and was interspersed with musketry—and Charge—yells and everything that goes to making up the indescribable battle of the best men on Earth, seemingly in the Fight to the Finish—At dark, our Cav Brig—2nd Brig 2" Div—was moved to the left—many wounded came in—Taken as a whole from all one can see from one point—it seems as tho our men—

1. **N.C.R.R.:** Northern Central Railroad.
2. **Picket firing:** When men on watch duty communicate with each other by firing rounds.

The Union Army—is rather overpowered and worsted—Lay on arms to rest—
Little chance to feed and eat.

July 3, 1863

Friday. Canonading commenced early—and battle was on again in full intensity at 10 ock we were ordered to the Front and Center, but immediately removed to the right of the Center—had some skirmishing. Pretty lively—Our squadron almost ran into a Rebel Battery with a Brigade of Cavalry maneuvering in the woods. They didn't want to see us, but moved left-ward and we held the woods all P-M.—All seemed rather quiet for several hours—From 1 1/2 til 4 P.M.—there was the heaviest canonading I ever have heard—One constant roar with rising and falling inflections—

Our Boys opened 54 guns at the same time on the Rebel lines and works from a little conical hill, Cemetary Ridge. We were picketing in the rear and on the right of it—Many shells came our way—some really quite near—But it is wonderful how few really made our acquaintance.

July 4, 1863

Saturday. The great battle closed and quieted with the closing day—Some firing at various points—

Our Regt layed on arms with Pickets out—on the ground where we had put in most of the day—Rather expecting attack momentarily—Rained furiously during the night—We had fed, eaten, and were standing "to horse" when about 6 ock NEWS CAME—"The Rebs are falling back!" and "Our Forces are following them" and our Regt went out towards Hunterstown reconnoitering. We found some confederates who had straggled, or were foraging, not knowing yet what had happened and was taking place—Of course, our Boys took them in—Making a little detour I captured two. Sergt. Major J. T. Richardson and Private Cox 9th Va Cav—disarming them and bringing them in—I guarded them—while the Regt gathered in some others—P.M. Captain Hughes came along and paroled them—and we were ordered to camp near Hanover—where we first lay on arriving near Gettysburg—Evening awfully muddy and disagreeable—I saw much of the destructiveness of the Johnies today—

July 5, 1863

Sunday. Rained awfully during the night. I got very wet—

Early we took up the march for Chambersburg—Crossing the battlefield—Cemitary Hill—The Great Wheat Field Farm, Seminary ridge—and other places where dead men, horses, smashed artillery, were strewn in utter confusion, the Blue and The Grey mixed—Their bodies so bloated—distorted—discolored on account of decomposition having set in—that they were utterly unrecognizable, save by clothing, or things in their pockets—The scene simply beggars description—Reaching the west side of the Field of Carnage—we virtually charged most of the way for 10 miles—to Cashtown—Frequently in sight of the Rebel rear guard—taking in prisoners—in bunches—We captured some 1,500 wounded men, and 300 stragglers—we went as far as Goodyears Springs, where we rested [*unclear:*] for the night. (I had to guard a Reb all night.)

July 6, 1863

Monday. Had a good breakfast. Turned my prisoner over to others. We took up the march—via Fayeteville for Quincy—I told Corp. Metz I intended going on—To Chambersburg—To see wife and Baby—and would report in the morning again. He understood and I slipped away—and was soon making time for home—I got a fine "10 oclock piece" at Heintzelmans—on approaching Chambersburg I was assured there were still squads of rebs about town—Near town I was met by townfolk inquiring about the battle. I was the first "blue coat" they had seen—and the first to bring direct news of the Enemy's defeat—as communications had been cut. As I struck the edge of town, I was told "The Rebel rear-guard had just left the Diamond." So I ventured out 2nd Street and ventured to strike Main near where Darling and Pussy lodged—and behold They were at the door—had been watching the Reb Rear leaving town—and Oh! The surprise and delight thus to meet after the awful battle they had been listening to for passing days—My horse was very soon stabled. My Cavalry outfit covered with hay—and myself in my citazens clothes—So should any final "rear" come along, I would not be discovered—To attempt to describe my joy and feelings at meeting and greeting my dear little family must prove a failure—We spent the P.M. and evening very sweetly and pleasantly, but only we had a few too many inquiring callers.

DIARY OF RACHEL CORMANY

June 16, 1863

Retired at 11 oclock. All was very quiet, so we concluded that all those reports must be untrue about the Reb's being so near, or that they had struck off in some other direction. Mr. Plough took his horse away so as to be on the safe side. So Annie and I were all alone. At 11 1/2 I heard the clattering of horses hoofs. I hopped out of bed & ran to the front window & sure enough there the Greybacks were going by as fast as their horses could take them down to the Diamond. Next I heard the report of a gun then they came back faster if possible than they came in. But a short time after the whole body came, the front ones with their hands on the gun triggers ready to fire & calling out as they passed along that they would lay the town in ashes if fired on again. It took a long time for them all to pass, but I could not judge how many there were—not being accustomed to seeing troops in such a body—At 2 oclock A.M. all was quiet again save an occasional reb. riding past. We went to bed again & slept soundly until 5 the morning. All seemed quiet yet. We almost came to the conclusion that the reb's had left again leaving only a small guard who took things quite leasurely. Soon however they became more active. Were hunting up the contrabands[3] & driving them off by droves. O! How it grated on our hearts to have to sit quietly & look at such brutal deeds—I saw no men among the contrabands—all women & children. Some of the colored people who were raised

3. **contrabands:** Escaped slaves.

here were taken along—I sat on the front step as they were driven by just like we would drive cattle. Some laughed & seemed not to care—but nearly all hung their heads. One woman was pleading wonderfully with her driver for her children—but all the sympathy she received from him was a rough "March along"—at which she would quicken her pace again. It is a query what they want with those little babies—whole families were taken. Of course when the mother was taken she would take her children. I suppose the men left thinking the women & children would not be disturbed. I cannot describe all the scenes—now—Noon—The Rebel horses with just enough men to take care of them & their teams, have just pased through town again on the retreat. Wonder what all this means. Just now the news came that the dismounted rebs are drawn up in line of battle out at McClures & expect a fight—so they sent their horses to the safe side of town in case a retreat is necessary. Some are walking or riding by every few minutes. The horses & wagons were taken back again. Evening—Had a good sleep this P.M. So had Pussy, & will retire trusting in God for safety.

June 17, 1863

. . . All was so quiet during the night that I veryly thought the Reb's had left—but they are still here. All forenoon they were carrying away mens clothing & darkeys. shortly after dinner their horses & wagons were taken on the retreat again. Yes Generals and all went. Saw Gen Jenkins, he is not a bad looking man—Some of the officers tipped their hats to us. I answered it with a curl of the lip. I knew they did it to taunt us. The one after he had tipped his hat most graciously & received in answer a toss of the head & curl of the lip took a good laugh over it. There were a few real inteligent good looking men among them. What a pity that they are rebels. After the main body had passed the news came that our soldiers were coming & just then some 1/2 doz reb's flew past as fast as their horses could take them. we learned since that one of them fired Oaks warehouse & that he was very near being shot by the citizens. Among the last to leave were some with darkeys on their horses behind them. How glad we are they are gone—None of our Soldiers came.

* * *

June 20, 1863

Went to bed early & slept well all night. This morning there is great excitement again. The report came last night that 40,000 or 50,000 infantry & some artillery have taken possession of Hagerstown—that the camps extend nearly to Greencastle—things surely look a little dubious. If we could only have regular mails. a mail came last night—but was not opened until this morning—Got a letter from My Samuel. it is but short. He is still safe—but were under marching orders again. it has been over a week on the way—I almost feel like getting out of this to some place where the mail is uninterupted, but then I fear, My Samuel might chance to come here & I would not see him so I shall stay—Will write to him now-.

* * *

June 26, 1863

12 1/2 oclock Cannon-waggons & men have been passing since between 9 & 10 this morning—42 Cannon & as many amunition waggons have passed—so now there are 62 pieces of artillery between us & Harrisburg & between 30,000 & 40,000 men. O it seems dreadful to be thus thrown into the hands of the rebbels & to be thus excluded from all the rest of the world—I feel so very anxious about Mr. Cormany—& who knows when we will hear from any of our friends again. It is no use to try to get away from here now—we must just take our chance with the rest—trusting in God as our Savior then come life come death if reconciled with God all is well—My God help me—I do wish to be a real true & living christian. Oh for more religion. Evening—called at Mrs Dickson a few minutes. Also at Mrs Clippingers. Numerous campfires could be seen on the fair ground.

June 27, 1863

Got up early & wakened Annie. And we flew round & put away our best bedclothes—before I got my things in order again Mrs. Clippinger came to go to Hokes where we got syrup & sugar. I also got me a lawn dress. Before we got started the rebels poured in already. they just marched through. Such a hard looking set I never saw. All day since 7 oclock they have been going through. Between 30 & 40 pieces of canno—& an almost endless trail of waggons. While I am writing thousands are passing—such a rough dirty ragged rowdyish set one does not often see—Gen's Lee & Longstreet passed through today. A body would think the whole south had broke loose & are coming into Pa. It makes me feel too badly to see so many men & cannon going through knowing that they have come to kill our men—Many have chickens as they pass— There a number are going with honey— robed some man of it no doubt— they are even carrying it in buckets. The report has reached us that Hooker & Sickel & Stoneman are after them. & at Harisburg the north has congregated en masse to oppose the invaders. Many think this the best thing in the word to bring the war to close—I hope our men will be strong enough to completely whip them— . . .

June 28, 1863

Slept well. Nowadays our cooking does not take much time—nowadays being we do all our eating by piecing. At 8 A.M. the rebels commenced coming again. Ga. troops. I was told this morning of some of their mean tricks of yesterday & before. They took the hats & boots off the men—Took that off Preacher Farney. Took $50. off Dr. Sneck & his gold watch valued very highly—took the coats off some, tetotally stripped one young fellow not far from town—Mr. Skinner. We have to be afraid to go out of our houses. A large wagon train & 500 or 600 Cavalry have just passed & it is now about 3 1/2 oclock. hope all are through now. Many of the saddles were empty, & any amount of negroes are along. This does not seem like Sunday. No church.

* * *

June 30, 1863

Nothing special transpired today. The Rebs are still about doing all the mischief they can. They have everything ready to set fire to the warehouses & machine shops—Tore up the railroad track & burned the crossties—They have cleared out nearly every store so they cannot rob much more—Evening—Quite a number of the young folks were in the parlor this evening singing all the patriotic & popular war songs. Quite a squad of rebels gathered outside to listen & seemed much pleased with the music—"When this cruel war is over" nearly brought tears from some. they sent in a petition to have it sung again which was done. they then thanked the girls very much & left—they acted real nicely.

* * *

July 2, 1863

At 3 A.M. I was wakened by the yells & howls of this dirty ragged lousy trash—they made as ugly as they could—all day they have been passing—part of the time on the double quick. At one time the report came that our men had come on them & that they were fighting—the excitement was high in town—but it was soon found out to be untrue—but the shock was so great that I got quite weak & immagined that I could already see My Samuel falling—I feel very uneasy about him—I cannot hear at all—They had quite a battle with Stuart[4]—I almost fear to hear the result in who was killed & who wounded—still I want to know.

July 3, 1863

Started out with Cora & a little basket on the hunt for something to eat out of the garden. I am tired of bread & molasses—went to Mammy Royers & got some peas & new potatoes—Cora got as many raspberries as she could eat. Came home put Cora to sleep then went to Mrs McG's for milk. got a few cherries to eat also a few for Cora when I got back Daddy Byers was standing at the gate. he came to see how I was getting along & told me how the rebels acted—they robbed him of a good deal—they wanted the horse but he plead so hard for him that they agreed to leave him & while one wrote a paper of securety others plundered the house. I guess Samuels silk hat & all that was in the box is gone. took Ellies best shoes—took towels sheets &c &c—After they were gone others came & took the horse too yet—they did not care for his security. Other of their neighbors fared worse yet. He would not stay for dinner. After dinner Henry Rebok came—he walked part of the way had an old horse but feared to bring him in—they were robbed of their horses and cattle up there—many had their horses sent away—one of J. Cormanys horses was taken. Henry wanted me to go along home with him but I could not think of leaving now—Samuel might come this way & if I were out there I would not get to see him. . . .

4. **Stuart:** J. E. B. Stuart, Confederate States Army general.

July 4, 1863

At daybreak the bells were rung—Then all was quiet until about 8 oclock when a flag was hoisted at the diamond. Soon after the band made its appearance & marched from square & played national airs—two rebels came riding along quite leisurely thinking I suppose to find their friends instead of that they were taken prisoners by the citizens—some 13 more footmen came and were taken prisoners. those were willing prisoners they had thrown their guns away before they reached this. The report has reached us that 6000 prisoners had been taken yesterday in Adams Co. near College Hill—also that Carlisle was shelled. It is getting very dark cloudy—I judge we will have a heavy rain. That Will Wampler does yell and cry like a panther. Evening We have had a powerful rain. Wild rumors of a dreadful fight are numerous.

July 5, 1863

I was roused out of sleep by Mr Early coming into Wampler & telling him something about wounded prisoners. so I got up took a bath dressed & went for a pitcher of water when I was told that 10, 4 or 6 horse waggons filled with wounded from the late battle were captured by citizens & brought to town—the wounded were put into the hospitals & the waggons & drivers were taken on toward Harisburg. Was also told that a great many more were out toward Greencastle—some went out to capture those but found that it was a train 20 miles long. P.M. A report has reached us that the whole rebel army is on the retreat—later that they are driven this way & are expected on soon—Have church S. School here today—seems like Sunday again Evening. At or after 4 P.M. I dressed myself & little girl and went to Mrs. Sulenbargers & while there we heard a fuss outside & when we got out lo our (Union of course) soldiers were coming in—she came along upstreet then to see them. They are of Milroys men—Just at dusk they went out the Greencastle road enroute to capture the waggon train which is trying to get over the river again. It is frightful how those poor wounded rebels are left to suffer. they are taken in large 4 horse waggons—wounds undressed—nothing to eat. Some are only about 4 miles from town & those that are here are as dirty and lousy as they well can be. The condition of those poor rebels all along from Getysburg to as far as they have come yet is reported dreadful. I am told they just beg the people along the road to help them—many have died by the way.

July 6, 1863

I was sitting reading, Pussy playing by my side when little Willie Wampler came running as fast as he could to tell me a soldier had come to see me & sure enough when I got to the door Mr Cormany just rode up. I was so very glad to see him that I scarcely knew how to act. He was very dirty & sweaty so he took a bath & changed clothes before he got himself dressed A. Holler & Barny Hampshire called—next Rev. Dixon & Dr Croft & others. Eve we went down into the parlor to hear some of the girls play—Mr. C was very much pleased with the music.

43

Fighting for the Union
Letters from Black Union Soldiers

The Civil War began with limited aims. The South sought independence to expand the plantation system to uncultivated lands to the West, while the North sought to preserve the Union and contain slavery. At first both sides wanted to limit the conflict to avoid disruption of the businesses, families, and institutions spread across the divide. This meant, among other things, excluding blacks from military service and leaving slavery intact.

Though African Americans had served in every war in U.S. history, an old militia law was invoked, leaving them out of the first Civil War battles. Abolitionists such as Frederick Douglass argued that this was a mistake and that the guerrilla war in "bleeding Kansas" in the 1850s showed this to be a life or death battle between two economic systems and two ways of life. They counseled Lincoln to end the war quickly by the four million enslaved African Americans in crippling the Southern economy by abandoning their masters to join the Union Army.

More moderate voices claimed that slaves were too servile and dependent on their masters to be reliable soldiers. Regardless of what Lincoln believed personally, his strategy was to preserve the Union by not antagonizing the five "border states" that had slavery, but remained loyal to the Union. This meant preserving slavery, keeping blacks out of the military, and reversing the actions of generals, like abolitionist David Hunter, who freed slaves taken in battle.

By 1862 states were struggling to provide enough soldiers to fight and started swearing in African Americans. Later that year Congress repealed the ban on blacks in the U.S. Army, and on January 1, 1863, Lincoln's Emancipation Proclamation signaled that the Civil War had become a war against slavery. African Americans deserted their masters by the thousands, swelling the Union Army by two hundred thousand soldiers, or 10 percent of the fighting force.

Black soldiers were not treated well in the army. They were poorly equipped and trained, paid less than white soldiers, and given the worst tasks. In the beginning they were excluded from combat, but after the heroic assault on Fort Wagner in July 1863 by the black 54th Massachusetts Regiment (portrayed in the movie Glory*), they became widely known as some of the Union Army's bravest soldiers. Lincoln described their services as "the heaviest blow yet dealt to the rebellion" and the Confederacy even came to recognize the central role of black slaves in the conflict, authorizing their enlistment on*

Edwin S. Redkey, ed., *A Grand Army of Black Men* (New York: Cambridge University Press, 1992).

February 18, 1865. How many might have fought for the South will never be known; it was clearly too little, too late.

The letters that follow are a small selection of the thousands written by black soldiers in the Union Army to friends and family, officers and officials, and African American newspapers in the North.

QUESTIONS TO CONSIDER

1. From the letters that follow, what can you glean about some of the concerns and hopes of African Americans serving in the Union Army? In what ways might these concerns and hopes have influenced their performance in war?

2. By the last year of the war, there were roughly two hundred thousand African Americans in the Union Army. What impact do you think that had on the way white Northerners and Southerners viewed the war?

3. How do you think the experience of serving in the army changed how African American soldiers viewed their place in American society? What impact do you think it had on the direction African American community life and political activity took after the war?

Near Petersburge [Virginia][1] August 19th 1864

Dear Madam   I receave A letter from You A few day Ago inquir in regard to the Fait of Your Son I am sarry to have to inform You that thear is no dobt of his Death   he Died A Brave Death in Trying to Save the Colors of Rige[ment] in that Dreadful Battil   Billys Death was unevesally [mourned] by all but by non greatter then by my self ever sins we have bin in the Army we have bin amoung the moust intimoat Friend   wen every our Rige[ment] wen into Camp he sertan to be at my Tent and meney happy moment we seen to gether Talking about Home and the Probability of our Living to get Home to See each other Family and Friend   But Providence has will other wise and You must Bow to His will   You and His Wife Sister and all Have my deepust Simppathy and trust will be well all in this Trying moment

You Inquired about Mr Young   He wen to the Hospetol and I can not give You eney other information in regard to Him

Billys thing that You requested to inquired about I can git no informa of us in the bustil of the Battil every thing was Lost

Give my Respects to Samual Jackson and Family not forgetting Your self and Family I remain Your Friend

G. H. Freeman

[Benton Barracks Hospital, St. Louis, Missouri, September 3, 1864. Spotswood Rice was an African American soldier writing to his children in captivity.]

---

1. Bracketed notes were provided by the original editor of these sources, Edwin S. Redkey.

My Children I take my pen in hand to rite you A few lines to let you know that I have not forgot you and that I want to see you as bad as ever now my Dear Children I want you to be contented with whatever may be your lots   be assured that I will have you if it cost me my life   on the 28th of the mounth. 8 hundred White and 8 hundred blacke solders expects to start up the rivore to Glasgow and above there thats to be jeneraled by a jeneral that will give me both of you   when they Come I expect to be with, them and expect to get you both in return. Dont be uneasy my children I expect to have you. If Diggs dont give you up this Government will and I feel confident that I will get you   Your Miss Kaitty said that I tried to steal you   But I'll let her know that god never intended for man to steal his own flesh and blood. If I had no confidence in God I could have confidence in her   But as it is If I ever had any Confidence in her I have none now and never expect to have   And I want her to remember if she meets me with ten thousand soldiers she [will?] meet her enemy   I once [thought] that I had some respect for them but now my respects is worn out and have no sympathy for Slaveholders. And as for her cristianantty I expect the Devil has Such in hell   You tell her from me that She is the frist Christian that Iever hard say that a man could Steal his own child especially out of human bondage

You can tell her that She can hold to you as long as she can   I never would expect to ask her ain to let you come to me because I know that the devil has got her hot set against that that is write   now my Dear children I am a going to close my letter to you   Give my love to all enquiring friends   tell them all that we are well and want to see them very much and Corra and Mary receive the greater part of it you sefves   and dont think hard of us not sending you any thing   I you father have a plenty for you when I see you   Spott & Noah sends their love to both of you   Oh! My Dear children how I do want to see you

[Spotswood Rice]

March 13, 1864

To the *Christian Recorder*

It is with pleasure that I now seat myself to inform you of our last battle . . .

The battle took place in a grove called Olustee, with the different regiments as follows: First there was the 8th U.S. [Colored Infantry]; they were cut up badly, and they were the first colored regiment in the battle. The next was the 54th Mass., which I belong to. . . . The firing was very warm, and it continued for about three hours and a half. The 54th was the last off the field. . . .

Now it seems strange to me that we do not receive the same pay and rations as the white soldiers. Do we not fill the same ranks? Do we not cover the same space of ground? Do we not take up the same length of ground in a grave-yard that others do? The ball does not miss the black man and strike the white, nor the white and strike the black. But sir, at that time there is no distinction made; they strike one as much as another. The black men have to go through the same hurling of musketry, and the same belching of cannonading as white soldiers do.

E.D.W. [Private]

[In August 1864 African American soldiers who had been free before the war began receiving equal pay. Units made up of former slaves did not receive full back pay until March 1865.]

June 20, 1864

To the *Weekly Anglo-African*

. . . Since I last wrote, almost half of the 5th Massachusetts Cavalry have been in several engagements, and about thirty have been killed and wounded. The first notice I had of going into the engagement was about 1 o'clock, a.m., Wednesday, the 15th. We heard the bugle, and sprang to our arms, and, with two days rations, we started towards Petersburg, and when about four miles on our way toward that city, at a place called Beatty's House, we came in front of the rebels' works. Here we formed a line of battle, and started for the rebs' works. I was with some thirty of my Company. We had to pass through the woods; but we kept on, while the shell, grape and canister came around us cruelly. Our Major and Col. [Henry F.] Russell were wounded, and several men fell—to advance seemed almost impossible; but we rallied, and after a terrible charge, amidst pieces of barbarous iron, solid shot and shell, we drove the desperate greybacks from their fortifications, and gave three cheers for our victory. But few white troops were with us. Parts of the 1st, 4th, 6th and 22nd [United States Colored Infantry] were engaged.

The colored troops here have received a great deal of praise. The sensations I had in the battle were, coolness and interest in the boys' fighting. They shouted, "Fort Pillow,"[2] and the rebs were shown no mercy.

[Private Charles Torrey Beman]

August 21, 1864

To the *Christian Recorder*

. . . I will say something about the prejudice in our own regiment when we returned from Olustee to Jacksonville. One of our captains was sick, and there was no doctor there excepting our hospital steward, who administered the medicines and effected a cure; he was a colored man, Dr. [Theodore] Becker, and a competent physician, and through the exertions of this recovered captain, there was a petition got up for his promotion. All the officers signed the petition but three, Captain [Charles] Briggs, and two lieutenants; they admitted he was a smart man and understood medicine, but he was a negro, and they did not want a negro Doctor, neither did they want negro officers. The Colonel, seeing so much prejudice among his officers, destroyed the document; therefore the negro is not yet acknowledged.

Notwithstanding all these grievances, we prefer the Union rather than the rebel government, and will sustain the Union if the United States will give us

---

2. At Fort Pillow in April 1864, Confederate troops shot prisoners, especially African Americans, who had surrendered. [Redkey's note.]

our rights. We will calmly submit to white officers, though some of them are no so well acquainted with military matters as our orderly sergeants, and some of the officers have gone so far to say that a negro stunk under their noses. This is not very pleasant, but we must give the officers of Company B of the 54th Massachusetts regiment, their just dues; they generally show us the respect due to soldiers, and scorn any attempt to treat us otherwise. . . .

"Fort Green" [54th Massachusetts Infantry]

October, 1865

To the *Weekly Anglo-African*

I have never before attempted to pen a line for your columns, but in this case I am compelled to, because I have been waiting patiently to see if I could see anything in regard to our noble Regiment, and have seen nothing. We have fought and captured Blakesly's Fort. We were only ten days on the siege, and had nothing to eat but Parched Corn. But as luck would have it, I crept out of my hole at night and scared one of the Jonnys so bad that he left his rifle pit, gun and accouterments, also one corn dodger and about one pint of buttermilk, all of which I devoured with a will, and returned to my hole safe and sound. After sleeping the remainder of the night, about day I was awakened by our turtle-backs that were playing with the enemy's works. At that time I forgot myself and poked my head out of my hole, and came very near getting one of Jonny's cough pills. We had to keep our heads down all the time or else run the risk of getting shot. So me and my friend of whom I was speaking had it all that day, shooting at each other. Finally, he got hungry and cried out to me, "Say, Blacky, let's stop and eat some Dinner." I told him, "All right." By the time I thought he was done eating, I cried, "Hello, Reb." He answered, "What do you want?" I said, "Are you ready" "No, not yet," he said. Then I waited for awhile. I finally got tired and cried for a chew of tobacco. He then shot at me and said, "Chew that!" I thanked him kindly and commenced exchanging shots with him.

I must not take too much time in relating all the incidents, for Parched Corn takes the day also. We have accomplished all undertakings, and excel in the drill. We ask nothing now but to be mustered out.

[Sergeant Cassius M. Clay Alexander]

April 12, 1865

To the *Christian Recorder*

I have just returned from the city of Richmond; my regiment was among the first that entered that city. I marched at the head of the column, and soon I found myself called upon by the officers and men of my regiment to make a speech, with which, of course, I readily complied. A vast multitude assembled on Broad Street, and I was aroused amid the shouts of ten thousand voices, and proclaimed for the first time in that city freedom to all mankind. After which the doors of all the slave pens were thrown open, and thousands came out shouting and praising God, and Father, or Master Abe, as they termed him. In this mighty consternation I became so overcome with tears that I could not stand up under the pressure of such fullness of joy in my own heart. I retired to gain strength, so I lost many important topics worthy of note.

Among the densely crowded concourse there were parents looking for children who had been sold south of this state in tribes, and husbands came for the same purpose; here and there one was singled out in the ranks, and an effort was made to approach the gallant and marching soldiers, who were too obedient to orders to break ranks.

We continued our march as far as Camp Lee, at the extreme end of Broad Street, running westwards. In camp the multitude followed, and everybody could participate in shaking the friendly but hard hands of the poor slaves. Among the many broken-hearted mothers looking for their children who had been sold to Georgia and elsewhere, was an aged woman, passing through the vast crowd of colored, inquiring for [one] by the name of Garland H. White, who had been sold from her when a small boy, and was bought by a lawyer named Robert Toombs, who lived in Georgia. Since the war has been going on she has seen Mr. Toombs in Richmond with troops from his state, and upon her asking him where his body-servant Garland was, he replied: "He ran off from me at Washington, and went to Canada. I have since learned that he is living somewhere in the State of Ohio." Some of the boys knowing that I lived in Ohio, soon found me and said, "Chaplain, here is a lady that wishes to see you." I quickly turned, following the soldier until coming to a group of colored ladies. I was questioned as follows:

"What is your name, sir?"
"My name is Garland H. White."
"What was your mother's name?"
"Nancy."
"Where was you born?"
"In Hanover County, in this State."
"Where was you sold from?"
"From this city."
"What was the name of the man who bought you?"
"Robert Toombs."
"Where did he live?"
"In the State of Georgia."
"Where did you leave him?"
"At Washington."
"Where did you go then?"
"To Canada."
"Where do you live now?"
"In Ohio."
"This is your mother, Garland, whom you are now talking to, who has spent twenty years of grief about her son."

I cannot express the joy I felt at this happy meeting of my mother and other friends. But suffice it to say that God is on the side of the righteous, and will in due time reward them. I have witnessed several such scenes among the other colored regiments. . . .

[Chaplain Garland H. White]

May 18, 1865

To the *Christian Recorder*

It is the first time in the history of my life that one so humble as myself ever attempted to write anything for publication through the columns of your most worthy journal; and it is with great reluctance that I attempt it on the present occasion, owing to my short stay at home in Park Co[unty], Ind[iana], on a furlough, where I found many friends to rejoice over, and many disadvantages upon the part of the colored people to mourn over. It seems very strange to me that the people of Indiana are so very indifferent about removing from their statute books those Black Laws, which are a curse to them in the eyes of God and man, and above all things in life, the most grievous to be borne by any people.

Shall the history of the old 28th [United States Colored Infantry], which was raised in that State, stand upon the great record of the American army second to none? Shall these brave sons return home after periling their lives for several years in the storm of battle for the restoration of the Union and to vindicate the honor and dignity of that fair Western State which is classed among the best composing this great nation, but to be treated as slaves? Shall it be said by the nations of the earth that any portion of the United States treated her brave defenders thus? I hope never to see the day; yet it is fast approaching.

Have we no friends at home among the whites to look this great injustice in the face, and bid its sin-cursed waves forever leave? Have we no colored friends at home who feel tired of the burden and are willing to pray to the thinking public to lighten it? As for us, we have done our duty and are willing to do it whenever the State and country call us; but after responding, are you not willing to pay the laborer for his hire? It is to be seen in all past history that when men fought for their country and returned home, they always enjoyed the rights and privileges due to other citizens. We ask to be made equal before the law; grant us this and we ask no more. Let the friends of freedom canvass the country on this subject. Let the sound go into all the earth. . . .

William Gibson, Corporal

44

Healing Wounds

Cornelia Hancock

Of about two million federal troops who served in the Civil War, 360,000 died. Among the more than one million who served in the Confederate military, some 250,000 also perished. Only one in three of these died of battle wounds; the others succumbed to disease or accident. About a half million were wounded, many of them severely.

A badly wounded man had only a precarious chance for survival. Little was known about infection, and military surgeons performed operations without taking sanitary precautions. Soldiers contracted gangrene and other deadly infections. Though anesthetics were known, doctors did not always have them on hand, and major surgery often resulted in shock, followed by death. Long delays occurred when transporting casualties to medical aid stations or hospitals. Soldiers suffered as well from the mosquitos, lice, and biting flies that infested the battlefront and that spread diseases such as malaria and yellow fever. Poor diet also undermined health, although the less well-supplied Confederate soldiers suffered from malnourishment to a far greater degree than Union troops.

Cornelia Hancock (1840–1927), from a New Jersey Quaker family, was one of thousands of women who worked to improve health care for the Union Army. In 1863, she volunteered to be a nurse, but Dorothea Dix, then Superintendent of Female Nurses, rejected her application, disapproving of nurses who were attractive or under thirty. Cornelia, twenty-three and pretty, simply traveled to Gettysburg, arriving on the third day of the battle and going right to work helping the wounded. Her account vividly renders the many horrors of Civil War battles. It also illuminates the reactions of friends at home to her decision to strike out on such an unladylike course.

QUESTIONS TO CONSIDER

1. How does Cornelia Hancock respond to the suffering around her?
2. Why do people at home complain about what Hancock is doing? What is her response to them?
3. How does Hancock respond to escaped slaves? How does her response compare to that of those around her?

Henrietta Stratton Jaquette, ed., *South after Gettysburg: Letters of Cornelia Hancock, 1863–1868* (New York: Crowell, 1956), 6–11, 17–19, 42–45, 58–60, 73–77, 91–94.

HANCOCK'S ACCOUNT OF HER
FIRST DAY AT GETTYSBURG

We arrived in the town of Gettysburg on the evening of July sixth, three days after the last day of battle. We were met by Dr. Horner, at whose house we stayed. Every barn, church, and building of any size in Gettysburg had been converted into a temporary hospital. We went the same evening to one of the churches, where I saw for the first time what war meant. Hundreds of desperately wounded men were stretched out on boards laid across the high-backed pews as closely as they could be packed together. The boards were covered with straw. Thus elevated, these poor sufferers' faces, white and drawn with pain, were almost on a level with my own. I seemed to stand breast-high in a sea of anguish. . . .

Learning that the wounded of the Third Division of the Second Corps, including the 12th Regiment of New Jersey, were in a Field Hospital about five miles outside of Gettysburg, we determined to go there early the next morning, expecting to find some familiar faces among the regiments of my native state. As we drew near our destination we began to realize that war has other horrors than the sufferings of the wounded or the desolation of the bereft. A sickening, overpowering, awful stench announced the presence of the unburied dead, on which the July sun was mercilessly shining, and at every step the air grew heavier and fouler, until it seemed to possess a palpable horrible density that could be seen and felt and cut with a knife. Not the presence of the dead bodies themselves, swollen and disfigured as they were, and lying in heaps on every side, was as awful to the spectator as that deadly, nauseating atmosphere which robbed the battlefield of its glory, the survivors of their victory, and the wounded of what little chance of life was left to them.

As we made our way to a little woods in which we were told was the Field Hospital we were seeking, the first sight that met our eyes was a collection of semi-conscious but still living human forms, all of whom had been shot through the head, and were considered hopeless. They were laid there to die and I hoped that they were indeed too near death to have consciousness. Yet many a groan came from them, and their limbs tossed and twitched. The few surgeons who were left in charge of the battlefield after the Union army had started in pursuit of Lee had begun their paralyzing task by sorting the dead from the dying, and the dying from those whose lives might be saved; hence the groups of prostrate, bleeding men laid together according to their wounds.

There was hardly a tent to be seen. Earth was the only available bed during those first hours after the battle. A long table stood in this woods and around it gathered a number of surgeons and attendants. This was the operating table, and for seven days it literally ran blood. A wagon stood near rapidly filling with amputated legs and arms; when wholly filled, this gruesome spectacle withdrew from sight and returned as soon as possible for another load. So appalling was the number of the wounded as yet unsuccored, so helpless seemed the few who were battling against tremendous odds to save life, and so overwhelming was the demand for any kind of aid that could be given quickly, that one's senses were benumbed by the awful responsibility that fell to the living. . . .

I need not say that every hour brought an improvement in the situation, that trains from the North came pouring into Gettysburg laden with doctors, nurses, hospital supplies, tents, and all kinds of food and utensils: but that *first* day of my arrival, the sixth of July, and the third day after the battle, was a time that taxed the ingenuity and fortitude of the living as sorely as if we had been a party of shipwrecked mariners thrown upon a desert island.

LETTERS

Gettysburg, Pa. July 7th, 1863

My Dear Cousin

I am very tired tonight; have been on the field all day — went to the 3rd Division 2nd Army Corps. I suppose there are about five hundred wounded belonging to it. They have one patch of woods devoted to each army corps for a hospital. I being interested in the 2nd, because Will [her brother] had been in it, got into one of its ambulances, and went out at eight this morning and came back at six this evening. There are no words in the English language to express the sufferings I witnessed today. The men lie on the ground; their clothes have been cut off them to dress their wounds; they are half naked, have nothing but hardtack to eat only as Sanitary Commissions, Christian Associations, and so forth give them. I was the first woman who reached the 2nd Corps after the three days fight at Gettysburg. I was in that Corps all day, not another woman within a half mile. Mrs. Harris was in first division of 2nd Corps. I was introduced to the surgeon of the post, went anywhere through the Corps, and received nothing but the greatest politeness from even the lowest private. . . . To give you some idea of the extent and numbers of the wounds, four surgeons, none of whom were idle fifteen minutes at a time, were busy all day amputating legs and arms. I gave to every man that had a leg or arm off a gill of wine, to every wounded in Third Division, one glass of lemonade, some bread and preserves and tobacco — as much as I am opposed to the latter, for they need it very much, they are so exhausted.

I feel very thankful that this was a successful battle; the spirit of the men is so high that many of the poor fellows said today, "What is an arm or leg to whipping Lee out of Penn." I would get on first rate if they would not ask me to write to their wives; *that* I cannot do without crying, which is not pleasant to either party. I do not mind the sight of blood, have seen limbs taken off and was not sick at all.

It is a very beautiful, rolling country here; under favorable circumstances I should think healthy, but now for five miles around, there is an awful smell of putrefaction. Women are needed here very badly, anyone who is willing to go to field hospitals, but nothing short of an order from Secretary Stanton or General Halleck will let you through the lines. Major General Schenk's order for us was not regarded as anything; if we had not met Miss Dix at Baltimore Depot, we should not have gotten through. It seems a strange taste but I am glad we did.

We stay at Doctor Horner's house at night — direct letters care of Dr. Horner, Gettysburg, Pa. If you could mail me a newspaper, it would be a great satisfaction, as we do not get the news here and the soldiers are so anxious to hear; things will be different here in a short time.

Cornelia

3rd Division — 2nd Army Corps Hospital
Gettysburg, Pa. July 26th [1863] — Sunday

My Dear Mother

Today is Sunday but there is no semblance of it here. It is now about five o'clock in the morning. Our hospital has been moved and our stores have given out. There is nothing to cook with, hence I have nothing to do, and therefore, have time to write.

... I have eight wall tents full of amputated men. The tents of the wounded I look right out on. It is a melancholy sight — but you have no idea how soon one gets used to it. Their screams of agony do not make as much impression on me now as the reading of this letter will on you. The most painful task we have to perform here is entertaining the friends who come from home and see their friends all mangled up. I do hate to see them. Soldiers take everything as it comes, but citizens are not inured. You will think it is a short time for me to get used to things, but it seems to me as if all my past life was a myth, and as if I had been away from home seventeen years.

... What I do here one would think would kill at home, but I am well and comfortable. When we get up early in the morning, our clothes are so wet that we could wring them. On they go, and by noon they are dry.

From thy affectionate daughter —
C. Hancock

Jan. 1864

Dear William [Cornelia's brother]

Where are the people who have been professing such strong abolition proclivity for the last thirty years? Certainly not in Washington laboring with these people whom they have been clamoring to have freed. They are freed now or at least many of them, and herded together in filthy huts, half clothed. And what is worse than all guarded over by persons who have not a proper sympathy for them. I have been in the Washington Contraband[1] Hospital for the past two months. It is in close proximity to the Camp of Reception [where the patients first arrived] — and I have had ample opportunity to see these people, the persons in charge of them, and the whole mode of proceeding with them. Their wants are great and appeal in every way for aid from the North.

---

1. **contraband:** A black slave who escaped or was brought to the North.

. . . Smallpox has raged here to a great extent but a separate hospital has been established for that now. The order now is to remove all contrabands south of the Potomac. It may be better there than here, but we remain under the same authority and let me state emphatically that nothing for the permanent advancement of these people can be effected until the whole matter is removed from the military authority and vested in a separate bureau whose sole object is the protection and elevation of these people.

. . . There is much charity being extended to our poor soldiers and I would note that any one should withhold one mite from them, but I maintain that persons living in their comfortable homes in the North should give liberally to those so sadly situated as these forlorn contrabands, as well as to the soldiers. A national Sanitary Commission for the Relief of Colored Persons of this class would save lives and a great deal of suffering. The slaves generally get free when our army advances; they come into our lines several hundred at a time, follow the army for a while, then come into Washington, some probably having walked 50 miles. One woman carried one child in her arms and dragged two by her side. Judge of the condition of that woman when she arrives. Should not some comfortable quarters await her weary body?

Thy sister,
Cornelia H.

[In February 1864 Cornelia became a nurse with the Army of the Potomac, then headquartered near Brandy Station, Virginia.]

3rd Div. 2 Corps Hospital
March 25, 1864

My Dear Sister
    . . . On Wednesday we received orders to send all the sick and wounded to Washington, along with the order came a snow storm, along with the snow storm came an orderly countermanding the previous order, along with him came a splendid morning, along with it, came another orderly ordering to move on Thursday; and at 8 o'clock we had them all loaded and on stretchers, and proceeded with the long train from the three hospitals to Brandy station. There the platform was strewed full of helpless men wounded at Morton's Ford. How like Gettys[burg] it seemed to me. I had all our worst cases put in a pile, took a whiskey bottle, and sat down and helped the poor souls to live while they were loaded. Two mortal hours we sat in the sun and heard the locomotive hiss, the cars back and go ahead, then back, etc., etc., etc., just what always happens at depots. One of our nice wounded wanted to give me some greenbacks right in the hubbub. There were two women who stay at the station with hot tea, etc. They supplied all hands and retired. There I sat, I suppose five hundred men staring at me, but Dr. Miller and our own steward and hospital boys were with me and I did not care. By dint of great perseverance a hospital car was provided for the worst cases and I went in and saw them lying comfortably upon the

stretchers, saw the cars trudge off with their groaning load, and think I to my-self, the idea of making a business of maiming men is not one worthy of a civi-lized nation. By the time I got home over the corduroy [a bumpy road] had a headache of the first water, went to bed, and there could lay, as my occupation is nearly gone now. . . .

from thy affectionate sister
Cornelia Hancock

3rd Div. 2 Corps Hosp.
March 27, 1864

My Dear Mother
     . . . Our hospital will soon fill up with sick unless they move. Then what will become of us is unknown — Ellen is fretting for fear I shall go on a march. My only answer to all such worriments is you ought to have confidence enough in my judgment to think I will do the best thing. After campaigning successfully for 9 months I ought to have some experience. In regard to Salem people think-ing I ought to have a woman to sleep with me, I am much better guarded than the lone widows and maids at Isabell's. Another woman is not needed nor would be allowed here. Mrs. Lee is within sending distance if I was sick, so calm all your fears. I go to sleep just as quick as I touch the bed, am used to being alone, like it, and never feel lonely and would not sleep with Mrs. Lee if I could. I am sorry you have any distress on my account, but I cannot help you any and I assure you it is all unnecessary.
     . . . Sarah Sinnickson wrote me a letter expressive of great concern from my "way of living." I wrote her a letter that she will not forget soon. They can-not expect everyone to be satisfied to live in as small a circle as themselves in these days of great events. She expresses it as the great concern of the whole family and her approaching sickness made her bold to express it. . . .

from thy daughter
Cornelia Hancock

[May 1864]

Dear Ellen
     . . . I am in Fredericksburg city. I do not know where Doctor is. On going ashore at Belle Plain we were met with hordes of wounded soldiers who had been able to walk from the Wilderness battlefield to this point. They were fam-ished for food and as I opened the remains of my lunch basket the soldiers be-haved more like ravenous wolves than human beings, so I felt the very first thing to be done was to prepare food in unlimited quantities, so with my past experience in arranging a fire where there seemed no possibility of one, I soon had a long pole hanging full of kettles of steaming hot coffee, and this, with soft bread, was dispensed all night to the tramping soldiers who were filling the steam boats on their return trip to Washington.

. . . when daylight came Dr. Detmold and Dr. Vanderpool, two eminent surgeons of New York, and I boarded [an ambulance] to go to Fredericksburg, where our hospital is established. On arriving here the scenes beggared all description and these two men, eminent as they are in their profession, were paralyzed by what they saw. Rain had poured in through the bullet-riddled roofs of the churches until our wounded lay in pools of water made bloody by their seriously wounded condition. On these scenes Dr. Detmold and Dr. Vanderpool gazed in horror and seemed not to know where to take hold. My Gettysburg experience enabled me to take hold. The next morning these two surgeons came to me and said: "If we open another church under better conditions than these, will you accompany us?" and I said "Yes." After they got their nerve their splendid executive ability asserted itself and they had the pews knocked to pieces; under the backs and seats put a cleat and made little beds to raise the wounded from the floor. 'Tis true the beds have no springs, but it keeps them from lying in the water. Here day by day things are improving. An amputating table is improvized under a tree in the yard where these two good men work indefatiguably.

[May 1864]

My Dear Mother
. . . I was the first and only Union woman in the city [Fredericksburg]. I believe today there were some of Miss Dix's nurses came thru. I have good quarters. We calculate there are 14,000 wounded in the town; the Secesh [rebel Southerners] help none, so you may know there is suffering equal to any thing anyone ever saw, almost as bad as Gettysburg, only we have houses and churches for the men. I am well, have worked harder than I ever did in my life. There was no food but hard tack to give the men so I turned in and dressed their wounds. It was all that could be done. I hear from my friends at the front one by one. Almost every one I knew was shot dead except the Doctor. Some of them are taken prisoners, Dr. Aiken for one. Dr. Dudley was safe last night. Lieut. Fogg was shot dead, so was Capt. Madison — this battle is still raging. I am glad I am here but I really thought my heart would break as one after another they told me was dead. If they only accomplish getting to Richmond. If not, it is a dear battle. There is very heavy firing today. I hope Dr. Dudley will get thru safe. He sent a Doctor to see me, told him he knew I would get thru. He is out on the front with his Regt. Oh, how awful, it seems as if the great judgment day was upon us now; the Secesh are still in town but we take possession of all churches and houses we want. I am well. Write to me in care of Dr. Davis, 1st Div. 2nd Corps. hospt., Fred'ksburg, Va. . . .

Thine in haste
Cornelia Hancock

45

African Americans during Reconstruction
Felix Haywood et al.

The Thirteenth (1865), Fourteenth (1868), and Fifteenth (1870) Amendments to the U.S. Constitution decreed an equality between the races that did not become a reality in African Americans' daily lives. At first the federal government established the Freedmen's Bureau and supported Reconstruction governments in Southern states, making vigorous efforts to help the freed slaves gain education, legal and medical services, reasonable employment contracts, and a measure of political power. But within about a decade those efforts were abandoned as the Northern public, tired of disorder in the South and wary of government intervention, abandoned freed slaves to their former masters. African Americans were left to respond however they could to the social revolution brought about by emancipation, the war's impoverishment of the South, and the violence of groups like the Ku Klux Klan. Historians have pieced together the story of their actions from a multiplicity of sources. Interviews with former slaves collected in the 1930s, of which you will here read a sample, are very illuminating of just how conditions really were for those living through them.

QUESTIONS TO CONSIDER
1. What, judging from these accounts, were the major problems that former slaves faced after the war?
2. What did these former slaves expect of freedom?
3. What role did the Ku Klux Klan play in former slaves' lives?
4. Why did some freedmen continue to work for their former masters?

FELIX HAYWOOD

San Antonio, Texas. Born in Raleigh, North Carolina. Age at interview: 88.

The end of the war, it come just like that — like you snap your fingers. . . . How did we know it! Hallelujah broke out —

> Abe Lincoln freed the nigger
>   With the gun and the trigger;
> And I ain't going to get whipped any more.
>   I got my ticket,

"African Americans React to Reconstruction," from B. A. Botkin, ed., *Lay My Burden Down: A Folk History of Slavery* (Chicago: University of Chicago Press, 1945), 65–70, 223–24, 241–42, 246–47.

> Leaving the thicket,
> And I'm a-heading for the Golden Shore!

Soldiers, all of a sudden, was everywhere — coming in bunches, crossing and walking and riding. Everyone was a-singing. We was all walking on golden clouds. Hallelujah!

> Union forever,
> Hurrah, boys, hurrah!
> Although I may be poor,
> I'll never be a slave —
> Shouting the battle cry of freedom.

Everybody went wild. We felt like heroes, and nobody had made us that way but ourselves. We was free. Just like that, we was free. It didn't seem to make the whites mad, either. They went right on giving us food just the same. Nobody took our homes away, but right off colored folks started on the move. They seemed to want to get closer to freedom, so they'd know what it was — like it was a place or a city. Me and my father stuck, stuck close as a lean tick to a sick kitten. The Gudlows started us out on a ranch. My father, he'd round up cattle — unbranded cattle — for the whites. They was cattle that they belonged to, all right; they had gone to find water 'long the San Antonio River and the Guadalupe. Then the whites gave me and my father some cattle for our own. My father had his own brand — 7 B) — and we had a herd to start out with of seventy.

We knowed freedom was on us, but we didn't know what was to come with it. We thought we was going to get rich like the white folks. We thought we was going to be richer than the white folks, 'cause we was stronger and knowed how to work, and the whites didn't, and they didn't have us to work for them any more. But it didn't turn out that way. We soon found out that freedom could make folks proud, but it didn't make 'em rich.

Did you ever stop to think that thinking don't do any good when you do it too late? Well, that's how it was with us. If every mother's son of a black had thrown 'way his hoe and took up a gun to fight for his own freedom along with the Yankees, the war'd been over before it began. But we didn't do it. We couldn't help stick to our masters. We couldn't no more shoot 'em than we could fly. My father and me used to talk 'bout it. We decided we was too soft and freedom wasn't going to be much to our good even if we had a education.

WARREN McKINNEY

Hazen, Arkansas. Born in South Carolina. Age at interview: 85.

I was born in Edgefield County, South Carolina. I am eighty-five years old. I was born a slave of George Strauter. I remembers hearing them say, "Thank God, I's free as a jay bird." My ma was a slave in the field. I was eleven years old when freedom was declared. When I was little, Mr. Strauter whipped my ma. It hurt me bad as it did her. I hated him. She was crying. I chunked him with rocks. He run after me, but he didn't catch me. There was twenty-five or thirty hands that worked in the field. They raised wheat, corn, oats, barley, and cotton. All the children that couldn't work stayed at one house. Aunt Mat kept the babies and small children that couldn't go to the field. He had a gin and a shop. The shop was at the fork of the roads. When the war come on, my papa went to built forts. He quit Ma and took another woman. When the war close, Ma took her four children, bundled 'em up and went to Augusta. The government give out rations there. My ma washed and ironed. People died in piles. I don't know till yet what was the matter. They said it was the change of living. I seen five or six wooden, painted coffins piled up on wagons pass by our house. Loads passed every day like you see cotton pass here. Some said it was cholera and some took consumption. Lots of the colored people nearly starved. Not much to get to do and not much houseroom. Several families had to live in one house. Lots of the colored folks went up North and froze to death. They couldn't stand the cold. They wrote back about them dying. No, they never sent them back. I heard some sent for money to come back. I heard plenty 'bout the Ku Klux. They scared the folks to death. People left Augusta in droves. About a thousand would all meet and walk going to hunt work and new homes. Some of them died. I had a sister and brother lost that way. I had another sister come to Louisiana that way. She wrote back.

I don't think the colored folks looked for a share of land. They never got nothing 'cause the white folks didn't have nothing but barren hills left. About all the mules was wore out hauling provisions in the army. Some folks say they ought to done more for the colored folks when they left, but they say they was broke. Freeing all the slaves left 'em broke.

That Reconstruction was a mighty hard pull. Me and Ma couldn't live. A man paid our ways to Carlisle, Arkansas, and we come. We started working for Mr. Emenson. He had a big store, teams, and land. We liked it fine, and I been here fifty-six years now. There was so much wild game, living was not so hard. If a fellow could get a little bread and a place to stay, he was all right. After I come to this state, I voted some. I have farmed and worked at odd jobs. I farmed mostly. Ma went back to her old master. He persuaded her to come back home. Me and her went back and run a farm four or five years before she died. Then I come back here.

LEE GUIDON

South Carolina. Born in South Carolina. Age at interview: 89.

Yes, ma'am, I sure was in the Civil War. I plowed all day, and me and my sister helped take care of the baby at night. It would cry, and me bumping it [in a straight chair, rocking]. Time I git it to the bed where its mama was, it wake up and start crying all over again. I be so sleepy. It was a puny sort of baby. Its papa was off at war. His name was Jim Cowan, and his wife Miss Margaret Brown 'fore she married him. Miss Lucy Smith give me and my sister to them. Then she married Mr. Abe Moore. Jim Smith was Miss Lucy's boy. He lay out in the woods all time. He say no need in him gitting shot up and killed. He say let the slaves be free. We lived, seemed like, on 'bout the line of York and Union counties. He lay out in the woods over in York County. Mr. Jim say all the fighting 'bout was jealousy. They caught him several times, but every time he got away from 'em. After they come home Mr. Jim say they never win no war. They stole and starved out the South. . . .

After freedom a heap of people say they was going to name theirselves over. They named theirselves big names, then went roaming round like wild, hunting cities. They changed up so it was hard to tell who or where anybody was. Heap of 'em died, and you didn't know when you hear about it if he was your folks hardly. Some of the names was Abraham, and some called theirselves Lincum. Any big name 'cepting their master's name. It was the fashion. I heard 'em talking 'bout it one evening, and my pa say, "Fine folks raise us and we gonna hold to our own names." That settled it with all of us. . . .

I reckon I do know 'bout the Ku Kluck. I knowed a man named Alfred Owens. He seemed all right, but he was a Republican. He said he was not afraid. He run a tanyard and kept a heap of guns in a big room. They all loaded. He married a Southern woman. Her husband either died or was killed. She had a son living with them. The Ku Kluck was called Upper League. They get this boy to unload all the guns. Then the white men went there. The white man give up and said, "I ain't got no gun to defend myself with. The guns all unloaded, and I ain't got no powder and shot." But the Ku Kluck shot in the houses and shot him up like lacework. He sold fine harness, saddles, bridles — all sorts of leather things. The Ku Kluck sure run them outen their country. They say they not going to have them round, and they sure run them out, back where they came from. . . .

For them what stayed on like they were, Reconstruction times 'bout like times before that 'cepting the Yankee stole out and tore up a scandalous heap. They tell the black folks to do something, and then come white folks you live with and say Ku Kluck whup you. They say leave, and white folks say better not listen to them old yankees. They'll git you too far off to come back, and you freeze. They done give you all the use they got for you. How they do? All sorts of ways. Some stayed at their cabins glad to have one to live in and farmed on. Some running round begging, some hunting work for money, and nobody had no money 'cepting the Yankees, and they had no homes or land and mighty little work for you to do. No work to live on. Some going every day to the city. That winter I heard 'bout them starving and freezing by the wagon loads. I never heard nothing 'bout voting till freedom. I don't think I ever voted till I come to Mississippi. I votes Republican. That's the party of my color, and I stick to them as long as they do right. I don't dabble in white folks' business, and that white folks' voting is their business. If I vote, I go do it and go on home.

I been plowing all my life, and in the hot days I cuts and saws wood. Then when I gets outa cotton-picking, I put each boy on a load of wood and we sell wood. The last years we got $3 a cord. Then we clear land till next spring. I don't find no time to be loafing. I never missed a year farming till I got the

Bright's disease [one of several kinds of kidney ailments] and it hurt me to do hard work. Farming is the best life there is when you are able. . . .

When I owned most, I had six head mules and five head horses. I rented 140 acres of land. I bought this house and some other land about. The anthrax killed nearly all my horses and mules. I got one big fine mule yet. Its mate died. I lost my house. My son give me one room, and he paying the debt off now. It's hard for colored folks to keep anything. Somebody gets it from 'em if they don't mind. . . .

TOBY JONES

Madisonville, Texas. Born in South Carolina. Age at interview: 87.

I worked for Massa 'bout four years after freedom, 'cause he forced me to, said he couldn't 'ford to let me go. His place was near ruint, the fences burnt, and the house would have been, but it was rock. There was a battle fought near his place, and I taken Missy to a hideout in the mountains to where her father was, 'cause there was bullets flying everywhere. When the war was over, Massa come home and says, "You son of a gun, you's supposed to be free, but you ain't, 'cause I ain't gwine give you freedom." So I goes on working for him till I gits the chance to steal a hoss from him. The woman I wanted to marry, Govie, she 'cides to come to Texas with me. Me and Govie, we rides the hoss 'most a hundred miles, then we turned him a-loose and give him a scare back to his house, and come on foot the rest the way to Texas.

All we had to eat was what we could beg, and sometimes we went three days without a bite to eat. Sometimes we'd pick a few berries. When we got cold we'd crawl in a brushpile and hug up close together to keep warm. Once in a while we'd come to a farmhouse, and the man let us sleep on cottonseed in his barn, but they was far and few between, 'cause they wasn't many houses in the country them days like now.

When we gits to Texas, we gits married, but all they was to our wedding am we just 'grees to live together as man and wife. I settled on some land, and we cut some trees and split them open and stood them on end with the tops together for our house. Then we deadened some trees, and the land was ready to farm. There was some wild cattle and hogs, and that's the way we got our start, caught some of them and tamed them.

I don't know as I 'spected nothing from freedom, but they turned us out like a bunch of stray dogs, no homes, no clothing, no nothing, not 'nough food to last us one meal. After we settles on that place, I never seed man or woman, 'cept Govie, for six years, 'cause it was a long ways to anywhere. All we had to farm with was sharp sticks. We'd stick holes and plant corn, and when it come up we'd punch up the dirt round it. We didn't plant cotton, 'cause we couldn't eat that. I made bows and arrows to kill wild game with, and we never went to a store for nothing. We made our clothes out of animal skins.

46

White Southerners' Reactions to Reconstruction

Caleb G. Forshey and
the Reverend James Sinclair

The Congressional Joint Committee of Fifteen, assembled to examine Southern represen-
tation in Congress, was named in December 1865 as part of the Republican Congress's re-
sponse to President Andrew Johnson's plan of Reconstruction. In 1866, the committee held
hearings as part of its effort to draft the Fourteenth Amendment. Despite the president's
veto, Congress had already enlarged the scope of the Freedmen's Bureau to care for dis-
placed former slaves and to try by military commission those accused of depriving freedmen
of civil rights. Republicans in Congress, in opposition to the Johnson administration, would
continue to evolve a Reconstruction policy that attempted to protect the freedmen's rights.

Of the two white Southerners whose interviews with the committee you will read
here, Caleb G. Forshey had supported secession while James Sinclair, although a slave-
holder, had opposed it. Sinclair was a Scottish-born minister who had moved to North
Carolina only in 1857; his Unionist sentiments had led to the loss of his church and then
to his arrest during the war. In 1865 he served on the Freedmen's Bureau.

QUESTIONS TO CONSIDER

1. What effect did Caleb Forshey anticipate from military occupation of Southern states?
2. How did he evaluate the effectiveness of the Freedmen's Bureau?
3. What were Forshey's beliefs about African Americans?
4. What were the strengths and weaknesses of the Freedmen's Bureau according to James Sinclair?
5. How does Sinclair's view of Southern opinion differ from Forshey's?

CALEB G. FORSHEY

Washington, D.C., March 28, 1866

Question: Where do you reside?
Answer: I reside in the State of Texas.
Question: How long have you been a resident of Texas?

The Report of the Committees of the House of Representatives Made during the First Session, Thirty-Ninth
Congress, 1865–1866, vol. 2 (Washington, D.C.: Government Printing Office, 1866); Forshey:
129–32; Sinclair: 168–71.

Answer: I have resided in Texas and been a citizen of that State for nearly thirteen years.

Question: What opportunities have you had for ascertaining the temper and disposition of the people of Texas towards the government and authority of the United States?

Answer: For ten years I have been superintendent of the Texas Military Institute, as its founder and conductor. I have been in the confederate service in various parts of the confederacy; but chiefly in the trans-Mississippi department, in Louisiana and Texas, as an officer of engineers. I have had occasion to see and know very extensively the condition of affairs in Texas, and also to a considerable extent in Louisiana. I think I am pretty well-informed, as well as anybody, perhaps, of the present state of affairs in Texas.

Question: What are the feelings and views of the people of Texas as to the late rebellion, and the future condition and circumstances of the State, and its relations to the federal government?

Answer: After our army had given up its arms and gone home, the surrender of all matters in controversy was complete, and as nearly universal, perhaps, as anything could be. Assuming the matters in controversy to have been the right to secede, and the right to hold slaves, I think they were given up tee-totally, to use a strong Americanism. When you speak of feeling, I should discriminate a little. The feeling was that of any party who had been cast in a suit he had staked all upon. They did not return from feeling, but from a sense of necessity, and from a judgment that it was the only and necessary thing to be done, to give up the contest. But when they gave it up, it was without reservation; with a view to look forward, and not back. That is my impression of the manner in which the thing was done. There was a public expectation that in some very limited time there would be a restoration to former relations. . . . It was the expectation of the people that, as soon as the State was organized as proposed by the President, they would be restored to their former relations, and things would go on as before.

Question: What is your opinion of a military force under the authority of the federal government to preserve order in Texas and to protect those who have been loyal, both white and black, from the aggressions of those who have been in the rebellion?

Answer: My judgment is well founded on that subject: that wherever such military force is and has been, it has excited the very feeling it was intended to prevent; that so far from being necessary it is very pernicious everywhere, and without exception. The local authorities and public sentiment are ample for protection. I think no occasion would occur, unless some individual case that our laws would not reach. We had an opportunity to test this after the surrender and before any authority was there. The military authorities, or the military officers, declared that we were without laws, and it was a long time before the governor appointed arrived there, and then it was sometime before we could effect anything in the way of organization. We were a people without law, order, or anything; and it was a time for violence if it would occur. I think it is a great credit to our civilization that, in that state of affairs, there was nowhere any instance of violence. I am proud of it, for I expected the contrary; I expected that our soldiers on coming home, many of them, would be dissolute, and that many of them would oppress the class of men you speak of; but it did not occur. But afterwards, wherever soldiers have been sent, there have been little troubles, none of them large; but personal collisions between soldiers and citizens.

Question: What is your opinion as to the necessity and advantages of the Freedmen's Bureau, or an agency of that kind, in Texas?

Answer: My opinion is that it is not needed; my opinion is stronger than that — that the effect of it is to irritate, if nothing else. While in New York city recently I had a conversation with some friends from Texas, from five distant points in the State. We met together and compared opinions; and the opinion of each was the same, that the negroes had generally gone to work since January; that except where the Freedmen's Bureau had interfered, or rather encouraged troubles, such as little complaints, especially between negro and negro, the negro's disposition was very good, and they had generally gone to work, a vast majority of them with their former masters. . . . The impression in Texas at present is that the negroes under the influence of the Freedmen's Bureau do worse than without it.

I want to state that I believe all our former owners of negroes are the friends of the negroes; and that the antagonism paraded in the papers of the north does not exist at all. I know the fact is the very converse of that; and good feeling always prevails between the masters and the slaves. But the negroes went off and left them in the lurch; my own family was an instance of it. But they came back after a time, saying they had been free enough and wanted a home.

Question: Do you think those who employ the negroes there are willing to make contracts with them, so that they shall have fair wages for their labor?

Answer: I think so; I think they are paid liberally, more than the white men in this country get; the average compensation to negroes there is greater than the average compensation of free laboring white men in this country. It seems to have regulated itself in a great measure by what each neighborhood was doing; the negroes saying, "I can get thus and so at such a place." Men have hired from eight to fifteen dollars per month during the year, and women at about two dollars less a month; house-servants at a great deal more.

Question: Do the men who employ the negroes claim to exercise the right to enforce their contract by physical force?

Answer: Not at all; that is totally abandoned; not a single instance of it has occurred. I think they still chastise children, though. The negro parents often neglect that, and the children are still switched as we switch our own children. I know it is done in my own house; we have little house-servants that we switch just as I do our own little fellows.

Question: What is your opinion as to the respective advantages to the white and black races, of the present free system of labor and the institution of slavery?

Answer: I think freedom is very unfortunate for the negro; I think it is sad; his present helpless condition touches my heart more than anything else I ever contemplated, and I think that is the common sentiment of our slaveholders. I have seen it on the largest plantations, where the negro men had all left, and where only women and children remained, and the owners had to keep them and feed them. The beginning certainly presents a touching and sad spectacle. The poor negro is dying at a rate fearful to relate.

I have some ethnological theories that may perhaps warp my judgment; but my judgment is that the highest condition the black race has ever reached or can reach, is one where he is provided for by a master race. That is the result of a great deal of scientific investigation and observation of the negro character by me ever since I was a man. The labor question had become a most momentous one, and I was studying it. I undertook to investigate the condition of the negro from statistics under various circumstances, to treat it purely as a matter of statistics from the census tables of this country of ours. I found that the free blacks of the north decreased 8 per cent.; the free blacks of the south increased 7 or 8 per cent., while the slaves by their sides increased 34 per cent. I inferred from the doctrines of political economy that the race is in the best condition when it procreates the fastest; that, other things being equal, slavery is of vast advantage to the negro. I will mention one or two things in connexion with this as explanatory of that result. The negro will not take care of his offspring unless required to do it, as compared with the whites. The little children will die; they do die, and hence the necessity of very rigorous regulations on our plantations which we have adopted in our nursery system.

Another cause is that there is no continence among the negroes.[1] All the continence I have ever seen among the negroes has been enforced upon plantations, where it is generally assumed there is none. For the sake of procreation, if nothing else, we compel men to live with their wives. The discipline of the plantation was more rigorous, perhaps, in regard to men staying with their wives, than in regard to anything else; and I think the procreative results, as shown by the census tables, is due in a great measure to that discipline. . . .

Question: What is the prevailing inclination among the people of Texas in regard to giving the negroes civil or political rights and privileges?

Answer: I think they are all opposed to it. There are some men — I am not among them — who think that the basis of intelligence might be a good basis for the elective franchise. But a much larger class, perhaps nine-tenths of our people, believe that the distinctions between the races should not be broken down by any such community of interests in the management of the affairs of the State. I think there is a very common sentiment that the negro, even with education, has not a mind capable of appreciating the political institutions of the country to such an extent as would make him a good associate for the white man in the administration of the government. I think if the vote was taken on the question of admitting him to the right of suffrage there would be a very small vote in favor of it — scarcely respectable: that is my judgment.

THE REVEREND JAMES SINCLAIR

Washington, D.C., January 29, 1866

Question: What is generally the state of feeling among the white people of North Carolina towards the government of the United States?

---

1. By this Forshey means that they did not rein in their sexual impulses.

Answer: That is a difficult question to answer, but I will answer it as far as my own knowledge goes. In my opinion, there is generally among the white people not much love for the government. Though they are willing, and I believe determined, to acquiesce in what is inevitable, yet so far as love and affection for the government is concerned, I do not believe that they have any of it at all, outside of their personal respect and regard for President Johnson.

Question: How do they feel towards the mass of the northern people — that is, the people of what were known formerly as the free States?

Answer: They feel in this way: that they have been ruined by them. You can imagine the feelings of a person towards one whom he regards as having ruined him. They regard the northern people as having destroyed their property or taken it from them, and brought all the calamities of this war upon them.

Question: How do they feel in regard to what is called the right of secession?

Answer: They think that it was right . . . that there was no wrong in it. They are willing now to accept the decision of the question that has been made by the sword, but they are not by any means converted from their old opinion that they had a right to secede. It is true that there have always been Union men in our State, but not Union men without slavery, except perhaps among Quakers. Slavery was the central idea even of the Unionist. The only difference between them and the others upon that question was, that they desired to have that institution under the aegis of the Constitution, and protected by it. The secessionists wanted to get away from the north altogether. When the secessionists precipitated our State into rebellion, the Unionists and secessionists went together, because the great object with both was the preservation of slavery by the preservation of State sovereignty. There was another class of Unionists who did not care anything at all about slavery, but they were driven by the other whites into the rebellion for the purpose of preserving slavery. The poor whites are to-day very much opposed to conferring upon the negro the right of suffrage; as much so as the other classes of the whites. They believe it is the intention of government to give the negro rights at their expense. They cannot see it in any other light than that as the negro is elevated they must proportionately go down. While they are glad that slavery is done away with, they are bitterly opposed to conferring the right of suffrage on the negro as the most prominent secessionists; but it is for the reason I have stated, that they think rights conferred on the negro must necessarily be taken from them, particularly the ballot, which was the only bulwark guarding their superiority to the negro race.

Question: In your judgment, what proportion of the white people of North Carolina are really, and truly, and cordially attached to the government of the United States?

Answer: Very few, sir; very few. . . .

Question: Is the Freedmen's Bureau acceptable to the great mass of the white people in North Carolina?

Answer: No, sir; I do not think it is; I think the most of the whites wish the bureau to be taken away.

Question: Why do they wish that?

Answer: They think that they can manage the negro for themselves: that they understand him better than northern men do. They say, "Let us understand what you want us to do with [the] negro — what you desire of us; lay down your conditions for our readmission into the Union, and then we will know what we have to do, and if you will do that we will enact laws for the government of these negroes. They have lived among us, and they are all with us, and we can manage them better than you can." They think it is interfering with the rights of the State for a bureau, the agent and representative of the federal government, to overslaugh[2] the State entirely, and interfere with the regulations and administration of justice before their courts.

Question: Is there generally a willingness on the part of the whites to allow the freedmen to enjoy the right of acquiring land and personal property?

Answer: I think they are very willing to let them do that, for this reason; to get rid of some portion of the taxes imposed upon their property by the government. For instance, a white man will agree to sell a negro some of his land on condition of his paying so much a year on it, promising to give him a deed of it when the whole payment is made, taking his note in the mean time. This relieves that much of the land from taxes to be paid by the white man. All I am afraid of is, that the negro is too eager to go into this thing; that he will ruin himself, get himself into debt to the white man, and be forever bound to him for the debt and never get the land. I have often warned them to be careful what they did about these things.

Question: There is no repugnance on the part of the whites to the negro owning land and personal property?

Answer: I think not.

Question: Have they any objection to the legal establishment of the domestic relations among the blacks, such as the relation of husband and wife, of parent and child, and the securing by law to the negro the rights of those relations?

Answer: That is a matter of ridicule with the whites. They do not believe the negroes will ever respect those relations more than the brutes. I suppose I have married more than two hundred couples of negroes since the war, but the whites laugh at the very idea of the thing. . . .

Question: What, in general, has been the treatment of the blacks by the whites since the close of hostilities?

Answer: It has not generally been of the kindest character, I must say that; I am compelled to say that.

Question: Are you aware of any instance of personal ill treatment towards the blacks by the whites?

Answer: Yes, sir.

Question: Give some instances that have occurred since the war.

Answer: [Sinclair describes the beating of a young woman across her buttocks in graphic detail.]

Question: What was the provocation, if any?

---

2. **overslaugh:** Block or impede.

Answer: Something in regard to some work, which is generally the provocation.

Question: Was there no law in North Carolina at that time to punish such an outrage?

Answer: No, sir; only the regulations of the Freedmen's Bureau; we took cognizance of the case. In old times that was quite allowable; it is what was called "paddling."

Question: Did you deal with the master?

Answer: I immediately sent a letter to him to come to my office, but he did not come, and I have never seen him in regard to the matter since. I had no soldiers to enforce compliance, and I was obliged to let the matter drop.

Question: Have you any reason to suppose that such instances of cruelty are frequent in North Carolina at this time — instances of whipping and striking?

Answer: I think they are; it was only a few days before I left that a woman came there with her head all bandaged up, having been cut and bruised by her employer. They think nothing of striking them.

Question: And the negro has practically no redress?

Answer: Only what he can get from the Freedmen's Bureau.

Question: Can you say anything further in regard to the political condition of North Carolina — the feeling of the people towards the government of the United States?

Answer: I for one would not wish to be left there in the hands of those men; I could not live there just now. But perhaps my case is an isolated one from the position I was compelled to take in that State. I was persecuted, arrested, and they tried to get me into their service; they tried everything to accomplish their purpose, and of course I have rendered myself still more obnoxious by accepting an appointment under the Freedmen's Bureau. . . .

Question: Suppose the military pressure of the government of the United States should be withdrawn from North Carolina, would northern men and true Unionists be safe in that State?

Answer: A northern man going there would perhaps present nothing obnoxious to the people of the State. But men who were born there, who have been true to the Union, and who have fought against the rebellion, are worse off than northern men.

Ruins in Charleston, South Carolina, 1865 or 1866
Photograph by George N. Barnard

The Civil War was the first modern war. Guns with rifled barrels could send a bullet accurately for long distances, and cannons loaded with grapeshot could kill and maim many men at one time. Railroads enabled armies to transport troops and supplies over vast distances, greatly increasing the size of battles — and the number of casualties. Not simply fought between professional armies, the war scarred large proportions of the population on both sides.

As photographs came to dominate the public's vision of the war, the technical limits of what the camera could depict defined the way people imagined battle. The photographic process was too cumbersome to allow "action" photographs: there are no Civil War photographs of actual battles. Nonetheless, skilled photographers such as George N. Barnard followed the Union Army closely, catching the preparations for battle, the sites where battles were fought, and the dreadful aftermaths of these events.

The following photograph is from a portfolio of images of Sherman's march by George N. Barnard, one of the best field photographers of the Civil War. His photographs show how photographic artists of the era selected subjects that might portray their own values. Barnard followed General Sherman's army as it fought its way through the South, photographing when the army paused long enough for him to take pictures, sketching when it moved too quickly for his bulky equipment. After the war, Barnard retraced the route of the army photographing "the principal events and most interesting localities" that he had not been able to capture during the actual march. Gathered together in The Photographic Views of Sherman's Campaign, *a portfolio of views that Barnard published in 1866, his photographs suggest both the power and the limits of the era's photography for evoking a vision of war.*

QUESTIONS TO CONSIDER

1. What mood does George Barnard create in his image of the "Ruins in Charleston, South Carolina"?
2. The South did not have the resources to support a photographic industry on the scale that was achieved by the North, and thus almost all our photographs of the war come from Northern sources. How might pictures taken by Southerners have been different? How would we view

---

George N. Barnard, *The Photographic Views of Sherman's Campaign* (1866; New York: Dover Publications, 1977), Plate 60.

the war differently if there were large numbers of photographs taken by Southerners?

3. Do you think audiences today view these images differently from Southern and Northern audiences immediately following the war? How?

4. How does this image compare with views of the destruction of wars with which you are familiar, such as scenes from Hiroshima and Nagasaki or from the Vietnam or Iraq wars?

"Ruins in Charleston, South Carolina," 1865 or 1866 by George N. Barnard.

Acknowledgments (continued from p. iv)

Bracketed numbers indicate selection numbers.

[2] "A Nahua Account of the Conquest of Mexico." From *We People Here: Nahuatl Accounts of the Conquest of Mexico*, edited and translated by James Lockhart. Published by the University of California Press. Reprinted by permission of James Lockhart.

[8] "Leaving an Abusive Husband." From *Religion and Domestic Violence in Early New England: The Memoirs of Abigail Abbot Bailey*, edited by Ann Taves. Copyright © 1989 by Indiana University Press. Reprinted by permission.

[17] "A Soldier's View of the Revolutionary War." From *Ordinary Courage: The Revolutionary War Adventures of Joseph Plumb Martin*, revised edition by James Kirby Martin. Copyright © 1999. Reprinted by permission of James Kirby Martin.

[19] "Secret Correspondence of a Loyalist Wife." From Catherine Van Cortlandt, *Secret Correspondence of a Loyalist Wife*, edited by H. O. H. Vernon-Jackson, in *History Today 14*, pp. 574–80. Copyright © 1964. Reprinted with permission of the publisher, History Today.

[22] "Casting Their Lot with the British." From *The Journal of Major John Norton, 1816*. The Publications of the Champlain Society. Copyright © The Champlain Society. Reprinted by permission of The Champlain Society.

[26] "Crossing the Continent." Excerpts from *The Journals of Lewis and Clark*, edited by Bernard DeVoto. Copyright © 1953 by Bernard DeVoto. Copyright © renewed 1981 by Avis DeVoto. Reprinted by permission of Houghton Mifflin Harcourt Publishing Company. All rights reserved.

[27] "The Trail of Tears." From *The Papers of Chief John Ross, Volume I, 1807–1839*, edited by Gary Moulton, pp. 169–75. Copyright © 1985. Reprinted with permission of University of Oklahoma Press.

[34] "The Lowell Textile Workers." From *Farm to Factory: Women's Letters, 1830-1860*, Second Edition, edited by Thomas Dublin. Copyright © 1993 Columbia University Press. Reprinted by permission of Thomas Dublin.

[36] A Family Torn Apart by Slavery." From *Narrative of the Life of Henry Box Brown, Written by Himself*. Electronic edition, *Documenting the American South*. Copyright © 1999 University of North Carolina. Reprinted by permission.

[39] "The Equality of All Men Before the Law, April 1865." *Speech at the Annual Meeting of the Massachusetts Anti-Slavery Society in Boston—What the Black Man Wants* by Frederick Douglass. Reprinted courtesy of Uncle Tom's Cabin & American Culture: A Multi-Media Archive.

[40] "A Slave Owner's Journal at the End of the Civil War." From *The Private Journal of Henry William Ravenel, 1859–1887*, edited by Arney Robinson Childs. Copyright © 1947 University of South Carolina Press. Reprinted with permission of University of South Carolina Press.

[42] "The Battle of Gettysburg: At War and at Home." Diaries of Samuel and Rachel Cormany (1863). Samuel Cormany's and Rachel Cormany's letters from *The Cormany Diaries: A Northern Family in the Civil War*, edited by James C. Mohr. Copyright © 1982. Reprinted by permission of the University of Pittsburgh Press.

[43] "Fighting for the Union." From *Grand Army of Black Men*, edited by Edwin S. Redkey. Copyright © 1992 Cambridge University Press. Reprinted with the permission of Cambridge University Press.

[44] "Healing Wounds." From *South After Gettysburg: Letters of Cornelia Hancock, 1863–1868*, by Cornelia Hancock. Copyright © 1956. Reprinted by permission of the University of Pennsylvania Press.

[45] "African Americans during Reconstruction." From *Lay My Burden Down: A Folk History of Slavery* by B. A. Botkin, editor. Copyright © 1945 by B. A. Bodkin. Reprinted by permission of Curtis Brown, Ltd.

Visual Portfolios and Documents

New World Images
[Figure 1] First European Attempt to Depict the Domestic Life of Native Americans. Spencer Collection, The New York Public Library, Astor, Lenox and Tilden Foundations.
[Figure 2] Drawing of Cortés and Malinche. Bibliothèque Nationale, Paris.
[Figure 3] The Manner of Their Fishing. Courtesy of the John Carter Brown Library at Brown University.
[Figure 4] Huron Woman. © British Library Board. All Rights Reserved.
[Figure 5] Return of English Captives during a Conference between Colonel Henry Bouquet and Indians on the Muskingum River. Rare Books Division, The New York Public Library, Astor, Lenox and Tilden Foundations.

[14] Amplissima Regionis Mississippi 1763. Courtesy of Hargrett Rare Book and Manuscript Library/University of Georgia.

Patriot and Loyalist Propaganda
[Figure 1] The Bloody Massacre. Anne S. K. Brown Military Collection Brown University Library/LOC.
[Figure 2] Join, or Die. The Granger Collection, New York.
[Figure 3] The Colonies Reduced. Library of Congress.
[Figure 4] The Edenton Tea Party. The Granger Collection, New York.
[Figure 5] Bostonians Paying the Excise Man. The Granger Collection, New York.
[Figure 6] The Able Doctor, or America Swallowing the Bitter Draught. Library of Congress.

[31] Miners during the California Gold Rush. California History Room, California State Library Association.
[38] Daguerreotype of John Brown, 1856. The Granger Collection, New York. Daguerreotype of John Brown, 1859. The Granger Collection, New York.

Slavery and Freedom
[Figure 1] United States: The South. From *Malte-Brun's School Geography*, 1836.
[Figure 2] Southern Man, His Two Daughters, and Nanny. J. Paul Getty Museum.
[Figure 3] Jack (Driver), a Slave in Columbia, S.C. Courtesy of the Peabody Museum of Archaeology and Ethnology, 35-5-10/53040.
[Figure 4] Delia, a Slave in Columbia, S.C. Courtesy of the Peabody Museum of Archaeology and Ethnology, 35-5-10/53044.
[Figure 5] Robert J. Wilkinson, Successful Businessman. Missouri Historical Society.
[Figure 6] Portrait of an Unidentified Woman. Library of Congress, National Portrait Gallery, Smithsonian Institution.
[Figure 7] The Africans of the Slave Bark "Wildfire." *Harper's Weekly*, June 2, 1860.
[Figure 8] Emancipated Slaves, White and Colored. *Harper's Weekly*, January 30, 1864.
[Figure 10] The "Peculiar Institution." Library of Congress.
[Figure 11] Price, Birch & Co., Dealers in Slaves, Alexandria, Va. National Archives.
[Figure 12] Interior View of the Price, Birch & Co. Slave Dealership, Alexandria, Va. National Archives.
[Figure 13] Solution of the Labor Question in the South. *Harper's Weekly* December 2, 1865.
[Figure 14] The Ebony Bridal—The Wedding Ceremony. *Frank Leslie's Popular Monthly*, October 1877.

[47] Ruins in Charleston, South Carolina, 1865 or 1866. Photo by George N. Bernard.